CHANCELLORSVILLE'S FORGOTTEN FRONT

The Battles of
Second Fredericksburg and
Salem Church, May 3, 1863

Chris Mackowski
& Kristopher D. White

SB

Savas Beatie
California

Library of Congress Cataloging-in-Publication Data

Mackowski, Chris.
Chancellorsville's forgotten front : the battles of Second Fredericksburg and Salem Church, May 3, 1863 / Chris Mackowski, Kristopher D. White. — First edition.
pages cm
Includes bibliographical references and index.
ISBN 978-1-61121-136-8
1. Fredericksburg, Battle of, Fredericksburg, Va., 1862. 2. Salem Church, Battle of, Va., 1863. I. White, Kristopher D., author. II. Title.
E474.85.M329 2013
973.7'33—dc23
2013007417

SB

Published by
Savas Beatie LLC
989 Governor Drive, Suite 102
El Dorado Hills, CA 95762

Phone: 916-941-6896
(E-mail) customerservice@savasbeatie.com

05 04 03 02 01 5 4 3 2 1
First edition, first printing

Savas Beatie titles are available at special discounts for bulk purchases in the United States by corporations, institutions, and other organizations. For more details, please contact Special Sales, P.O. Box 4527, El Dorado Hills, CA 95762, or you may e-mail us at sales@savasbeatie.com, or visit our website at www.savasbeatie.com for additional information.

Proudly published, printed, and warehoused in the United States of America.

Kris: *For Sarah; and for all those who stood beside me.*

Chris: *To Kristopher Douglas White, of course. This book has been his dream for as long as I've known him.*

We jointly dedicate
this book to our friend Don Pfanz

Confederate dead behind Fredericksburg's Sunken Road atop Marye's Heights.

Table of Contents

Table of Contents (continued)

Table of Contents (continued)

Foreword

Each year, thousands of people visit Chancellorsville. Some come simply to enjoy a natural landscape that is fast vanishing amid a proliferation of subdivisions, gas stations, and shopping centers. Others come to see where a great battle transpired or because they are following the movements of an ancestor who fought on that bloody field. A small number of professional soldiers, however, come to study the battle, to learn the lessons of strategy and tactics that it can teach—for Chancellorsville was no ordinary battle. For students of the war, especially devotees of Robert E. Lee, it *was* the battle: a tactical masterpiece forged from necessity and carried out with incredible boldness.

Yet often forgotten by those studying the battle is the pivotal role played by Maj. Gen. John Sedgwick's VI Corps. In a way, this is surprising, since three of the four battles encompassed by the campaign were fought by the VI Corps. Sedgwick's operations constitute a campaign within a campaign, one in which communications played fully as much a role as fighting. It is this fascinating yet complex piece of the campaign that Chris Mackowski and Kristopher White skillfully record in their book, *Chancellorsville's Forgotten Front: The Battles of Second Fredericksburg and Salem Church.*

Historians agree that, for all Lee's brilliance in the campaign, his bold gambit could not have succeeded had it not been for the blunders of his opponent, "Fighting Joe" Hooker, a scheming man of loose morals, who exuded confidence prior to the campaign only to lose his nerve once the fighting started. The Union commander had started well enough. While his cavalry under Brig. Gen. George Stoneman severed Lee's lines of communication and supply with Richmond, a secondary force under Maj. Gen. John Sedgwick crossed the Rappahannock River below Fredericksburg, focusing Lee's attention on the east. Hooker, meanwhile, led the balance of the army upriver, crossing the Rappahannock beyond Lee's left flank and gaining his rear at Chancellorsville. As April 1863 came to a close, Hooker seemed poised to crush Lee's army between the two wings of his massive army.

Then Hooker's plan began to unravel. Rather than retreating southward, as Hooker expected, Lee accepted Hooker's challenge and marched out to give battle at Chancellorsville. Surprised by Lee's audacity, the Union commander surrendered the initiative and fell back to a defensive position around the Chancellorsville crossroads. From that point on, Lee had it his own way. On May 2, he sent his incomparable lieutenant, "Stonewall" Jackson, to attack Hooker's exposed right flank.

Hooker was still reeling from Jackson's successful blow when Lee ordered an all-out assault on the Army of the Potomac's position. In four and one-half hours of savage fighting on the morning of May 3, approximately one man fell for every second of combat, making that day the second-bloodiest of the Civil War, after only Antietam.

Hooker attempted to hold his ground, but as the pressure mounted he once again lost his nerve and ordered his army to fall back toward the river. From that point on, Hooker had just one thought: re-cross the river and save his army. It mattered not that he still outnumbered Lee by a margin of two to one, that he held a strong defensive position, or that Stoneman and Sedgwick continued to threaten Lee's flank and rear; Hooker had had enough. He was, in the estimation of his second-in-command, Maj. Gen. Darius Couch, "a whipped man." Twelfth Corps commander Henry Slocum put it more strongly still. Hooker, he asserted, sunk to the level of "a poor drivelling cur."

It was a modern David-versus-Goliath tale, and—like all epic tales—it had an element of tragedy. On the second day of the battle, at the height of his most successful attack of the war, "Stonewall" Jackson fell mortally wounded, the accidental victim of a point-blank volley delivered by his own men in the shadows of the dark forest. He died eight days later at Guinea Station.

Lee's boldness and Jackson's death came to define the battle. And yet it might have been very different. Had Hooker not abandoned the offensive on May 1, had he not misinterpreted Jackson's flank movement as a retreat on May 2, had he committed his reserves on May 3, Hooker could have turned the battle around. What has come down in history as Lee's greatest victory might just as easily be remembered as his greatest defeat. In fact, starting on April 30, Hooker made at least one crucial blunder every day of the campaign. Many of those blunders involved the handling of his force at Fredericksburg.

At the center of the drama was the VI Corps' commander, Maj. Gen. John Sedgwick. At the age of 50, the Connecticut native was a thorough soldier. A graduate of West Point in 1837, he was serving with Robert E. Lee in the Second United States Cavalry when, in 1861, the Civil War caused the two men to pursue different paths. While Lee catapulted to command of the Army of Northern Virginia, Sedgwick steadily made his way up the Union chain of command to become a leading officer in the Army of the Potomac. Chancellorsville was his first battle at corps level. Popular with his colleagues and with the men of his command, who affectionately called him "Uncle John," Sedgwick was a steady figure in the Army of the Potomac's uneven panoply of generals. He was not one to make mistakes, but he was not particularly creative or aggressive either. He was dependable, but hardly dynamic.

Hooker was not unduly concerned by Sedgwick's shortcomings, for he envisioned a largely static role for the commander of his left wing. Sedgwick's job, as Hooker saw it, was simply to engage Lee's attention while he and the rest of the army turned his flank at Chancellorsville and attacked him from the rear. By Hooker's reckoning, Sedgwick was to be the anvil and he was to be the hammer. But when "Fighting Joe" lost his nerve at the outset of the battle, the offensive derailed. Hammer and anvil would never meet.

Instead, they swapped roles. After falling back to Chancellorsville, Hooker found himself under relentless assault by Lee and Jackson. On May 2, Jackson's men fell like an avalanche on Hooker's exposed right flank, routing Maj. Gen. Oliver O. Howard's XI Corps and threatening the Army of the Potomac's communications with Washington.

His confidence shaken by this second surprise in as many days, Hooker called on Sedgwick to brush aside the Confederates confronting him on Marye's Heights and drive westward to his support. By then,

Hooker had siphoned off all the troops in Sedgwick's left wing except Brig. Gen. John Gibbon's division of the II Corps and Sedgwick's own VI Corps, leaving him a force of approximately 27,000 men. Facing him were four Confederate brigades amounting to fewer than 13,000 men, led by Maj. Gen. Jubal A. Early. Although outnumbered by a factor of more than two to one, Early held a strong position on the heights south and west of Fredericksburg, the same ridge successfully defended by Lee five months earlier. Farther west, Hooker had approximately 90,000 men under his direct command at Chancellorsville and was opposed by some 45,000 Confederates personally led by Lee. Unlike Sedgwick, though, Hooker stood on the defensive. Under his new plan, he would become the anvil, and Sedgwick the hammer.

It was a role unsuited to the VI Corps commander, but Sedgwick dutifully attempted to comply with his superior's orders. Unfortunately, communications between the army's two wings was sorely lacking. Because of the distance between himself and Sedgwick, Hooker relied on the telegraph to communicate his wishes to his subordinate. The messages traveled over wire via United States Ford to army headquarters at Falmouth, where Hooker's chief of staff, Maj. Gen. Daniel Butterfield, forwarded the messages to Sedgwick a few miles farther downriver.

From the outset, the system failed. Weak signals and damaged and broken wires hampered transmissions. Messages arrived hours late, when they arrived at all. Confronted with a flurry of outdated and sometimes confusing orders, Sedgwick became cautious. When the enemy troops in front of him mistakenly evacuated Marye's Heights on May 2, Sedgwick failed to take advantage of their blunder to seize the Heights. It was one of the great missed opportunities of the campaign. And things only got worse from there.

Because of the ongoing troubles with the telegraph, when Hooker, on the evening of May 2 in the wake of Jackson's flank attack, called on Sedgwick to act, Sedgwick did not receive his orders until shortly before midnight. Hooker wanted Sedgwick to take Marye's Heights, brush aside any resistance he might encounter, and press on to Chancellorsville, attacking the rear of Lee's army early on May 3. To comply with this order, Sedgwick would have to clear Fredericksburg of Confederate troops, carry an extremely strong position, and march the 10 miles to Chancellorsville—all in about eight hours' time, most of it in darkness.

The assignment was patently impossible, but Sedgwick did his best to comply. About midnight he began moving north from his bridgehead below Fredericksburg in an effort to flush Confederate troops from the town. It was slow going. Vision was limited and resistance stubborn. Nevertheless, by early morning Sedgwick's troops were in possession of the town.

Beyond it was Marye's Heights. A preliminary assault confirmed what every soldier in the army knew all too well: the Heights would be a hard nut to crack. With that in mind, Sedgwick methodically set about making preparations to storm them. To his credit, he succeeded, but at the cost of several hours' time. At the hour he was supposed to be thundering into Lee's rear at Chancellorsville, Sedgwick was still 10 miles away, gearing up for his assault on Marye's Heights. He compounded his tardiness by halting for an hour after taking the Heights before resuming his advance. He did this in order to bring up Brig. Gen. William T. H. Brooks' division from its position below Fredericksburg. Sedgwick anticipated hard fighting before day's end, and he wanted fresh troops to lead his advance to Chancellorsville.

While Brooks was moving to the front, Confederate troops were making preparations to resist Sedgwick's advance. If there was a hero on either side in the Second Fredericksburg and Salem Church operations, it was Brig. Gen. Cadmus M. Wilcox. Wilcox led a brigade of Alabama troops posted at Banks' Ford, roughly midway between Fredericksburg and Chancellorsville. Disappointed at being left behind to guard the ford while the rest of Lee's army engaged Hooker at Chancellorsville, Wilcox chafed for action. When he heard combat erupt at Fredericksburg on May 3, he led his brigade east to join Early's forces at Fredericksburg. By the time he arrived, however, the Confederate line was giving way. Rather than join Early, who was falling back toward Richmond on the Telegraph Road, Wilcox took it upon himself to impede Sedgwick's advance to Chancellorsville.

Wilcox made his stand four miles west of Fredericksburg at a roadside sanctuary called Salem Church. There he was joined by four additional brigades led by Maj. Gen. Lafayette McLaws sent by Lee from Chancellorsville. Together, McLaws and Wilcox repulsed Sedgwick's late-afternoon attack. Even so, Lee's rear would not be truly secure as long as Sedgwick remained on the south side of the river. With Hooker passively digging in near United States Ford, Lee pulled Maj. Gen. Richard

Anderson's division out of line at Chancellorsville and led it eastward to join McLaws and Wilcox at Salem Church. At the same time, Jubal Early recaptured Marye's Heights, cutting Sedgwick off from Gibbon's division, which had remained in Fredericksburg.

Hemmed in by Confederates on three sides and with his back to the Rappahannock River, Sedgwick feared for the safety of his corps. He wished to retreat, but Hooker was adamant that the VI Corps remain south of the river. Yet, even as Lee massed fully half his infantry against Sedgwick, Hooker remained strangely inactive back at United States Ford. When one of his subordinates urged him to seize the initiative and attack the Confederates who remained at Chancellorsville while Lee's attention was focused on Sedgwick at Salem Church, Hooker demurred. He would give Lee one more day to attack him, Hooker asserted with a pretense of fight, and after that, well, the Confederate commander had better watch out!

Meanwhile, Lee was struggling to mount an attack against Sedgwick. The Southern leader's blood was up, and he was determined to drive Sedgwick into the Rappahannock. Unfortunately, his subordinates were not up to the task. Lee left it to McLaws and Early to make a coordinated attack against Sedgwick's position, but both men waited for the other to act; in the end, neither did. It remained for Lee to take the reins and sort things out. By the time he was ready to go forward, there was little daylight left. His attacks late in the afternoon of May 4 pushed Sedgwick back toward the river but failed to crush his corps. That night, the VI Corps slipped back across the river at Banks' Ford. For Sedgwick and his men, the campaign was over.

Reluctant to attack the Army of Northern Virginia when it was divided, Hooker was not about to fight it when it presented a united front. Two days later, against the advice of the majority of his corps commanders, he withdrew his right wing to the north side of the river. The campaign was over.

For the Army of the Potomac, it had been a campaign fraught with errors. Even the lowliest private recognized that someone had blundered. The question was, who? In the weeks following the campaign Hooker, true to form, attempted to pin the blame on his subordinates. Stoneman, Howard, and Sedgwick all came in for a share of criticism, and indeed each, in his own way, had contributed to the result through negligence, incompetence, or overcaution. In retrospect, Sedgwick seems the least culpable of the three, although, as Mackowski and White point out, his performance was far from flawless. He failed to act with the aggression expected of him by Hooker, he failed to seize Marye's Heights when Confederates mistakenly abandoned the high ground on May 2, and he moved far too deliberately after finally carrying the heights on May 3. But when compared with the number and magnitude of Hooker's blunders, Sedgwick's mistakes seem minor.

As years passed and the legend of Lee and Jackson grew, the fighting at Second Fredericksburg and Salem Church received less attention. They became seen as a mere sideshow to the main fighting at Chancellorsville rather than the pivotal actions they were. Consequently, little of the land encompassed in the VI Corps operations was preserved. When a parsimonious Congress established Fredericksburg and Spotsylvania County National Military Park in 1927, it did not save a single acre of the Salem Church battlefield, and it set aside just a few small scraps of the Second Fredericksburg battlefield. (Congress purchased the latter only because they also happened to be key sites in the December 1862 battle.) The National Park Service has picked up a few acres since that time, but these tiny parcels stand like isolated islands amid a sea of development.

Unfortunately, that will not change. What hopefully will change is the emphasis that Second Fredericksburg and Salem Church receive in future studies of the campaign. In their book *Chancellorsville's Forgotten Front*, authors Chris Mackowski and Kris White remind us that these battles were not just prominent features of the campaign, but critical ones. Thanks to their efforts, Chancellorsville's forgotten front is forgotten no longer.

Donald Pfanz
March 2013

Acknowledgments

Jointly

We cannot thank Ted Savas enough for supporting this effort from day one. Ted allowed us to bring to life a story we are both highly passionate about. From the bottom of our hearts: thank you, Ted.

We would also like to thank Rob Ayer, Lindy Gervin, Veronica Kane, the indispensible Sarah Keeney, and Yvette Lewis of Savas Beatie. The support they've offered to this book, and to us as authors, has been deeply gratifying. Thanks also have to be extended to our cartographer, Hal Jespersen. His maps are an outstanding addition to this book.

Finally, we would like to thank Lawrence "Larry" Hjalmarson. Larry is a descendent of Capt. Sewell Gray, of the 6th Maine. If it were not for Larry donating a transcription of Gray's diary to Fredericksburg and Spotsylvania National Military Park, this book may have never existed. Once Kris unwittingly found this very thin green folder wedged between two books in the Fredericksburg library, our passion for the battles was truly born. Larry and his wife, Ginny, were kind enough to travel from Texas to Virginia in the summer of 2009 for a Second Fredericksburg tour led by Kris. At that time, Larry handed us a beautifully transcribed copy of the diary; included in this transcription were portraits of the young officer as well as pictures of the actual pages of the diary itself. We can't thank Larry enough for his support in this long endeavor.

From Kris

In the summer of 2006, I was a young seasonal park ranger at Fredericksburg and Spotsylvania National Military Park (FSNMP) in Fredericksburg, Virginia. I had just completed my undergraduate degree in history and was looking to make my mark in the world of Civil War history. As I searched for the right project, I sat down with my friend, mentor, and fellow ranger/historian Frank O'Reilly. For nearly an hour, he and I kicked around idea after idea before he finally suggested that I take a look at the Second Battle of Fredericksburg. I was well aware of the battle because I led daily walking tours down the famous Sunken Road, but I was not sure whether there was enough there to spark my interest.

However, I began delving into the topic. And the more I read in secondary sources, the more fascinated I became. The story of the men, the battle, and the impact on the Chancellorsville campaign as a whole was either glossed over or ignored altogether in many contemporary and secondary works.

After numerous meetings with Frank, I set to work. Without his guidance in the early days, months, and years of this project, I would have gotten nowhere. I cannot thank him enough for his support and encouragement throughout this project.

Thanks must be extended, too, to historian Noel Harrison. Noel was and still is the reigning expert at FSNMP on the Second Battle of Fredericksburg and Salem Church. I spent countless hours in his office—which is also the library—pulling sources, studying maps, and picking his brain. Noel always wanted to know what I'd dug up, and his enthusiasm for the project was heartwarming and genuine.

Donald Pfanz at FSNMP is a rare treasure—a scholar and a gentleman. When I needed a source or had a lead, he always knew where to find what I was looking for. Don is truly a great person and even better friend. He reminded me time and again that others had attempted to bring a Second Fredericksburg manuscript to life, but up until this point none of those efforts had seen the light of day. His words helped motivate me, and his meticulous reading of our manuscript meant the world to both me and my co-author, Chris Mackowski. This project truly never would have seen the light of day—becoming instead yet another addition to the long list of failed manuscripts about the campaign—were it not for Don.

By 2009 I had gathered much of the material that would be used in creating this work, though I still was not at the point of putting pen to paper. Greg Mertz and John Hennessy at FSNMP allowed me to take what research I had and turn it into the park's first-ever History at Sunset tour, built purely around the Second Battle of Fredericksburg. This tour was not only one of the highlights of my National Park Service career, it allowed me to hash out the story and sources into a comprehensive story line and present it to a crowd of over 250—a great, yet frightening way to present the latest research on the topic.

Over the years, others have been more than supportive of this endeavor, be it through their words of encouragement or their efforts in helping in the research of the project. They always stood beside me through thick and thin, and I will never forget them for it: Joseph Haydon (US Army, Retired); the late Major General Thomas Cleland; my dear friend Dr. James Good; the always-entertaining Richard Chapman (FSNMP); the ever-boisterous Jake Struhelka; the incomparable Ray Castner; Becky Cumins (FSNMP); Randy Washburn (FSNMP); Ryan Longfellow (FSNMP); Beth Parnicza (FSNMP); Eric Mink (FSNMP); Matt Stanley; Greg Kurtz; Thomas Breen; Lee Wolfe; Royce and Ginny Cook; Kin Glover; J. D. Cribbs; Conway Richardson; Kati Engel; John Cummings; Jon Gerlach; Mark Allen; Dick Fleming; and Ben "Huggybear" Lamb. Thanks also to my longtime brothers and friends from western Pennsylvania, Roger Doty, Doug Wilson, Pat Larkin, and the rest of the men of the 140th Pennsylvania. Finally, my thanks to the man who always knows where he is, Joseph Obidzinski.

To Gregg Kneipp, Craig Johnson, Chuck Lockhart, Keith Kelly, Regina Carrico, and Kate Sargent: thank you! You went above and beyond, and I would not be where I am today without all of you.

We have to thank the historians who took the time to read and critique the manuscript during its development: Daniel Davis, formerly of FSNMP; Phill Greenwalt, ranger/historian at the George Washington Birthplace; Rea Redd at Waynesburg University; Dr. James Broomall at the University of North Florida; Clint Schemmer at the Fredericksburg *Free-Lance Star*; Steward Henderson (FSNMP), a great friend and historian Patrick Larkin; historian Edward Alexander at Pamplin Park; Greg Mertz Supervisory Historian (FSNMP) and the aforementioned Donald Pfanz.

I cannot give enough thanks to my colleague, co-author, and best friend, Chris Mackowski. Chris and I met at the FSNMP in the summer of

2005. At the time, I was an underpaid and overenthusiastic intern and he was a volunteer from New York state who brought his daughter Stephanie to volunteer at the park. In our first day on the line together, a friendship was formed almost instantly. Since then, he and I have trekked across numerous battlefields in varying states of weather. We have written numerous articles and books, created a website for emerging Civil War authors, and formed a friendship that transcends research and writing. He was the best man at my wedding, and I couldn't ask for a better partner in all of our writing projects. If it were not for his encouragement and motivation, this project would never have seen the light of day. His constant enthusiasm for the Civil War and for writing is contagious. I am eternally grateful that he agreed to be a part of this seven-year project and endure the hardships that go along with a work of this breadth.

Finally, I have to thank my family. My parents Donna and Evan have always nurtured my love for history. If it were not for my father's love of cars, I would never have stepped foot on the Gettysburg battlefield and found my love for history. Their constant and unwavering support make all of my projects possible.

My sisters Karen and Kim are my biggest fans and do whatever they can to help advertise projects. They push me to be the best I can be. My nephews Colton and Trevor inspire me with their love of history and support of my projects. My brothers-in-law Joe and Jeff have always been there for me and have supported me in every way possible. My brother Kevin took me across battlefields on overnight and day trips when I was young. Our adventures across those fields and to many flea markets on the way have filled me with stories beyond my years. My Aunt Nancy and Uncle Gerry took me to battlefields and historic places I had never heard of as a kid, from Droop Mountain to Philippi and every little place in between. My in-laws have embraced my love and endured trips across many a field with me.

Last but not least, I have to thank my wife, Sarah, and our dog, Dobby. I have known my wife almost as long as I have worked on this project. She has been the constant strength in my life and my rock. Too many nights and weekends I have been pulled away from her by the lure of Second Fredericksburg. She has patiently listened to my triumphs when I find a great source and my frustration when I find five sources on the same thing that all say something different. With her, I am a better person, and for her love and support, I can never thank her enough.

From Chris

Most of my thanks are worked into Kris' list, above, because together he and I have had the privilege of working with some wonderful colleagues. In the spirit of avoiding redundancy, I won't repeat the list, but two people in particular merit special attention. Like Kris, I wouldn't be writing about the Civil War if it wasn't for our friend and mentor, Frank O'Reilly, who shared with us a tradition of scholarship and writing that sprang from the inestimable Bob Krick. Frank is also the person who first took me into Salem Church, a rare and splendid treat that opened my eyes to this forgotten story. He and his wife, Amy, are gems. I also need to thank Greg Mertz for years of support. He has continually enabled and encouraged my professional growth as a historian, allowing me to branch out in all kinds of ways, for which I am deeply grateful. This book is very much the latest culmination of that growth. Also from Kris' list, I will give a special shout-out to Don Pfanz because the book is dedicated to him: "Don is the *Man*!"

During the writing of this book, I spent a lot of time on the Fredericksburg battlefield with former park ranger/historian Caity Stuart. Caity is a pacifist, and that she worked at a battlefield was an irony never lost on her. Her attempts to reconcile those two perspectives, though, allowed her to tell deeply humane stories and raise powerful questions that helped me see the battlefields in new ways. It is my great fortune that we explored those battlefields together, and I am thankful for the energy and spirit of adventure she brought to those explorations.

Above and beyond Kris' list, I would like to thank my colleagues at the Russell J. Jandoli School of Journalism and Mass Communication at St. Bonaventure University, especially Dean Pauline Hoffmann and my colleague (and ever-diligent personal editor) Patrick "Mr. Bad Example" Vecchio. A tip of the hat, too, to my former colleague and Civil War aficionado, John Hanchette.

I've spent more time on battlefields with my daughter, Stephanie, than with any other person (Kris included). They have been among the best times of my life. She and my son Jackson continue to be my life's great blessings. I love them both and thank them for tolerating my long hours in front of the computer screen, trying to tell the stories of the fields we've walked together—even though telling those stories has meant time apart.

The person I probably owe the greatest debt of thanks to for this book died on the Second Fredericksburg battlefield late on the morning of May 3, 1863. Capt. Sewell Gray of the 6th Maine left behind a diary with a tragically ironic last entry: "Sabbath, and a lovelier day never overtook a soldier. . . . If we fall God strengthen the bereaved." The poignancy of Sewell's entry—and, yes, I have come over time to know him as "Sewell"—led to my first writing project about the battle, a piece Kris and I did based on Sewell's diary for *Fredericksburg History & Biography*. The kinship I felt for Sewell as we researched his life and death made it one of the most gratifying projects of my career.

This project now ranks up there with it. It is always a privilege and pleasure to work with Kris, but this book has been his baby for as long as I've known him, so it is particularly meaningful. I cannot express how pleased I've been to help him see it to fruition. Kris and I have written hundreds of thousands of words together, yet I still can't seem to find the right ones to express my admiration and respect for him. "Thanks" just doesn't seem to cut it—but I know he knows what I mean when I say it. Sometimes it's the things we can't articulate that mean the most. Kris, this one's for you.

Prologue

Two New Jersey soldiers stand sentinel on either side of Virginia State Route 3 as it runs westward from I-95 through a landscape of commercial sprawl. The Garden State boys, both hewn of New Hampshire granite and perched high on pillars, have spent more than a century keeping watch over the battlefield, but they have been powerless to do anything as the farmlands have given way to strip malls, fast food joints, and parking lots.

It's easy to miss the Jersey men. The man on the north side of the road, from the 15th New Jersey, is hemmed in on three sides by trees. One could easily mistake him for a bushwhacker, ready to charge out of the brush.

Opposite, on the south side of the road, a soldier from the 23rd New Jersey faces north. A cemetery dots the hillside around him, so at first pass he looks like another grave marker, albeit a bit grander than the others. It's hard to slow down for a better look because the eight lanes of traffic move in a steady stream, and many of the drivers are trying to beat the light at the crest of the hill.

It's easy to miss Old Salem Church, nestled on the southeast corner of the intersection by that traffic light. The historic building sits back from the road, screened on the west side by a line of trees planted by the National Park Service in 1981 as a last line of defense against the modern world. On the property's north side, a split-rail fence runs along the edge as a token form of resistance against Route 3.

Visitors cannot get to Old Salem Church from either road that borders it, though. They need to drive south a few hundred yards on Salem Church Road past the bank and the Advance Auto Parts store and the

A modern view of the 23rd New Jersey monument on the
Salem Church Battlefield.

Kristopher D. White

Arby's, then take a left at the next light, then curl left again on Old Salem Church Road, which dead-ends a few hundred yards away at a small parking area. A footpath leads from there to the church, which usually remains closed. Volunteers from "new" Salem Church, built in 1954, sometimes staff the older building on weekends in the summer, although few visitors find their way in.

In the old church, rows of pews face front, toward where a preacher standing at the pulpit would be framed by a large window. Plenty of natural light spills in, making the white-walled interior feel even more stark. Boot heels echo up from the floor, past the balconies that line both sides of the room, and bounce back down from the high ceiling. Between two windows under the northern balcony, soldiers scrawled graffiti, still visible today thanks to the National Park Service's preservation efforts. The NPS could save little of the land around the church, but it saved the graffiti inside it.

Outside, the façade still bears the scars of battle: bullet holes pock-mark the salmon-colored bricks. On the eastern wall, a crack from a lightning strike zigzags downward.

At the intersection by the traffic light, a brown Park Service sign advertises to motorists that they're passing through the Salem Church battlefield; but a smaller sign should be mounted beneath it that warns, "Don't blink or you'll miss it."

Old Salem Church sits on a parcel that measures only 2.76 acres. It's all that's left of a battlefield that has otherwise been forgotten.

*   *   *

Built in 1844 by a Baptist congregation under the pastorship of the Reverend Joseph A. Billingsley, Salem Church sat along the Orange Turnpike four miles outside the city of Fredericksburg. When civil war struck the city in December of 1862, refugees flooded westward along the Orange Turnpike, and many of them took shelter in the church.

In the spring, the war shifted several miles to the west of Salem Church, into the "dark close wood" known as the Wilderness. There, at a crossroads clearing known as Chancellorsville, Union and Confederate forces clashed May 1-3, 1863. As part of that action, the Union VI Corps, stationed in Fredericksburg, drove west along the turnpike to come to the aid of the rest of the army. Elements of the Army of Northern Virginia

Salem Church today. In the foreground is a monument to the battle placed
by the United Daughters of the Confederacy.

Kristopher D. White

moved eastward to check the Federal movement. They took up positions
in and around Salem Church because it sat along a north-south ridge that
provided a strong military position.

The VI Corps, bruised by its morning victory in Fredericksburg,
stalled in its advance when it discovered the Confederates on the ridge.
Both sides took turns assaulting each other on May 3 and 4, but eventually
the stunned Federal force slipped across the river at Banks' Ford, just to
the north.

Today, most of the ridge is gone, hauled away in the late nineties and
early two-thousands by earth movers. "Someone came in here and did a
study and found out that, subconsciously, shoppers don't like to pull *up*
into a parking lot—they like to pull *down*," explained one NPS historian,
the disdain in his voice hardly disguised at all. "So they came in and

literally bulldozed the ridge and hauled it away so people could pull down into a parking lot for that strip mall on the north side of the road."[1]

Also on the north side of Route 3, below the level of the roadbed, hulks the multi-million-dollar Faith Baptist Church, constructed in 2008. It is *not* Salem Church, although its massive size certainly calls much attention to itself.

New Salem Church, a congregation of about 500 members, sits on the south side of the road, much smaller, much more modest. The congregation's cemetery sits between the new church and the historic church. There, too, stands the shaft of granite topped by the soldier from the 23rd New Jersey.

The monument, built with funds provided by the state of New Jersey, was dedicated in 1906. "Reconciliation and reunion were the themes of the day," NPS historian Donald Pfanz said.[2] During dedication ceremonies, one of the speakers, Col. Alexander S. Bacon of the New York National Guard, praised the soldiers of both sides. "With the North and South standing shoulder to shoulder," he said, "we can whip any two nations on the face of the globe."[3] The plaque on the monument's east face honors the fallen men of New Jersey and bears witness "to the valor of the men who opposed them on this field." The plaque's north face bears an inscription "Dedicated to national unity and perpetual peace."[4]

The monument, and the parcel it rests upon, was the first piece of property set aside in the area to commemorate the battle.

Two years later, the 15th New Jersey erected its monument across the street. It likewise bears "a generous tribute to the foes in whose memory it was reared":[5]

1 Frank O'Reilly, interview by Chris Mackowski, June 2, 2011.

2 Donald Pfanz, *History Through Eyes of Stone* (Fredericksburg, VA, 2006), 146.

3 Ibid., 36-37.

4 Text quoted from the monument of the 23rd New Jersey on the Salem Church battlefield.

5 Newspaper article, *Fredericksburg (VA) Daily Star*, May 7, 1907.

TO THE BRAVE ALABAMA BOYS, OUR
OPPONENTS ON THIS FIELD OF
BATTLE, WHOSE MEMORY WE HONOR,
THIS TABLET IS DEDICATED[6]

In August of 1932, the state of Virginia transferred responsibility for the monuments to the United States Department of War, which was then overseeing the creation of the new Fredericksburg and Spotsylvania National Military Park (FSNMP). Established by an act of Congress on February 14, 1927, the park includes areas associated with four major battles: Fredericksburg, Chancellorsville, the Wilderness, and Spotsylvania Court House.

At the time, park boundaries were set following what was known as "The Antietam Plan." In 1902, when Congress created the Antietam National Battlefield, the plan called for procuring "those essential land strips along roadways and narrow tracts delineating the actual lines of battle" rather than "an entire battlefield land area."[7] Everyone believed that the farmland around Antietam would always be farmland, so there was no need to buy it in order to preserve it; its perpetual use as farmland would be protection enough. Such thinking guided them in Spotsylvania, too: the farmland between the city and the 70-square-mile "region of gloom" known as the Wilderness, ten miles to the west, would always remain devoted to agriculture. As a result, no land was set aside for actual preservation at Salem Church.

"Unfortunately," said researcher Eric Martin, "because of its failure to anticipate the threat of future urban population growth and sprawl within the county, this plan's critical assumption would later sow the seeds for the future destruction of the vast rural setting surrounding Salem Church."[8]

In 1954, the Salem Church congregation built a new building a few hundred yards east of its original structure, on property adjacent to the far

---

6 Text quoted from the monument of the 15th New Jersey on the Salem Church battlefield.

7 Eric B. Martin, *Salem Church Heights: The Loss of a Park Battlefield*, 2003, in the Fredericksburg and Spotsylvania National Military Park bound manuscript collection.

8 Ibid., 6.

side of the cemetery. In 1962, it donated the old church and just over an acre of land to the Park Service, which had taken over administration of the park. Along with the monuments, the Salem Church battlefield consisted of just over two acres of federally protected property.

Around that time, plans got underway for the creation of Interstate 95, which would run north-south between Washington, D.C., and Richmond, Virginia. In anticipation, the state decided to widen Route 3. The project caused the first significant disruption to the land around Salem Church, even necessitating the shifting of the 15th New Jersey monument several dozen yards to the north to make way for the wider westbound lane. "Once the interstate was built," said Martin, "the result over the next ten years was to slowly transform Virginia State Route 3 from a mostly quiet, rural, and pastoral thoroughfare into a noisy, busy, commercial strip corridor."[9]

The NPS responded by trying to establish new administrative boundaries for the Salem Church battlefield, but when the property finally came up for sale in November 1977 at an asking price of $300,000, the Park Service declined to act, saying the parcel was overpriced by $25,000. So the landowner chose to develop the property, putting a Star Petroleum station on a corner across from Old Salem Church.

"The Star Petroleum gas station's construction and placement within the heart of the park's authorized boundary, in the summer of 1981, ultimately ensured the loss of the historical integrity of the Old Salem Church battlefield to commercial development," Martin concluded.[10]

The Park Service's protests fell on deaf ears. "Spotsylvania County, at the time, one could say, really had no vested (long-term) interest in promoting the idea of 'protecting and preserving' its lesser-known Civil War battlefields," Martin wrote. "[T]he local government leaders of Spotsylvania County, beginning in the 1970s, were almost solely concerned with promoting and embracing development. . . . [T]he Spotsylvania County Board of Supervisors, almost all of the time, were either indifferent to or neutral toward any efforts by the park's local

9 Ibid., 10.

10 Ibid., 23.

officials to procure 'protective zoning' or 'conservation easements' near Old Salem Church."[11]

As Spotsylvania County's population continued to balloon—it more than doubled between 1970 and 1980, for instance—development opportunities abounded in the stretch between the new I-95 interchange and Salem Church. The spot where Federal artillerists unlimbered so they could bombard Confederates on the ridge turned into a parking lot. One of the historic houses from the battlefield was replaced by a Rax restaurant; later, that too was razed to make way for a CVS pharmacy.

In the ongoing struggle between preservation and development, the modern battle for Salem Church was as lopsided a loss as the Federal charges against the stone wall at Fredericksburg.

*   *   *

Most visitors to the Fredericksburg battlefield do not realize that Union soldiers *did* manage to break through the Confederate position behind the stone wall—in May of 1863.

Instead, visitors focus on the futile Union charges against the position that took place on December 13, 1862. Major General Ambrose E. Burnside sent seven waves of men against the wall in an effort to support his main attack at the south end of the field against Confederates on Prospect Hill; the latter field of attack is known today as Slaughter Pen Farm. As that attack unfolded, then sputtered out, the demonstrations against the stone wall took on a horrible life of their own, resulting in some 8,000 Union casualties on the north end of the field. (In comparison, Confederates there suffered just under 1,000 casualties, many of whom were victims of accidental friendly fire.)[12]

---

11 Ibid., 22.

12 Frank O'Reilly, *The Fredericksburg Campaign: Winter War on the Rappahannock* (Baton Rough, LA, 2003). O'Reilly delves into the topography of the Sunken Road sector and the effect it had on the Confederate defensive line there. Brigadier General Thomas R. R. Cobb's Georgia brigade, specifically the 24th Georgia and Phillip's Legion, received friendly fire from men of the 15th and 46th North Carolina of Brig. Gen. Robert Ransom's brigade. The Georgians were forced to send two runners to the rear in an attempt to tell the Tar Heels to stop firing into their backs. The fire also left evidence in the form of battle scars that still exist on the Innis House. The friendly fire ended when the North Carolinians shifted into the Sunken Road itself to reinforce their Georgia counterparts.

The infamous Sunken Road at Fredericksburg.

Kristopher D. White

A walk along the Sunken Road and stone wall today is a little like walking back in time. In 2004, the city of Fredericksburg relinquished its right-of-way on the Sunken Road, turning over possession to the NPS, which promptly initiated efforts to restore the road to its wartime appearance. Through extensive archeology and with the help of old photos, the Park Service recreated the stone wall and the gravel road itself.

The wall, as it turned out, was far sturdier than the fieldstone wall constructed back in the 1930s by the Civilian Conservation Corps along the southernmost stretch of the road. The original wall was constructed from quarried stone. Two feet thick and four and a half feet high, it provided the Confederates with a formidable shield.

Visitors might be familiar with a post-battle photo of the stone wall and Sunken Road that shows Confederate dead lying in the road. Abandoned muskets and other detritus of battle—an overturned haversack, an unfurled bedroll, a canteen—are scattered around them. The body closest to the foreground, twisted, blackened from gunpowder, frequently gets cropped out.

The image, taken by Andrew J. Russell, came in the wake of the May battle, not the battle in December—but most visitors don't even know the May battle took place. All eyes in May focus to the west, beyond Salem Church, to the crossroads at Chancellorsville in the heart of the Wilderness—a 70-square-mile "region of gloom" that sprawled across north Spotsylvania and Orange counties.

Yet this second battle of Fredericksburg proved the one bright spot in Maj. Gen. Joseph Hooker's otherwise dismal experience that May. At Second Fredericksburg, the Union VI Corps overran a Confederate position that had, until that point, grown legendary in the minds of Federal soldiers because they were defeated on that same ground, in front of that same stone wall, four and a half months earlier. By taking the position, "[t]he troops behaved most nobly, and were duly praised," observed one newspaper correspondent.[13] The Federals drove off some of the Confederacy's scrappiest officers—Maj. Gen. Jubal Early and Brig. Gen. William Barksdale—and positioned themselves perfectly for a strike at the rear of the main Confederate army at Chancellorsville. "Ah, we anticipated a good time," wrote a New York private.[14]

But as the VI Corps moved westward, things unraveled. "How different everything might, nay, would have been, if we had had the cooperation of even a small part of the immense force with Fighting Joe Hooker [at Chancellorsville]!" wrote R. F. Halsted, a member of Maj. Gen. John Sedgwick's staff.

> Why did he not keep Lee occupied so that he would not have dared to turn his back to Chancellorsville, to fall upon us? Or if, finding that he had so left him, why did he not know it and act accordingly; fall upon the rear of his column as it came down upon us? What was Hooker there for? To entrench himself, with six corps under his command, and expect and even order one single corps to march right through the enemy, to 'crush and destroy,' were the words of his order to the General, 'any force which might oppose itself to' our march?[15]

13 *Albany(NY) Evening Journal*, May 20, 1863.

14 Jacob Bechtel to Candis Hannawalt, 59th New York, May 13, 1863, in the Fredericksburg and Spotsylvania National Military Park bound manuscript collection.

15 R. F. Halsted to "Miss Sedgwick," in Carl and Ellen Battelle Stoeckel, eds., *Correspondence of John Sedgwick Major-General*, 2 vols. (New York, NY, 1903), vol. 2, 124-125.

"Thus we find the army paralyzed at the very time when the capture of Fredericksburg Heights by Sedgwick, and his approach to the rear of Lee, should have been a signal to us for the redoubling of efforts," wrote Col. Charles S. Wainwright in his diary. He called it "the decisive moment." "Everything could yet have been saved," he wrote; "yet all was lost."[16]

"All was lost"—Wainwright had no idea how prophetic those words would be, considering just how much of the story has been forgotten: how Second Fredericksburg has been subsumed by First Fredericksburg; how the grisly images of the dead have been cropped from photos in an effort to sanitize them; how the battlefield at Salem Church has been bulldozed and paved and commercialized; how the very terrain itself has been hauled away in dump trucks, forever altering the topography.

The battle of Chancellorsville hinged on the VI Corps' movement at Second Fredericksburg and Salem Church, and Hooker's ability to take advantage of the opportunities opened by these operations. Yet in the shorthand of history, the actions at Second Fredericksburg and Salem Church get noticed only as a footnote when critics cast aspersions at Sedgwick in an attempt to scapegoat him—a tradition that dates back to Fighting Joe Hooker himself, who tried to salvage the nearly mortal blow his reputation suffered in the middle of the Wilderness.

We owe it to those New Jersey boys who still stand sentinel over the battlefield, and all their comrades who fought and fell there—to the men of the North and to the South—to look more closely at the battles of Second Fredericksburg and Salem Church, the forgotten front of Chancellorsville.

16 Allan Nevins, ed., *A Diary of Battle: The Personal Journals of Colonel Charles S. Wainwright, 1861-1865* (New York, NY, 1998), 198.

Chapter One

Mr. Lincoln's Principal Army:

The Army of the Potomac

A small knot of officers and dignitaries looked out over a vast plain filled with men-at-arms. Two horsemen stood out in particular. One, seated on a fine white horse, wore full military regalia—Maj. Gen. "Fighting Joe" Hooker, now in his third month in command of the Army of the Potomac. The other rider, sitting atop a black horse, looked "pale, haggard and care-worn," one observer said, "but seemed to have a gleam of happiness about him. . . . You could discern by his countenance that he felt deeply interested in the army and the salvation of the Union; that his mind was deeply absorbed in the duties devolving upon him as the Chief Magistrate of the Nation."[1]

"Mr. Lincoln is one of the plainest of men," a III Corps soldier said.

He has a kindly expression that made us forget his plainness. Mr. Lincoln on horseback is not a model of beauty such as an artist would select. A more awkward specimen of humanity I cannot well imagine. It shows him off at a horrible disadvantage. There was a fearful disproportion between the length of

---

1 From an article written on April 15, 1863, by an unidentified VI Corps soldier. The article appeared in the April 24, 1863, edition of the *Hunterdon (NJ) Republican*, in the Fredericksburg and Spotsylvania National Military Park bound manuscript collection, vol. 109.

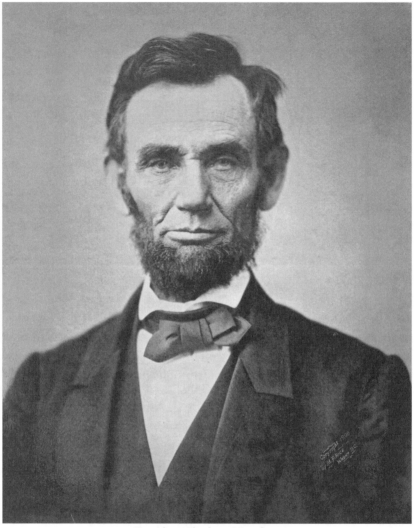

President Abraham Lincoln.

Library of Congress

his legs and the height of his horse. It seemed as if nothing short of tying a knot in them would prevent them from dragging the ground.[2]

2   Ruth L. Silliker, ed., *Rebel Yell & the Yankee Hurrah: The Civil War Journal of a Maine Volunteer: Private John W. Haley, 17th Maine Regiment* (Bangor, ME, 1985), 75.

Despite his awkward appearance and careworn expression, Lincoln seemed to be enjoying himself immensely.[3] Some 80,000 men from the II, III, V, and VI corps stretched out in front of him in martial glory. "It was a grand sight to see so many soldiers, all with guns and bayonets gleaming in the air," wrote a Michigan soldier in a letter home the next day.[4] A correspondent from the *Cincinnati (OH) Daily Gazette* described "[t]he proud, elastic, but firm military tread, the exact and uniform movement, as if every company and every regiment were moved by one impulse and inspirited by one soul, demonstrated that these men had the spirit of the true soldier."[5]

The spectacle provided quite a contrast to Lincoln's arrival three days earlier on April 5. He, his wife and son, and a small party of guests that included Attorney General Edward Bates and newspaper correspondent Noah Brooks had arrived during a heavy snow squall. "I only regret that your party is not as large as our hospitality," Hooker had told him.[6] Hooker's chief of staff, Maj. Gen. Daniel Butterfield, installed the dignitaries in three large tents next to Hooker's headquarters.[7]

Over the ensuing days, Lincoln made calls around the army. Aside from meetings with Hooker and Butterfield, Lincoln also met with Maj. Gen. Daniel Sickles, a man of considerable political influence in both New York and Washington who had recently been promoted to command of the III Corps. Lincoln also went to the front lines along the Rappahannock River to view the enemy and then to the rear of the army to see the refugee camps of newly freed slaves. Mrs. Lincoln visited the army's field hospitals, "giving little comforts to the sick, without any

---

3 William E. Doster, *Lincoln and Episodes of the Civil War* (New York, NY, 1915), 190-191.

4 Edgar W. Clark, 3rd Michigan, to Wife, April 9, 1863, in the Fredericksburg and Spotsylvania National Military Park bound manuscript collection, local index.

5 Rufus Robinson Dawes, *Service with the Sixth Wisconsin Volunteers* (Marietta, OH, 1890), 131. While Dawes served in the I Corps' First Division, they were on review at the same time as the VI Corps.

6 Noah Brooks, *Washington in Lincoln's Time* (New York, NY, 1896), 158.

7 Jane Hollenback Conner, *Lincoln in Stafford* (Fredericksburg, VA, 2006), 56-59.

display or ostentation, like a gentle, kind-hearted lady, as she is," noted VI Corps commander Maj. Gen. John Sedgwick in a letter to his sister.[8]

Once the ground dried out a bit from the snowfall, Hooker began to assemble parts of his reorganized army for Lincoln's review. On April 6, the reorganized cavalry corps under Brig. Gen. George Stoneman marched by. Now, on April 8, the heart of the Army of the Potomac—the army's four biggest corps—had assembled for him: II, III, V, and VI. "The formation was in three 'lines of masses' of two corps each," wrote the historian of the 140th Pennsylvania. "The length of each line was estimated to be more than a mile, and the depth of the three lines from front to rear, including the spaces between, at about one-fifth of a mile. The number of men present was estimated at 80,000."[9] The I Corps was scheduled for review the next day, April 9, and the army's most recent additions, the XI and XII corps, would march for the president on April 10.

The men looked crisp and refreshed despite their harrowing experience at Fredericksburg in December 1862; the disastrous "Mud March" of January 1863; and a long winter in Stafford County, Virginia. Lincoln saw the life Joe Hooker had breathed back into the army. "In truth," XI Corps commander Maj. Gen. Oliver Otis Howard later wrote in his autobiography, "during February, March, and April, the old, cheerful, hopeful, trustful spirit which had carried us through so many dark days, through so many bloody fields and trying defeats, returned to the Army of the Potomac; and Hooker's success as a division and corps commander was kept constantly in mind as an earnest of a grand future."[10]

Morale was generally as high among the enlisted men as it was among the officers and the president's party. "The army has again got the good old spirit and the enthusiasm of last spring is surely returning, and old Hooker is getting to be a second McClellan," wrote musician Erasmus W.

---

8 John Sedgwick to Emily Sedgwick Welch, April 12, 1863, *Correspondence of John Sedgwick Major-General*, eds. Carl and Ellen Battelle Stoeckel, 2 vols. (New York, NY, 1903), vol. 2, 90.

9 Robert L. Stewart, *History of the One Hundred and Fortieth Pennsylvania Volunteers* (Pittsburgh, PA, 1912), 46.

10 Oliver Otis Howard, *Autobiography of Oliver Otis Howard: Major General United States Army*, 2 vols. (New York, NY, 1908), 348.

Reed of the 96th Pennsylvania a few days prior to the president's review. "He has a fine army to back him. If it be God's will he must be successful."[11]

"Gen. Hooker is gaining strength and popularity every day with the army," echoed an officer from the 7th Maine, "and we hope and expect that he will not be found wanting when the day of trial comes."[12]

*   *   *

Lincoln had chosen Hooker for command only reluctantly, in part as a capitulation to radicals in his own Republican party. He believed Hooker to be "a brave and skillful soldier" and praised Hooker because "you do not mix politics with your profession," but he knew of Hooker's role in undermining his predecessor, Ambrose Burnside.

> [Y]ou have taken counsel of your ambition, and thwarted him as much as you could, in which you did a great wrong to the country. I have heard, in such a way as to believe it, of your recently saying that both the Army and the Government needed a Dictator. Of course it was not for this, but in spite of it, that I have given you the command. Only those generals who gain successes, can set up dictators. What I now ask of you is military success, and I will risk the dictatorship.[13]

In the same letter, Lincoln warned Hooker to "beware of rashness." It was an admonition Hooker apparently ignored, at least in his boasting. At one point during Lincoln's visit in April, the president began to suggest that if Hooker made it to Richmond. . . . "Excuse me, Mr. President," Hooker interrupted, "but there is no '*if*' in the case. I am going straight to Richmond if I live." Lincoln later grumbled that Hooker's overconfidence was "about the worst thing I have seen since I have been down here."[14]

---

11 Erasmus W. Reed to Parents, Brothers and Sisters, April 3, 1863, in the Fredericksburg and Spotsylvania National Military Park bound manuscript collection, local index.

12 Lieutenant Colonel Selden Connor to Father, March 25, 1863, in the Fredericksburg and Spotsylvania National Military Park bound manuscript collection, local index.

13 Paul M. Angle, *Abraham Lincoln's Letter to Major General Joseph Hooker Dated January 26, 1863: A Facsimile Reproduction of the Letter with Explanatory Text by Paul M. Angle* (Chicago, IL, 1942), 2-4.

14 Walter H. Hebert, *Fighting Joe Hooker* (Lincoln, NE, 1999), 183.

Hooker was a Hadley, Massachusetts-born Yankee who began his military career as a member of West Point's class of 1837, in which he graduated 29th out of 49.[15] Commissioned a second lieutenant upon graduation, he was assigned to the 1st U.S. Artillery in Florida, where he served in the Second Seminole War. Later, he was transferred back to West Point to serve as adjutant.

During the Mexican War, he was attached to numerous generals, including Maj. Gen. Gideon Pillow. Though serving as a staff officer, Hooker managed to make his way into the fight somehow, and was brevetted for bravery at the battles of Monterey, National Bridge, and Chapultepec. He also managed to make a few enemies, including Maj. Gen. Winfield Scott, the most famous army officer of his day. During court-martial proceedings against Pillow, who was one of Scott's chief rivals, Hooker testified on Pillow's behalf.

Following the Mexican War, Hooker was assigned to an outpost in California, but the monotony of the peacetime army caught up with him. In 1854, Hooker resigned his commission to take up farming, politics, and militia duty in California and Oregon, where he toiled in relative obscurity. When civil war broke out, Hooker came east and rejoined the United States Army, but the newly re-commissioned lieutenant colonel had difficulties obtaining a command because his former run-in with Scott had left him on the wrong side of an army power struggle. Discouraged, Hooker began thinking of heading back west.

While Hooker languished, the Union army came to grief on the plains of Manassas, Virginia. In the wake of the July 1861 defeat, the lieutenant colonel gladly took on the role of armchair general, telling anyone who would listen, including the president, that if he had been in charge, the battle would have been a victory. "I was anxious to pay my respects to you, sir, and express my wish for your personal welfare, and for your success in putting down the rebellion," Hooker told Lincoln when they finally met. "And, while I am about it, Mr. President, I want to say one thing more, and that is, that I was at the battle of Bull Run, the other day, and it is neither vanity nor boasting in me to declare that I am a better

---

15 H. Edwin Tremain, *In Memoriam Major General Joseph Hooker* (Cincinnati, OH, 1881), 4.

Major General Joseph "Fighting Joe" Hooker.

National Archives

general than you, sir, had on that field."[16] Lincoln placed his hand on Hooker's shoulder and told the transplanted Californian: "Stay. I have use for you and a regiment for you to command."[17]

By the end of August 1861, Hooker found himself newly minted as a brigadier general of volunteers. He at first assumed command of a brigade near Bladensburg, Maryland, but was quickly promoted to head the 2nd Division of the newly created III Corps under then-Brig. Gen. Samuel P. Heitzelman. Hooker's division defended the approaches to the capital in southern Maryland.[18]

The following spring, the division joined the largest troop movement ever undertaken on the continent up until that point, relocating to the Virginia Peninsula and joining the Army of the Potomac, then commanded by Maj. Gen. George B. McClellan. On the Peninsula, Hooker led his men with distinction at the battle of Williamsburg in May 1862, where his division at first stood alone against Confederate Maj. Gen. James Longstreet's brigades. Hooker's men fought well but were roughly handled until reinforcements arrived on the field.

Following Williamsburg, Hooker's division fought in the subsequent Seven Days battles around Richmond. It was there on the Peninsula that Hooker earned his famous nickname. A newspaper correspondent sent a dispatch of Hooker's that concluded "I am still fighting—Joe Hooker," but the telegrapher left out the dash. As a result, the final headline read "Fighting Joe Hooker." Hooker lost his punctuation but gained dash of another sort, although the general hated it. "People will think I am a highwayman or a bandit," he said.[19] His men loved it, though, because they felt the name captured their hard-fighting spirit and that of the man who led them.

Hooker's reputation as a fighter continued to grow after his men performed well in late August 1862 at the battle of Second Bull Run, even though they were again roughly handled. Hooker earned promotion to command of the I Corps. Less than a month later at Antietam in

16 Ibid., 5.

17 Ibid., 5-6.

18 Ibid.

19 John Bigelow, *The Campaign of Chancellorsville* (New Haven, CT, 1910), 6.

Maryland, Hooker opened the action in the Miller cornfield and North Woods. As the action seesawed on the north end of the field, Hooker was wounded in the foot and had to be evacuated from the field.

When Burnside rose to command of the Army of the Potomac in early November, he reorganized the army into "Grand Divisions" and appointed Hooker to command the Center Grand Division, which consisted of the III and V corps. When the battle of Fredericksburg unfolded in mid-December, Hooker had to split his Grand Division, so he ended up sending corps to both major sectors of the field: most of the III Corps fought at the southern end of the field in the Prospect Hill sector, helping to stem a Southern counterattack by Lt. Gen. Thomas J. "Stonewall" Jackson; the V Corps fought on the northern end of the field, in the Marye's Heights sector, where, like so many other Federal troops, they bled out in front of Longstreet's divisions.[20]

The battle of Fredericksburg was a debacle for Burnside, and it cost the army commander the confidence of the men and generals under his command. "The three months he exercised the command of the Army it never degenerated so rapidly," Hooker later recalled of his predecessor. "His administration was a blunder, and worse than a blunder for not less than one third of his Army had disappeared from the field [through desertion], and those that remained were despondent and disheartened. . . . The trouble with Burnside appeared to be that his thoughts were always woolgathering. . . . "[21]

Convinced that the Army of the Potomac's "end was close at hand," Hooker began to surreptitiously but actively campaign against Burnside. He was not alone. In fact, generals John Newton and John Cochrane went to Lincoln directly to press the campaign.

The weather, as much as anything, finally proved to be Burnside's undoing. He planned a wide flank march to the north and west, from where he could drop down behind the Confederate army still ensconced on the far side of the Rappahannock River. No sooner did the movement get underway, though, than a downpour started, bogging down the entire

---

20 Edward J. Stackpole, *The Fredericksburg Campaign: Drama on the Rappahannock* (Harrisburg, PA, 1991), 172-198.

21 Joseph Hooker to Samuel Bates, June 29, 1878, in the Fredericksburg and Spotsylvania National Military Park bound manuscript collection, vol. 406.

Hooker's rival and predecessor Maj. Gen. Ambrose Burnside. Burnside lasted a mere 77 days as commander of the Army of the Potomac.

Library of Congress

army. At first, Burnside insisted on pressing forward, but it soon became apparent that was impossible: "it rained as if the world was coming to an end."[22] Confederates on the far side of the river mocked the Federals by mounting a wooden sign with big letters that read, "Burnside stuck in the Mud."[23]

The Mud March, as it became known, was the last straw. Burnside asked to be removed and Lincoln quickly took him up on the offer. The Army of the Potomac's top leadership was shuffled. On January 26, 1863, Hooker got the nod from Lincoln. "Beware of rashness," Lincoln counseled—an admonition he repeated twice in the letter, and which surely must have rankled "Fighting Joe"—"but with energy and sleepless vigilance, go forward, and give us victories."[24]

The men of the army, jaded by a string of battlefield disappointments that dated back to the start of the war, greeted the news of Hooker's ascension with mixed reaction. "Burnside, Sumner, and Franklin relieved and Hooker assumes the command. The news creates no excitement, is hardly a subject of gossip," wrote Capt. Sewell Gray of the 6th Maine in his diary.[25] I Corps artillery chief Charles Wainwright shared Gray's ambivalence. "The appointment of 'Fighting Joe Hooker' to the command of the Army of the Potomac has given great satisfaction and raised great expectations in the civilian world; the papers are loud in praise," Wainwright wrote in his diary. "I cannot say that my own expectations are so high."[26]

Captain Henry Abbott of the 20th Massachusetts had lower expectations even than that of his fellow Bay Stater. "Hooker is nothing more than a smart, driving, plucky Yankee, inordinately vain & I imagine

22 Russell C. White, ed., *The Civil War Diary of Wyman S. White: First Sergeant Company F. 2nd United States Sharpshooters* (Baltimore, MD, 1993), 121.

23 Robert K. Krick, *Civil War Weather in Virginia* (Tuscaloosa, AL, 2007), 82.

24 Angle, *Abraham Lincoln's Letter*, 2-4.

25 Sewell Gray, Diary of Sewell Gray, transcription in the Library of Fredericksburg and Spotsylvania National Military Park, 26.

26 Nevins, ed., *Personal Journals of Colonel Charles S. Wainwright*, 161.

Officers of the 61st New York Infantry in their winter
encampment near Falmouth, Virginia.

Library of Congress

from the way he has converted himself to the Administration, entirely unscrupulous," he said.[27]

It came as a huge surprise, then, when Hooker quickly proved himself a master of administration and morale. He reorganized the army, abolishing the failed Grand Divisions and bringing back the old corps system: 7 infantry corps in total, plus a massive artillery reserve of 12 batteries, consisting of 56 light and heavy guns.[28] He also organized the

27 Richard F. Miller, *Harvard's Civil War: A History of the Twentieth Massachusetts Volunteer Infantry* (Lebanon, NH, 2005), 225.

28 Robert N. Scott, ed., *The War of the Rebellion: A Compilation of the Official Records of the Union and Confederate Armies*, 128 vols. (Washington, D.C., 1890-1891), vol. 25, pt. 1, 246-253. (All subsequent references will refer to the Official Records as *OR* 25, pt. 1 or 2.) The Union artillery was a massive beast to carry into the wilderness near Chancellorsville. According to Brig. Gen. Henry Hunt, the Army of the Potomac's artillery branch consisted of 412 guns, 980 artillery carriages, 9,543 men and officers, and 8,544 horses. These numbers do not include the ammunition trains attached to the army.

cavalry into a single corps, instead of breaking it into small squadrons, regiments, and brigades and spreading them among the army infantry corps. Hooker then assigned each of the corps an identifying insignia, the forerunner of the modern-day divisional patch, which gave the men in each corps a common symbol to rally behind. The patches quickly boosted esprit de corps. II Corps historian Francis Walker said the badges "became very dear to the troops, as a source of much emulation on the part of the several commands, and a great convenience to the staff, in enabling them, quickly and without troublesome inquiries, to identify a division upon the march or along the line of battle."[29]

Hooker improved the quality and quantity of supplies and rations, and he had bake ovens installed to provide fresh bread to the men in the camps and on picket duty. The general health of the camps improved, too, due largely to Dr. Jonathan Letterman, the army's chief medical officer, to whom Hooker gave free rein to upgrade campsites, properly place latrines, and implement an innovative way of dealing with the wounded by introducing what we know today as triage. Hooker granted furloughs, allowing men who had not seen home in months—some more than a year—to get much-needed time with their families. And new uniforms were issued; many of the men who had participated in the failed "Mud March" were in need of such clothing.

According to the historian of the 140th Pennsylvania, "During the three months which were spent in winter quarters, under command of Major-General Hooker, the men of all branches of the service gained greatly in discipline, effectiveness, military bearing, and the army as a whole was hopeful, loyal and in splendid condition."[30]

Other officers and men agreed. "When Hooker . . . was placed in command of the army, many of us were very much surprised," wrote Maj. Gen. Darius N. Couch, commander of the II Corps.

> I think the superior officers did not regard him competent for the task. He had fine qualities as an officer, but not the weight of character to take charge of that army. Nevertheless, under his administration the army assumed wonderful

---

29 Francis A. Walker, *History of the Second Army Corps In the Army of the Potomac* (New York, NY, 1886), 204.

30 Stewart, *History of the One Hundred and Fortieth Pennsylvania Volunteers*, 45.

Aquia Landing, also known as Aquia Harbor, was the backbone of Hooker's supply system. At its peak, while supplying the Army of the Potomac, the port was reportedly the 5th busiest harbor in the world.

Library of Congress

vigor. I have never known men to change from a condition of the lowest depression to that of a healthy fighting state in so short a time.[31]

*   *   *

This is what Lincoln had come to see for himself. He had been well aware when he appointed Hooker of the malaise and discontent that had pervaded the army. Now he saw for himself the army restored in spirit and invigorated.

"[Hooker] has renewed it, in courage, strength, spirit, confidence," wrote Attorney General Bates in a letter to a former colleague when he returned from the review. "He told me with emphasis that he had as many

31 Darius N. Couch, "Chancellorsville Campaign," in *Battles and Leaders of the Civil War*, 4 vols. (New York, NY, 1956), vol. 3, 119.

Major General Darius Couch, II Corps commander and
Hooker's second-in-command.

men as he wanted, & good men. . . . [S]eeing what Hooker has done in the
rehabilitation of that army, I do not doubt that he will use it as effectively
as he has reformed & inspired it."[32]

Spirits seemed high all the way around—the exact effect such a pageant
was supposed to inspire. "It was a beautiful day, and the review was a

32 Edward Bates to James Eads, April 1863, in the Fredericksburg and Spotsylvania
National Military Park bound manuscript collection, vol. 268.

stirring sight," recalled Couch. "Mr. Lincoln, sitting there with his hat off, head bent, and seemingly meditating, suddenly turned to me and said: 'General Couch, what do you suppose will become of all these men when the war is over?' And it struck me as very pleasant that somebody had an idea that the war would sometime end."[33]

The ground around Belle Plains, where the review took place, was within "easy sight and almost within cannon range of the heights occupied by the enemy beyond the Rappahannock," noted New York engineer Wesley Brainerd.[34] The review was in plain view of the Confederate signal stations, too.[35] Confederates by the thousands crowded Marye's Heights to gaze upon the spectacle that was their foe.[36] "What must have been their feelings," Brainerd wondered, "as they witnessed our solid columns wheel and march past the reviewing Officers hour after hour as they did nearly all that day?" A single defiant cannon shot from the Confederates, fired as the review drew to a close, might have been an indication. It was, Brainerd said, "as much to say 'Come on, we are ready for you.'"[37]

Lincoln spent two more days reviewing troops. The experience affected him profoundly. "As Mr. Lincoln rode by," wrote John Haley of the 17th Maine, assigned to escort the president following his review of the XI and XII corps on April 10, "I noticed that he was weeping. Why he wept I know not—whether he was thinking how many had fallen, or how many will soon fall. It might be neither. But this I do know: under that homely exterior is as tender a heart as ever throbbed, one that is easily moved toward the side of the poor and downtrodden. He is probably aware that a battle cannot long be deferred."[38]

Hooker knew it, too. "With his habitual modesty, he has remarked that with a certain force he could 'drive the Rebels to Hell or anywhere

---

33 Couch, "Chancellorsville Campaign," 120.

34 Ed Malles, ed., *Bridge Building in Wartime: Colonel Wesley Brainerd's Memoirs of the 50th New York Volunteer Engineers* (Knoxville, TN, 1997), 193.

35 Stewart, *History of the One Hundred and Fortieth Pennsylvania Volunteers*, 46.

36 Ibid., 46.

37 Malles, *Bridge Building in Wartime*, 193.

38 Silliker, *Rebel Yell & the Yankee Hurrah*, 75.

else,'" Haley observed. "The administration's plan doesn't involve so extensive a campaign, only that we go as far as Richmond."[39]

In fact, Lincoln made a special point of impressing his expectations upon Hooker one final time before heading back to Washington. Couch, as Hooker's senior corps commander and de facto second-in-command, sat in on the meeting at Lincoln's request. "Gentlemen," the president told them, "in your next battle put in *all* your men."[40]

For his part, Hooker was keeping things close to the vest. "My plans are perfect," he had boasted to subordinates on March 29, "and when I carry them out, may God have mercy on Robert E. Lee, for I shall have none."[41]

Lincoln was not necessarily buying it. "That is the most depressing thing about Hooker," he confidentially told Noah Brooks. "It seems to me he is overconfident."[42]

---

39 Ibid., 71.

40 Couch, "Chancellorsville Campaign," 120. In his account of the meeting, Couch went on to add: "Yet that is exactly what we did not do at Chancellorsville."

41 H. Seymour Hall, *Fredericksburg and Chancellorsville: In the Military Order of the Loyal Legions of the United States: War Talks in Kansas* (Kansas City, MO, 1906), 194.

42 Brooks, *Washington in Lincoln's Time*, 52.

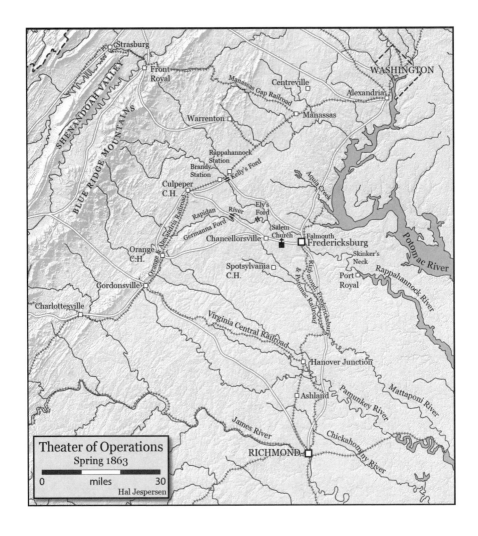

Theater of Operations
Spring 1863

0 miles 30

Hal Jespersen

Chapter Two

The Bedraggled Foe:

The Army of Northern Virginia

"**If** the Enemy does not run, God help them," Hooker had boasted following the review of his XI Corps on March 19.[1] As it was, the "enemy," Gen. Robert E. Lee's Army of Northern Virginia, sat on the west side of the Rappahannock, ensconced in formidable field fortifications it had constructed since the battle of the previous December. A "dark line of rifle pits and earthworks frowned from the bluffs for miles up and down the banks, commanding every available crossing," one Federal observed.[2]

We think Lee to be the greatest general in the world, and his army invincible. Hence, if the Yankees come again, we make no other calculation than to whip them," wrote one South Carolinian, whose opinion was pretty typical.[3]

By mid-January, Lee had about 78,000 men stretched along a front nearly 30 miles long, covering all possible Union approaches from the far

---

1 Bigelow, *The Campaign of Chancellorsville*, 108; *New York Tribune*, March 21, 1863.

2 Winthrop Sheldon, *The Connecticut War Record*, 362, in the Fredericksburg and Spotsylvania National Military Park bound manuscript collection, local index.

3 T. D. Gwin, February 12, 1863, *Southern Enterprise (Greenville, SC) in the Fredericksburg and Spotsylvania National Military Park bound manuscript collection, MS. 05128.*

shore. Lee had other motives for the widely dispersed front, too. His army, encamped in the area for so long, acted like a plague of locusts on the Spotsylvania County countryside: they consumed everything. They even pillaged the city of Fredericksburg itself, having a more devastating effect than the Federal looting that had taken place back in December.[4] "The conduct of our soldiers is most disgraceful," wrote Douglas H. Gordon, owner of the antebellum home Kenmore. "[O]ur troops are plundering and defiling every house in town."[5]

By late winter, supplies for the men and forage for the horses were precariously low. "The men can do very well but our animals suffer terribly," Lee wrote to his wife.[6] To alleviate the situation, Lee detached two divisions from Lt. Gen. James Longstreet's First Corps—the divisions of major generals George Pickett and John Bell Hood—in mid-February and sent them south, first to Richmond, from there toward the southeast corner of the state, to forage for supplies for the rest of the army. Longstreet himself commanded the detachment. By April 11, he was in position to lay siege to the city of Suffolk, Virginia, pinning Federal troops there while his men continued to gather supplies to send north. "I consider it of the first importance to draw from the invaded districts every pound of provision & forage we can," Lee told his Old Warhorse near the start of the mission.[7]

That left Lee in Fredericksburg with Longstreet's other two divisions, those of major generals Richard Anderson and Lafayette McLaws, as well as his entire Second Corps, commanded by Lt. Gen. Thomas J. "Stonewall" Jackson. In all, Lee had perhaps 60,000 men at his ready

---

4   Douglas H. Gordon to Ann E. Gordon, letters of January 13, 27, and 30, 1863, in the Fredericksburg and Spotsylvania National Military Park bound manuscript collection, vol. 19. Gordon, a civilian, was upset by the way Confederate soldiers treated the property of the civilians of the area. Many Confederate soldiers and officers set a double standard by complaining in letters home that the Yankee hordes had descended upon the town, stolen, destroyed, and left devastation behind; yet many southern soldiers performed the same acts against their own civilian population.

5   Douglas H. Gordon to Ann E. Gordon, January 13, 1863; Ibid.

6   Robert E. Lee to Mary Custis Lee, February 23, 1863, in the Fredericksburg and Spotsylvania National Military Park bound manuscript collection, vol. 19.

7   Robert E. Lee to James Longstreet, March 27, 1863, in the Fredericksburg and Spotsylvania National Military Park bound manuscript collection, vol. 19.

disposal—which left him severely undermanned. Even so, he still wished to seize the initiative if and when circumstances allowed, although the overall situation disheartened him. "[T]he most lamentable part of the present condition of things is the impossibility of attacking them with any prospect of advantage," he wrote to Confederate President Jefferson Davis. "The rivers & streams are all swollen beyond fording. We have no bridges, & the roads are in a liquid state & nearly impracticable. In addition, our horses & mules are in that reduced state that the labor & exposure incident to an attack would result in their destruction, & leave us destitute of the means of transportation."[8]

Lee knew the area well, having been born some 35 miles east of Fredericksburg on the Northern Neck of Virginia at his family's ancestral home, Stratford Hall. As a scion of one of Virginia's "First Families" and the son of Revolutionary War hero "Light Horse Harry" Lee, young Robert seemed predestined for a career in the military. He graduated second in the West Point class of 1829, then served in the army as an engineer. During the Mexican War, he served as an engineer and personal aide to army commander Winfield Scott and was thrice brevetted for distinguished service. Following the war, he served a three-year stint as superintendent of West Point before accepting an assignment to the Second United States Cavalry in Texas. It was, finally, the kind of combat position he had always wanted.

In October 1859, while home on leave, he was tasked with suppressing an armed raid on the Federal arsenal at Harper's Ferry. When he and future Confederate general James Ewell Brown "Jeb" Stuart arrived on the scene, they found abolitionist John Brown and 21 of his men holed up in a firehouse. Lee, in command of a contingent of Marines, ordered his men to storm the building and end the standoff.[9]

Eighteen months later, at the outbreak of civil war, Lee was called to Washington and, because of his reputation and the confidence shown in him by his former commander, "Old Fuss and Feathers" Winfield Scott, was offered command of the entire Federal army. That same night,

8 Robert E. Lee to Jefferson Davis, February 16, 1863, in the Fredericksburg and Spotsylvania National Military Park bound manuscript collection, vol. 19.

9 James M. McPherson, *Ordeal by Fire: The Civil War and Reconstruction* (New York, NY, 2001), 125-127.

General Robert Edward Lee.

Library of Congress

however, Virginia voted to secede from the Union, prompting Lee to turn down Lincoln's offer and resign from the army. "I shall never bear arms against the Union," he had told a subordinate, "but it may be necessary for me to carry a musket in the defense of my native state, Virginia, in which case I shall not prove recreant to my duty."[10]

Lee's early war record for the Confederacy was spotty. In September 1861, in present-day West Virginia, he suffered defeat while leading troops into combat for the first time in the battle of Cheat Mountain, tarnishing his reputation. He was then transferred to Georgia and tasked with bolstering the defenses of forts Jackson and Pulaski. Lee arrived on the scene just as Union Capt. Quincy Gilmore, employing mortars and rifled cannon, brought down the brick-and-mortar walls of a fort nearly everyone had assumed was impregnable. With yet another defeat hanging over his head, Lee was called to Richmond to take a desk job as Jefferson Davis' chief military adviser.

Lee's luck changed in the flash of a single artillery shell. On May 31, 1862, the commander of the Confederate army defending the capital, Gen. Joseph E. Johnston, was wounded by an exploding shell at the battle of Seven Pines. That evening, Davis appointed Lee as Johnston's replacement. The first thing the new commander did was set to work on the capital city's defenses. Under his engineer's eye, Confederates dug miles of new trenches, reinforced by forts and redoubts. All the digging earned Lee one of his early-war nicknames, "The King of Spades." But once the city was thus fortified, "the King" went on the offensive, changing Confederate fortunes almost instantly.

In the months since, Lee had taken the war from the gates of Richmond to the outskirts of Washington, earning a stellar reputation as a battlefield commander in the process. His lopsided victory at Fredericksburg in December 1862 capped off his string of unprecedented battlefield feats.

But at 56, Lee had already gone white from the stresses of the war. Waiting out the winter added to the strain, with the Union army just across the river and meager supplies an ever-constant worry. In late March 1863, he came down with a cold, and it turned severe. Even worse, he was waylaid by an attack of pericarditis, a heart ailment that causes acute chest

---

10 Douglas Southall Freeman, *Lee*, ed. Richard Harwell (New York, NY, 1997), 425.

pain. By mid-April, though, he was feeling better. "I am able to ride out every day, & now that the weather has become good, I hope I shall recover my strength," he wrote to his daughter.[11]

He knew he would need his strength. Already he was getting reports of movement on the far side of the river, although he had no clear picture of what those reports meant. Hooker, it seemed, was waking up his army. Lee had to rest his hope on his home field advantage in Virginia: if the Federal army started to make a clear move, he hoped he would get tipped off in time to concentrate his own widely dispersed army.

"I owe Mr. F. J. Hooker no thanks for keeping me here in this state of expectancy," Lee wrote to his wife, making a derisive reference to "Fighting Joe's" nickname. "He ought to have made up his mind long ago what to do."[12]

*   *   *

"General Hooker seems to be very sanguine of success," wrote V Corps commander Maj. Gen. George Gordon Meade, "but is remarkably reticent of his information and plans; I really know nothing of what he intends to do, or when or where he proposes doing anything."[13]

Meade understood the need for secrecy. "For my part, I am willing to be in ignorance, for it prevents all criticism and faultfinding in advance," Meade conceded. "All I ask and pray for is to be told explicitly and clearly what I am expected to do, and then I shall try, to the best of my ability, to accomplish the task set before me."[14]

Hooker boasted that no human being in the army or in Washington knew the details of his plan.[15] In fact, though, it wasn't too different from

---

11 Robert E. Lee to Agnes Lee, April 11, 1863, in the Fredericksburg and Spotsylvania National Military Park bound manuscript collection.

12 Robert E. Lee to Mary Custis Lee, February 23, 1863, in the Fredericksburg and Spotsylvania National Military Park bound manuscript collection.

13 George Gordon Meade, *The Life and Letters of George Gordon Meade: Major General United States Army*, ed. George Gordon Meade, Jr., 2 vols. (New York, NY, 1913), 367.

14 Ibid., 369.

15 Ibid., 367.

Major General George Gordon Meade, V Corps Commander.

Library of Congress

the one Burnside had tried to execute when he bogged down in the Mud March.

The first phase of Hooker's plan would be to deploy his newly reorganized cavalry as a raiding force "for the purpose of turning the enemy's position on his left, and of throwing [the] command between him and Richmond, and isolating him from his supplies, checking his retreat, and inflicting on him every possible injury which will tend to his discomfiture and defeat."[16] To carry out his orders, Hooker called on newly appointed cavalry corps commander Brig. Gen. George Stoneman.

The New York-born Stoneman was a career cavalryman. He had graduated 23rd in the famed West Point class of 1846.[17] While at "the Point," he shared a room with future Confederate luminary Thomas J. "Stonewall" Jackson. Instead of service in the Mexican War, Stoneman saw service on the western frontier in various capacities for 15 years. By 1861, Stoneman was commanding Fort Brown in Texas; following the bombardment of Fort Sumter, he was forced to uproot his command and make for friendly territory.[18]

Like his commanding officer, Hooker, Stoneman was promoted to brigadier general in August 1861. The Empire State general then assumed command of the growing cavalry forces around the Washington, D.C., area attached to the new Army of the Potomac. During the Peninsula Campaign, though, army commander Maj. Gen. George B. McClellan misused the cavalry, and Stoneman's men were humiliated as their Confederate counterparts rode around the entirety of McClellan's army, raiding as they went. As a result, Stoneman was demoted to command an infantry division in the III Corps—a corps that, by virtue of his seniority, he ended up commanding during the battle of Fredericksburg. His time in the infantry was unimpressive at best, though, so when Hooker found himself in need of an experienced cavalry chief, he turned back to Stoneman.[19]

---

16 Bigelow, *The Campaign of Chancellorsville*, 142-143.

17 John C. Waugh, *The Class of 1846 From West Point to Appomattox: Stonewall Jackson, George McClellan and their Brothers* (New York, NY, 1994), 46.

18 Ibid., 405.

19 Ibid.

A quiet and unassuming leader, Stoneman did not fit the bold mold typical of a cavalry officer; yet he had the confidence of his men.[20] "We believe in his judgment, his courage, and determination," wrote Capt. Charles Francis Adams. "We know he is ready. . . . He will take good care of us and won't get us into places from which he can't get us out."[21]

Hooker wanted the cavalry to strike out northwest toward the Confederate left flank and cross the Rappahannock and Rapidan rivers. From there, Stoneman was to move south to the Virginia Central Railroad, destroying all the bridges, stations, and rolling stock he could. Following the rail line east to Hanover Junction, the force would destroy the junction, then begin on the Richmond, Fredericksburg & Potomac Railroad. The hope was to destroy Lee's supply lines and lines of communication and cause as much panic and consternation in and around Richmond as possible. Hooker told Stoneman, "Let your watchword be fight. . . ."[22]

To support Stoneman's raid, Hooker assigned colonels Judson Kilpatrick and Percy Wyndham to strike out from Tappahannock, Virginia, about 45 miles southeast of the main army encampment. Like Stoneman's force, Kilpatrick's would aim for the Virginia Central Railroad. Wyndham would strike the Richmond & York Railroad, which came into the Confederate capital from the east. If all went as planned, there would be nearly 10,000 Union horsemen in Lee's rear, a formidable force—if they were able to interpose themselves between Lee and Richmond.[23]

Hooker was well aware of the supply problems Lee faced, thanks to intelligence forwarded to him from Samuel Ruth, a Union sympathizer at the head of the Richmond, Fredericksburg & Potomac Railroad.[24] This allowed the Federal commander to tamper with the amount of food and fodder reaching the Army of Northern Virginia. Hooker had other spies,

20 Ibid., 406.

21 Charles F. Adams, *A Cycle of Adams Letters, 1861-1865*, 2 vols., ed. Worthington Chauncey Ford (Boston, MA, 1920), vol. 2, 8.

22 Ibid.

23 Ben F. Fordney, *Stoneman at Chancellorsville: The Coming of Age of Union Cavalry* (Shippensburg, PA, 1998), 1-8.

24 Thomas Allen, *Intelligence in the Civil War* (Washington, D.C., 2008), 22-23.

Brigadier General George Stoneman.

Library of Congress

too, whose efforts were coordinated by a newly appointed chief intelligence officer, Col. George Sharpe. Sharpe, a prewar lawyer from New York who served with the 120th New York, was so good at his job that, by the time Hooker's army stepped off in late April, the Union high command had a working order of battle for Lee's army, complete with unit strengths and locations.[25]

Just as Hooker split his cavalry into two separate forces, he planned to split his infantry as well. He intended to lead the V, XI and XII corps, nearly 60,000 men, northwest around Lee's left flank. Like Stoneman's cavalry, Hooker's infantry would cross the Rappahannock and Rapidan rivers, but instead of moving south, the head of the column would turn east, doubling back toward Fredericksburg. Hooker's hope was to move as quickly as possible and use the element of surprise to gain Lee's rear.

As daring as this plan was, the lack of any substantial cavalry force would leave the Army of the Potomac essentially blind. Hooker retained one undersized brigade to lead his right wing into the Wilderness of Orange and Spotsylvania Counties. This handful of regiments was to clear the roads ahead of the main column of enemy horsemen, gather intelligence, deal with prisoners of war, and rally troops in the forthcoming campaign—a tall task for a brigade numbering only 1,157 men.[26]

The success of the movement all depended on the other portion of Hooker's army, his left wing, which he would leave across the river from Fredericksburg. The men of the I, III, and VI corps, consisting of another 65,000 men, would act as a diversionary force under the command of Maj. Gen. John Sedgwick. It would be Sedgwick's first major independent command.

Hooker expected Sedgwick to cross at Fredericksburg and demonstrate in front of Lee's army to keep Lee looking east. Hooker, moving in from the west, could then smash Lee between the wings of his army. At the very least, the powerful Fredericksburg line would become untenable for Lee, forcing the Confederates to either surrender or withdraw. If Lee retreated south, toward Richmond, it was up to Sedgwick's force to pursue.

Hooker exuded supreme confidence in his plan. "Hooker seems very confident of success," Meade noted, "but lets no one into his secrets."[27] He

---

25 Ibid.

26 Bigelow, *The Campaign of Chancellorsville*, 194.

27 Meade, *The Life and Letters of George Gordon Meade*, vol. 1, 369.

The dense second-growth forest known as "The Wilderness"
was a nearly impenetrable barrier in many areas.

Library of Congress

worried that such secrecy "may be carried too far, and important plans
may be frustrated by subordinates, from their ignorance of how much
depended on their share of work."[28]

In fact, Hooker brought even Couch, his second in command, into his
full confidence about the plan's details only after the movement had
begun. At that point, Hooker also outlined the plan to XII Corps
commander Maj. Gen. Henry W. Slocum, who was to lead the march
westward. However, Hooker did not take the time to meet with
Sedgwick, the man in command of the entire left wing. Hooker merely took
the time to issue written orders to his left wing commander, which only outlined a
vague sketch of Hooker's grander scheme for the campaign ahead.

Meade's worries would become prophetic.

28 Ibid., 367.

Chapter Three

Under the Greek Cross:

The Federal VI Corps

D espite any charges his critics leveled at him following the Chancellorsville campaign, John Sedgwick started the campaign with excellent timing.[1] He had been away on medical leave recovering from injuries sustained during an ill-fated advance into the West Woods at Antietam the previous September. His return to the army came just as Joe Hooker was doing some housecleaning.

Following Burnside's debacle at Fredericksburg in December 1862, a number of officers approached President Lincoln with their reservations about the army commander. Among the malcontents was Maj. Gen. William B. Franklin, commander of Burnside's "Left Grand Division." Franklin had a brilliant mind but a loud mouth, with a habit of taking issue with his commanding officers. He proved to be unreliable in important commands. He was an outspoken critic of the way the Lincoln

---

1 One could argue that Sedgwick ended his career with an uncanny sense of timing, too. On May 9, 1864, while standing beside the fortifications his men were constructing outside Spotsylvania Court House, his men urged him to seek cover from the Confederate sharpshooters who were harassing them. "They couldn't hit an elephant at that distance," Sedgwick said. Seconds later, the sharpshooters proved him wrong, killing Sedgwick with a bullet to the head. William D. Matter, *If It Takes All Summer: The Battle of Spotsylvania* (Chapel Hill, NC, 1988), 102-103.

Major General William Buell Franklin.

Library of Congress

administration was handling the war. And he was a McClellan man, to boot.

At Fredericksburg, Franklin was responsible for the fight on the left end of Burnside's army, with nearly 60,000 men under his direct command—about one-half of the Army of the Potomac. His task was to assault Prospect Hill, where he and his men were to push the Confederate forces to the west and north, away from Richmond. At the same time, he was to keep a heavy reserve of troops ready to exploit the opening and march toward Richmond, interposing themselves between Lee's army and the Confederate capital.

Franklin failed miserably. In the weeks following the battle, he twice testified in front of the Joint Committee on the Conduct of the War, and the committee found inconsistencies in his testimony. "I put in all the troops that I thought it proper and prudent to put in," he told the committee. "I fought with the whole strength of my command, as far as I could, and at the same time keep my connection with the river open."[2] In other words, he committed as many troops as he felt comfortable with while still maintaining a line of retreat.

After considering the testimony of numerous officers, the committee found Franklin one of the people most culpable for the debacle at Fredericksburg. "From the testimony it would appear that the attack was

2 Joint Congressional Committee on the Conduct of the War, *Report of the Congressional Committee on the Operations of the Army of the Potomac: Causes of its Inactions and Ill Success. Its Several Campaigns. Why McClellan was Removed. The Battle of Fredericksburg. The Removal of Burnside* (New York, NY, 1863), 24.

in reality made by one of the smallest divisions in Gen. Franklin's command—the division of Gen. Meade, numbering about 4,500 men," the findings read. "This division was supported on its right by Gen. Gibbon's division of about 5,000 men."[3] In the end, Franklin's main assault consisted of fewer than 10,000 men. Apparently, he had believed he needed 50,000-plus men to watch his rear.

The committee also found that Franklin had disobeyed direct orders from Burnside, and that his disobedience had cost the army dearly.[4] "The testimony of all the witnesses before [this] Committee proves most conclusively that, had the attack been made upon the left with all the force which Gen. Franklin could have used for that purpose, the plan of Gen. Burnside would have been completely successful, and our army would have achieved a most brilliant victory," the committee wrote.[5]

Even before the committee released its findings, Franklin set his cronies to work trying to push the blame elsewhere. Generals John Newton and John Cochrane went directly to Washington the week following the battle. Cochrane was a highly connected political general, and he searched for anyone who would listen. The man he found was Secretary of State William Seward, a fellow New Yorker. Seward obtained an audience for the two generals with the president himself, usurping the chain of command by bypassing Burnside and the derisive general in chief of the army, Maj. Gen. Henry "Old Brains" Halleck. The generals informed Lincoln that the "dispirited condition of the army was the want of confidence in the military capacity of Gen. Burnside."[6]

However, the finger-pointing and backstabbing did not sit well with the men in Washington, nor with the head of the army. Lincoln informed Burnside of the visit, but would not name names.

Despite his efforts, Franklin's days were numbered—but so were Burnside's. In the end, both were ousted. When Hooker abolished the "Grand Division" organizational structure that Burnside had created, the

3 Ibid., 24.

4 Ibid., 24-25.

5 Ibid., 25.

6 Ibid.

Major General Henry Wager "Old Brains" Halleck.

Library of Congress

new corps structure left no place for Franklin, who was quietly shuffled out of the picture.

Franklin, unlike Burnside, blamed others for his failures. After Fredericksburg, Franklin ranted, "The moral I wish to draw from Halleck's prevarication is, that the administration intended that Burnside should move forward at any cost, and did not care how many lives were lost, or what good were done only so that there was a fight. In other words it was determined to pander to the radical thirst for blood which has lately been so rife."[7]

One of Franklin's chief conspirators was his subordinate, VI Corps commander William F. "Baldy" Smith. A brigadier general, Smith had been brevetted major general, but his confirmation languished in the U.S. Senate, in part because of his role in trying to oust Burnside. Smith was well-loved by his men, but Hooker recognized him as an instigator—which smacked of the pot calling the kettle black—and wanted him gone. Hooker began looking around for an appropriate replacement—just when Sedgwick, the army's senior division commander, returned to active service.

"One day a grizzled, bluff major-general rode up to our quarters with an aide-de-camp as handsome as Romeo," observed a VI Corps staff officer

---

7   Mark A. Snell, *From First to Last: The Life of Major General William B. Franklin* (New York, NY, 2002), 163.

on February 4. "General [Sedgwick] dismounted and disappeared in General Smith's tent."[8] Orders were passed. Sedgwick assumed command.

"None who witnessed the farewell reception of General Smith, will forget the scene at corps head-quarters," wrote one observer.

> The two generals, the old and loved leader of the Second division and of the corps, and the new commander, stood side by side. General Smith, tall, well dressed, his regulation coat buttoned closely about him, his easy and graceful manner and conversation; General Sedgwick, of stouter build, wearing a loose blouse and coarse blue pants, such as are furnished the private soldier, strong and manly in his appearance, and somewhat abrupt in his manner.[9]

Major General John Newton, commander of the VI Corps' 3rd Division, said Sedgwick "looked a soldier every inch."[10]

*　　*　　*

Born in Cornwall Hollow, Connecticut, on September 13, 1813, John Sedgwick was a career soldier, and the son of a Revolutionary War general.[11] Although poorly prepared—the examination board told him "he could never pass the second [entrance] examination"—Sedgwick entered West Point.[12] There he worked hard, finally graduating in 1837, ranking 24th in a class of 50.[13] Like many of his contemporaries, Sedgwick saw a great deal of action in the Seminole Wars, Canadian border disputes,

---

8 Thomas W. Hyde, *Following the Greek Cross or Memoirs of the Sixth Army Corps* (Boston, MA, 1894), 119.

9 George T. Stevens, *Three Years in the Sixth Corps: A Concise Narrative of Events in the Army of the Potomac, From 1861 to the Close of the Rebellion, April, 1865* (Albany, NY, 1866), 186-187.

10 William B. Styple, ed., *Generals in Bronze: Interviewing the Commanders of the Civil War* (Kearny, NJ, 2005), 74.

11 Mark Hughes, *The New Civil War Handbook: Facts and Photos for Readers of All Ages* (New York, NY, 2011), 28.

12 Emily Sedgwick Welch, *A Biographical Sketch of John Sedgwick Major-General* (New York, NY, 1899), 9-10.

13 Richard E. Winslow III, *General John Sedgwick: The Story of a Union Corps Commander* (Novato, CA, 1982), xi.

Major General John Sedgwick.

Library of Congress

and the Mexican War. In Mexico, the young lieutenant was brevetted for bravery at Churubusco and Chapultepec.[14] Following the war, Sedgwick was transferred to the plains and served in both the artillery and cavalry.

14 Welch, *A Biographical Sketch of General John Sedgwick Major-General*, 11.

Throughout his army service, Sedgwick maintained a steady flow of correspondence with his family in Connecticut, particularly with his sister, Emily Sedgwick Welch. He sent home letters, mementos, and, most importantly, money. This became especially important in the early 1850s, when Sedgwick's father fell on hard times. To help the family out, Sedgwick bought the family homestead. Tragically, the house later burned, taking with it most of Sedgwick's personal possessions. Undaunted, he took leave from the army, traveled home to Cornwall Hollow, and rebuilt.[15]

With the coming of the Civil War, Sedgwick's career went into high gear. In early 1861, he was promoted several times in the span of a few short weeks as Southern officers resigned their commissions. One of those resignations, that of Col. Robert E. Lee, opened a path for Sedgwick's promotion to lieutenant colonel. Lee, as it later turned out, had a tough time getting Sedgwick's many promotions to stick in his mind; as late as May of 1863, Lee still referred to his former subordinate as "Major Sedgwick."[16]

As 1861 wore on, Sedgwick eventually earned promotion to brigadier general and was placed in charge of a brigade in Samuel Heintzelman's division. Following the Union debacle at Ball's Bluff in October, Sedgwick assumed command of Brig. Gen. Charles P. Stone's division. When army commander George McClellan shifted the Army of the Potomac to the Peninsula for spring operations, Sedgwick's division went as part of Brig. Gen. Edwin V. "Bull" Sumner's II Corps. There his troops fought well, and Sedgwick earned yet another promotion, on July 25, 1862, to major general.[17]

Sedgwick's meteoric rise stalled in the West Woods of Antietam when Sumner sent Sedgwick's division forward without ample reconnaissance or support. To make matters worse, the battle formation stacked Sedgwick's three brigades one behind the other at close intervals—with both flanks exposed. His men drove into the West Woods, but at a fearful cost: of the 5,400 men in Sedgwick's division, 2,225 of them became

---

15 Ibid., 20-23.

16 Robert Stiles, *Four Years Under Marse Robert* (Marietta, GA, 1995), 177-179.

17 Styple, *Generals in Bronze*, 431.

casualties in less than 20 minutes. Sedgwick himself was wounded three times in the assault. He returned to Connecticut to convalesce.

By the time Sedgwick was well enough to rejoin the army, his division was being led by the aloof Brig. Gen. Oliver Otis Howard. However, Sedgwick's standing as the ranking division commander made him the perfect candidate for Hooker's organizational shuffle.

Corps command suited Sedgwick well, and he expressed no wish to rise higher in the ranks. He "thought that his limit was reached in command of a corps, and so declined offers of advancement," a staff officer later revealed.[18]

"It is impossible to do justice or convey an adequate impression of a character like General Sedgwick's," the officer, Capt. Charles Whittier, wrote. "People recognize his simplicity, geniality and kindness of heart."[19]

Lieutenant Colonel Martin Thomas McMahon, Sedgwick's chief of staff, described Sedgwick as "tall; ruddy complexion; blue eyes; a very smooth silky voice; his hair growing rather long on his forehead, with a large mustache and side whiskers. He always wore his boots under his pants. He wore an old fashion pair of brass spurs-never taking them off. His coat he kept open with his swordbelt underneath."[20]

Sedgwick was a soldier's soldier who did not stand for the pomp and circumstance of war, unlike his VI Corps predecessors. He was low-key and frequently kept to himself, enjoying games of solitaire. His men loved him and called him "Uncle John."

According to most accounts, the corps quickly took to Sedgwick, which was good: he had a great deal of work ahead.

*   *   *

The VI Corps was a damaged machine of war when Sedgwick assumed command, though not because of battlefield losses. As the product of George McClellan's machinations—it was not one of the original four

---

18 Charles Whittier, Diary, undated entry, in the Fredericksburg and Spotsylvania National Military Park bound manuscript collection, vol. 266, 6.

19 Ibid.

20 Styple, *Generals in Bronze*, 84.

corps of the Army of the Potomac, but something McClellan cooked up—it had to weather political as well as military battles.

In his ongoing power struggles with President Lincoln, Radical Republicans, and his own corps commanders, McClellan, a popular Democrat, realized he needed additional political clout. For starters, the four corps commanders whom McClellan's army employed in early 1862—Irvin McDowell, Edwin Sumner, Samuel Heintzelman, and Erasmus Keyes—were not of his choosing, which did not sit well with the haughty McClellan. He considered them inept. "[N]ot willing to be held responsible for the present arrangement," McClellan petitioned Lincoln and the War Department for permission to create two new army corps, led by commanders of his choosing.[21] McClellan was soon granted his wish, and in an order dated May 18, 1862, McClellan designated his two new army corps as "the Fifth and Sixth Provisional Army Corps."[22] At the head of the V Corps McClellan installed Brig. Gen. Fitz John Porter, and at the head of the VI Corps he installed Franklin. Both officers were staunch Democrats and loyal McClellan followers.

The VI Corps saw action on the Peninsula at Gaines' Mill and Savage's Station. Later in the summer, one brigade was engaged and roughly handled during the Second Manassas campaign.[23] Then, during the Maryland campaign, the VI Corps found itself engaged in the battle of South Mountain, but two days later, at Antietam, only one brigade again saw action. During the first battle of Fredericksburg, the corps crossed south of the city and, in reality, only a handful of regiments were engaged, mainly in an ill-fated reconnaissance into the Landsdowne Valley late in the day.

So, by 1863 the VI Corps was not an especially battle-tested corps. Nonetheless, it was the largest corps in the army, numbering 23,667 officers and men, and it consisted of quality units, such as the 121st New York ("Upton's Regulars"), the 102nd Pennsylvania, and the 6th Maine.

---

21 Stephen W. Sears, ed., *The Civil War Papers of George B. McClellan: Selected Correspondence 1860-1865* (Cambridge, MA, 1989), 258.

22 *OR* 11, pt. 3, 181.

23 Camille Baquet, *History of the First New Jersey Brigade, New Jersey Volunteers: From 1861 to 1865 Compiled Under the Authorization of Kearny's First New Jersey Brigade Society* (Princeton, NJ, 1910), 35-36.

Brigadier General William T. H. "Bully" Brooks.

Generals in Blue

The corps also included the famed New Jersey Brigade, once commanded by the one-armed, tough-as-nails Phil Kearny, and the tough-as-granite Vermont Brigade. The corps also produced such quality officers as Winfield Scott Hancock, Henry Slocum, Romeyn Ayres, Emory Upton, and Joseph Bartlett. All would distinguish themselves in combat; Hancock and Slocum would both rise to corps command, and Slocum would eventually command the Army of Georgia.[24]

The VI Corps originally consisted of two divisions, but by the time Sedgwick took command a third had been added.

Brigadier General William T. H. "Bully" Brooks commanded the 1st Division, which was, by all accounts, the most stable division, with two solid brigades under Brig. Gen. Joseph J. Bartlett and Brig. Gen. David A. Russell. Brooks was an Ohio-born graduate of the West Point class of 1841, a class that produced 20 general officers who served either North or South. Brooks was with the VI Corps from its inception in 1862, serving as a brigade commander from the Peninsula through Antietam, with Smith as his division commander. Brooks acquired a great deal of battlefield acumen during that time. With the promotion of William Franklin to Grand Division command during the Fredericksburg campaign, Smith received promotion to fill Franklin's slot at the corps level, and Brooks succeeded Smith as division commander. Brooks' division saw little action during the debacle at Fredericksburg, but Brooks was nonetheless an

24 Slocum was in command of the Army of Georgia at the end of the war.

outspoken opponent of Burnside—which led to his arrest in January 1863.[25] Brooks managed to weather the storm, however, and by the spring he was back at the head of his division.[26]

Sedgwick's 2nd Division was under Maine native Brig. Gen. Albion P. Howe. Like Brooks, Howe was a graduate of the West Point class of 1841; unlike Brooks, Howe graduated near the top of the class, ranking 8th out of 52. (Brooks ranked 46th of 52.) Prior to the war, Howe served in the field and as an instructor of mathematics at West Point. He joined the VI Corps, assuming command of the 2nd Division, for the Fredericksburg campaign.[27]

The 3rd Division was under Maj. Gen. John Newton, a Virginia-born Yankee. Newton graduated from West Point one year after Brooks and Howe, in the class of 1842. Newton saw very limited prewar action, but joined the VI Corps on the Peninsula as a brigade commander, serving in that capacity until his promotion to division command following the Maryland campaign. Like the other VI Corps divisions, his men saw little action at Fredericksburg. Like Brooks, he conspired against Burnside; in fact, Newton went so far as to travel to Washington to lay the grievances of "the army" at the feet of President Lincoln.[28]

While other members of the anti-Burnside cabal ended up on the outside, Newton and Brooks were survivors; both maintained their commands within the corps. Although they were the last remaining malcontents in the VI Corps' high command, both proved to be capable combat leaders. Their experience, along with Howe's, would be absolutely critical as the VI Corps prepared to enter the spring campaign, providing the backbone that would compensate for Sedgwick's lack of experience at the corps level.

The corps faced a lack of experience at the brigade level, too. Newton's 3rd Division had lost all three of its brigade commanders in the months leading to the campaign. Howe's 2nd Division, meanwhile, lost

---

25 Meade, *The Life and Letters of George Gordon Meade*, vol. 1, 344-345.

26 Ezra J. Warner, *Generals in Blue: Lives of the Union Commanders* (Baton Rouge, LA, 2006), 47.

27 Ibid., 239-240.

28 *OR* 28, pt. 1, 998-999.

Brigadier General Albion P. Howe.

Library of Congress

one brigade, which was renamed the "Light Division" and reassigned. His famed Vermont Brigade would enter the fight with a new brigade commander, Col. Lewis A. Grant. The third brigade, Phil Kearney's old

Major General John Newton.

Library of Congress

New Jersey Brigade—tough fighters, no doubt—entered the campaign under Col. Henry Brown of the 3rd New Jersey.

The "Light Division," as it was called, was actually not a division at all but rather a brigade. Formed on February 3, 1863, the brigade consisted of the 6th Maine, 31st New York, 43rd New York, 61st Pennsylvania, 5th Wisconsin, and 3rd New York Independent Light Artillery. The division was under the command of Brig. Gen. Calvin Pratt.[29]

Pratt was not a career military man, but he did have a militia background, having served in the Massachusetts National Guard with the Worcester Light Infantry. He was later promoted to major of the 10th Massachusetts.[30] By 1861, Pratt was in Brooklyn, New York, where he funded and organized the 31st New York. He was appointed colonel of the regiment, fought at First Bull Run, and was wounded in the face at Mechanicsville (the round remained lodged in Pratt's face until it was finally removed in 1891).[31] The Bay Stater was promoted to brigadier general of volunteers in September 1862 and commanded the 2nd Division of the VI Corps at Fredericksburg.[32] In February, Pratt was given command of the Light Division, and the regiments and battery under his command were issued a green Greek Cross, denoting their designation as the 4th Division of the VI Corps—the only units at Chancellorsville to have a green divisional badge. "The regiment is going into a Flying Brigade," Pvt. John Honey of the 6th Maine wrote proudly. "This is a great honor mother to be selected from the great Army of the Potomac as part of a brigade in which none but the best troops in the country can enter."[33]

The idea was to have a mobile organization that could move quickly to seize a position or act as shock troops during an assault. While the regiments did not have specialized training, they did move lightly. When on the march, the units used pack mules instead of traditional supply wagons, and normally carried only one day's rations instead of the typical three.[34] Major Joel Haycock claimed that the purpose of the Light

---

29 Ibid., 166.

30 Obituary, *New York Times*, August 4, 1896.

31 Ibid.

32 Warner, *Generals in Blue*, 385.

33 James H. Mundy, *No Rich Men's Sons: The Sixth Maine Volunteer Infantry* (Cape Elizabeth, ME, 1994), 106.

34 Kerry A. Trask, *Fire Within: A Civil War Narrative from Wisconsin* (Kent, OH, 1995), 170.

Division was "to harass and annoy the enemy when and wherever we can cut off their communications and supply trains."[35] Although the men's intended role on the field of battle was never made entirely clear, Haycock's remark intimates that they would act as a flying column, fan out as skirmishers, take the enemy in rear or flank, or act as shock troops in a brisk assault. Regardless of their role, the men in the division were proud to be selected.

It took much of the winter for the VI Corps, indeed the entire army, to adjust to Hooker's many changes. Thomas Hyde noted that "[t]he winter of '62 and '63 was marked by the hard work of organizing and improving the army. Constant drills, reviews, and inspections followed each other." Hooker could only hope that the hard work and reorganization would pay dividends in the campaign to come.[36]

*   *   *

Hooker's plan for the coming campaign relied heavily on the VI Corps—and on John Sedgwick himself. Sedgwick would command the entire left wing of the army, which included not only his VI Corps but Maj. Gen. John F. Reynolds' I Corps, Maj. Gen. Daniel E. Sickles' III Corps, and a division detached from the II Corps under Brig. Gen. John Gibbon. In all, Sedgwick would command nearly 65,000 men—a considerable bump-up from the 5,000 men he had last commanded in combat at Antietam.

As outlined in Hooker's plan, Sedgwick was to force a crossing below Fredericksburg with elements of the I and VI corps. Using an amphibious assault, Federals would establish a bridgehead across from Lee's line near Prospect Hill, then move a sizeable portion of Sedgwick's force across so as to hold Lee's attention. Meanwhile, Hooker's wing of the army would position itself in the rear of Lee's army. Thus, when battle came, Lee would not know which force was the feint and which force the threat.

If Hooker had reservations about Sedgwick, he did not express them at the time. But in a revisionist effort after the war, the commander pointed out Sedgwick's,

35 Mundy, *No Rich Men's Sons*, 106.

36 Hyde, *Following the Greek Cross*, 120.

utter deficiency in the topographical faculty, and consequently his great distrust of himself in exercising on the field important commands. I was well aware of the weakness in his character when I detailed him and his Corps for independent command around Fredericksburg, but as his Corps was encamped in full view of the enemy, any movement of him would awaken suspicions in the enemy which I did not want to arouse.[37]

Given those concerns, Hooker easily could have given the command to Darius Couch, who was not only an experienced corps commander but also Hooker's second in command. He chose not to. Likewise, Hooker could have addressed any concerns by simply meeting with Sedgwick, but, as noted earlier, there is no record of him doing that, either. As a result, Hooker's postwar protestations seem disingenuous.

It is also possible that Hooker left the VI Corps in its diversionary role for entirely different reasons. Possibly weighing on his mind were the problems the VI Corps had posed for Burnside after Fredericksburg. It was possible that Hooker left the VI Corps along the Rappahannock to keep them at arm's length, so if anything did go wrong, Newton and Brooks would not be on hand to witness Hooker's foul-ups.

As history would later show, however, there would be plenty of finger-pointing to go around.

---

37 Joseph Hooker to Samuel Bates, November 29, 1878, in the Fredericksburg and Spotsylvania National Military Park bound manuscript collection, vol. 406.

Chapter Four

Bridging the Rappahannock:

The Federal River Crossing

Shaking the stiffness from its limbs after a winter of inactivity, the Army of the Potomac was, once again, finally, on the move.

On April 27, Hooker and his V, XI, and XII corps, a force of about 45,000 men, moved out for their long, sweeping march around the Confederate flank. The few cavalry regiments he had retained led the way. Meanwhile, the II Corps sat for the time being with the 18,721 men of the III Corps at and around the small village of Falmouth, with orders to join the march once the column advanced. By the time everyone caught up, including the artillery reserve, some 70,000 men would be available for the first phase of Hooker's maneuver.[1]

While the right wing of Hooker's army maneuvered, the I Corps, consisting of 16,908 officers and men, stayed in place to hold the left end of the Federal position. Sedgwick's VI Corps stayed as well. Both had been stationed along the river, in view of Confederates on the far side, and so needed to maintain their positions in order to hold Confederate attention. Once Hooker had advanced far enough, though, Sedgwick was to swing behind Reynolds' I Corps and move south, skirting the Rappahannock

---

1 Although it would not be for a few more days, the I and III corps would join Hooker, as would William Averill's cavalry division, bringing the Union right wing total to nearly 90,000 men.

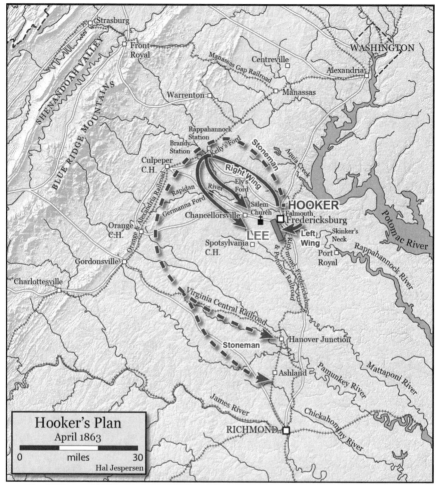

Hooker's grand offensive incorporated his cavalry moving south in a raid against Richmond, while one wing of his army tied Lee in place, as the other slammed into the enemy from behind.

while using the rolling terrain and deep valleys to cover the VI Corps movements. Both Reynolds and Sickles would join in. Between the three corps and the engineers and artillery attached to them, Sedgwick had nearly 65,000 men. They were to cross the Rappahannock at two points south of the city in the pre-dawn hours of April 29 and put themselves in a position to threaten Lee. As Sedgwick kept all Confederate eyes on him, Hooker could slip into position to the west, behind Lee, unnoticed—and pin the Confederates to the river or force them to flee.

The two corps commanders working closest with Sedgwick could not have been more different from one another. I Corps commander Maj. Gen. John Fulton Reynolds was a well-respected Keystone State officer who had graduated in the West Point class of 1841 and, like Sedgwick, had made a career as a military man. He was a veteran of the Mexican War as well as western outpost duty, and he headed the Corps of Cadets at West Point in the months leading to the war. In August of 1861, like so many others, Reynolds received his general's star. He was shuffled through multiple assignments until he found himself attached as a brigade commander in Brig. Gen. George McCall's Pennsylvania Reserves Division.

In the spring of 1862, Reynolds' Civil War career brought him for the first time to the sleepy town of Fredericksburg, where he served as military governor of the occupied city. Reynolds made his headquarters at Belmont, the future home of artist Gari Melchers. Reynolds soon earned a reputation among the citizens of Fredericksburg for being fair-minded, and when the general was later captured during the Peninsula Campaign, the citizens of the city petitioned the authorities in Richmond to release him.[2]

Following his release, Reynolds was promoted to command the Pennsylvania Reserves Division and eventually the I Corps.[3] In that capacity, he returned with the army to the Fredericksburg area in November 1862, and in December he and his men fought for Prospect Hill and across what is today known as the Slaughter Pen Farm. His men, led by division commander Meade, were the only ones to crack Lee's line during the battle.

Although opinion on Reynolds' overall combat leadership was mixed, he was nonetheless the only experienced corps commander in the left wing. He was not in command of the operation because, by seniority if not experience, Sedgwick outranked him.

III Corps commander Maj. Gen. Daniel Sickles was cut from a different cloth entirely. As a politician, not a military man, the New York

2 Marsena Rudolph Patrick, *Inside Lincoln's Army: The Diary of General Marsena Rudolph Patrick, Provost Marshall General, Army of the Potomac*, ed. David E. Sparks (New York, NY, 1964), 8.

3 Warner, *Generals in Blue*, 396-397.

Major General John F. Reynolds.

Library of Congress

City native felt right at home amidst the corrupt political machine of Gotham. In the mid-1850s, Sickles had been elected to the state senate of New York and then to the United States Congress.

While in Washington, Sickles' young wife, Teresa Bagioli Sickles, took a lover, Philip Barton Key II, the son of Francis Scott Key, the man who penned the Star-Spangled Banner.[4] The love affair was no secret to Washington's high society. At parties, Mrs. Sickles and Mr. Key were often seen off in a corner together, enjoying one another's company.[5] This was too much for the hotheaded Sickles—himself a notorious philanderer—to handle. In February 1859, Sickles approached Key outside of Lafayette Park in Washington and, in broad daylight and in cold blood, shot Key.[6] For his trial, Sickles hired attorney Edwin Stanton—the future secretary of war—to defend him. Stanton built his defense around an innovative new tactic, a claim of temporary insanity, which the jury accepted. It was the first successful use in United States history of such a defense to exonerate a defendant.[7]

Although his reputation was damaged by the scandal, Sickles still had friends in high places. At the outbreak of the war he was able to approach New York Governor Edwin Morgan and offer his services as a regimental commander. Morgan did Sickles one better: he gave the ex-politician an entire brigade of four regiments, collectively known as the Excelsior Brigade.[8]

What he lacked in morals and military training, Sickles more than made up for in bravery. He led his brigade on the Peninsula but missed the Second Manassas and Antietam campaigns— ostensibly on a military recruiting campaign back in New York State, although it looked much more like an effort to test the waters for another possible run at a Congressional seat.[9] By Fredericksburg, though, Sickles was serving at the head of an entire III Corps division, and in the spring Hooker promoted his friend and political ally to head the III Corps, making him

4 Thomas Keneally, *American Scoundrel: The Life of the Notorious Civil War General Dan Sickles* (New York, NY, 2002), 66.

5 Ibid., 148-149.

6 Key supposedly died grasping part of the black iron-rail fence surrounding the park—a fence that, today, stands as the barrier between Gettysburg National Cemetery and the Evergreen Cemetery in Gettysburg, Pennsylvania.

7 Keneally, *American Scoundrel*, 204-209.

8 Ibid., 218-220.

9 Ibid., 250.

Major General
Daniel E. Sickles.

Library of Congress

the only non-West Pointer
commanding a corps in the
campaign. The promotion
did not sit well with Maj.
Gen. O. O. Howard, who
ranked the political
general and should have
been next in line to
command a corps.

Howard, who would
soon receive a promotion
of his own, was not the
only officer rankled by
Hooker's elevation of
Sickles. "I believe Hooker is a good soldier," lamented Maj. Gen. George
Meade, commander of the V Corps; "the danger he runs is of subjecting
himself to bad influences, such as Dan Butterfield and Dan Sickles, who
being intellectually more clever than Hooker, and leading him to believe
they are very influential, will obtain an injurious ascendancy over him and
insensibly affect his conduct."[10]

XII Corps division commander Brig. Gen. Alpheus Williams, in a
letter to his daughters, showed similar disdain for Sickles. "A 'Sickles'
would beat Napoleon in winning glory not earned. He is a hero without a
heroic deed! [His reputation was] [l]iterally made by scribblers."[11]

*   *   *

---

10 Meade, *The Life and Letters of George Gordon Meade*, vol. 1, 351.

11 Alpheus S. Williams, *From the Cannon's Mouth: General Alpheus S. Williams*, ed. Milo
M. Quaife (Lincoln, NE, 1995), 203.

Word came down to Sedgwick on the morning of April 28: time to go. Between 10:00 a.m. and noon, the VI Corps commander mobilized his four divisions, located in the vicinity of White Oak Church, and pointed them east and south along the Rappahannock. They were to make for the mouth of a stream called Deep Run, to an area that had become known as Franklin's Crossing. Word went to Reynolds and Sickles to get their corps on the march, as well. Reynolds, like Sedgwick, did his best to tuck his behemoth corps into the ravines and valleys near the Rappahannock while staying out of sight of the enemy. Sickles, meanwhile, quietly withdrew his corps to the east through the village of Falmouth and turned his column south by southeast to assume a supporting position about a quarter of a mile to the right rear of Sedgwick's right flank.

The Federals marched through a countryside that had been blighted by the winter-long Union occupation but was now trying to refresh itself under the call of spring. "The spring is very backward here," wrote Edgar Clark of the 3rd Michigan, part of Sickles' III Corps. "The peach trees are just in blossom. The wild onions just begin to peep out of the ground. The buds are beginning to start on the trees. There is nobody to work the land, consequently there is nobody plowing, no fixing up a bit. All the fences has been consumed for wood this winter by the army."[12] Yet even though the fields were largely untended, they were greening. Pear and apple trees were in bloom. Temperatures were seasonable, but a light drizzle fell. "[T]he roads and fields swarming with columns of troops moving in the same direction, one of the most glorious sights I ever saw," wrote a Massachusetts man.[13]

Union observation balloons had been making periodic ascents since March, and now another floated overhead. Hooker did not put much faith in the so-called Balloon Corps' ability to gather useful intelligence, but he thought their presence added to the ruse that the Federal status quo remained unbroken. Meanwhile, on the ground, Sedgwick's infantry continued to trudge southward. With them, engineers struggled to move the pontoon boats the army would need for a river crossing. Veterans

12 Edgar Clark to Parents, Brothers and Sisters, April 27, 1863, in the Fredericksburg and Spotsylvania National Military Park bound manuscript collection, vol. 54.

13 Charles Brewster to Sister, May 10, 1863, in the Fredericksburg and Spotsylvania National Military Park bound manuscript collection, vol. 70.

understood that moving toward the river meant they were moving toward the enemy.

Franklin's Crossing was well known to the I, VI, and at least a portion of the III corps. Here, Burnside the previous December had ordered the construction of three pontoon bridges as part of his failed battle plan. Unlike the crossing under fire in the city itself, the troops who crossed here did so virtually unmolested. Leaders and men of the various corps strode across the bridges in confidence on December 11 and 12, only to trudge back across the spans a few days later following the debacle of December 13.

Reynolds positioned his corps a mile south of Sedgwick, near Pollock's Mill, and Sickles' corps assumed its reserve position tucked in behind Tyler's Hill. The ridges and valleys along Stafford Heights filled with Union soldiers. Units settled in, were shifted, then shifted again. Much of their activity still remained hidden, though, "by ravines . . . to

Two Federal pontoon bridges at Franklin's Crossing. Each bridge spanned approximately 440 feet of river.

Library of Congress

conceal large numbers of men."[14] Still, the men were under orders not to light any campfires.

Sedgwick planned to start crossing at around 3:30 a.m., and he hoped to avoid the same terrible mistakes that had so confounded Burnside when engineers tried to bridge the river in December. In December, the engineers who performed the actual construction of the pontoon bridges had infantry and artillery lined up behind them to offer protection as they worked, but when Confederates in the city of Fredericksburg hotly contested the crossing, the engineers—specially trained, highly skilled, and hard to replace—took heavy casualties. Federal infantry on the river's edge, lined up in mass formations out in the open, responded, but their volleys had little success at dislodging the Confederate marksmen from their positions.

After nearly eight hours of ineffective skirmishing, the Union high command had changed tactics. Brig. Gen. Henry Hunt, in charge of the Federal artillery, approached Burnside with a plan. He proposed placing infantry from Michigan, New York, and Massachusetts in pontoon boats and sending them across the river to force a landing. The plan worked. With a beachhead established on the far shore, Burnside's engineers were able to finish their work. Although it seems like a logical tactic to use today, it was the first riverine crossing under fire in American military history. Like so many commanders before and after him, Hunt had to rewrite the rulebook as the battle unfolded.

Now in May, the VI Corps' staff officers, preparing for their own crossing, had learned from Burnside's hard lessons. Their plans called for sending infantry across in pontoon boats first, before the engineers started building. Forcing a landing on the hostile shore, Federal infantry would drive back the Confederates and allow the engineers to work relatively unmolested on the otherwise vulnerable bridges. Infantry and artillery on the Federal-controlled near shore would provide additional support as necessary.

The Confederates were well entrenched on the far riverbank, and their presence made it difficult for the Federals to operate in continued

---

14 R. F. Halsted to Sedgwick's sister, May 13, 1863, in Carl and Ellen Stoeckel, eds., *Correspondence of John Sedgwick: Major-General*, 2 vols. (New York, NY, 1903), vol. 2, 112.

secrecy. In fact, the Southerners could see much of the movement because the land had been so denuded of ground cover over the winter. Soldiers on both sides had collected all the wood they could to build winter huts and burn for fuel. Trees had been cleared from the banks of the Rappahannock River, over the top of Stafford Heights, then deeper along the hills and valleys of Stafford County.

From Marye's Heights to the spires of Fredericksburg, curious Confederates tried to spy a glimpse of what was transpiring on the Federal side of the river. Captain William J. Seymour of Brig. Gen. Harry Hays' staff went into the city on the morning of April 28 with Col. Leroy Stafford of the 9th Louisiana. The pair

> [a]scended the spire of [St. George's] Episcopal Church, from which elevated position we had a fine view of the Yankee camps and forces, and a most animating & bustling sight it was. Camps were going through the process of demolition; tents were being struck, and the immense parks of waggons were unfolding themselves into long lines, whose directions could be discovered by the clouds of dust which rose from the roads they traversed. In front of this moving spectacle, and nearer the River, could be seen the hosts of the enemy, drawn up in battle array, their burnished arms glistening in the sunlight and their banners floating proudly in the breeze.[15]

Concealing the movement of tens of thousands of soldiers had been difficult enough for the Union army. Now, Federals had to get their bridge-building materials down to the river without tipping their hand. The pontoons were 1,500-pound boats that measured 31 feet long and nearly 6 feet wide. In the water, an engineer would float a pontoon into position and others would lash it into place with ropes, planks, and support beams. After that, engineers would float the next pontoon into place and, in that way, a floating bridge would extend across a river. On land, though, the pontoons were so cumbersome that engineers needed specialized wagons to transport them and move them into position. Several wagons together were called pontoon trains, which also included

---

15 Terry L. Jones, ed., *The Civil War Memoirs of Captain William J. Seymour: Reminiscences of a Louisiana Tiger* (Baton Rouge, LA, 1991), 47.

chess wagons that carried the plank boarding for the bridges, as well as trestle wagons, abutment wagons, and tool wagons.[16]

The rattling of wagons moving down to the riverfront would be a dead giveaway to the Confederate soldiers on the far bank of the river. If the Federals blew their cover or could not move enough soldiers across the river to solidify their foothold on the western bank, Hooker's offensive could grind to a screeching halt.

As evening set in, soldiers tried to steal some rest; they had orders to be on arms at 11:00 p.m. Meanwhile, Hunt supervised the placement of the artillery, concealing his guns in belts of woods behind the crest of Stafford Heights. He would roll them out in the pre-dawn hours, just before the crossing. At Franklin's Crossing, Hunt positioned 34 rifled guns above and below the bridging site: four 4.5-inch siege rifles, six 20-pounder Parrott guns, twelve 10-pounder Parrott guns, and twelve 3-inch ordnance rifles. A dozen Napoleons sat in reserve, and twelve more guns were positioned on the riverbank itself to create a crossfire on the Confederate trenches across the river. The guns at Franklin's Crossing were under the able command of VI Corps artillery chief Col. Charles Tompkins.[17]

At Pollock's Mill, Hunt placed the guns of the I Corps under the command of the haughty Col. Charles Wainwright. Wainwright positioned twenty 3-inch ordnance rifles above the mill, while below it he placed fourteen 3-inch ordnance rifles and six Napoleons.[18]

Covering the Federal left flank about a mile below Pollock's Mill were 16 more rifled guns: four 20-pounder Parrott's and twelve 3-inch ordnance rifles under the command of Lt. Col. E. R. Warner. Unlike Wainwright and Tompkins, whose job it was to cover the bridges and infantry during the crossing, Warner's men were to deter Confederate reinforcements from approaching the bridges from the south and west along the Bowling Green Road.[19]

Arguably, the artillery of the left wing of the army had the easiest task of anyone. Open fields of fire led from the Federal side of the

16 O'Reilly, *The Fredericksburg Campaign*, 45.

17 *OR* 25, pt. 1, 246.

18 Ibid., 247.

19 Ibid.

Brigadier General Henry J. Hunt.

Library of Congress

Rappahannock River to the main Confederate line along Prospect Hill. The long arm of Hooker's army could blanket the flat, open fields that Confederate reinforcements would have to cross. The artillerymen were aware that many of their guns on Stafford Heights could not depress their barrels low enough to hit enemy infantry along the riverbank, although they solved this problem by deploying guns on the riverbank itself. The only major issue the artillerists might have to deal with, then, would be the thick morning fog that was prone to cover the Rappahannock Valley. The infantry and the engineers, meanwhile, would have the much tougher job of forcing a crossing and then consolidating their gains in hostile territory.

At 11:30 p.m., preparations for bridge-building got underway. To reduce the noise, infantrymen were tasked with carrying the unwieldy boats to the riverbank, a distance of half a mile. Forty-four boats were to be carried to the I Corps crossing point alone.[20]

At Franklin's Crossing, much of the work was handled by men of the 5th Wisconsin and 61st Pennsylvania, although units slated to participate in the assaults also lent their strength. "We were called in line and marched to our pontoon train," wrote Cpl. William B. Westervelt of the 27th New York. "Here, as many as could take hold of the side of a boat, were placed on each side, and picking up the boat we started for the river."[21] It took 75 men to carry each one—and they had to do it in the dark.

The entire ordeal was recalled by a member of Col. Alexander Shaler's brigade:

> To the five regiments composing the first brigade of the third divisions, was assigned the arduous duty of carrying the pontoon boats and placing them on the banks of the stream. This was a difficult job. These special engineers had to be thus detailed, as the pioneer brigade had duties similar to perform elsewhere. The regiments were divided, each given a number of squads; these unslung their knapsacks, slung their rifles on their backs, and tackled the pontoons about a mile and a half from the

---

20 Ibid., 253.

21 William B. Westervelt, *Lights and Shadows of Army Life: As Seen by a Private Soldier of 27th N.Y. Infantry and 17th N.Y. Veteran Zouaves* (Marlboro, NY, 1886), 39.

riverbank, along the line the boats would have to be taken.[22] This was to obviate all noise, and halloing of tipsy teamsters. . . . During the night we pulled, hauled, lifted, laid down, took up, and carried these huge pontoons. . . . So quietly had the movement been conducted, that it is doubtful whether the pickets of the enemy mistrusted what was being transacted on the Federal shore.[23]

"The pontoons, not drawn on noisy, rumbling trucks, as they were in the former attempt by Burnside, were quietly born upon the shoulders of the light brigade and placed in the river at intervals of twenty or thirty feet," wrote Joseph Brown of the 16th New York. He noted, though, that there was "no attempt being made to construct a bridge."[24] As he would soon find out, that was because the 16th was bound for the far shore.

Likewise, Westervelt's 27th was bound for the far shore, too—but, like Brown's 16th, they had to hurry up and wait. Brown and his mates hauled their pontoons all the way to the riverbank before, "by some misunderstanding of orders, we were halted and kept waiting until daybreak." He added: "I don't pretend to know where rests the responsibility of delaying us until it was light enough for the enemy to use us for target practice; but it looked like criminal imbecility somewhere, for we were all ready to go several hours before we were ordered, and with darkness to favor us our task would have been comparatively easy and our loss light."[25]

Responsibility for the delay, it turned out, rested with Brig. Gen. David A. Russell of Brooks' 1st Division. Russell, a hard-nosed, no-nonsense type of commander, was in charge of the assault force. The 42-year-old Russell was a West Point graduate whose prewar trials had

---

22 The distance varies account to account. Some of the pontoon trains were closer to the river, given their proximity to the ravines and valleys they were stationed in. Nonetheless, men carried the boats from a quarter of a mile to almost a mile and a quarter to the river front. The engineers did their best to get as close to the front as possible.

23 William B. Styple, *Writing & Fighting the Civil War: Soldiers Letters from the Battlefront* (Kearny, NJ, 2004), 187.

24 Joseph M. Brown, *Historical Sketch of the Sixteenth Regiment, N.Y. Volunteer Infantry: From April 1861 to May 1863*, in the Fredericksburg and Spotsylvania National Military Park bound manuscript collection, vol. 356, 23-24.

25 Westervelt, *Lights and Shadows of Army Life*, 39.

Brigadier General David Russell.

*Fredericksburg and Spotsylvania
National Military Park*

taken him to Mexico, where he was
brevetted for gallantry, and to the
Pacific Northwest for service on
the frontier. Staff officer Theodore
Lyman described Russell as "brave
& straightforward a soldier as ever
was; and short of manners."[26] The
general seemed to fear nobody—
not even Lt. Gen. Ulysses S. Grant,
as it turned out. In 1864, Russell
would have a run-in with Grant's
cook, who was forcibly taking sugar from a woman near Richmond.
Russell proceeded to pick up "the biggest stick at hand, [and] did whack
him most soundly," depriving Grant's mess of the sugar.[27]

Here on the banks of the Rappahannock, the New York native was
about to embark on the dangerous mission of crossing the river in boats in
the face of the enemy. It would be up to him and his men to protect the
engineers as they built the bridges. The problem was, the officer in charge
of the engineers—indeed, in charge of the entire bridge-building project
and in charge of coordinating with the infantry to get it done—was
rip-roaring drunk. And Russell would have none of it.

That officer was 50-year-old Brig. Gen. Henry W. Benham,
commander of the Army of the Potomac's Engineer Brigade, which
consisted of the 50th New York Engineers, the 15th New York Engineers,
and the United States Engineer Battalion—nearly 1,700 skilled men.[28]

26 Theodore Lyman, Diary, May 25, 1864, in the Fredericksburg and Spotsylvania
National Military Park bound manuscript collection, vol. 405.

27 Ibid.

28 State of New York Historian, *Third Annual Report of the State Historian of the State of
New York, 1897: Transmitted to the Legislature March 14, 1898* (Albany, NY, 1898), 60.

Benham had graduated first in the West Point class of 1837 and was a career engineer prior to the war, serving with distinction in Mexico. In the early phases of the Civil War, he served in western Virginia in a combat role, but was removed from combat leadership following the botched battle of Secessionville in June 1862. Now under Joe Hooker, Benham had a chance to redeem himself. "Perhaps the change [in command] may be beneficial to our brigade," thought Maj. Ira Spaulding of the 50th New York Engineers, "but there is the possibility that it may prove disastrous."[29] So far, the latter had turned out to be the case: Benham had underwhelmed everyone in his new role as the head of the Engineer Brigade.

While Benham busied himself with last-minute preparations for the crossing, he took to the bottle. By one account, the general steeled himself with two glasses of sherry added to his canteen;[30] others said he was drinking whiskey.[31] Regardless of his beverage, Benham was, according to Capt. Wesley Brainerd, "in a beastly state of intoxication."[32] One VI Corps staff officer went so far as to say that Benham "was deficient in physical courage, and needed stimulant."[33]

Benham had a great deal of work on his plate: the bridges had to be laid by 3:30 a.m.[34] That way, the Union infantry and artillery could begin rolling across the bridges before daylight and be in a position to surprise Lee's men.

The drunken master of ceremonies made his way to the infantry units of the VI Corps that were supposed to cross the river and protect his engineers. Boats had been carried down to the river's edge, where Russell's men were to embark and make for the opposite shore—except Russell's men were not in position.

---

29 Ira Spaulding to Mrs. Dunklee, April 22, 1863, in the Fredericksburg and Spotsylvania National Military Park bound manuscript collection, vol. 394.

30 Winslow III, *General John Sedgwick*, 65.

31 Nevins, *A Diary of Battle*, 186.

32 Malles, *Bridge Building in War Time*, 141.

33 Whittier, Diary, n.d., 6-7.

34 *OR* 25, pt. 1, 205.

Brigadier General Henry Benham.
Benham was to oversee the bridging
operations, which was made
impossible by his "beastly
state of intoxication."

Library of Congress

Benham sought out Russell and ordered him to move his men to the front and prepare for the assault on the southern shore. Russell, already unhappy about the prospect of a pre-dawn assault, refused, unhappy with Benham's state of inebriation. This led to "some hard talk between . . . the generals."[35]

Frustrated, Benham proceeded to arrest Russell, then looked to "Bully" Brooks for help in getting the infantry going. By the time Benham found him, though, the operation was falling behind schedule, although much of that had to do with the fact that it took more than the estimated one hour to carry the boats from the staging area to the river.

Brooks was none too amused: Benham was not in control of the situation. In fact, Benham was hardly in control of himself—in his drunken stupor, he had fallen from his horse and cut his face. "He had allowed the blood to dry upon his face, which gave him an extremely savage and repulsive appearance," recorded Capt. Brainerd.[36] Lieutenant Stephen Weld observed "General B.[enham] drunk as could be, with a bloody cut over his left eye, and blood all over that side of his face and forming a disgusting sight altogether."[37]

35 Gray, Diary, April 28, 1863.

36 Malles, *Bridge Building in War Time*, 141.

37 Stephen Weld, Diary, n.d., in the Fredericksburg and Spotsylvania National Military Park bound manuscript collection, vol. 187-188.

Brooks' fiery temper, mixed with the unfathomable behavior of Benham, led to a blow-up between the two men. Brooks supported Russell, his junior officer; when asked whether Brooks acknowledged Benham's right to command the crossing, Brooks responded "No!"[38] The fuming engineer informed Brooks that he was now responsible for the crossing.[39]

But Benham did not stick to this new arrangement. He stormed off to find Sedgwick, who seemed to do his best to avoid the engineer and allow his staff officers to deal with the unruly drunk. Sedgwick's staff officer, Capt. Charles Whittier, came upon Benham "lying on the ground, his face badly scratched and bruised."[40] When Whittier informed the inebriated brigadier that Sedgwick hoped the bridges would be laid without delay, Benham tore into the young officer, then went on to say that Brooks and Russell would not follow his orders. The two men set out in search of the infantry commanders, a quest that took them to the riverfront. There Benham broke down again, clutching the staff officer's arm and wailing, "Captain Whittier, Captain Whittier look at all these men on the riverbank. The enemy will certainly fire on us. Dear me, dear me, what shall I do?"[41] He "bellowed like a mad man," said one witness.[42] Benham's sad display did not seem to surprise those under his command, though. "General Benham did not disappoint my expectations of him," Brainerd said.[43]

Despite the commotion, the operation still made progress. By 4:20 a.m., near dawn, the 15th New York Engineers were at the riverfront. So was the maverick David Russell with men of the 18th and 32nd New York

38 Francis E. Pinto, *History of the 32nd Regiment, New York Volunteers in the Civil War, 1861-1863 and Personal Recollections During that Period*, 137, in the Fredericksburg and Spotsylvania National Military Park bound manuscript collection, vol. 370.

39 Ibid.

40 One account from the May 3, 1863, edition of the *Sunday Mercury* states that Benham was wounded while the assault on the Rebel shore was taking place. He was along the river, screaming, "'Then fill the boats! fill the boats! Go to the rescue of your comrades! My staff, to the right, this way!' And then a bullet struck him near the nose, just biting out a chunk of flesh."

41 Whittier, Diary, n.d., 6.

42 Pinto, *History of the 32nd Regiment*, 137.

43 Malles, *Bridge Building in War Time*, 141.

and the 49th, 95th, and 119th Pennsylvania regiments, ready to board boats for the landings ahead. Russell took the time to call his regimental commanders together for a short briefing on the operation.[44]

Downriver at the I Corps crossing site, Brig. Gen. James Wadsworth had men of his 1st Division on the shore ready to cover the engineers' pending venture there. Wadsworth commanded some of the finest fighting men in the Army of the Potomac, the men of the Iron Brigade.

As a soldier, the 55-year-old Wadsworth defied convention. He was not a West Point graduate, nor was he a career politician like many other generals; he was a millionaire New Yorker from Geneseo who had answered his country's call to arms and had even refused pay for his service.

Prior to the war, Wadsworth had studied law at Harvard and dabbled in politics. During the First Manassas campaign, he proved a capable staff officer to Brig. Gen. Irvin McDowell. The following month, in August of 1861, Wadsworth was promoted to brigadier general and held the post of military governor of Washington, D.C. In 1862, while serving in the army, he ran for New York's governorship but lost. With the reorganization of the I Corps, Wadsworth was assigned to command its first division even though he lacked combat experience.[45]

"Wadsworth has never done anything in his military capacity to deserve credit," lamented Robert Robertson of the 93rd New York. "He has never taken the field nor exposed his life in the country's service, but the sphere of his duties are confined to Willard's Hotel and a comfortable office, so what has he done."[46] Wadsworth had much to prove.

*   *   *

By 4:20 a.m., as the sun tried to brighten the drizzle-gray sky across the Rappahannock River Valley, the engineers were already at work placing the bridge abutments on the northern shore. The infantry were in position. Men of the 49th and 119th Pennsylvania would lead the first

---

44 Pinto, *History of the 32nd Regiment*, 137.

45 Warner, *Generals in Blue*, 532-533.

46 Robert S. Robertson to Parents, October 29, 1862, in the Fredericksburg and Spotsylvania National Military Park bound manuscript collection, vol. 219.

Brigadier General James Wadsworth.

Library of Congress

wave. Forty to 45 infantrymen piled into each boat, with engineers of Col. Clinton Colgate's 15th New York Engineers acting as oarsmen.

"At the first streak of day our pontoons were launched," wrote Sewell Gray of the 6th Maine, who watched the action from the Federal shore, "and in the face of an entrenched enemy were filled with men and started out for the Land of Dixie."[47]

Pontoons were designed to be highly stable and highly buoyant in order to support the heavy weight of men and material; they were not designed for speed. The flat noses of the boats worked against the engineers who powered them, by sheer muscle, to the far side of the river, a distance of nearly 440 feet. It was slow going. The flat noses had one major advantage, though: they made pontoon boats perfect as landing craft, much like the Higgins boats of World War II. The pontoons could be driven right up onto shore and the men in their heavy woolen uniforms could jump out on dry land.

"So stealthily had the operation been conducted that the enemy's pickets did not sound the alarm till they saw boat loads of armed men approaching," wrote Brown.[48] And that was close, indeed—the morning "was as foggy as you ever saw it," one Confederate later recounted, providing plenty of cover for the assault force.[49] The boats of the 49th Pennsylvania were near to shore before shots finally rang out from the Confederate lines. "The gallant Pennsylvanians reached the Rebel shore," wrote one witness. "[They] jumped from the boats, many going to the waist in the water, and charged up the embankment. The Rebel pickets were taken altogether by surprise. . . . [T]he onset was so sudden, bold, and dashing, that the Butternut dogs, after firing a few ill-aimed volleys, fled in dismay."[50] Most of the Rebel shots went high, missing the Federals' boats.

As the Pennsylvanians began to slide ashore, the Confederates on the riverbank, of the 54th North Carolina, fell back about 100 yards to a line

47 Gray, Diary, April 29, 1863.

48 Joseph M. Brown, *Historical Sketch of the Sixteenth Regiment*, 23-24.

49 Lt. Col. Charles W. McArthur, 61st GA, to James Vaughn, May 23, 1863, in the Fredericksburg and Spotsylvania National Military Park bound manuscript collection, vol. 129.

50 Styple, *Writing & Fighting the Civil War*, 187.

of works.[51] Colonel William Irwin, commander of the 49th, was one of the first out of the boats. He had been standing like a "mast" in the boat while his men squatted to avoid fire, but as soon as it hit the bank he scrambled ashore. As Irwin attempted to form his men into a battle line along the riverbank, a bullet struck him in the leg, making him perhaps the first Union officer wounded by enemy fire in the campaign.[52]

As more Union men made their way out of the boats, losses began to mount. Quickly, men of Company B made their way toward a house about 50 yards from their position and flushed out Confederates from inside.

The 119th Pennsylvania had a tougher time making their way across the foggy river. Several of their boats caught in the current and drifted downstream and into one another.[53] Undeterred, the engineers rowed as hard and fast as they could, bringing the 119th ashore just moments after the 49th Pennsylvania. As they did, the second wave of Pennsylvanians struggled with "the steep and slippery banks made doubly so by the rain."[54] Next came the 95th Pennsylvania.

Moments later, Brig. Gen. Russell himself landed and directed the action in person. More boats slid ashore. In all, 23 boats made the initial crossing, carrying some 1,000 Union soldiers across the Rappahannock.

The boats that made the initial landing turned back to the friendly shore and refilled with more human cargo, comprised mostly of members of Bartlett's 2nd Brigade. "[T]he order was given, and quickly the boats were pushed into the water, filled with men, the oar manned, and we started," recalled William B. Westervelt of the 27th New York. "No sooner did we start than the enemy opened fire, and we being packed so close in the boats could hardly return it; but if we ever pulled an oar we did then. . . . "[55]

51 Robert S. Westbrook, *History of the 49th Pennsylvania Volunteers: A Correctly Compiled Roll of the Members of the Regiment and Its Marches From 1861-1865* (Altoona, PA, 1898), 144.

52 Ibid.

53 Larry B. Maier, *Rough & Regulars: A History of Philadelphia's 119th Pennsylvania Volunteer Infantry, The Gray Reserves* (Shippensburg, PA, 1997), 36-37.

54 Ibid., 38.

55 Westervelt, *Lights and Shadows of Army Life*, 39.

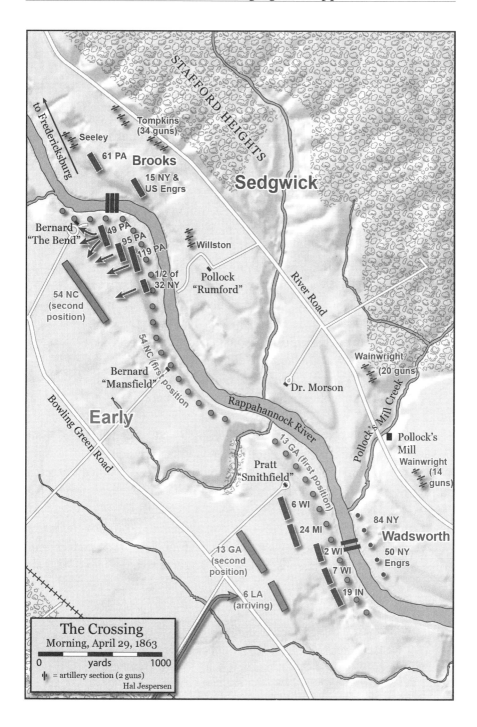

The Crossing

Morning, April 29, 1863

0   yards   1000

⊪ = artillery section (2 guns)

Hal Jespersen

"The sudden zigzag blaze of the enemy's fire lit up the darkness," added Brown of the 16th New York, also part of the second wave, "and it was a thrilling moment midway of the stream, in crowded boats, moving slowly—a target for a thousand rifles."

On the far bank, "about twenty feet high . . . and so steep we could only ascend by catching hold of some small trees and bushes and pulling ourselves up," the fresh reinforcements joined the melee. According to Brigadier General Brooks, his entire division crossed the river in this fashion.[56]

Confederates, many of whom had been living along the riverbank on picket duty since December and had perhaps gotten a little complacent, soon found themselves overwhelmed. The Federals "made very short work of capturing the enemy's works and about all the troops it contained," crowed Westervelt. "Very few tried to escape, and those who did had a long, level plain to cross, and were exposed all the way to our fire. . . ."[57] Some Federals made their way to Mansfield, the Bernard family home. One member of the 5th Wisconsin described the property as being owned by "grand, wealthy secessionists and they tried last fall to escape from our lines into those of the rebels."[58] On the property some scavenging Union soldiers unearthed a box containing $100,000 of Southern scrip.[59]

Aside from two men captured, the North Carolinians escaped. The Federals, meanwhile, suffered one fatality and ten wounded.

As the infantry secured the beachhead, Capt. Chauncey Reese's United States Engineer Battalion and the 15th New York Engineers worked feverishly to build bridges for the VI Corps crossing. It was not long before a competition developed between the two groups of engineers. "There was always a strife between these two branches of the service—the volunteers and the regulars—and here was a chance to test their skill," said one witness:

---

56 *OR* 25, pt. 1, 566.

57 Westervelt, *Lights and Shadows of Army Life*, 39.

58 Letter from a soldier in the 5th Wisconsin to the *Wisconsin Daily Patriot*, May 20, 1863, in the Fredericksburg and Spotsylvania National Military Park bound manuscript collection, vol. 149.

59 Ibid.

They had plenty of spectators, as the army on either bank were watching their movements, and this served as an incentive for them both to do their best. Boats were quickly anchored, and the men who carried the string pieces and plank would not think of walking; but while carrying their load, or returning empty, would run their best. The morning was cool, but the sweat ran off their faces. Still they kept on. . . . [60]

The volunteers won by a six-minute margin, a feat "received with hearty cheers by thousands who lined the banks on either side."[61]

The bridges, each nearly 440 feet long, lay about 140 yards from each other. Troops soon began flooding across. It was 9:30 a.m.

Downriver, Reynolds was having a much tougher go.

*   *   *

Sedgwick, in his inexperience as a wing commander, had not yet gotten the hang of communicating with his fellow commanders. So, as effective as Sedgwick's new method for crossing the river was, it did Reynolds little good—Sedgwick had failed to share his idea with him. So the I Corps commander set about crossing the river in the original Burnside fashion: infantry would stand on the Federal side of the river and blast away at Confederates on the far side as the engineers worked feverishly in the crossfire.

It is possible that Reynolds anticipated an easy crossing. After all, when he first crossed the river back in December, he had met little resistance. The United States Sharpshooters and one regiment of the Pennsylvania Reserves had proved sufficient to keep Confederate soldiers at bay because the Confederates in this sector had not enjoyed the same kind of cover their comrades enjoyed in the city of Fredericksburg to the north. Reynolds had no reason to expect anything different now.

In any event, the lack of communication between Reynolds and Sedgwick meant the two would not reach the hostile shore simultaneously, as they should have. Responsibility for this lack of

60 Westervelt, *Lights and Shadows of Army Life*, 39.

61 Ibid.

coordination falls on Sedgwick, who had relied on the drunken Benham. Since Benham could not even stay on his horse, how was he supposed to coordinate such a large military operation? Sedgwick's refusal to deal with Benham only compounded the problem.

The Confederate infantry along the riverfront had spent the winter digging rifle pits and entrenchments, and on the morning of April 29 the works were manned by Col. James Smith's 13th Georgia. The Georgians peppered the far shoreline with gunshot. "Their fire was so sharp and destructive, and their cover so secure, that we had great difficulty in laying the bridges," wrote one of Reynolds' staff officers.[62] "Yet the bridge must be laid," another observed sullenly, "however great the sacrifice."

Reynolds first employed Wainwright's cannon in an attempt to blast the Georgians away, but to no avail. Instead, it merely tipped off the Confederates to the fact that the Federals intended to cross in force at the mouth of Pollock's Mill Creek. If Confederate reinforcements flooded into the area, it would prevent Reynolds from crossing at all—which would mean that Brooks' division, already across upriver, could be taken in the flank and destroyed.

Reynolds called on Brig Gen. Wadsworth and his 1st Division to break the stalemate. Wadsworth, in turn, turned to his 6th Wisconsin and 24th Michigan regiments to buy time for the rest of the Iron Brigade to deploy. "The plan was simple and fully comprehended by the men," wrote Lt. Col. Rufus Dawes of the 6th Wisconsin. "A line of troops was to be moved forward to the edge of the riverbank who would fire over our heads at the enemy while we crossed the river in the boats."[63] With only 20 boats in the water and the element of surprise gone, the Federals on the exposed riverbank did what they could.[64] Just to their right rear, on a small crest overlooking the river, deployed the 19th Indiana as well as the 2nd and 7th Wisconsin. The men in front were ordered to lie down, so the 6th Wisconsin and 24th Michigan pulled back, aligned themselves, and went prone. The 84th New York, a Zouave regiment also known as the 14th

---

62 Charles H. Veil, *An Old Boy's Personal Recollections and Reminiscences of the Civil War* (Dillsburg, PA, 1958), 38-39.

63 Dawes, *Service with the Sixth Wisconsin Volunteers*, 136.

64 *OR* 25, pt. 1, 261.

Brooklyn, pushed down to the riverfront, deploying as skirmishers rather than in line of battle so as to present less of a target.

"About 20 boats lay in the water," wrote Capt. William Speed of the 24th Michigan, "& upon a concerted signal the 6th & 24th rushed to the river & into the boats & pulled for the opposite shore as fast as possible. The Artillery opened fire & other Rgts came down to the river bank & protected us all they could. Oh! These were fearful moments. The balls flew about like hail."[65]

"The men plunged into the boats and threw themselves upon the bottom," Dawes wrote. The orders were given to "Heave off your boats! Up with the oars!"[66] The men of the Iron Brigade rowed with all their might. The plan was to cross below the Georgians' right flank, turn it, and drive the rebels back from the river. As the boats made their way across the river, Wadsworth leapt into action. Reynolds' staff officer, Charles Veil, claimed that the white-haired general "jumped his horse off the bank and swam the river with the men. His son, Captain [Craig] Wadsworth, who was an aide on General Reynolds' staff, seeing what his father was doing, put spurs to his horse and, too, plunged into the river and swam over after his father."[67] Other accounts suggest Wadsworth crossed in less flamboyant style, in a boat, pulling his swimming horse along behind.

"When we got across the river, we jumped into the mud and water, waist deep, waded ashore, crawled and scrambled up the bank, laying hold of the bushes," Dawes wrote. "Very few shots were fired before the rebels were throwing down their arms or running over the plain."[68]

By the time the badgers and wolverines came aground, the men of the 13th Georgia had exhausted their ammunition. Relief was on the way, though, from the 6th Louisiana. The Louisianans had started their morning in the area of Hamilton's Crossing, about a mile from the Georgians' location, when "we were aroused from our peaceful slumbers,

65 Captain William Speed to Charlotte Speed, May 10, 1863, in the Fredericksburg and Spotsylvania National Military Park bound manuscript collection, vol. 278.

66 Dawes, *Service with the Sixth Wisconsin Volunteers*, 137.

67 Veil, *An Old Boy's Personal Recollections and Reminiscences of the Civil War*, 39.

68 Dawes, *Service with the Sixth Wisconsin Volunteers*, 137.

by the rattling of musketry on our picket lines on the Rappahannock."[69] The 6th formed a line of battle near Hamilton's Crossing, upon which their brigade commander, Brig. Gen. Harry Hays, ordered them to the front to relieve the Georgians. The remainder of the brigade formed a line of battle along the railbed of the Richmond, Fredericksburg & Potomac Railroad.

"When the brigade had been formed and I was sitting on my horse at the head of the column an affecting incident occurred of which I was the subject," recalled staff officer Seymour. "An Irish woman rushed out of her hut in the camp of the 6th [Louisiana] Regt., in demi-toilette, with her red shock of hair unkempt and disordered, and coming up to me raised her long, bony arms to Heaven and fervently called upon the Almighty to cover me with His shield in the day of battle and preserve me from the hands of the enemy. [Though] the woman was hideously ugly, there was an earnestness and solemnity in her manners. . . . She was a laundress in my Father's Regt. & revered his memory—hence her blessing upon me."[70]

As the 6th Louisiana made its way forward, the men took artillery fire from Wainwright's guns on Stafford Heights. With the fog lifting, the Federal guns could dominate the open fields that led to the river's edge. That, in turn, made it impossible for the 13th Georgia to pull out of the front lines. Although out of ammunition, they did what they could to

---

69 Waxia, *Richmond (VA) Sentinel*, May 14, 1863, in the Fredericksburg and Spotsylvania National Military Park bound manuscript collection, vol. 373. "Waxia" was the correspondent's pen name.

70 Jones, *The Civil War Memoirs of Captain William J. Seymour*, 48. Seymour's father Isaac was not a career soldier, but served the United States in the Seminole Wars and the Mexican-American War. Prior to the American Civil War, Isaac moved his family to New Orleans and was an editor of the *Commercial Bulletin*. At the outbreak of the war, Isaac assumed command of the 6th Louisiana infantry and William stayed behind to run the newspaper. Isaac was killed in action at Gaines' Mill in 1862. William left the business behind to become a volunteer aide to Brig. Gen. Johnson Kelly Duncan. Duncan was in command of the coastal defenses in New Orleans. Seymour was among the Confederate soldiers who surrendered Fort Jackson to Federal forces on April 28, 1862. The young staff officer was paroled and went back to his paper, but ran afoul of Maj. Gen. Benjamin Butler, who was in command of the Union occupying forces in New Orleans. By the spring of 1863, Seymour had found another staff position, this time with Brig. Gen. Harry Hays in the Army of Northern Virginia.

support the Creoles. Under a withering fire, the 6th Louisiana took position in the rifle pits.[71]

Captain Seymour remembered: "The 6th Regt. was ordered to the River to relieve a Georgia Regt. that reported their ammunition exhausted. It marched up to the position under a galling fire from the hills on the other side of the River and took their places in the rifle pits."[72]

The Union soldiers crossing in the boats "landed without much difficulty and rushed up the bank," one soldier recalled.[73] Another recorded, "they jumped out and went up the hill with a yell and charged bayonets. The rebs thought that the DEVIL was after them the way they ran away."[74] Colonel Edward Bragg of the 6th Wisconsin claimed, "without fear of contradiction, that the Sixth Wisconsin Volunteers first scaled the bank and their colors first caught the breeze on the southern bank of the Rappahannock on the morning of the 29th."[75] Bragg's men were the first members of Reynolds' corps to set foot on the Confederate shore.

They were not the last, though—more Union soldiers kept coming. Once the boats were unloaded on the hostile shore, they, like their counterparts at the upper crossing, turned back to reload with reinforcements. Meanwhile, Wainwright's guns dominated the riverfront and the fields to the Confederate rear. The 6th Louisiana was in a hot place.

Still, they did what they could to slow the Midwesterners. "It was evidently not the intention of our Generals to prevent their crossing, but merely to hold them in check until we could have our lines formed," one of the Louisianans recalled.[76] Outnumbered and out-gunned, they held out until about 10:30 a.m. when, finally, their commander, Col. William

---

71 Chester, "Letter from the Sixth Louisiana: The Storming of Marye's Heights," *Mobile (AL) Advertiser & Register*, June 4, 1863, in the Fredericksburg and Spotsylvania National Military Park bound manuscript collection, vol. 270.

72 Jones, *The Civil War Memoirs of Captain William J. Seymour*, 48-49.

73 Nevins, *A Diary of Battle*, 186.

74 Mair Pointon to unknown recipient, May 11, 1863, in the Fredericksburg and Spotsylvania National Military Park bound manuscript collection, vol. 353.

75 *OR* 25, pt. 1, 272.

76 Chester, "Letter from the Sixth Louisiana."

Pontoon boats similar to this ferried troops of the I and VI Corps
across the Rappahannock River.

Fredericksburg and Spotsylvania National Military Park

Monaghan, gave the order to retreat. "They fell back . . . to the
Fredericksburg and Port Royal Turnpike, a sunken road equidistant from
the River & our fortifications," he recalled.[77]

The 6th Louisiana paid a heavy price for its tenacious resistance, losing
7 killed, 12 wounded, and 78 captured, including its lieutenant colonel.[78]
"[T]his was totally unavoidable, however, as the entire regiment was
deployed as skirmishers," said a member of the 6th, explaining why so
many of his comrades had been captured. "[I]t was therefore impossible,
on the extreme ends of the line, to hear the command [to withdraw]."[79]

With the Confederates finally driven from the riverfront, the bridging
commenced. By midday two more spans were across the Rappahannock,
and Wadsworth's division was pouring across. To the north, at Franklin's

77 Jones, *The Civil War Memoirs of Captain William J. Seymour*, 49.

78 Stephen W. Sears, *Chancellorsville* (New York, NY, 1996), 158.

79 Chester, "Letter from the Sixth Louisiana."

Crossing, Maj. Gen. John Newton had ordered a third span across the river there.[80]More than 10,000 Union soldiers were now on the south bank of the Rappahannock.

As the army spilled across the open plain on the west side of the Rappahannock, Wadsworth's division of I Corps and Brooks' division of VI Corps took up positions halfway between the river and the Bowling Green Road, filling the fields of Arthur Bernard's and Thomas Pratt's sprawling plantations. Two full divisions were poised to strike out toward the Confederate lines, and, for all the Confederates knew, thousands more men dressed in blue would cross behind them in support.

"The scene was exceedingly magnificent," wrote VI Corps staff officer Thomas Hyde as he stood on the east side of the river watching the mass of blue soldiers streaming across the newly laid bridges. "Imagine yourself standing on a high range of hills at our Head Quarters, overlooking the beautiful green valley of the winding Rappahannock, dotted with country seats and alive with troops; the pontoon bridges; ten-thousand men holding with watchful care the opposite bank; the city off to the right; the batteries of both sides roaring and flashing at each other."[81]

Although it had suffered a rocky start, Hooker's diversionary force had crossed the river with relatively few casualties. Although still on edge, many of the Union soldiers were relieved that the crossing had gone so well. Abraham Hilands of the 49th Pennsylvania perhaps said it best: "[W]e crossed the 'Rubicon.'"[82]

Now they had to be ready for whatever Robert E. Lee had waiting for them on the other side.

80 *OR* 25, pt. 1, 213.

81 Thomas Hyde to Mother, May 7, 1863, in the Fredericksburg and Spotsylvania National Military Park bound manuscript collection, vol. 404.

82 Abraham Hilands to Mary Hilands, May 3, 1863, in the Fredericksburg and Spotsylvania National Military Park bound manuscript collection, vol. 412.

Chapter Five

To Call Hooker's Bluff

Confederate troops along the western heights had been listening to Union artillery firing into their riverfront most of the morning, but the fog had obscured the view. As the last of it burned away by 9:00 a.m., they could see a blue landscape of Union soldiers congregating on the open plains below. There was no way to tell yet how many there were, but the sheer size of the host made it clear that something was up. "I have been in hopes that the enemy would let us alone here but it seems that he is determined to have a fight," wrote one Confederate captain.[1]

"[S]omething was going to happen," wrote Pvt. David Holt. "Every fellow cleaned up his gun and fixed up his accouterments, for we did not have a single inspection of armies at that camp."[2]

As his comrades began preparing for the looming battle, Marion Hill Fitzpatrick, a private with the 45th Georgia, snuck out toward the Federal position for a closer look. "I went down there this morning and could see and hear them plain," he wrote in a letter home. "I went over the ground

1 Ujanirtus Allen to Wife, April 28, 1863, *Campaigning with "Old Stonewall": Confederate Captain Ujanirtus Allen's Letters to His Wife*, ed. Randall Allen and Keith S. Bohannon (Baton Rouge, LA, 1998), 230.

2 David Holt, *A Mississippi Rebel in the Army of Northern Virginia* (Baton Rouge, LA, 1995), 162.

Major General Jubal Anderson Early: "Lee's Bad Old Man."

Cooke Collection, Valentine Museum

we fought on before and saw the place where I was wounded. . . . The field is literally covered with graves now. I saw the arm of a dead Yankee sticking out of a grave that had not decayed."[3] Confederates and Federals alike worried that there would be fresh graves soon enough.

Major General Jubal A. Early, the Confederate division commander at the southernmost end of the field, began preparations for what might come next. Couriers flew back and forth with orders and reports as Early steeled his men for a possible assault against his portion of the Confederate line.

Jubal Anderson Early was Lee's junior ranking division commander. A West Point graduate of the class of 1837 whose classmates included Joe Hooker and the man leading the Union left wing, John Sedgwick, Early had left the army to pursue a career as a lawyer and politician. Although he voted against the secession of Virginia, he soon embraced the Confederate cause. Initially, Early—who became known as "Old Jube"—commanded the 24th Virginia, but he quickly rose to brigade command. He saw action at Williamsburg, where he was wounded, Malvern Hill, Cedar Mountain, and Second Manassas. During the Sharpsburg campaign, he took the reins of a Confederate division. In that capacity at Fredericksburg, he earned distinction—and risked earning the ire of his commander, Stonewall Jackson—by disregarding an order so that he could protect the Confederate right flank, a decision that, some said, saved Jackson's line.

Lee playfully referred to Early as "my bad old man."[4] Reportedly, Early was the only Confederate officer in the Army of Northern Virginia with the temerity to curse in Lee's presence—an orneriness not even the gentle presence of the army commander could repress. John Brown Gordon, who served as a general officer under Early, described his commander as "a bachelor, with a pungent style of commenting on things he did not like; but he had a kind heart and was always courteous to women."[5] Many people had a difficult time getting along with him,

---

3 Jeffrey Lowe, ed., *Letters to Amanda: The Civil War Letters of Marion Hill Fitzpatrick, Army of Northern Virginia* (New York, NY, 2003), 66-67.

4 Phax, *Mobile (AL) Advertiser & Register*, May 15, 1863, in the Fredericksburg and Spotsylvania National Military Park bound manuscript collection, vol. 270. "Phax" was the correspondent's pen name.

5 John B. Gordon, *Reminiscences of the Civil War* (Dayton, OH, 1985), 318.

though, as Early was quick to anger and held grudges for life, as Brig. Gen. William Barksdale would soon find out.[6]

Conversely, if Early liked a person, that person could do no wrong, and nowhere was that more apparent than in his near-worship of his senior officers, Lee and Jackson. Unlike Lee and Jackson, though, Early drank, cursed, and was not a religious man. Lee's adjutant, Col. Walter Taylor, wrote of Old Jube to his fiancée, "Don't tell anyone I say so, but I have feared our friend Early would not accomplish much because he is such a Godless man. He is a man who utterly sets at defiance all moral laws & such a one Heaven will not favour."[7]

Still, Early was thus far in the war proving himself an above-average combat leader, and what he lacked in experience he made up for in aggressiveness. "Early was undoubtedly one of the strongest and ablest of Lee's lieutenants," observed Confederate artillerist Maj. Robert Stiles:

> He was not perhaps the brilliant and dashing soldier that A. P. Hill was, nor a superb, magnetic leader like Gordon, and possibly he could not deliver quite as a majestic blow in actual battle as Longstreet; but his loyal devotion, his courage, his native intellect, his mental training, his sagacity, his resource, his self-reliant, self-directing strength, were all very great, and the commanding general reposed the utmost confidence in him.[8]

Now, with tension building in the fog below, Early mobilized his troops into position and sent word to his corps commander. However, battle was the furthest thing from Stonewall Jackson's mind.

*   *   *

---

6 Gordon, undoubtedly Early's ablest subordinate, would eventually discover Early's life-long tendency to hold grudges. In their postwar writings, they would get into a feud over who was to blame for the delay in launching an attack on the evening of May 6, 1864, in the Wilderness.

7 R. Lockwood Tower, ed., *Lee's Adjutant: The Wartime Letters of Colonel Walter Herron Taylor, 1862-1865* (Columbia, SC, 1995), 177.

8 Stiles, *Four Years Under Marse Robert*, 188-189.

Shortly before the December battle in Fredericksburg, Jackson had received a letter from home, written in his sister-in-law's hand but with a decidedly different voice.

> My own dear Father, . . . I know that you are rejoiced to hear of my coming, and I hope that God has sent me to radiate your pathway through life. I am a very tiny little thing. I weigh only eight and a half pounds, and Aunt Harriet says I am the express image of my darling papa. . . . My hair is dark and long, my eyes are blue, my nose straight just like papa's. . . . My mother is very comfortable this morning. She is anxious to have my name decided upon, and hopes you will write and give me a name, with your blessing. . . . [9]

Julia Thomas Jackson, named for Jackson's mother, had been born on November 23, and she represented her father's dearest wish come true. In what seemed a lifetime ago, he had lost his first wife, Ellie, in childbirth—along with their unnamed son. After remarrying, Jackson and his second wife, Mary Anna, lost a daughter only a few weeks old. As someone who had been orphaned himself at an early age, he wanted nothing more than a family of his own, and yet that wish had been denied and denied again. Now, with the birth of Julia, his wish had come true.

His frequent letters home gushed over his "little comforter," but he did not get to revel in fatherhood until the following spring. On April 20, a rainy Monday, Mary Anna and Julia arrived by train from Richmond at the Confederate rail depot at Guinea Station, Virginia. Jackson, umbrella aloft, waited to meet them. "His face was all sunshine and gladness," Mary Anna later recalled. "[I]t was a picture, indeed, to see his look of perfect delight and admiration as his eyes fell on that baby!"

Jackson spent an idyllic eight days with his wife and daughter—the happiest time of his life, which would make the events to come all the more tragic. Jackson installed his family in the stately brick plantation house of Thomas Yerby. The home, Belvoir, sat aslope a hill that provided an expansive view of the local landscape, and it was conveniently located about a mile from Jackson's field headquarters. In December, Belvoir had

---

9 Mary Anna Jackson, *Memoirs of Stonewall Jackson: By his Widow Mary Anna Jackson* (Louisville, KY, 1895), 374.

Confederate Second Corps commander Lieutenant General
Thomas J. "Stonewall" Jackson.

Library of Congress

been used as a Confederate field hospital; Maxcy Gregg, the Confederate brigadier general mortally wounded trying to stop the Union breakthrough during the battle of Fredericksburg, had died in the home.

The Jacksons were still asleep when Early's adjutant, Maj. Samuel Hale, Jr., rode up to the house. His heavy boot steps on the front steps woke the general, who dressed quickly and met with the courier. Apprised of the situation, he gave directions for his wife and daughter to pack their things, then swept out the door to his horse, Little Sorrel, and off to the front he rode.

*   *   *

By 8:00 a.m., Jackson was riding out from Prospect Hill toward the line along the railroad line held by Hays' Louisiana Tigers. "Jackson rode in front of our Brigade, amid the loud cheers of our men, and proceeded to the road along which our advanced regiments [the 5th and 6th Louisiana] were stationed," recalled staff officer William J. Seymour. "[F]rom that point he cooly reconnoitered the positions of the enemy and exhorted our men to hold at all hazards."[10]

Jackson eyed the Federal operations. Around him, shells burst at random intervals as Federal artillerists began to bombard the line. "Though the picket firing was very brisk at the time and the balls fell thick and fast around him, he providentially escaped unhurt, much to our relief who were fearfully looking to see him fall from his horse every moment," Seymour said.[11] Although his staff began to get concerned, Jackson, as was his custom, paid the shells little heed, focusing his attention instead on the growing number of Federals on his side of the river. Hooker was crossing in force, he concluded, and sent word to Lee's headquarters. Jackson's adjutant, Lt. James Power Smith, passed along the message. "Well I thought I heard firing," Lee replied with good-natured charm, "and was beginning to think it was time some of you young fellows were coming to

10 Jones, *The Civil War Memoirs of Captain William J. Seymour*, 49.

11 Ibid.

tell me what it was all about. Tell your good general that I am sure he knows what to do. I will meet him at the front very soon."[12]

In Fredericksburg, the peal of the bells in the Episcopal church tower alerted residents and soldiers alike that something was happening. Lee made his way to Jackson's position amid great clamor as Confederate infantrymen readied for . . . they knew not what. Neither did Lee until he had the chance to inspect the situation for himself.

By the time Lee arrived, Early had already sent forward four brigades to take up position along the tracks of the Richmond, Fredericksburg & Potomac Railroad. He had also sent a picket line about a half a mile forward of that. Other troops, too, were soon on the move. Jackson sent word for division commanders Robert E. Rodes, Raleigh E. Colston, and A. P. Hill to converge on the area around Prospect Hill, some five miles south of the city. The units had been spread out over the countryside during the winter as part of the effort to meet the demand for supplies.

From Prospect Hill, Lee and Jackson simply watched.[13] It was clear by the number of troops involved that the Federals certainly planned something, but rather than pile-drive straight across the field while the Confederates scrambled to consolidate their position, the Federals instead just sat there. What started out with a roar was quickly petering out into something much less impressive.

The Chancellorsville campaign was barely a day and a half old, and Fighting Joe Hooker had already given up the initiative—or so it seemed. It is important to note that Hooker had been well aware of the Confederate dispositions, thanks to the outstanding and accurate intelligence gathered for him prior to the campaign by Colonel Sharpe. Hooker knew the Confederates were strung out from Fredericksburg southward. There is no record, however, that Hooker shared any of that detailed knowledge with Sedgwick nor any of the other commanders in the army's left wing. Sedgwick, then, had no idea of the possible opportunity he was unintentionally squandering; he was just following Hooker's orders.

---

12 Couch, "Chancellorsville Campaign," 203.

13 Some Confederates refer to Prospect Hill as "Jackson's Hill" since Stonewall used the hill during First Fredericksburg as a command post, as well as the focal point of his defense-in-depth.

Lee now considered whether to fall on Sedgwick and his growing bridgehead with the full force of Jackson's Second Corps or wait and see how the situation played out. He had no idea what Hooker's intentions might be. His own army was under-strength and still precariously spread out to the south through Caroline, Hanover, and Louisa counties, nearly down to Richmond. He still faced supply issues. He had also begun to receive word that a Federal force of indeterminate size was moving north of the Rapidan River. He received word, too, that Federal cavalry—Stoneman's corps—was working its way west.

To counter any Federal threat from that direction, Lee dispatched three brigades of Maj. Gen. Richard H. Anderson's division toward the Chancellorsville area. Anderson was to take up a defensive position to block any advance into the Confederate rear. At first, the brigades of William "Little Billy" Mahone, Carnot Posey, and Ambrose R. Wright took up positions around the crossroads, but Anderson quickly realized the area was not conducive to defensive operations—a fact Hooker seemed to miss—so he ordered most of his men back toward the Zoan Church Ridge, three miles east of Chancellorsville. Pickets of the 12th Virginia were left back in the Chancellorsville area to warn of any Federal advance.

Rumors began to spread among the Confederate soldiers that Lee and Jackson were going to order a retreat. Jackson dismissed the gossip testily. "No, sir, we have not a thought of retreat," he said. "We will attack them!"[14]

But it seems Lee quietly dismissed that idea. He could already tell that the Federals had deployed an overwhelming number of artillery pieces overlooking the bridgehead, which made a Confederate attack over the open fields nearly suicidal. He could also see, on further inspection, that the Federals had begun to entrench: he could see light fortifications springing up along the Bowling Green Road. Federal artillery dueled with Jackson's guns, a few probing skirmishes took place in the Landsdowne Valley, but nothing even resembling a major assault was brewing. Since the Federals seemed to pose no immediate threat, Lee saw no pressing need to take the fight to them, at least not until he had a clearer picture of what was taking shape around him.

---

14 Lacy narrative, Dabney Papers, University of North Carolina, in the Fredericksburg and Spotsylvania National Military Park bound manuscript collection.

"I hope if any reinforcements can be sent they may be forwarded immediately," Lee telegraphed to Jefferson Davis. In a second message, he requested that Longstreet's divisions be recalled from the southern part of the state and asked for the forwarding of supplies.[15] However, Longstreet, Lee's second in command, and his two combat-tested divisions—numbering more than 14,000 badly needed men—were more than 150 miles away.

Lee also asked his division commanders at hand to get ready. "Caution your officers to be vigilant & energetic," he told one of them. "We may be obliged to change our position."[16]

15 Robert E. Lee to Jefferson Davis, Dispatches, April 29, 1863, in the Fredericksburg and Spotsylvania National Military Park bound manuscript collection, vol. 19.

16 Robert E. Lee to Lafayette McLaws, Dispatches, April 29, 1863, in the Fredericksburg and Spotsylvania National Military Park bound manuscript collection, vol. 19.

Confederate First Corps commander Lieutenant General James "Pete"
Longstreet, Lee's second-in-command.

National Archives

Chapter Six

The Enemy in Front and Rear

"T he papers will of course tell you the army has moved," wrote George Gordon Meade to his wife on April 30, 1863. "I write to tell you that there is as yet but a little skirmishing; we are across the river and have out-maneuvered the enemy, but are not yet out of the woods."[1]

Meade could not have been more prophetic, or more literal. At the time of his letter, his V Corps, along with Howard's XI Corps and Slocum's XII Corps, were all moving through the thick, second-growth forests of Spotsylvania's Wilderness. One of Slocum's marchers described it as "a thick growth of scraggly and stunted timber, growing in many places so rank as to be almost impassable to man or beast." It was, the New Yorker said, "a dreary and deserted country."[2]

In the early fog-filled morning of April 30, Meade's men had successfully completed their crossing at Ely's Ford. Three squadrons of the 8th Pennsylvania Cavalry clashed with Company H of the 12th Virginia Infantry in some brisk but brief skirmishing near the Bullock Farm less than a mile north of the Chancellorsville crossroads, but otherwise the Federal movement went unopposed. Meade advanced one

---

1 Meade, *The Life and Letters of George Gordon Meade*, 370.

2 K. Jack Bauer, *Soldiering: The Civil War Diary of Rice C. Bull* (Novato, CA, 1995), 41.

division toward the Chancellorsville crossroads and sent elements of the 8th Pennsylvania Cavalry and Maj. Gen. George Sykes' division to secure the United States Ford a little to the east.[3]

Howard and Slocum, meanwhile, had crossed about ten miles to the west at Germanna Ford. Confederate cavalry briefly harried the movement with a few artillery shots, but was quickly chased off. Slocum pushed forward toward Chancellorsville, converging there with Meade in order to secure the crossroads and the surrounding open fields. "We arrived at a clearing larger than we had seen since we crossed the Rapidan," said New Yorker Rice Bull. "This was a plantation of several hundred acres. . . . The cleared land was on both sides of the turnpike and near the center was a large and rather pretentious mansion."

It was about 11:00 a.m. and the ladies of the house stood on the mansion's front porch, "not at all abashed or intimidated," recalled a Pennsylvanian. They "scolded audibly and reviled bitterly. They seriously condemned the stoppage. . . . "[4] Neither Meade, nor Slocum when he appeared, seemed to mind. The general officers occupied the front porch, displacing the women. "Gen. Meade was lavish in praise of Hooker," said one Federal soldier. "He considered the movement thus far to have been a great success."[5] When Slocum arrived to meet him, Meade suggested they press the advantages they had gained through their march and push onward toward Lee's unsuspecting army in Fredericksburg. In fact, Meade had already sent Brig. Gen. Charles Griffin's 1st Division forward to clear the way.

Slocum, however, had been given express orders from Hooker not to advance beyond the crossroads. He ordered his XII Corps to dig in. "There was a lot of fallen timber that we gathered and placed lengthwise, then dug a trench behind, with the dirt thrown over the logs," wrote Rice Bull. "The trench was over two feet deep, wide enough for the line to stand in

3 Bigelow, *The Campaign of Chancellorsville*, 213-214.

4 Survivors Association, *History of the Corn Exchange Regiment 118th Pennsylvania Volunteers: From Their First Engagement at Antietam to Appomattox* (Philadelphia, PA, 1888), 171-172.

5 Alexander S. Webb, "Meade at Chancellorsville," in *Campaigns in Virginia, Maryland, and Pennsylvania, 1862-1863*, 3 vols. (Boston, MA, 1903), vol. 3, 228-229, in the Fredericksburg and Spotsylvania National Military Park bound volume collection, vol. 53.

and with the embankment the total depth was five feet. These works were quite strong and would protect the men against attack. . . . "[6]

At the rear of the marching column, the XI Corps settled into position near Dowdall's Tavern, about two miles to the west of the crossroads, essentially acting as Hooker's reserve.[7]

Meade's disappointment was obvious. "[H]e considered it a great mistake," said a staff officer. "[H]is corps was in splendid condition and was ready for anything, and [he said] 'that we ought to get into the open country beyond.'"[8] Disheartened, Meade sent orders to Griffin to pull back.

Griffin, as it turned out, had already pushed his way eastward along the turnpike several miles, nearly as far as Zoan Church. There, light Confederate resistance under Mahone tried to bluff the Federals into stopping. "There they stood facing each other, neither firing, and no one speaking," said a Pennsylvanian. "Finally the Confederates fell back, neither side firing a shot."[9] No wonder, then, that Griffin was "much chagrined at the peremptory order to stop"—so chagrined, in fact, that "some hot, plain, determined words were spoken" and Griffin even offered to surrender his commission should things go wrong.[10]

His appeals were for naught. Inexplicably, at least as far as the Confederates were concerned, although just as inexplicably to Griffin's men, the Federals withdrew from their advanced position, falling back to the Chancellorsville clearing.

"The soldiers were as discomfited as if they had been checked by a serious repulse," the Pennsylvanian said. "All enthusiasm vanished, all the bright hopes of success disappeared. The belief that had grown to conviction that the campaign would culminate in the utter rout of the enemy was changed to sullen disappointment. The spirits of at least the

6   Bauer, *Soldiering*, 43.

7   Howard, *Autobiography of Oliver Otis Howard*, 355-356.

8   James C. Biddle to Alexander Webb, November 21, 1886, in Webb, "Meade at Chancellorsville," 228-229.

9   Survivors Association, *History of the Corn Exchange Regiment*, 171-172.

10 Ibid.

advance of the Army of the Potomac were sadly broken. . . . Somebody had again blundered."[11]

But in actuality, Hooker could not have been happier. His army had successfully maneuvered through hostile territory and had placed itself in the rear of the Confederate army, essentially unopposed. Since Sedgwick still had Lee's attention, Hooker wanted to use April 30 to consolidate his forces around Chancellorsville before the final thrust at Lee.

"It is with heartfelt satisfaction the commanding general announces to the army that the operations of the last three days have determined that our enemy must ingloriously fly, or come out from behind his defenses and give us battle on our own ground, where certain destruction awaits him," Hooker wrote in a general order issued to his men that evening. "The operations of the Fifth, Eleventh, and Twelfth Corps have been a succession of splendid achievements."[12]

To bolster his position at Chancellorsville, Hooker called on Sickles' III Corps, which was acting as Sedgwick's reserve.[13] He also summoned two divisions from Couch's II Corps. By 10:00 am on May 1, Hooker would have nearly 70,000 men in and around Chancellorsville.

From Chancellorsville, Hooker had the ability—and the will—to drive toward Lee's rear. Three major roads led to Fredericksburg from the crossroad: the River Road, the Orange Plank Road, and the Orange Turnpike. Control of the roads, coupled with the size of his army, gave Hooker a strong tactical advantage, but his immediate position in the Wilderness around Chancellorsville was a weak one. Although there was open ground around the Chancellorsville crossroads, the area was not conducive to fighting a major battle. The heavy woods of the Wilderness made it nearly impossible for infantry units to hold their formations; cavalry had little room to maneuver; artillery had little room to deploy and hardly any open fields of fire. Thus, Hooker's army would have to move quickly to get out of the Wilderness if it was going to flush out the wily Lee before the Gray Fox could react.

11 Ibid.

12 *OR* 25, pt. 2, 359-360.

13 Ibid.

"This is splendid," Meade said to Slocum. "We are on Lee's flank and he does not know it."[14]

*   *   *

Hooker had spent the morning at his headquarters in Falmouth, carefully following the progress of his marching column while also monitoring the situation south of Fredericksburg. With the Army of Northern Virginia situated directly between his two wings, able to move against either of them, Hooker felt an acute need for intelligence. At 8:30 a.m. Hooker sent orders to Sedgwick through Hooker's chief of staff, Maj. Gen. Daniel Butterfield, to

> make a demonstration on the enemy's lines in the direction of Hamilton's Crossing at 1 o'clock, the object being simply to ascertain whether or not the enemy continues to hug his defenses in full force; and if he should have abandoned them, to take possession of his works and the commanding ground in their vicinity. In his [Hooker's] opinion a corps should be used for this service, a portion of it advanced, while the balance is held in supporting distance, and your whole force held in readiness to spring to their relief. . . . This demonstration will be made for no other purpose than that stated. The enemy must not be attacked behind his defenses, if held in force. . . . As soon as the required information is obtained the column can return. Look well after the defenses at your bridge-heads during this movement.
>
> If you are certain that the enemy is in full force in your front, I am instructed by the commanding general to say that the demonstration herein directed will not be made. The general must know the position of the affairs and be advised fully. . . . [15]

The orders to Sedgwick were a confusing mixture of aggression and ambivalence. Sedgwick was to move a corps across the open fields in front of Jackson's fortified lines, where his men would be in full view of the enemy and well within the range of Confederate artillery. To complicate

14 Sears, *Chancellorsville*, 180.

15 *OR* 25, pt. 2, 306.

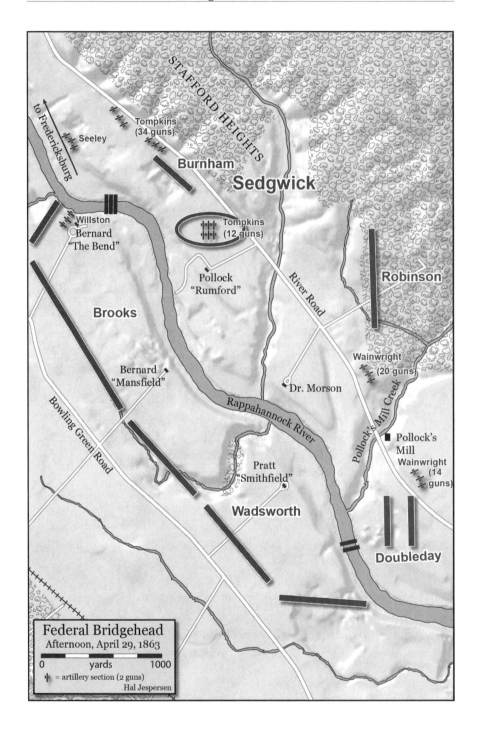

Federal Bridgehead
Afternoon, April 29, 1863

0   yards   1000

= artillery section (2 guns)

Hal Jespersen

matters further, Sedgwick did not yet even have a full corps across the river. Sedgwick would have to move at least two more divisions across. Although it could be done easily enough, the bridgehead area would become a massed target of blue—particularly problematic because the Southern artillery could easily reach the bridges. In fact, rebel shells had punched holes in a number of the pontoon boats already.[16]

The bridgehead had remained essentially unchanged since midday of April 29th. "Bully" Brooks' division still held the northern sector, with his right flank anchored on the Rappahannock River near "The Bend." From the river, the line then ran southwest and eventually dog-legged southeast near the long carriage road that led to Arthur Bernard's home, Mansfield. Just south of the carriage road, the left of Brooks' division met with the right of Wadsworth's I Corps division. "Old Waddy's" line continued southeastward through the front yard of Thomas Pratt's home, Smithfield, until the left flank of the division refused eastward and anchored itself on the Rappahannock just short of the Alsop home.

The main Federal line, which had scratched out a low line of trenches during the afternoon and evening of April 29th, still did not reach as far forward as the Bowling Green Road, although skirmishers positioned themselves in and about it. They also found a bit of cover in the III Corps trenches cut the previous December.

With their backs to the river and little room to maneuver, the I Corps men looked to improve their line any way they could. Many of Wainwright's guns stood atop Stafford Heights, but to bolster morale and the defensive strength of the main battle line, two I Corps batteries were moved across the bridges at Fitzhugh's Crossing: the six guns of Capt. James Stewart's Battery B, 4th United States Artillery, and the four guns of Capt. Dunbar Ransom's Battery C, 5th United States Artillery. (Ransom was actually a North Carolina native who stuck with the Union during the war.) The two batteries, comprised of ten 12-pounder Napoleons, would provide perfect cover should Lee launch an attack on the bridgeheads. Even though the guns did not have the range of the rifled pieces atop Stafford Heights, they could be employed with deadly accuracy if a retreat was forced across the bridges. Their double loads of

16 Nevins, *A Diary of Battle*, 188.

This photograph of soldiers on the front line was taken near the bridgehead at Franklin's Crossing. The troops are of Brooks' VI Corps division, which was the first to cross on April 29, 1863. Photos in the field like this were rare.

Library of Congress

canister could cut swaths in enemy formations while buying precious time.

Although the order called for the entire corps to advance across the fields, only a portion of the corps was supposed to engage, and it would have to do so over muddy fields. "It rained a good part of last night," wrote Colonel Wainwright. "The roads are very bad, and the fields so soft as to make the moving of batteries difficult."[17] Meanwhile, the portion of the corps not engaged would likely have to sit idly by, subject to Confederate artillery fire.

Some of the I Corps officers, including Colonel Wainwright, climbed the rooftop of Smithfield, which gave them an excellent vantage point to

17 Ibid.

Colonel Charles Wainwright, I Corps Chief Artillery.

Fredericksburg and Spotsylvania National Military Park

look across the relatively flat and open fields that led to the Confederate position at Prospect Hill and along the Richmond, Fredericksburg & Potomac Railroad. Such information was not enough, however, and Sedgwick prepared to send out the reconnaissance mission as ordered.

The reconnaissance actually had the potential to end the Confederate occupation of Fredericksburg. If Hooker moved in from Chancellorsville

The Smithfield Plantation circa 1930s. Today, Smithfield is home
to the Fredericksburg Country Club.

Fredericksburg and Spotsylvania National Military Park

fast and hard with the right wing of the Federal army, pressure from the
reconnaissance might be enough to flush out the Confederates. In the end,
though, that was not Hooker's plan. He simply wanted to know whether
Lee was there or not.

Hooker's motives might seem a little befuddling because, after all, the
Confederate lines were easily visible from Stafford Heights on the east side
of the Rappahannock. Federals also took to the skies in balloons. Others
climbed the roofs of local plantations.[18] All signs from all lookouts were
about the same: the enemy's dispositions had changed little since the
29th—had changed little since the start of winter, for that matter.

However, there was a great deal of rail movement along the
Richmond, Fredericksburg & Potomac Railroad. Reynolds reported "a

18 Ibid., 190.

train of passenger cars just gone down the road toward Bowling Green."[19] Reynolds reported seeing platform cars as well. What could that movement mean? Were troops making their way to or from Richmond? Even with all the observation points at the Federals' disposal, no one could be fully certain what Lee and Jackson were up to. Confederate trains could make their way no farther than Hamilton's Crossing at the southern base of Prospect Hill. There, Southern forces were clearly at work along the rail line constructing earthworks. Although the men looked as if they had hunkered down to stay, they might actually be covering the railhead while Lee and Jackson withdrew their forces to the south, using the Richmond, Fredericksburg & Potomac Railroad.

Aeronaut James Allen sent a report that complicated things even further. Allen reported that "[t]he woods directly opposite our bridge on the left full of rebel troops. The extensive camp still remains 6 miles directly south from this point. . . . " If true, Allen's information directly contradicted what Reynolds was witnessing from his vantage point.[20]

Either way, Sedgwick was not about to move across the fields to the waiting Confederates with his back to the Rappahannock.

Hooker exacerbated the situation further by sending orders to engineer Benham, simultaneously copying both Sedgwick and Reynolds: "The commanding general [Hooker] directs that you have one of the bridges at Franklin's Crossing and one of the bridges at Reynolds' Crossing [Fitzhugh's Crossing] taken up to-night, and in position to be laid at Banks' Ford before daylight to-morrow [May 1]. . . . This movement must be concealed from the enemy, and nothing be done that betray the movement before dark to-night."[21] Sedgwick was now losing two bridges. If the enemy made an assault, the I Corps would be especially vulnerable because it would be down to only one bridge should it need to withdraw.

That evening, to the riverfront went the men of the 50th New York Engineers. Along with the men of Col. Thomas M. Bayne's 136th

---

19 *OR* 25, pt. 2, 313.

20 Ibid., 311.

21 Ibid., 308.

Pennsylvania, they pulled up the bridge at Fitzhugh's Crossing.[22] At the upper crossing, meanwhile, the 15th New York Engineers set to work dragging bridges from the water there. Their work was aided by Col. Andrew Morrison's 26th New Jersey.[23]

Adding to Sedgwick's heavy burden, the nearly 18,000 men of Sickles' III Corps were being reassigned. The order to Sickles arrived at 12:30 p.m. on the 30th:

> Upon the receipt of this order you will proceed with your corps, without delay, by the shortest road, concealed from view of the enemy, to the United States Ford. The batteries taken from your command, placed in position to cover the crossing, will be relieved. It is expected in time to join you. . . . The greatest promptness is expected of you. As much of your corps as can cross on the bridges at United States Ford to cross to-night, and all to cross by 7 a.m. to-morrow. . . . General Couch [with two divisions of II Corps] precedes you, and the [V Corps] batteries left by General Meade also. After crossing, you will take up your line of march toward Chancellorsville. . . . [24]

Now, not only was Sedgwick losing bridges, he was also losing his reserve corps. Still, even with the loss of Sickles' corps, Sedgwick had the I and VI corps plus Brig. Gen. John Gibbon's II Corps division near Fredericksburg and a detachment of guns from the artillery reserves—nearly 45,000 men in all. Yet Sedgwick, in finest George McClellan fashion, worried that would not be enough. "General Reynolds is satisfied that the enemy have not weakened their force in infantry or artillery, and that a demonstration will bring on a general engagement on the left," he wrote. "General Brooks thinks the infantry force in his front is undiminished and strong. He can see nothing of their batteries."[25]

Although Sedgwick provided no definitive answer as to exact enemy strength or dispositions, his message convinced Hooker that it would be futile to attack the Confederate position at Fredericksburg. From

---

22 *OR* 25, pt. 1, 213, 253-255.

23 Ibid.

24 *OR* 25, pt. 2, 314.

25 Ibid., 310.

everything he had heard from Sedgwick and Reynolds throughout the day, the commander doubted that the Confederates had abandoned the position.

As their commanders dithered, the soldiers in the I and VI corps had little to occupy themselves on April 30 beyond the occasional cannonading, mixed with camp gossip. "Raining this morning, foggy all quiet at 12 noon. We received word that Hooker has been whipped on their left," wrote Pvt. Lewis Luckenbill of the 96th Pennsylvania. "At 1 ½ o'clock p.m. cannonading commences. On our left the balloon up near the river."[26]

One VI Corps soldier in Shaler's brigade, using the pen name "Sergeant Drill," wrote home to his local newspaper:

> We are lying in line of battle, ready for the word. The sun has emerged from behind the clouds, it is very hot. The entire scene from the adjoining heights is magnificent in the extreme. We are utterly ignorant of what is to take place, but look for commencement of the engagement at any moment. This note is written in the midst of the field, surrounded by the general hubbub.[27]

Reynolds sought to develop the situation without endangering his men's lives. The I Corps commander called to Henry Hunt and requested that a battery of 20-pounder Parrott guns be attached to his command so he could shell the enemy. The ammunition for the guns that Reynolds already had on hand, 10-pounder Parrott guns, was "not good, or the gunners [were not good], I don't know which."[28] In response to Reynolds' request, Capt. Elijah Taft's 5th New York Independent Artillery rolled into battery and shelled the Confederates.

Shortly thereafter, Reynolds received reports that the Confederates were on the move. They were "passing troops to our right; that is they are massing, and then moving troops up the valley beyond on the shortest line to Fredericksburg and above. . . . [Taft's battery] shelled them out of one

---

26 Lewis Luckenbill, Diary, April 29, 1863, in the Fredericksburg and Spotsylvania National Military Park bound manuscript collection, vol. 399.

27 Styple, *Writing & Fighting the Civil War*, 188.

28 *OR* 25, pt. 2, 311.

part of the railroad, and they had to take a longer road to Fredericksburg."[29] No one could quite make out what the Confederates were up to, though, and the two Federal corps commanders disagreed on their enemy's intent. Whereas Reynolds saw the Confederates shifting to the right, Sedgwick thought they were "forming for an attack."[30] Later, Reynolds changed his mind and agreed with Sedgwick that the Southerners were massing for an offensive.

By now it was 2:30 p.m. Costly in lives or not, the Federals desperately needed a reconnaissance. Their left wing was sinking into confusion, Reynolds nearly going so far as to say he did not know what he was witnessing from the enemy. He and Sedgwick, far from being on the same page, sent conflicting messages to army headquarters, where Hooker seemed content to manage the situation passively. Instead of giving the final order for Sedgwick's men to move forward for reconnaissance, Hooker took his leave and headed west to join the rest of the army at Chancellorsville.

*   *   *

Had Hooker forced Sedgwick to make even a small reconnaissance, it could have pinned Lee in place and prevented the Confederate commander from sending reinforcements west to Zoan Church. As it was,

Artist Alfred Waud's sketch of the Federal
Bridgehead at Franklin's Crossing.

Library of Congress

29 Ibid., 313.

30 Ibid., 313-314.

Lee had a free hand to move—and the intelligence coming to him all day had finally given him an idea of Hooker's intentions.[31]

First came the report that Anderson's men had engaged the lead elements of Meade's corps. "I hope you have been able to select a good line and can fortify it strongly," Lee responded. "Set all your spades to work as vigorously as possible."[32] Next came word from cavalry commander Jeb Stuart, who said he was fighting his way back to the army, slowing the advance of Howard and Slocum as best he could.[33] Facts also began rolling in about the size of the Federal force at Chancellorsville. Coupled with the odd inactivity in front of the lines at Fredericksburg, Lee began to better understand Hooker's intentions. "Object evidently to turn our left," he concluded at the end of a letter written that afternoon to Jefferson Davis. "If had Longstreet's division, would feel safe."[34]

Lee set about mobilizing his army. First, he attached the 3rd Virginia and 2nd North Carolina cavalry regiments to Anderson. The troopers were to picket the roads leading to Anderson's position.[35] Next, Lee dispatched the division of Maj. Gen. Lafayette McLaws west to reinforce Anderson, less one brigade left to the rear of the city of Fredericksburg.[36] The two divisions—representing the only men from Longstreet's corps

31 Lee kept a close watch on Sedgwick's wing of the Union Army from Prospect Hill throughout April 30. Lee, Jackson, A. P. Hill and a variety of lower-ranking generals and officers came and went from the hill. The actions were closely monitored by their own men, who documented the comings and goings of their general officers as they tried to glean any information of what might happen next. Jones, *The Civil War Memoirs of Captain William J. Seymour*, 46-48.

32 Robert E. Lee to Richard H. Anderson, April 30, 1863, in the Fredericksburg and Spotsylvania National Military Park bound manuscript collection, vol. 19.

33 Gary W. Gallagher, ed., *Fighting for the Confederacy: The Personal Recollections of General Edward Porter Alexander* (Chapel Hill, NC, 1989), 195.

34 Robert E. Lee to Jefferson Davis, April 30, 1863, in the Fredericksburg and Spotsylvania National Military Park bound manuscript collection, vol. 19.

35 Bigelow, *The Campaign of Chancellorsville*, 232-233.

36 *OR* 25, pt. 1, 762.

available to Lee—could field roughly 14,000 men.[37] That would be enough to slow, but not stop, any advance Hooker might make from the west.

Lee's orders went on to direct the bulk of Jackson's Second Corps—nearly 29,000 more men—to Zoan Church on the morning of May 1. Jackson was to leave behind one division to hold the line at Fredericksburg.[38] That division would have the support of the brigade left behind by McLaws, plus support from the 56 guns of the Confederate artillery reserve.[39]

When Reynolds reported movement along the Confederate line, he was witnessing Confederate ambulances, supply wagons, ammunition wagons, and artillery shifting out of the way so Jackson's men would have a clear line of march. He was witnessing the withdrawal of McLaws' division and the preparations Jackson's men were making for the next day's march.

A Federal reconnaissance would have put a halt to all of it. Instead, Federal inaction allowed Lee to mobilize his countermeasures freely and prepare an unexpected greeting for "Mr. F. J." Hooker.

"The rebel army is now the legitimate property of the Army of the Potomac," Hooker had boasted earlier that day.[40] Lee was about to contest ownership.

---

37 Although recalled from Suffolk, Longstreet's remaining two divisions—Hood's and Pickett's—as well as Longstreet himself, would not reach the front in time to take part in the battle.

38 *OR* 25, pt. 1, 762.

39 Jennings Cropper Wise, *The Long Arm of Lee*, 2 vols. (Lincoln, NE, 1991), vol. 2, 452-454.

40 Edward G. Longacre, *The Commanders of Chancellorsville: The Gentleman and the Rogue* (Nashville, TN, 2005), 155.

Chapter Seven

Lee's "Bad Old Man"

As Jackson's senior division commander, Maj. Gen. A. P. Hill would have been the logical choice to hold the line in Fredericksburg as the rest of the Confederate Second Corps prepared to move west to counter the Federal advance. He was the most seasoned of Jackson's four subordinates: two of them, Colston and Rodes, were new to division command, and the third, Early, had seen action as a division commander only once before, at the first battle of Fredericksburg. Hill, by contrast, had ably served at the head of the so-called Light Division since May of 1862, and had racked up an impressive record of service, highlighted by his end-of-the-day appearance on the field at Antietam the previous September, appearing at just the right time and place to stem a Federal advance and prevent a Confederate collapse.

Although Jackson and Hill had a strained relationship, Jackson nonetheless recognized Hill's qualities as a fighter and his fitness for independent command. It had been left to Hill, for instance, to oversee the final surrender of the Federal garrison at Harper's Ferry on September 16, 1862, while Jackson moved the rest of the Second Corps to Antietam.[1]

---

1 One might be tempted to interpret this as evidence that Jackson did not want Hill with him in a fight. However, following the battle of Second Manassas, Jackson and Hill squabbled so badly over marching orders that Jackson placed Hill under arrest for insubordination. If Jackson truly did not want Hill with him during the fight at

Only after tying things up there was Hill able to march north—just in the nick of time, as it turned out.

Yet when it came time to execute Lee's orders, Jackson assigned not Hill but Early to hold the Fredericksburg fortifications. The decision probably had more to do with the relative positions of the generals' divisions: Early's was at the far end of the line and so would not require as much maneuvering to get into place; likewise, Hill's could get on the road west more quickly. "[L]ate on the afternoon of the 30th I was instructed by General Jackson to retain my position on the line," Early later recalled, "and, with my division and some other troops to be placed at my disposal, to watch the enemy confronting me while the remainder of the army was absent."[2]

Early's troops had been the first to engage Sedgwick's crossing force; now they would be Lee's last line of defense should Hooker's left wing fall upon the Southern forces.

The command "Old Jube" had at his disposal was eclectic, to say the least. Along with his four brigades of infantry, consisting of 8,596 men, he also had the brigade of Brig. Gen. William Barksdale, of Lafayette McLaws' division. And he had 56 guns from the First and Second corps and from the Confederate artillery reserve, all under the command of Brig. Gen. William N. Pendleton. In total, the hodgepodge rear guard mustered in at just over 10,000 men. With the exception of Pendleton, Early was the only West Point graduate among the ragtag command staff.

Fortunately for Early, his division was well rested from the winter, and three of his four brigade commanders were cut from fighting cloth.

Early's largest brigade consisted of the six Georgia regiments under the command of Brig. Gen. John Brown Gordon. Gordon was a

---

Antietam, Jackson could have simply left Hill under arrest. Instead, Jackson released him so the division commander could take part in operations. Leaving Hill to mop up at Harper's Ferry after the surrender might also be interpreted as evidence that Jackson did not want Hill with him in a fight, but Jackson readily understood that Hill's "Light Division," the most mobile of his divisions, would be best able to make the distance to Antietam quickly should it need to—which, as it turned out, it did.

2   Jubal Anderson Early, *Jubal Early's Memoirs: Autobiographical Sketch and Narrative of the War Between the States* (Baltimore, MD, 1989), 196.

31-year-old lawyer and coal mine developer from Georgia.[3] Well educated and well liked, Gordon was elected captain of a company dubbed the "Raccoon Roughs" at the outbreak of hostilities. Apparently the "Roughs" were too rough for Georgia, because when they offered their services to their home state, Georgia turned them down.[4] Undaunted, Gordon petitioned other Confederate states; eventually Alabama accepted him and his men into service.

Assigned to the 6th Alabama, the "Roughs" and their young leader performed admirably. Gordon was soon promoted to colonel and his regiment was attached to Brig. Gen. Robert Rodes' brigade of Maj. Gen. Daniel Harvey Hill's division.

Gordon performed well at the head of the 6th. During the Peninsula campaign, he saw vicious fighting, particularly at Seven Pines, where his regiment sustained 59 percent casualties and lost all but one field officer—Gordon.[5] By the end of the Seven Days' battles, when fatigue was wearing on both armies, Gordon took temporary command of Rodes' brigade at Malvern Hill.[6]

In August 1862, the brigade missed out on the move north toward Second Manassas but by September was back with the army in time for the battle of Antietam. There, Rodes' brigade was tasked with holding Lee's center at the Bloody Lane. Over the course of the day's fight Gordon was wounded five times, and by day's end lay unconscious, face-down in a hat that was filling with his blood. Supposedly, a fortuitous bullet hit the hat and produced a hole, allowing the blood to drain, preventing Gordon from drowning. Surviving his wounds, he was made a brigadier general in April and given command of the six Georgia regiments in Early's division. "Col. Jn. B. Gordon most richly deserved promotion for his brilliant service in D. H. Hill's desperate fighting at Seven Pines, Malvern, &

---

3   Ezra J. Warner, *Generals in Gray: Lives of the Confederate Generals* (Baton Rogue, LA, 2006), 111.

4   Larry Tagg, *The Generals of Gettysburg: The Leaders of America's Greatest Battle* (Cambridge, MA, 2003), 262.

5   Stephen W. Sears, *To the Gates of Richmond: The Peninsula Campaign* (New York, NY, 1992), 127-128. A field officer is one of the ranking officers within a regiment, i.e., with the rank of colonel, lieutenant colonel, or major.

6   Douglas Southall Freeman, *Lee's Lieutenants: A Study In Command*— In One Volume, ed. Stephen W. Sears (Old Saybrook, CT, 1998), 136-139.

Brigadier General John B. Gordon.

Battles and Leaders

Sharpsburg [Antietam]," wrote Confederate artillerist E. Porter Alexander. "At Sharpsburg he had received 5 wounds & not to promote him would have been a *scandal*."[7]

Early's second brigade consisted of five Louisiana regiments under Brig. Gen. Harry T. Hays. The Tennessee native was 43 years old at the time of the battle. Educated at St. Mary's College in Baltimore, the young man soon thereafter relocated to New Orleans to practice law. During the Mexican War, Hays served as a lieutenant in the 5th Louisiana.[8] After the war, Hays returned to his New Orleans law practice and was active in the Whig political party.[9]

When the Civil War broke out, Hays was appointed colonel of the 7th Louisiana. The unit was assigned to the eastern theater of the war and saw extensive service in Stonewall Jackson's 1862 Valley campaign. At Port Republic, Hays sustained a wound that kept him out of action until just prior to the Antietam campaign. Upon his return to the army, he was promoted to brigadier general and assumed command of the five Louisiana regiments.

Hays' new command was a rough-and-tumble one. Many of the men were wharf rats from the docks of New Orleans; others were British and Irish seamen stranded in Creole country by the Union blockade.[10] The unit's uniforms were as diverse as the men in its ranks. Men of the 6th Louisiana wore Sicilian caps, the 8th Louisiana wore brown jackets and trousers, and others wore brownish-gray wool-and-cotton twill cloth with green piping.[11] During the winter of 1862-3, Hays' men took to stealing anything that was not bolted down, which did not sit well with Jackson or the testy Early.[12] What Hays' men lacked in manners, though, they more than made up for in fighting prowess.

---

7   Gallagher, *Fighting for the Confederacy*, 193.

8   Tagg, *The Generals of Gettysburg*, 259.

9   Warner, *Generals in Gray*, 130.

10 Joseph H. Crute, Jr., *Lee's Intrepid Army: A Guide to the Units of the Army of Northern Virginia* (Madison, GA, 2005), 58-62.

11 Ibid., 59-61.

12 Bradley M. Gottfried, *Brigades of Gettysburg: The Union and Confederate Brigades at the Battle of Gettysburg* (Cambridge, MA, 2002), 502.

Brigadier General Harry T. Hays.

Fredericksburg and Spotsylvania National Military Park

Brigadier General Robert F. Hoke headed Early's third brigade, which consisted of four North Carolina regiments and a battalion of North Carolina sharpshooters. At 25, Hoke was Early's youngest brigade commander and, unlike the others, had actual military training.[13] The North Carolina native had attended the Kentucky Military Institute, and prior to the war had managed his family's iron and cotton mills. When hostilities erupted, he was appointed second lieutenant in the 1st North Carolina, then took part in the action at Big Bethel in June 1861. Later, Hoke accepted the lieutenant colonelcy of the 33rd North Carolina and then the colonelcy of the hard-fighting 21st North Carolina.[14] After Fredericksburg, Hoke received his brigadier general's commission. His service with many units at various command levels meant the young Hoke had seen combat in every one of the army's battles since the Seven Days', battles making him a tried and tested leader.

The final brigade in Early's division was led by Brig. Gen. William Smith. Smith had been born in the eighteenth century, in 1797, less than 30 miles from the army's current position near Fredericksburg, on the Northern Neck of Virginia. This made him, at 65, the oldest general in Lee's army. Like Early, Hays, and Gordon, Smith had served as a lawyer prior to the war, with offices in Fredericksburg and nearby Culpeper. Elected to the state senate, he served there for six years, then as Virginia's governor during the Mexican War.[15] Smith also served five terms in the U.S. Congress. During his time in Washington, he earned the infamous nickname "Extra Billy" for the kickbacks he received from a postal route he oversaw between Washington and Milledgeville, Georgia.

Kickbacks or not, Smith's popularity in Virginia and his political connections brought him command of the 49th Virginia. As one of the political generals who plagued both armies, Smith had no respect for West Point or its graduates. He referred to West Pointers as "those West P'int

---

13 Warner, *Generals in Gray*, 140.

14 Ibid.

15 Smith would start a second term as governor on January 1, 1864. He would serve until May of 1865, when he was removed from office and arrested, although he would be paroled less than a month later. In the late 1870s, he served a single term in the Virginia House of Delegates. A statue of Smith stands on the grounds of Virginia's capitol building.

Brigadier General William "Extra Billy" Smith.

Library of Congress

fellows."[16] Despite Smith's lack of military experience, his regiment fought well at First Manassas, and Smith himself showed bravery in the face of the enemy. "It is said that he used to drill his regiment at Manassas," said Maj. Robert Stiles, "sitting cross-legged on the top of an old Virginia snake fence, with a blue cotton umbrella over his head and reading the orders from a book. On one occasion he was roused by the laughing outcry, 'Colonel, you've run us bang up against the fence!' 'Well then boys,' said the old Governor, looking up and nothing daunted; 'Well, then, of course you'll have to turn around or climb the fence."[17]

At Chantilly in September 1862, Smith went into battle with his umbrella. During the battle, a heavy thunderstorm broke out. As the rain poured down and the fighting swirled around him, Smith walked the line with his umbrella above him and a beaver-skin hat atop his head, for Smith also hated military uniforms.[18] As another of his affectations, he typically rode in a carriage instead of on a horse.

Later that month at Antietam, Smith assumed brigade command and was wounded three times. After leaving the army to recuperate, he was promoted to brigadier general—more for his political prowess than his battlefield acumen. The promotion put him in charge of Early's old

16 Stiles, *Four Years Under Marse Robert*, 111.

17 Ibid.

18 Tagg, *The Generals of Gettysburg*, 265.

brigade, although two of the brigade's six regiments were on detached duty in northwestern Virginia.[19] Smith tried to balance his duties as brigade commander with another run at the Virginia governorship, which irked Early, who was already hostile toward Smith. Early would do his best to keep Smith away from major combat in this and future campaigns.

Early's 56 guns were under the command of the 53-year-old Pendleton, father of Jackson's adjutant Sandie Pendleton. The elder Pendleton was a West Point graduate, class of 1830, who then served in the army for three years before ill health forced him to resign his commission. Pendleton took to the cloth and was an ordained Episcopal minister, serving as rector of the Grace Church in Lexington, Virginia. There he met many up-and-coming officers at the Virginia Military Institute, including Maj. Thomas Jackson.[20]

When war came, Pendleton was quickly elected to command the Rockbridge Artillery. He dubbed his four guns Matthew, Mark, Luke, and John. He and his men performed with distinction at First Manassas, drawing the praise of both Jackson and then-Brig. Gen. Joseph E. Johnston. This was arguably Pendleton's finest battle of the war. By late March 1862, Pendleton had been promoted to brigadier general.

During the Seven Days' battles, a different Pendleton showed up—one who would be, it turned out, the "real" Pendleton. In command of the reserve artillery of Lee's new army, Pendleton failed to bring his guns onto the field at Malvern Hill, costing Lee's men greatly. E. Porter Alexander did not look kindly on Pendleton's failure. "His report will convict him of having practically hidden himself out all day where nobody saw him, & no orders could find him," Alexander wrote.[21] Alexander was not alone in his assessment; the minister's continued weak performance earned him the nickname "Granny Pendleton." "He was too old, & had been too long out of army life to be thoroughly up to all the opportunities of his position," Alexander later pronounced.[22]

19 Early, *Jubal Early's Memoirs*, 191.

20 Warner, *Generals in Gray*, 234-235.

21 Gallagher, *Fighting for the Confederacy*, 112.

22 Ibid., 336.

Brigadier General William "Granny" Pendleton.

Library of Congress

Most of the men under Early's command were familiar with the ground they had to defend. Early's division had fought at the December 1862 battle of Fredericksburg, where, through quick action, they had helped save Jackson's faltering line. Confederate occupation of the area since then had allowed them to fortify the position, which stretched for nearly seven miles. The left of the line was anchored on a bend in the Rappahannock River near Beck's Island. From there the line ran south, terminating at the Confederate railhead at Hamilton's Crossing.

"The world has never seen such a fortified position," wrote the younger Pendleton in a letter that spring:

As I go to [Moss Neck, Jackson's headquarters] I follow the lines, and have to ride the trenches. These are five feet wide and two and a half feet deep, having the earth thrown towards the enemy, making a bank still higher. They follow the contour of the ground and hug the bases of the hills as they wind to and from the river, thus giving natural flanking arrangements; and from the tops of the hills frown the redoubts for the sunken batteries and barbette batteries ad libitum, far exceeding the number of guns; while occasionally, where the trenches take straight across the flats, a redoubt stands out defiantly in the open plain to receive our howitzers, and deal destruction to the Yankees, should their curiosity tempt them to an investigation.[23]

From December 1862 through March 1863, Confederates had cut roads through the surrounding woods to link different parts of their lines, and a few existing pre-Revolutionary War roads were improved.[24] The better road network allowed reinforcements to move from one place to another with ease along the interior lines the long defensive position allowed for. Artillery, too, could shift quickly into new positions, and what few supplies the Confederates had could be readily moved to or removed from the front.

By far the strongest part of the line was the four-mile stretch immediately south of the river, a series of five hills on the western edge of the city of Fredericksburg collectively known as Marye's Heights. The first of the ridges, Taylor's Hill, began at the river and extended south to Stansbury Hill, named after John Stansbury, whose hilltop home, Snowden, overlooked the 521 acres of land he controlled.[25]

Next in line was Cemetery Hill, also known as Willis Hill. Atop Willis Hill sat Brompton, the home constructed in 1824 by John Marye.[26] Marye's 780 acres ran both south and westward from the Telegraph Road

23 Alexander S. Pendleton to unknown correspondent, April 26, 1863, *Papers of the Military Historical Society of Massachusetts*, vol. 3, 244.

24 Ibid., 82-83.

25 Noel G. Harrison, *Fredericksburg Civil War Sites*, Volume Two: December 1862–April 1865 (Lynchburg, VA, 1995), 220.

26 Ibid., 141. Today Brompton is owned by the Commonwealth of Virginia and is the residence of the president of the University of Mary Washington. The home and grounds are not open to the public.

at the base of the hill, known today as the Sunken Road. The heights and road together made for a formidable position. To aid in bringing reinforcements over and around Willis Hill, the Confederates had cut a road up and around it.[27]

Less than a half mile to the south of Willis Hill sat Telegraph Hill. In the December 1862 battle, Lee used the formidable position as his headquarters. At 243 feet above sea level, Telegraph Hill was the highest point along Marye's Heights, which provided an excellent field of vision

Postwar view of Marye's Heights. Notice how the hill was terraced after the war. This was done to create the Fredericksburg National Cemetery.

Fredericksburg and Spotsylvania National Military Park

27 Ibid., 158.

to the southern commander. (Willis Hill, by comparison, was about 140 feet above sea level.)[28]

Connected by a small swale was the last hill in line, Howison's Hill, part of the 600 acres owned by John Howison. The Howison home, Braehead, built in 1859, sits on the eastern face of the hill. While the heights curve away westward, Howison Hill slopes southward toward the low ground of Deep Run and the relatively flat Landsdowne Valley.

Criss-crossed by the small tributaries of Deep Run and spotted with swampy lowlands and wooded thickets, the Landsdowne Valley stretches southward for three miles before gently rising to another piece of high ground, Prospect Hill. Although not a dominating hill compared to the heights at the northern end of the line, the small rise made for an excellent artillery position because it overlooked nearly a mile of open fields leading down to the Union position along the river.

Prospect Hill did have inherent weaknesses. To the northeast of the rise lay a swamp, where Union forces had punched through the previous December and flanked the Confederate forces on the hill. To the south was Hamilton's Crossing, a natural target for Union infantry and artillery because it served as the terminus of the Richmond, Fredericksburg & Potomac Railroad and the end of the Confederate defensive line.

The Confederates had done what they could to cover up the weaknesses of the position. They scratched infantry earthworks into the military crest of the rolling hill, and commanders positioned themselves in command bunkers dug within yards of the front lines.[29] Fourteen pieces of artillery, protected by lunettes, had been placed in support atop the hill; the guns easily covered the forward approaches, and a handful of them could be turned obliquely to the left and fired toward the front of the swamp.[30] South of Hamilton's Crossing more Confederate guns faced

---

28 Ibid., 152.

29 To properly lay out a line of earthen fortifications on a hillside, one should set the main line of works in front of and below the actual crest of a hill. This prevents the defenders from being silhouetted atop the crest of the hill. It also allows the defenders to have a fallback position; if pushed from the military crest, they have a rallying position atop the hill.

30 French for "little moon," a lunette was a crescent-shaped earthen fortification surrounding three sides of an artillery piece. The gun and gunners were protected while

north and northeast to cover the fields in front of Prospect Hill and the swamp, enfilading any attacking force moving across their front.[31]

A little over a mile to the north of Prospect Hill sat Bernard's Cabin, a slightly misnamed collection of slave quarters that sat atop a small knoll. The knoll, which sat about a quarter mile in front of the Confederate main battle line, gave Confederate gunners yet another artillery platform from which to fire. The guns there could be positioned to face east and southeast, covering the approaches to the swamp and Prospect Hill and, like their counterparts two miles to the south, enfilading any attack column. However, the guns at Bernard's Cabin were dangerously exposed to Federal fire from across the river, diminishing their effectiveness.

Still, the winter had afforded Southern forces the opportunity to fortify the artillery and infantry line along the hill, and Early did what he could to bolster the lines even further. He massed most of his division at Prospect Hill and Hamilton's Crossing, ordering his men to pull up railroad ties and use them in their fortifications. He spread Hays' brigade in a thin line from Deep Run to the north side of Howison Hill. "On going into the trenches we found we had so large a space to cover that we were placed in one rank, with an interval of about a pace between the men," said one of Hays' men.[32]

North beyond Hays' brigade, Barksdale's brigade filled the Confederate line past Telegraph Hill—where Barksdale was now making his headquarters—and on toward the Sunken Road and beyond, nearly all the way to Stansbury Hill where it reconnected with another portion of

---

the rear of the fortification was open so that the gun could be withdrawn quickly if overrun.

31 Enfilading fire occurs when an attacker gains access to the flank, or end, of an enemy line, enabling the attacker to fire perpendicular down the axis of the line. This maneuver was made famous in the December battle by the young horse artillerist Maj. John Pelham. With one Napoleon strategically placed near an intersection in a hedgerow, he was able to stall the Left Grand Division's assault on Prospect Hill for nearly two hours. Pelham also received assistance from a Blakely gun. Since the Blakely was not concealed like the Napoleon, it was quickly sighted in by Union artillery on Stafford Heights and disabled. Only a lack of ammunition and the dissipation of the morning fog stopped the heroic stand of the "Gallant Pelham."

32 Chester, "Letter from the Sixth Louisiana."

Hays' Brigade.[33] Barksdale also had men in the city picketing the waterfront.

Barksdale, 41, was a Tennessee native educated at the University of Nashville. Like so many others in Early's command, he had practiced law before the war, making his home and practice in Columbus, Mississippi. In 1852, he was elected to Congress from Mississippi and built a reputation as a firebrand, favoring states' rights and secession.[34] At the outbreak of hostilities, Barksdale went to war at the head of the 13th Mississippi. He and his men fought at First Manassas and Savage's Station; at the latter Barksdale assumed brigade command. From there he fought at Malvern Hill, Antietam, and Fredericksburg, where his brigade held the city against artillery and infantry assaults on December 11. Now Barksdale was again in a strong position, with a fight on the horizon.[35]

By 10:00 p.m., with Early doing everything he could to prepare his men, Jackson and the rest of the Second Corps were readying themselves to head west. They moved at night to avoid the aeronautic eyes of Lowe's balloonists. "By the light of a brilliant moon, at midnight, that passed into early dawn of dense mist, the troops were moved, by the Old Mine Road, out of sight of the enemy," wrote James Power Smith, "and about 11 A.M. of Friday, May 1st, they reached Anderson's position, confronting Hooker's advance from Chancellorsville. . . . "[36]

Back in Fredericksburg, Jubal Early watched and waited to see what his old West Point classmate, John Sedgwick, would do next.

33 Gary W. Gallagher, "East of Chancellorsville: Jubal A. Early at Second Fredericksburg and Salem Church," in Gary W. Gallagher, ed., *Chancellorsville: The Battle and Its Aftermath* (Chapel Hill, NC, 1996), 40-45.

34 Warner, *Generals in Gray*, 16-17.

35 Stackpole, *The Fredericksburg Campaign*, 133-135.

36 James Power Smith, "Stonewall Jackson's Last Battle," in *Battle and Leaders of the Civil War*, 4 vols. (New York, NY, 1956), vol. 3, 203.

Chapter Eight

The Errant Order

Perhaps the fog was to blame; perhaps it was wishful thinking. Whatever the reason, things appeared calm along the banks of the Rappahannock River on the morning of May 1. "The enemy appear to remain in their position and as far as we can learn, have not changed," John Reynolds reported. "The fog is so thick we can do little but be ready to meet an attack. . . . "[1]

That was just the news Joe Hooker wanted to hear from the left wing of his army. The Confederates, it seemed, had not moved from their fortifications outside Fredericksburg, still distracted by the Union I and VI corps hunkered down along the west bank of the river. He had the Rebels right where he wanted them.

Except, of course, he didn't. The Confederates had been mobilizing since the previous evening. "Our whole corps was moved from in front of the enemy with bands playing and colors flying," wrote a surgeon with the 3rd North Carolina, "and we were marching at a brisk pace in the direction of Chancellorsville."[2] The movement was, he admitted, shrouded in secrecy—secrecy imposed on Southerners by Stonewall Jackson's "strictest orders" and on Northerners by the morning fog.

---

1   Bigelow, *The Campaign of Chancellorsville*, 238.

2   Thomas F. Wood, Memoir, in the Fredericksburg and Spotsylvania National Military Park bound manuscript collection, 65-66.

Jackson's men had struck west under the cover of darkness, following
Mine Road until, near Tabernacle Church, those at the head of the column
turned west onto the Orange Plank Road, where they soon met up with
Anderson's and McLaws' divisions already entrenched in hastily dug
fortifications along the ridge near Zoan Church. Jackson, riding ahead of
his column, arrived on the scene by 8:30 a.m. The Second Corps started
filing in behind him shortly after 10:00 a.m., by which time Jackson had
conceived a scheme for taking the offensive.

By then, the morning sun had burned off the fog, allowing Thaddeus
Lowe, in his observation balloon high above the Federal army's former
headquarters in Falmouth, to watch the Confederate panorama unfold.
According to the aeronaut,

> heavy columns of the enemy's infantry and artillery . . . now moving up
> the river, accompanied by many army wagons. . . . " Later, he reported
> that "the guns had been taken from the earthworks to the right of
> Fredericksburg. Another train; wagons moving to right. . . . Enemy's
> barracks opposite Banks' Ford are deserted. Largest column of enemy is
> moving on road toward Chancellorsville. The enemy on opposite
> heights, I judge, considerably diminished. Can see no change under the
> heights and rifle-pits. No diminution in the enemy's tents.[3]

Lowe tried as early as 9:30 a.m. to get word to Hooker about the
Confederate movement, but problems with the telegraph line, which
would cause significant problems for the army over the next few days,
prevented Lowe's messages from ever getting through.

Hooker, ignorant of the shifting military situation to his east, ordered
his men forward at 10:00 a.m. Spirits were high, and the men were ready.
"I never saw my troops in better condition, never more anxious to meet
the enemy," wrote Brig. Gen. Alpheus S. Williams of the XII Corps. "The
poor fellows, marching on an average of fifteen miles a day over hard,
muddy roads and carrying sixty pounds on their backs for four days, were
not only not weary or disheartened, but they seemed panting to meet the
Rebels. . . . Surely we had promise of success."[4]

---

3   *OR* 25, pt. 2, 324.

4   Williams, *From the Cannon's Mouth*, 186.

Hooker planned a three-pronged attack: two divisions of the V Corps were to take the River Road skirting the Rappahannock; a third division of the V Corps was to take the Orange Turnpike due east toward Fredericksburg; the XII Corps was to take the meandering Orange Plank Road, which curved south a little before swinging east. He expected the two-corps front to sweep away the few Confederates who had plunked down to his east near the Zoan Church; that would allow him an easy advance toward the rear of the Army of Northern Virginia. Hooker expected "the heights of Fredericksburg to be carried at 2 p.m."[5]

He was not, of course, expecting to run smack into stout Confederate resistance. Shortly after striking out on the turnpike, though, the lead elements of Sykes' V Corps division stumbled into the division of Lafayette McLaws. "& here the hot work began," later wrote a private in the 11th U.S. Regulars.[6] First contact came just a few minutes past 11:00 a.m. The battle of Chancellorsville was underway.

Sykes' division held its own at first, but soon Confederate numbers began to prevail. Meanwhile, just to the south on the Orange Plank Road, Jackson had ordered Anderson's division to advance, and it ran head-on into Slocum's marching column. Along the turnpike, Sykes finally got help from Hancock's hard-fighting II Corps division, which arrived in time to cover Sykes' withdrawal. Slocum, meanwhile, had to battle it out alone.

To the north, along the River Road, Meade's other two divisions had advanced without a single bit of resistance. In fact, they advanced well beyond McLaws' position, far into the Confederate rear.

"All was going capitally," wrote George Thayer of the 2nd Massachusetts, fighting with the XII Corps along the southern Orange Plank Road.[7]

And then everything shifted.

---

5 *OR* 25, pt. 2, 330-333.

6 Sears, *Chancellorsville*, 205; George Merryweather to Parents, May 9, 1863, in Timothy J. Reece, *Sykes Regular Infantry Division 1861-1864: A History of Regular United States Infantry Operations in the Civil War's Eastern Theater* (Jefferson, NC, 1990), 210-212.

7 George A. Thayer, *History of the Second Massachusetts Regiment of Infantry* (Boston, MA, 1882), 16.

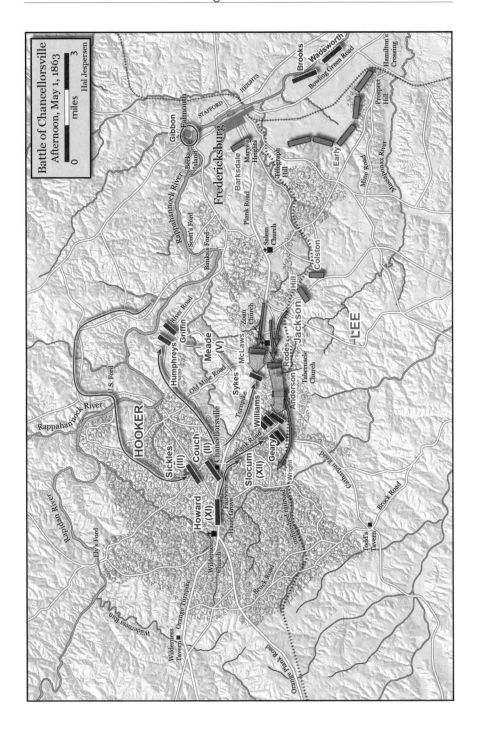

Instead of sending Maj. Gen. William French's II Corps division into the fray, Hooker sent orders to his corps commanders to withdraw from the fight, to pull back into a defensive position around Chancellorsville.

Slocum was "astounded, and declined to take a verbal command for such an ignominious step. . . . "[8] He rode back to headquarters for personal confirmation, believing Hooker had misinterpreted the situation. Other officers bridled as well. Griffin, leading Meade's column on the River Road, had advanced as far as Banks' Ford. He scoffed at the idea of falling back to Chancellorsville. "Call that a position?" he exclaimed bitterly. "Here I can defy any force the enemy can bring against me."[9] Meade was equally astounded. "My God, if we can't hold the top of a hill, we certainly cannot hold the bottom of it!"[10]

"We all received the orders of retreat with astonishment: 'Go back to the old position!'" wrote Howard, whose XI Corps men were already in the rear of the Union army, as far away from the fighting as possible, because of their place in the order of march. "It gave to our whole army the impression of a check, a failure, a defeat."[11]

After the war, Hooker tried to explain away his decision. "The field of operations was in what is called the Wilderness, but of which I had not adequate conception. It was impossible to maneuver, on which I had largely depended on for success," he wrote in 1877.[12] "[W]hile still upon the narrow roads in these interminable forests, where it was impossible to maneuver my forces, [I was] met by Jackson with a full two-thirds of the entire Confederate army," he added. "I had no alternative but to turn back, as I had only a fragment of my command in hand, and take up the position about Chancellorsville. . . . "[13]

---

8 Ibid.

9 Webb, "Meade at Chancellorsville," 229.

10 Walker, *History of the Second Army*, vol. 2, pt. 4, 224.

11 Howard, *Autobiography of Oliver Otis Howard*, vol. 1, 361.

12 Joseph Hooker to Samuel Bates, April 2, 1877, Hooker Papers, in the Fredericksburg and Spotsylvania National Military Park bound manuscript collection, vol. 406.

13 Samuel Bates, "Hooker's Comments on Chancellorsville," in *Battles and Leaders of the Civil War*, 4 vols. (New York, NY, 1956), 218.

His hindsight seems disingenuous. Rather than "only a fragment of my command," Hooker had four corps on hand—the bulk of II Corps and all of V, XI, and XII corps—and the corps commanders of the engaged units—II, V, and XII—had all reported that they occupied good positions. III Corps, meanwhile, had arrived near the Chancellorsville crossroads around 11:00 a.m. Although fatigued from the long, circuitous march, Sickles' more than 18,000 men were ready for action. Furthermore, large portions of the II, V, and XII corps and the entire XI remained unengaged. Only Gibbon's division, elements of the Artillery Reserve, and the I and VI corps, holding down the Fredericksburg front, were not immediately available.

However, the I and VI Corps were, as it turned out, dealing with Confederate surprises of their own.

* * *

"The day is warm and beautiful—a real summer day," wrote artillerist Lt. George Breck. "Fleecy clouds are floating in the air, the birds are caroling their sweetest notes, and as I write, 12 o'clock, everything is very quiet."[14]

"Not a gun was fired in our vicinity," wrote Sewell Gray of the 6th Maine. He called May 1 "A most lovely day. . . . We rested all day and matters remained about as the last day left them."[15] Other Union men echoed Gray's assessment. "To-day we are resting, and the weather is warm and pleasant," wrote Marshall Stull of the 15th New Jersey.[16] His regimental colleague, S. W. Gordon, thought the men were "in fine spirits."[17]

Sedgwick and his men sat in the meager earthworks they had scratched in the earth, waiting for orders. The Union's artillery—Tompkins' VI

14 Lt. George Breck, Reynolds' Battery, *Union & Advertiser* (Rochester, NY), May 6, 1863.

15 Gray, Diary, 44.

16 Marshall B. Stull to the *Sussex (NJ) Register*, May 1, 1863, in the Fredericksburg and Spotsylvania National Military Park bound manuscript collection, vol. 352.

17 S. W. Gordon, Diary, May 1, 1863, in the Fredericksburg and Spotsylvania National Military Park bound manuscript collection, vol. 71.

Corps Artillery and Wainwright's I Corps guns—stood silent.[18] Along the Confederate positions opposite, Pendleton's guns also stood silent, and the Confederates' thinking ran along the same lines. "All is quiet along our portion of the line—both sides busily engaged in strengthening their fortifications and batteries," one of them wrote.[19]

Although Hooker did not envision a role for the left wing in the grand offensive, and he did not want Sedgwick to initiate one of his own, he did want Sedgwick to keep up the pressure on the eastern front. "Direct Major-General Sedgwick to threaten an attack in full force at 1 o'clock," Hooker ordered, "and continue in that attitude until further orders. Let the demonstration be as severe as can be, but not an attack."[20] Hooker's chief of staff, Butterfield, cut the orders at 11:30 a.m.—but they took more than six hours to make the circuitous route from Hooker's headquarters at Chancellorsville, north across the rivers, around through Falmouth, and then south to Sedgwick's position. The problem, again, lay in the telegraph lines. Not only had the lines been strung and restrung over the winter—victims of poor weather and guerilla tampering—but the wires themselves were poorly insulated. Woefully unreliable, the recycled wires repeatedly disrupted Hooker's communications.[21]

Once Hooker's orders finally arrived at the left wing commander's headquarters, Sedgwick ordered the wing to life. John Newton's third division was shifted across the river. So, too, was the Light Division, acting as the fourth division of the corps, which moved from Stafford Heights across the river to the bridgehead on the Confederate shore.[22]

The Light Division was now under the command of the 6th Maine's commanding officer, Col. Hiram Burnham, a pre-war coroner known as "Grizzly" to his friends. Brigadier General Calvin Pratt, the Light Division's commander since its inception, had tendered his resignation on April 25, 1863. Speculation remains over the reason for Pratt's decision.

18 John F. L. Hartwell, Diary, May 1, 1863, in the Fredericksburg and Spotsylvania National Military Park bound manuscript collection, vol. 23.

19 Jones, *The Civil War Memoirs of Captain William J. Seymour*, 50.

20 *OR* 25, pt. 2, 327.

21 Donald E. Markle, ed., *The Telegraph Goes to War: The Personal Diary of David Homer Bates, Lincoln's Telegraph Operator* (Hamilton, NY, 2003), 1-8.

22 *OR* 25, pt. 2, 343.

The most logical is that a facial wound he had sustained on the Peninsula was too much to deal with in the field. There is, though, another theory, less plausible: that he was upset with the plan for crossing the Rappahannock. Because he tendered his resignation three days before the move, the timing makes that motivation unlikely.[23] In any event, Pratt's resignation was accepted on April 27th, and word had reached the front during the campaign that the general could return to New York.

The VI Corps units on the front line did what they could to make themselves look as though they were readying for battle, although their confines made it difficult because there was only so much space to maneuver. It would not take long for the Confederates to realize their enemy was not pushing to attack.

Reynolds, meanwhile, opted not to cross any I Corps troops to the Confederate bank—a wise choice, since the small bridgehead was rapidly filling with troops already. In contrast, by adding the third and fourth divisions to the VI Corps units already across the river, Sedgwick was crossing nearly 10,000 more men, horses, and accompanying accouterments. Now down to just three bridges, and with little reliable information from Hooker's headquarters related to the enemy and their movements near Chancellorsville, a massacre could have taken place had the Confederates attacked. The small size of Early's force made such an attack impracticable, but neither Sedgwick nor Reynolds knew that.

Reynolds instead opted to shift his troops, marching the divisions of Maj. Gen. Abner Doubleday and Brig. Gen. John C. Robinson up and down the River Road to create the impression the Federals were on the move to attack. Wadsworth's division at the front followed suit, adding to the deception.

All the hollow gesturing—the additional river crossing, the change in dispositions, the marches along the River Road—was for naught. In the time it took Hooker's orders to arrive, the tactical situation in front of Sedgwick had changed dramatically. The aeronauts had continued to try—with only limited success—to send word about the Confederate shift west. "There is also a reduction of force in railroad cut and trenches from

23 Obituary of Calvin Pratt in the *New York Times*, August 4, 1898, in Warner, *Generals in Blue*, 385.

Brig. Gen. Hiram Burnham

Colonel Hiram Burnham.

Fredericksburg and Spotsylvania National Military Park

the city to a mile south of it," Lowe reported. "The trench in rear of Howison's is evacuated between that house and Hazel Run."[24]

As if the intelligence Lowe gathered, coupled with the difficulties he had relaying what he had learned, was not confounding enough, Confederate prisoners taken along the Fredericksburg front made it

24 *OR* 25, pt. 2, 323.

worse: they deliberately sowed misinformation. "From deserter, just in," Butterfield wrote to Hooker, "that Jackson's whole corps is opposite Franklin's Crossing."[25] If that was true, with whom was Hooker slugging it out in the Wilderness?

The lack of cavalry units on both wings of the Army of the Potomac was having dire consequences for the current campaign. Sedgwick had only two companies of cavalry attached to his headquarters, Company L of the 1st New Jersey Cavalry and Company H of the 1st Pennsylvania Cavalry. These "squadrons" of troopers were normally used as message-runners for headquarters, as guards for prisoners, and as safety escorts for "Uncle John"; they were not used as intelligence-gathering units. The lack of clear intelligence might have suggested a need to rethink this use of his cavalry, but—as Sedgwick had already demonstrated through his difficulties pulling up the bridges—he was not a man to think "outside the box."

When Hooker had boasted that his movement would force his enemy to "ingloriously fly" or "come out from behind his defenses and give us battle on our own ground," he apparently had not considered a third choice—a square punch in the nose—impelled by Lee's well-known audacity and aggressiveness. Lee was not playing to Hooker's perfect plans after all, and Hooker was not rolling well with the punches.

A well-timed strike by Sedgwick to coincide with Hooker's advance, or even a vigorous demonstration on time as originally planned, would have done much to develop the situation in a way that would have given Hooker much-needed information, and it might have done much, too, to pin the Confederates down. Instead, Hooker allowed the left wing of the army to languish in the backwater of the campaign.

Something else may have been at work in Hooker's mind, as well. In a postwar visit to Fredericksburg and the surrounding battlefields, he remarked to Pennsylvania historian Samuel Bates that "I never think of this ground but with a shudder."[26] He was referring to the December battle in front of Marye's Heights:

---

25 Ibid., 322.

26 Bates, "Hooker's Comments on Chancellorsville," 215.

The whole scene is indelibly fixed in my mind, as it appeared on that fatal day. Here on this ground were ranged the enemy's cannon, and the heights farther to his left were thickly planted with pieces; all the infantry he could use was disposed behind earthworks and stonewalls. How this could have been selected as the point, above all others for attack, and followed up until four whole divisions had been sacrificed, I cannot comprehend.[27]

Still, Sedgwick's overwhelming force, nearly 40,000 men, almost certainly could have crushed Early's 10,000-man force. The United States Military Academy at West Point taught the Corps of Cadets that an assault on an entrenched enemy required that attackers outnumber defenders by at least three to one for any chance of success; by that measure, Sedgwick had the odds in his favor.[28] Whatever Hooker's reason for not ordering such an assault, his decision played into Southern hands. Jubal Early should have considered himself lucky.

But the next day, May 2, nearly cost Jubal Early all his luck.

*   *   *

May 2 dawned "clear and very warm."[29] To the west, Stonewall Jackson had begun a march around the Federal right flank while Robert E. Lee kept Federal attention fixed on him through vigorous demonstrations conducted by the divisions of Anderson and McLaws—the same sorts of demonstrations Hooker had originally envisioned for Sedgwick.

Somewhere among the crossed wires on May 1, Hooker got the impression that Sedgwick had moved his entire force back to the east side of the river. In a return dispatch to Federal headquarters at 11:00 p.m., Sedgwick tried to clarify by outlining the dispositions of the two corps under his command following the demonstration. The dispatch read, "General Reynolds has Wadsworth's division over the river occupying the rifle-pits. General Newton, with Brooks' division, occupies the upper

27 Ibid.

28 James L. Morrison, Jr., *"The Best School": West Point 1833-1866* (Kent, OH, 1998), 87-89, 163-169.

29 Luckenbill, Diary, May 2, 1863.

crossing with Light Brigade, 9,600 men. Inexpedient to cross a larger force. The railroad line has been strengthened by rifle-pits both along and front of it."[30]

Rather than try to push Sedgwick forward against the Confederate line, Hooker sent a telegram at 1:00 a.m. directing Sedgwick to pull up all the pontoons at Franklin's and Reynolds' crossings before daybreak and send Reynolds' I Corps to Chancellorsville. Hooker intended to use Reynolds to secure the army's right flank, plugging the gap between the XI Corps and the Rapidan River. However, the courier carrying the order got lost, so it did not arrive until nearly 5:00 a.m. Butterfield, passing the order on to Reynolds, called the delay "one of the most unfortunate things that has occurred. . . . If you were now with the general, I think there would be no doubt as to the result of the operations of to-day." The delay would have catastrophic consequences. In the meantime, Reynolds complied with the order as best he could. He, however, had to make his move in full view of Confederate spotters; the fog that had hidden Jackson's similar movement the previous day did not rise from the river again to provide Reynolds with like cover.

Sedgwick, meanwhile, felt baffled by Hooker's order; he was concerned that pulling up the bridges would leave his men vulnerable on the west bank of the river. Sedgwick sent a dispatch to the army commander for clarification, explaining that he "dare not take up the upper bridges as it would relieve the enemy at once," giving Confederates

Sketch by artist Alfred Waud depicting the troops of Reynolds' Corps at the bridgehead.

Library of Congress

30 *OR* 25, pt. 2, 343.

more flexibility to maneuver against Brooks' isolated division.[31] Hooker sent no reply.

As the back-and-forth between the wings of the army continued, things otherwise remained generally quiet along the Fredericksburg front. Some Union soldiers fished in the Rappahannock, catching their breakfast.[32] The only excitement had come the night before, when Confederate pickets raised a clamor of "halloaing and shouting," which was soon matched, all along the line, by Sedgwick's and Reynolds' men. "One regiment on the left would commence a kind of half cheer and holloa, and another would take it up, pass it along to the rest, and soon way up to the right, when it would be repeated back in the same manner," wrote a New York lieutenant. "Secesh very shortly subsided, and introduced quite an illumination of camp fires, perhaps to make us believe how strong they were in numbers, and how defiant."[33]

"[T]he boys did not know what to think of the officers when they were told they were on a hollering detail but appeared to be quite fond of it," a Georgia private wrote.[34]

This was all part of Early's ongoing attempt to make the Confederate trenches seem full. For that same reason, the rest of Jackson's corps never struck their tents when they marched off to Chancellorsville, so it would look as if Confederate camps remained populated. Early also sent a pair of Louisianans through the lines to the Union side, posing as deserters, to continue the disinformation campaign. They told tales of Jackson's entire corps still encamped across the way and, even more alarming, of the return of Hood's division from the south.

On the morning of May 2, Early—hoping to feel out the Federals a bit more—got more aggressive in his attempts at bluster, in the form of an artillery barrage.[35] His opponents' response would then dictate his next move: if they did not respond, Early could disengage a portion of his force and march to Lee at Chancellorsville; if they did respond, provoked into

31 Sears, *Chancellorsville*, 229.

32 Ibid.

33 *Union & Advertiser* (Rochester, NY), May 11, 1863.

34 Sears, *Chancellorsville*, 215.

35 *OR* 25, pt. 1, 811.

an attack by the firing, Early would have to fight like hell to hold the line. Either way, Early wanted to get back into the war.

Around 10:00 a.m., Confederate cannon shot began raining down on the Union bridgehead. Pendleton's gunners had the range they needed, and punched holes in a number of the pontoon boats, even sinking one.[36] "[T]errible cannonading to our right," wrote Lewis Luckenbill of the 96th Pennsylvania.[37] Federal artillery soon responded in kind. Blue skirmishers rushed to the front, preparing to receive an enemy attack. However, Early was aggressive, not stupid. He would not risk his outnumbered infantry out in the open. Instead, he remained content to let the long arm of his forces address the Federals.

As the artillery dueled, two opposing bands struck up a duel of their own. "The sky was clear, the air soft and still, when . . . from the rebel lines came the clear notes of a band playing the air of 'Dixie,' a favorite tune with the Confederates," a member of the 5th Maine recalled. "Three or four times they played it through, and then stopped. In a moment, a band in our own army commenced the 'Star Spangled Banner.'"[38]

Like his Confederate counterpart on the heights beyond Fredericksburg, Sedgwick, too, was looking for a way to gauge the situation along the line and possibly shake things up. He bolstered the bridgehead by committing his final division, under Albion Howe, to march to the far shore. Following Howe's division was the remainder of the VI Corps' artillery. Now with nearly 23,000 men and 54 cannon on hand, if Sedgwick was forced to pull up his bridges he would have the full weight of the VI Corps on the enemy side of the river.[39]

Hooker had sent him new orders that morning, via Butterfield: "[I]f an opportunity presents itself with reasonable expectations of success . . . attack the enemy in his front. . . . It is impossible for the general [Hooker] to determine here whether it is expedient for him to attack or not. It must

36 Ibid., 259, 172-179, 557-558,

37 Luckenbill, Diary, May 2, 1863.

38 George W. Bicknell, *History of the Fifth Regiment of the Maine Volunteers: Comprising Brief Descriptions of its Marches Engagements, and General Services from the Date of its Muster in, June 24, 1861 to the time of its Muster Out, July 27, 1864* (Portland, ME, 1871), 216.

39 *OR* 25, pt. 1, 563.

be left to his [Sedgwick's] discretion."[40] The orders were vague in regards to what Sedgwick should do if he was successful in his assault, but they at least gave Sedgwick an opportunity to break out from his bridgehead and take an active role in the campaign.

* * *

Even as Early was ramping up the stakes with his artillery barrage, and even as Sedgwick was considering a possible advance, Lee's chief of staff, Col. Robert H. Chilton, appeared on the scene as a wild card.

Chilton was either the unluckiest staff officer of the war on either side, or the worst. On more than one occasion during the Peninsula campaign, he botched orders from Lee; the subsequent confusion blunted Confederate effectiveness. During the Maryland campaign, Chilton lost Special Order 191, which fell into Federal hands, bringing Lee's offensive to a premature close.[41] Now, once more, Chilton was in over his head.

To the west, Jackson had started his flank march. Lee, with just two divisions to hold the Federals' attention, hoped Early might be able to provide a little extra muscle. He invited Early to withdraw all but one brigade from the Fredericksburg front and bring the infantry to his aid at Chancellorsville. Early was also supposed to move his reserve artillery to the rear. Any force left behind at Fredericksburg was to hold out as long as possible, then withdraw to the south toward Spotsylvania Court House, putting themselves into a blocking position to help slow any Federal thrust toward the Confederate capital.[42]

Lee's order was discretionary, however, depending on whether Early felt it would be advantageous to the Confederates and whether Early could execute the movement safely in the face of Sedgwick's forces. Chilton, however, misinterpreted Lee's intentions and, when giving the order to Early, insisted the order was preemptory, not discretionary. "This order

40 *OR* 25, pt. 2, 362.

41 Many blame Maj. Gen. Daniel Harvey Hill for losing Lee's Special Order 191. However, Hill claimed on numerous occasions that he was not the one who lost the order and went so far as to produce his copies of the orders from the campaign. Joseph L. Harsh, *Sounding the Shallows: A Confederate Companion for the Maryland Campaign of 1862* (Kent, OH, 2000), 74-75.

42 Early, *Jubal Early's Memoirs*, 200.

took me very much by surprise," remembered Early.[43] There was, after all, no advantage: the morning's artillery duel showed that Sedgwick was still south of the town in force.

Early pointed out the flaws in the new orders:

> Before leaving, General Lee instructed me to watch the enemy and try to hold him; to conceal the weakness of my force and if compelled to yield before overpowering numbers, to fall back towards Guiney's depot where our supplies were. . . . I was further instructed to join the main body of the army in the event that the enemy disappeared from my front. . . . I remarked to Colonel Chilton that I could not retire my troops without their being seen by the enemy, whose position on Stafford Heights not only overlooked ours, but who had one or two balloons which he was constantly sending up from the heights. . . . [44]

Chilton should have seen the problem immediately, because the situation, as Early described it, was laid out across the landscape in front of him, as obvious as the daylight. But Chilton's aloof response to Early showed the poor grasp he had of his commander's intent. "General Lee understood all this," Chilton replied, "but it was much more important for him (Lee) to have the troops where he was, than at Fredericksburg, and if he defeated the enemy there he could easily retake Fredericksburg. . . . "[45]

Chilton and Early had been 1837 classmates at West Point (along with Sedgwick, Hooker, and Benham). Unlike his peers, however, Chilton had not yet risen to the level of general officer despite the full support of Lee—a telling fact that speaks volumes. However, here he was, debating with Early over confounding orders that Chilton assumed were clear-cut. Thus a heavy burden fell on the shoulders of Jubal Early.

Reluctantly, the division commander ordered all but Hays' Louisiana Brigade, the 21st Mississippi, and the reserve artillery out of the trenches and onto the road. "The orders were given at once and the withdrawal

---

43 Ibid., 200.

44 Ibid., 197.

45 Ibid., 200-201.

commenced, but it had to be made with great caution so as to attract as little attention as possible," Early wrote.[46]

"At 1 o'clock P.M. three brigades of our Division Gordon's, Hoke's & Smith's marched out of the breastwork in the direction of Spotsylvania Court House, leaving Hays' & Barksdale's Brigades to hold the enemy in check," wrote William Seymour. "The design of General Lee evidently was to concentrate his whole army in the vicinity of Chancellorsville, whip Hooker and then turn upon Sedgwick and cut his force to pieces."[47] This of course was not the case. Federal spotters quickly noticed the move, though, and reports began fluttering back and forth between Hooker, Butterfield, and Sedgwick.

With great trepidation, the Rebel column moved from Hamilton's Crossing to the Telegraph Road, across an intersecting back road, and finally to the Orange Plank Road. The movement took much of the afternoon. Hays, meanwhile, did his best to redeploy his men to block any Union advances. He strung his men from the southern base of Howison Hill to the southern extent of Stansbury Hill. He shifted the 6th and 9th Louisiana to the hills directly behind the city. In the direct front of the VI Corps line were Hays' remaining three regiments, the 5th, 7th, and 8th Louisiana, supported by John B. Richardson's battery of the Washington Artillery. In the city was the lone regiment of Barksdale's brigade left behind, the 21st Mississippi, tasked with acting as the forward skirmish line along the Rappahannock. "Watch your flanks, hold the picket line as long as you can, then fall back along the Spottsylvania Court-House Road, and hunt for your brigade," Barksdale had told the 21st's commander, Col. Benjamin Humphreys.[48]

Then, much to Jubal Early's chagrin, word came from a panicked Pendleton that Sedgwick had started to attack.

*   *   *

46 Ibid., 202.

47 Jones, *The Civil War Memoirs of Captain William J. Seymour*, 51.

48 Benjamin Humphreys, Mississippi State War Records, *Recollections of Fredericksburg: From the Morning of 20th April to the 6th of May, 1863.*

An attack by Sedgwick at that moment would have allowed him to easily overtake the Creoles and Mississippians, then strike the rest of Early's division in the rear and in column—exactly the kind of opportunity Sedgwick and Hooker had hoped for. Pendleton's alarm, however, was nothing more than a case of "Chicken Little-ism." Without a direct order pushing him forward, Sedgwick seemed determined to stand fast in McClellan-like fashion.

Pendleton raised his alarm based on reports from Confederates ensconced in the cupola of the Slaughter House—the home owned by Fredericksburg's mayor—and in a stately home south of the city called Ferneyhough. Spotters in both locations watched the final few elements of the VI Corps cross from the east bank of the river and misinterpreted the movement.

Humphreys knew that, if they were attacked in force, there was little his Mississippians would be able to do to resist. His fellow officers thought the same. Before pulling out of Fredericksburg, Humphreys received a letter from one of his peers, the fractious Col. W. D. Holder of the 17th Mississippi: "Tell the Colonel [Humphreys] farewell; the next time I hear from him will be from Johnson's Island [a Federal prisoner of war camp]."

"My nerves were not much strengthened," Humphreys admitted.[49]

The 53-year-old Humphreys was a native of Mississippi who had been dismissed from West Point. He then studied law, worked as a planter, and finally took to politics. In 1861, he became captain, then colonel, of the 21st and commanded the regiment in all its battles leading up to Chancellorsville.

When Humphreys got word of the possible Federal attack, he deployed his men closest to the enemy in the best position he could. "I immediately threw back the right of my picket line, composed of Company E, under Lieut. McNeely of Wilkinson County, and Company G under Lieut. Mills of Leak county, and established it from the gas-house up Hazel Run to the railroad toward Hamilton Station, connecting with Gen. Early's pickets," he reported.[50]

49 Ibid.

50 Ibid.

Colonel Benjamin Humphreys, 21st Mississippi Infantry.

Fredericksburg and Spotsylvania National Military Park

With the additional VI Corps units arriving at the bridgehead, Sedgwick looked to bring more real estate into Federal hands. Around 5:00 p.m., near the Bend, Sedgwick's skirmish line, under Brig. Gen. Joseph Bartlett, tangled with Col. Davidson Penn's 7th Louisiana along the Bowling Green Road, driving the Confederates back to the cover of the railbed of the Richmond, Fredericksburg & Potomac Railroad.

In the vicinity of Mansfield, just south of Franklin's Crossing, the 21st New York deployed in a heavy skirmish line. The New Yorkers pushed to the left of a large ravine on the Bernard property toward the Bowling Green Road, supported by the 6th Maine, 5th Wisconsin, and 61st Pennsylvania.[51] The four units pushed the thinner Confederate skirmish line back across the Bowling Green Road, thus securing the approaches to the bridgehead via the Bowling Green Road from the south.

The Federals looked to expand northward as well, but the two companies of the 21st Mississippi were too well placed for the Federals to dislodge them. "The enemy's pickets . . . advanced and engaged my pickets, but being supported by a line of infantry, failed to drive them from their position," Humphreys said.[52]

*   *   *

With the exception of that sparring along the Bowling Green Road south of the city, the situation remained low-key along the Rappahannock—panicked words from Pendleton notwithstanding.

Still, always itching for a fight, Barksdale turned his brigade back; Gordon did as well. Early then made the decision to turn the whole column back in order to meet the supposed threat. The news of Early's force turning back to man its former battle line brought cheers from the skeleton crew remaining there. "Bully for Barksdale! bully for Hays! bully for the Washington Artillery! bully for old Bob!"[53] Chilton's mix-up could have led to disaster for the Army of Northern Virginia. Instead, Early's luck, bolstered by Pendleton's ineptitude, held long enough for his men—all the wearier for the extra marching—to file back into the positions they had abandoned hours earlier.

None too soon, either: Hooker had cut new orders for the VI Corps. "The major-general commanding directs that General Sedgwick cross the

---

51 *New York Herald*, May 5th, 1863.

52 Humphreys, *Recollections of Fredericksburg.*

53 Ibid.

river as soon as indications will permit; capture Fredericksburg with everything in it, and vigorously pursue the enemy."[54]

Near Chancellorsville, the Federal commander thought he had the Confederates on the run, and it was time for Sedgwick to at last get in on the action. "We know that the enemy is fleeing, trying to save his trains," Hooker's order explained. "Two of Sickles' divisions are among them."[55]

The "fleeing enemy" Hooker was supposedly harrying would turn out to be Jackson's marching column, and the tables at Chancellorsville would quickly turn. Reynolds' I Corps, delayed from leaving the Fredericksburg front, would not be in place to secure the army's right flank when Jackson's "foot cavalry" rolled out of the Wilderness and slammed into Howard's ill-prepared XI Corps. When Hooker sent his orders to Sedgwick, though, Jackson's surprise attack still lay in the future.

From Hooker's current perspective, his perfect plan was working out after all: the enemy was ingloriously flying. And Sedgwick was being called upon to help give chase.

54 *OR* 25, pt. 2, 363.

55 Ibid.

Chapter Nine

Calling on Uncle John

Hooker sent his orders at 4:10 p.m. for Sedgwick to move. Butterfield passed them on to Sedgwick at 5:50 p.m. In that timespan, Jackson launched his surprise flank attack, throwing much of the right wing of the Union army into turmoil. As a result, subsequent communications between Hooker and Butterfield suffered from an almost absurd time delay. Even as the army reeled under the Confederate assault, Butterfield was painting a rosy picture. "Everything working well," he wrote to John Gibbon at 8:25 p.m. "Sickles is in the enemy's trains. Sedgwick is pursuing here. Be ready to spring with your full supplies whenever you receive the order. Expect it at any moment."[1]

Gibbon, a North Carolinian who had stayed loyal to the Union at the outbreak of the war, was a career military man. A member of the West Point class of 1847, he graduated with such men as A. P. Hill and Ambrose Burnside. He served in Mexico and then in the Seminole Wars. Later he taught artillery tactics at West Point, where he literally wrote the book on the subject: the *Artillerist's Manual*, a treatise later used by both North and South.

During the early stages of the war, Gibbon served as Irvin McDowell's chief of artillery, but in May 1862 he was promoted to brigadier general

1 *OR* 25, pt. 2, 368.

and assumed command of the Iron Brigade. The hard discipline of their new commander chafed many of the Midwestern men. Gibbon looked to whip them into soldiers as good as the regulars. He held inspections, ordered drill, and forced the men to wear gaiters—white leggings that were hot, uncomfortable, and, above all, impossible to keep white. One morning, the general emerged from his tent to find his horse wearing gaiters. Yet although the men grumbled about their commander's ways, he transformed them from civilians into tough-as-nails soldiers.

Gibbon's solid service during the war eventually elevated him to command of the I Corps' 2nd Division just prior to the December 1862 battle of Fredericksburg. There, across ground that later became known as the Slaughter Pen Farm, Gibbon assaulted a Confederate position defended by soldiers from his home state, including three of his brothers. Wounded in the wrist by a shell fragment, Gibbon spent a few months recovering, battling a light infection that refused to go away.

He had been back since March and was now on light duty with his new division in the II Corps, a command that had once belonged to John Sedgwick. At Antietam, Sedgwick had led that division into the West Woods, where he had been felled by three wounds that knocked him out of the war for months. The men, meanwhile, went on without him to see hard action at Fredericksburg, where they were called upon to assault the southern shoreline in boats and engage in house-to-house fighting. Two days later, they took part in the assaults against Marye's Heights. The year 1862 had been hard on the division in general, and by May 1863 it was down to 3,300 men, a mere shadow of its former self.

The division had quality units, including the 7th Michigan, 1st Minnesota, and 20th Massachusetts, but they had lacked a quality division commander since the wounding of Sedgwick.[2] In December, they had been "led" into battle by the aloof and inept Oliver Otis Howard. Now, with Gibbon, they had a solid leader capable of making tough decisions on the spot. A soldier in the 19th Maine described him as "a good looking officer, and never appeared nervous or excited."[3]

---

2   The 1st Minnesota was the first unit accepted into Federal service in 1861 and was the only unit from the state of Minnesota to fight at Fredericksburg or Chancellorsville.

3   Tagg, *The Generals of Gettysburg*, 44.

Brigadier General John Gibbon.

Library of Congress

The division's task in the campaign thus far had been to stay in the army's old position in Falmouth and maintain the ruse that the army still occupied its winter camps. The Union right wing had slipped away, gaining the head start Hooker needed, and Gibbon's men had had little to do since.

The information accompanying the new orders from Butterfield made it seem as if everyone was not only on the move but scoring impressive offensive gains. Soon, it would be Gibbon's turn to get in on the action.

* * *

By that point, of course, Sickles was not in the enemy's trains at all, nor had he ever been—he had been harrying Jackson's flanking column, which had since turned on the Federal right flank with disastrous results. On the Fredericksburg front, Sedgwick had yet to pursue anyone anywhere.

It was not necessarily for lack of trying. When Sedgwick got his afternoon orders, he immediately set his massive corps into motion. He had 23,600 men under his command, which meant that even without Reynolds' I Corps he still outnumbered Early by some 17,000 men, including the support of Gibbon's 3,300-man division. But by the time Sedgwick got his corps moving, another confusing order came from Butterfield, timed at 5:15 p.m.: "The major-general commanding directs you to pursue the enemy on the Bowling Green Road."[4] Although Hooker seemed at least to know which side of the river Sedgwick was on, the order was confusing in that the Bowling Green Road ran north-south, whereas the Confederate position lay due west. Sedgwick sent to Butterfield's command post in Falmouth for further clarification, but neither he nor Butterfield had any idea how preoccupied Hooker was at the moment.

In fact, in a dispatch to Sedgwick at 8:00 p.m., Butterfield conveyed the same optimism he had shown in his dispatch to Gibbon. "Your opportunities are grand beyond question," he wrote. "I know you will

---

4 *OR* 25, pt. 2, 363.

Major General Daniel Butterfield,
Hooker's chief of staff.

Library of Congress

improve them."[5] And, he added, there was no news from Hooker. (Little wonder.)

By that point, Sedgwick reported that he had sent Brooks' division forward to clear Bowling Green Road and drive back Confederate pickets, and had sent Newton's division southwestward toward Hamilton's Crossing. Once that was accomplished, he proposed to settle into position for the night. "Can't you take Fredericksburg tonight?" Butterfield asked.[6]

Word finally came from Hooker at 9:00 p.m. It carried a much different tone:

> The major-general directs that General Sedgwick crosses the Rappahannock at Fredericksburg on the receipt of this order, and at once take up his line of march on the Chancellorsville Road until [he] connect with us, and he will attack and destroy any force he may fall in with on the road. He will leave all his trains behind . . . and march to be in our vicinity at daylight. He will probably fall upon the rear of the forces commanded by General Lee, and between us we will use him up. . . . Be sure not to fail. Deliver this by your swiftest messenger.[7]

Hooker now looked toward playing the anvil to Sedgwick's hammer. Despite later critics who suggested that Hooker acted like a whipped man,

5 Ibid., 364.

6 Ibid., 365.

7 Ibid., 365.

his dispatch to Sedgwick suggests that he still saw himself in a position of strength. While Jackson's flank attack had certainly caught him off guard, Hooker recognized that he still outnumbered the precariously divided Confederate army. From the Federal perspective, the Confederates had gambled big and, in doing so, had endangered themselves—and Hooker still had Sedgwick up his sleeve.

Nonetheless, Hooker's expectations for Sedgwick were ludicrous. He expected his VI Corps commander to march the three miles to Fredericksburg, brush past whatever opposition waited there, march twelve more miles, and then strike Lee in the rear at Chancellorsville at dawn. Even under the best conditions, such a sequence of tasks would have been Herculean—but executing a night march, engaging the enemy, and then bringing 23,000 men online to strike a foe of unknown strength and disposition?

After the battle, Sedgwick sought to defend himself from many critics, including Hooker's lackey, Butterfield. "I had been informed repeatedly by Major General Butterfield, Chief of Staff, that the force in front of me was very small," Sedgwick wrote, "and the whole tenor of his many dispatches would have created the impression that the enemy had abandoned my front and retired from the city and its defenses, had there not been more tangible evidence than the dispatches in question that the Chief of Staff was misinformed."[8]

Sedgwick nonetheless determined to try to follow Hooker's directions, which he received at 10:10 p.m. Shortly thereafter, a follow-up arrived that said the orders "must be fully carried out to the very letter. This is vitally important."[9] Sedgwick dispatched orders of his own to his division and brigade commanders.[10] On the front line, the officers whispered to the men so as to awaken them but not the suspicion of the enemy.[11]

With the Bowling Green Road secure, Sedgwick planned to move his column north, deploy flankers and skirmishers, and march into

8   *OR* 25, pt. 1, 558.

9   *OR* 25, pt. 2, 365.

10 *OR* 25, pt. 1, 558.

11 Bicknell, *History of the 5th Regiment of the Maine Volunteers*, 217.

Fredericksburg, where he would unite with Gibbon's division. The VI Corps would then turn west on the Plank Road and head straight toward the rear of Lee's army. Butterfield and Hooker were convinced by now that only three enemy regiments blocked the path westward.[12]

Sedgwick called together his division commanders to discuss the march. "Not long after the order was received," claimed division commander Albion Howe, "General Sedgwick said to Newton, 'Newton, you move on; Howe will follow, and Brooks and I will take a little nap.'"[13]

Newton's 3rd Division, led by Col. Alexander Shaler's 1st Brigade, took point, followed by Burnham's Light Division, which was now attached to the 3rd Division. Howe, then Brooks, followed. "[A]s the long dark columns of troops moved off with the moon light flashing from the bright barrels and bayonettes of the guns it was magnificent," wrote a Massachusetts man.[14]

"The weather was very warm, uncomfortably warm," wrote an officer with the 6th Maine.[15] A private from the 5th Maine saw the evening a little differently. "It was a beautiful night," he wrote, "almost too lovely in which to engage in blood and carnage."[16] The movement toward the city was slow going. "The road was bad for artillery, and our progress was slow," wrote R. F. Halsted of Sedgwick's staff.[17] Foliage on the trees darkened the way.[18]

Delaying the column's advance north were Companies E and G of the 21st Mississippi, while Company F manned the old December defenses on

---

12 Stoeckel, *Correspondence of John Sedgwick Major-General*, vol. 1, 116.

13 Samuel Bates, *The Battle of Chancellorsville* (Meadville, PA, 1882), 185.

14 Charles Brewster to Sister, May 10, 1863, in the Fredericksburg and Spotsylvania National Military Park bound manuscript collection, vol. 70.

15 Chris Mackowski and Kristopher D. White, "From Foxcroft to Fredericksburg: Captain Sewell Gray of the Sixth Maine Infantry," in *Fredericksburg History & Biography* (December 2008), vol. 7, 140.

16 Ibid.

17 Stoeckel, *Correspondence of John Sedgwick Major-General*, vol. 1, 116.

18 Huntington W. Jackson, "Sedgwick at Fredericksburg and Salem Heights," in *Battles and Leaders of the Civil War*, 4 vols. (New York, NY, 1956), 225.

Colonel Alexander Shaler.

Library of Congress

the city's waterfront, facing Gibbon's men.[19] Although the three companies hardly constituted a substantial force, they had knowledge of the terrain. They knew, for instance, what poor condition the road was in and how much the dark forest crowded it in places. They knew they had a good pair of natural defensive barriers they could use: Deep and Hazel runs. In the city, they knew the streets and where they led. They also had fortifications that had been constructed prior to and after the battle of Fredericksburg, and they had buildings they could use as cover.

With Confederates harrying them in the darkness, Shaler's men moved with glacial speed. "It was 'poky' work creeping along in the dark, with a lively spattering of picket firing going on in front," wrote a member of the 122nd New York.[20] The short-tempered Newton looked to rectify the situation. Newton was alongside Shaler's brigade as the herky-jerky, stop-and-go column made its way north. Newton called for one of his aides, Lt. Col. Huntington Jackson, and directed him to "ride ahead and tell Colonel Shaler to brush away the enemy's pickets."[21] Jackson found the road filled with Federal soldiers. Some of the men had spread out blankets and were trying to sleep; others were resting on their arms.[22] He found Shaler with Lt. Col. Joseph Hamblin conversing near Hazel Run. The aide conveyed the order to Shaler, who turned to Hamblin and said, "Colonel Hamblin, you have heard the order from General Newton?"[23] Hamblin, a prewar insurance broker, unleashed his regiment, the 65th New York, known as the "United States Chasseurs," on the Mississippians.[24] Jackson later recalled "the noise of hurrying feet . . . a

19 Ibid.

20 Stuart McDonald to the *Weekly Recorder* (Fayetteville, NY), May 9, 1863, in the Fredericksburg and Spotsylvania National Military Park bound manuscript collection, vol. 358.

21 Jackson, "Sedgwick at Fredericksburg and Salem Heights," 225-227.

22 Ibid., 227.

23 Ibid., 225-227.

24 Edmund J. Raus, Jr., *A Generation on the March: The Union Army at Gettysburg* (Gettysburg, PA, 1996), 69.

shout, a bright, sudden flash, a roll of musketry followed, and the road was open."[25]

Humphreys' men were driven from the banks of Hazel Run and made their way back to the southern end of the city. Eventually the two companies pulled back to the cover of the Richmond, Fredericksburg, & Potomac Railroad embankment.

But even with Humphreys' two companies out of the way, the VI Corps still made slow progress. It was not until just before dawn on May 3 that lead elements of Newton's division entered the foreboding streets of the once-stately city.

* * *

By May of 1863, the city of Fredericksburg had seen two Federal occupations, and was now about to embark on a short-lived third.

Nestled on the banks of the Rappahannock River, the colonial city sat almost exactly halfway between the nation's capital, Washington, D.C., and Virginia's state capital, Richmond. Founded in 1727, the city was named after Frederick, Prince of Wales, the son of King George II. George and Frederick had loathed one another.

The city's streets reflected its rich colonial history and bore the names of the English-German House of Hanover. William Street and Hanover Street ran west from the city toward Marye's Heights. Princess Anne Street, Caroline Street (the city's main street), and others ran parallel to the river. At its widest point, the city was barely seven blocks across.

Prior to the Civil War, Fredericksburg was home to many state and national luminaries. George Washington's family owned and operated a ferry crossing on the Rappahannock at the lower end of the city. George's mother, Mary Washington, spent the last 17 years of her life in the city. His sister, Betty, lived in the impressive mansion Kenmore, just a short walk from their mother's home. President James Monroe practiced law in the city, as did Virginia governor/Confederate general William Smith. Revolutionary War hero John Paul Jones lived in the city, as did fellow revolutionary Hugh Mercer, who ran an apothecary shop on Caroline Street.

25 Jackson, "Sedgwick at Fredericksburg and Salem Heights," 227.

The City of Fredericksburg from Stafford Heights.

Library of Congress

As the last navigable spot in the ascension of the Rappahannock, Fredericksburg boasted a bustling port, established in 1788.[26] Farmers brought goods from Virginia's piedmont to the port, and from Fredericksburg sail ships and steamers made their way downriver to Chesapeake Bay; most of the ships would turn north and head for Fredericksburg's sister city of Baltimore, Maryland.

To enhance river commerce even further, local entrepreneurs installed the Rappahannock Canal on the north end of the city to bypass the rocks of the river's fall line. The idea for a canal—to stretch from northern Fauquier County, Virginia, along the Rappahannock River, to terminate at Fredericksburg—came about in 1816. Construction on the canal did not begin until 1829, though, and took 20 full years to

26 Noel G. Harrison, *Fredericksburg Civil War Sites, Volume One: April 1861–November 1862* (Lynchburg, VA, 1995), 40.

complete.[27] The Rappahannock Canal brought produce, gold, and other wares around to the city docks, where they could be sold at market in Fredericksburg or shipped from the port.[28] However, tolls on the canal were not enough to sustain the upkeep and maintenance on the 50-mile waterway; thus, in 1853, the owners of the canal declared bankruptcy and closed it. However, parts of the canal were still viable by the outbreak of war, including a slack-water pond from the canal, which also provided water to a millrace that powered factories along the city's riverfront.[29]

The city's transportation network also boasted three major roads: the Bowling Green Road, the Telegraph Road, and the Orange Turnpike, which overlapped in places with the Orange Plank Road. The Bowling Green Road led from Fredericksburg 55 miles south to Richmond. The Orange Turnpike led west to Orange Court House and Culpeper. The Telegraph Road was the Interstate 95 of its day, leading from Washington to Richmond. The city also had a rail line, the Richmond, Fredericksburg, & Potomac Railroad.

Prewar downtown Fredericksburg had an impressive courthouse constructed in 1852, a sash and blind factory constructed in 1859, two banks, a market house, and the Masonic Cemetery and Lodge.[30] The city also had three major churches and many smaller ones, thirteen confectioners, two book dealers, and a number of grocers and dry goods dealers.

"The town is one of those rare spots, solely to be found, so far as the North American Continent is concerned, in the Southern states, and chiefly in Virginia, which has hardly had a building added to it for 50 years," wrote the London *Times*. "It has long boasted itself as possessing a refined society; which may be interpreted as a society satisfied with the

27 Robert Hodge, "The Story of the Rappahannock Canal," *The Fredericksburg (VA) Times*, January 1978.

28 Harrison, *Fredericksburg Civil War Sites*, Volume Two, 120.

29 Ibid.

30 Harrison, *Fredericksburg Civil War Sites*, Volume One, 50, 113.

possession of moderate competency, unambitious, devoid of Yankee restlessness and greed."[31]

The edges of the city featured large plantation houses, including Brompton, the Marye family home, located on the heights to the west. To the east was Chatham, the home of J. Horace Lacy. To the south stood Smithfield (today the Fredericksburg Country Club) and, before Confederates accidentally burned it down in April 1863, Mannsfield; their sprawling fields ran contiguously toward Prospect Hill and the Landsdowne Valley.

"The city of Fredericksburg was an aristocratic and wealthy town," said David Chamberlain of the 4th Michigan. "There was more taste and comfort exhibited in their dwellings than any place I have ever seen south of our Northern cities. The town was lighted with gas and well supplied with good water. The streets and sidewalks in good order, the general location is superb, a valley about two miles wide gradually rising up . . . until you reach the first range of hills, then running off into a country beautifully rolling."[32]

To Northern soldiers, the attitude of the citizenry was not as beautiful as the landscape. During the first Federal occupation of Fredericksburg in the spring of 1862, a soldier of the 2nd Wisconsin wrote, "The women of this place look as if they could swallow the entire army of live Yankees. . . . Their 'pouting' and effeminate scowls are amusing to our troops who nearly kill the poor 'secesh creatures' with their Yankee smiles. . . . " The soldier went on to say, "Had Barnum's Big Show been in town it would not have attracted half the attention that our distinguished country men did."[33]

Other Union soldiers were not impressed with the area *or* people. Charley Goddard of the 1st Minnesota described the small village of Falmouth, just across the river from Fredericksburg, as "one of the most

31 London *Times*, January 1, 1863, in the Fredericksburg and Spotsylvania National Military Park bound manuscript collection, vol. 270.

32 David Chamberlain to editor Hudson, *Michigan Gazette*, December 23, 1862, in the Fredericksburg and Spotsylvania National Military Park bound manuscript collection, vol. 414.

33 W. M. P. Taylor to *The Herald*, May 2, 1862, in the Fredericksburg and Spotsylvania National Military Park bound manuscript collection, vol. 481.

The ruins of Mannsfield, the home of Arthur Bernard.

Fredericksburg and Spotsylvania National Military Park

Godforsaken places I ever saw in my life. . . . The inhabitants that are around the street standing or leaning up against the corners look as if they had not a friend in the world and if you asked them how they like these visitors, 'Right smart,' will be the answer and you can't get another word out of them."[34]

Federals had spent much of the spring of 1862 in and around Fredericksburg. As George McClellan made his way to the Peninsula near Richmond, soldiers of the I Corps of the Army of the Potomac tromped into Fredericksburg to secure the city as a staging area. Some 40,000 Union troops would eventually converge on the city to support McClellan's movement by threatening the Confederate capital from the north. Stonewall Jackson's movements in the Shenandoah Valley, however,

34 Richard Moe, *The Last Full Measure: The Life and Death of the First Minnesota Volunteers* (New York, NY, 1993), 207.

A sketch of Union soldiers attempting to avoid flying chamber pots during the spring 1862 occupation of Fredericksburg.

Fredericksburg and Spotsylvania National Military Park

froze the Federals in Fredericksburg; if Jackson moved on Washington, the troops in Fredericksburg would be needed to protect the capital.

From April through June of 1862, the Union soldiers had free rein of the city, and a number of famous units and generals spent time there. Brigadier General John Gibbon and his yet-to-be-named Iron Brigade camped on Stafford Heights. Brigadier General John Reynolds acted as the military governor. President Lincoln, Brig. Gen. Irvin McDowell, and Brig. Gen. Rufus King all visited or were stationed near the city, as well.

The 40,000 Yankees in their midst did not sit well with the local population, who felt the hard hand of war like few others. If the Union Army was not bombarding or looting the city, the Confederate protectors were wreaking havoc themselves. The street fighting between opposing forces piled on additional destruction. Refugees who lost their homes were taken in by other families but, after a while, had to be turned out because they were a burden.[35] In the city, food became scarce. Southern soldiers who camped on local farms foraged there instead, wearing out the land.

35 Alfred Randolph to S. G. Randolph, February 26, 1863, in the Fredericksburg and Spotsylvania National Military Park bound manuscript collection, vol. 387.

A knot of Confederate soldiers massed atop the destroyed railroad bridge in Fredericksburg.

Library of Congress

Civilians avoided all soldiers as much as possible—for fear they would catch lice.[36]

By the spring of 1863, "Fredericksburg presented a most desolate appearance," recalled a member of the VI Corps. "Nothing has been done to repair the serious injuries it received during the engagement of last December. Nearly every prominent building is more or less hurt by shot, shell and minie balls. Ruins of once elegant residences are seen on every hand."[37]

On the edge of the city, where the fairgrounds once stood, cows grazed on the spring grass. Mixed among the cows were the buried bones of 2,000 Union soldiers, according to some of the locals. On the side of one road, most likely Prussia Street, boys kicked the skull of a Union soldier as if it were a ball.[38]

This was the wasteland upon which Sedgwick's men descended.

* * *

The VI Corps had seen little action in the December 1862 battle and had never entered the city itself. Thus, when those at the head of Newton's division led the way into Fredericksburg in May 1863, they were entering unknown territory. Butterfield had ordered Sedgwick to "Seize the mayor of Fredericksburg [Montgomery Slaughter] or any citizen. Put them ahead as guides, on pain of death for false information. Meanwhile I will send

36 Alfred Randolph to S. G. Randolph, April 20, 1864, in the Fredericksburg and Spotsylvania National Military Park Bound Manuscript Collection, vol. 387.

37 Letter from soldier in the 5th Wisconsin to the *Wisconsin Daily Patriot*, May 20, 1863, in the Fredericksburg and Spotsylvania National Military Park bound manuscript collection, vol. 149.

38 Ibid.

you one, if I can."[39] Shortly thereafter, Butterfield informed Sedgwick that "I send you a contraband, who knows the Plank road leading to Chancellorsville. Push on [to Hooker] without delay. . . . "[40]

Local guides seemed in short supply. According to Henry Francis of the 7th Massachusetts, the city "is deserted only a few niggers living there."[41] The historian of the 102nd Pennsylvania remembered:

> I rode back through the old city, and found it almost wholly deserted of its inhabitants; the doors and windows all open. The desolate quietness was almost painful. Passing over the lower skirts of the city, a long and beautifully shaded gravel carriage-way was seen, leading to a fine old mansion. Riding along it to the dwelling, a strange poetic, and fairly-like scene presented itself. The grounds and gardens were beautifully laid out and adorned with a great variety of ornamental trees and shrubbery, all now budding into leaf and bloom. . . . The front door of the capacious old mansion stood open. I entered, and the sound of my footsteps and voice echoed through the empty halls. . . . Poor Virginia. The far reaching terrors of this great revolution are as yet scarcely realized by any."[42]

The VI Corps cautiously moved through the beleaguered city. Confederates fired down the streets from the open heights to the west. To avoid being hit, Federal units had to scurry through intersections close to the old killing field. "[W]e were in the midst of the city of Fredericksburg," wrote Charles Brewster of the 10th Massachusetts, "round the corner we went up a long street to the Rail Road, turned up the track and into the Depot where we halted in plain sight of the terrible heights rifle pits and

---

39 *OR* 25, pt. 2, 366.

40 Ibid. "Contraband" was an euphemism for a slave who was freed—or who freed him- or herself—from bondage. The usage came from the working assumption that such slaves became confiscated property.

41 Henry W. Francis to Sister, May 11, 1863, in the Fredericksburg and Spotsylvania National Military Park bound manuscript collection.

42 Alexander Morrison Stewart, *Camp, March, and Battle-Field or Three and a Half Years with the Army of the Potomac* (Philadelphia, PA, 1865), 312.

fortifications behind the city which the centre Grand Division could not take last December."[43]

As the VI Corps made its way northward, Gibbon's division was supposed to meet it. "Your command must cross the river to Fredericksburg to-night," Butterfield had ordered. "Pontoon bridge now at the Lacy house. Get under way soon. General Sedgwick is ordered to move through Fredericksburg toward Chancellorsville. . . . You must see to the laying of the bridges."[44] Butterfield also warned him to beware of any accidental contact that might trigger a friendly fire incident.

The Lacy House, known as Chatham, was the home of J. Horace Lacy, an ardent secessionist and "the most dangerous Rebel in the county," according to Maj. Gen. Abner Doubleday.[45] The home, constructed between 1768 and 1771, had hosted George Washington, Thomas Jefferson, and Abraham Lincoln. During the Federal occupation in the spring of 1862, it had served as headquarters for Irvin McDowell; during the battle of Fredericksburg, it had served as headquarters for Maj. Gen. Edwin Voss Sumner. It served, too, as a hospital, where Clara Barton nursed soldiers back to health.[46]

Gibbon's division was to move from a position near Chatham to the riverfront and then, with the aid of engineers, bridge the river, and seize the city for Union operations. The 50th New York Engineers had been given the same bridge-building task back in December. Likewise, the 2nd Division had been called on then to assault the city—defended, then as now, by Mississippians.

Through the night, boats were placed in the water and the bridge constructed. The Confederates were aware of the crossing almost immediately. At around 2:00 a.m., Lt. Cicero Denman of the 21st Mississippi spotted a signal rocket thrown from the roof of one of the

---

43 Charles Brewster to Sister, May 10, 1863, in the Fredericksburg and Spotsylvania National Military Park bound manuscript collection, vol. 70.

44 *OR* 25, pt. 2, 368.

45 A. Wilson Greene, *J. Horace Lacy: The Most Dangerous Rebel in the County* (Richmond, VA, 1988), 6.

46 Harrison, *Fredericksburg Civil War Sites*, Volume One, 102-111.

buildings in the city. He sent word to the heights behind the town, where the blast of three signal guns warned of the Federal crossing.[47]

Company F of the 21st Mississippi, along the riverfront, fired into the night. The jumpy engineers slowed their progress but pushed on steadily. If pressure continued, a detachment of the 34th New York and a detachment of 25 men from Company F, 1st Minnesota, would rush the far bank, eliminating any resistance.[48] However, by the time Gibbon's men moved across the new bridges, the Mississippians of Company F had pulled out; Newton's division, by entering the town from the south, had made the riverfront position of the rebels untenable.

Near dawn, Gibbon and Newton successfully united. Sedgwick was now at full strength for his push westward.

For the third time in the war, the city of Fredericksburg was in Union hands. And for a second time, a forlorn assault would have to be made against Marye's Heights.

---

47 Humphreys, *Recollections of Fredericksburg.*

48 *OR* 25, pt. 1, 356.

Chapter Ten

The Failed Reconnaissance

Morning fog, made translucent by the rising sun, filled the streets of Fredericksburg, and a preternatural calm settled over the city. Although thousands of Union soldiers filed up from the Bowling Green Road, they did so slowly, as the night of marching and intermittent skirmishing had wearied them. There was surprisingly little other movement in the city. Many houses stood empty. Homes that had been re-occupied following the December battle had again been abandoned by residents fleeing the approach of Sedgwick's men. Civilians who stayed tried to keep their heads down. "They took refuge in the cellars while the fight was going on," wrote William Allison of the 61st Pennsylvania. "They are of intensely secesh sentiments, but treated our men with all possible kindness."[1]

Not all Northerners were as charitable in their assessment. "The city looks as all rebel cities should, battered to pieces and used up," wrote a New Jersey soldier the following day. "It contains two very fine churches, but other music than the peal of their bells has floated on this Sabbath's

---

1 William A. Allison to a Friend, May 10, 1863, in the Fredericksburg and Spotsylvania National Military Park bound manuscript collection, vol. 359.

air." He added that "[t]he houses are completely riddled, and are in very truth good samples of perforated board and worsted work!"[2]

Street by street, Alexander Shaler's brigade searched out the enemy, but the Confederates had all but vanished into the morning mist. Men of Col. Henry Browne's brigade served the Union forces as a protective screen. "We reached Fredericksburg early in the morning," wrote the historian of the 7th Massachusetts, "and were, with the 36th New York, detached from the brigade, and put in position to hold the city against any attack the enemy might make against the division on the Telegraph and Plank Roads."[3]

The VI Corps had overpowered the two companies of the 21st Mississippi, but the delay had cost precious time. Sedgwick was now far behind schedule and needed to move quicker if he had any hope of threatening the rest of Lee's army. Yet somewhere out in the fog on the heights west of town, an enemy force of unknown size still blocked his way. "[P]ush through every obstacle in your path," read orders issued to Sedgwick at 1:45 a.m. "The enemy will no doubt make every effort to delay and stop your force by a smaller one. . . . "[4]

The fog made it difficult not only to assess the situation but to communicate. It masked the visual signals Sedgwick and Butterfield had been using to send messages back and forth across the river. During daylight, they had been using flags; at night, they switched to torches. "I don't want any signal," Butterfield ordered shortly after 2:00 a.m. "It will betray the movement for miles. The enemy reads our signals."[5] Just how Sedgwick was expected to communicate while moving through enemy territory against an unknown force while trying to coordinate with Hooker's wing of the army seemed to be something Butterfield did not

2 E. P. Ackerman, "Wreaths of Smoke from the Battle Field," *Newark (NJ) Daily Advertiser*, May 6, 1863 and May 8, 1863, in the Fredericksburg and Spotsylvania National Military Park bound manuscript collection, vol. 193.

3 Nelson V. Hutchinson, *History of the Seventh Massachusetts Volunteer Infantry in the War of the Rebellion of the Southern States Against Constitutional Authority, 1861–1865* (Taunton, MA, 1890), 124-125.

4 *OR* 25, pt. 2, 384.

5 Ibid.

consider. They resorted to the use of couriers—one more slow process to further impede an already-slow movement.

To make matters worse, Sedgwick had two staff officers breathing down his neck. Near 11:30 p.m. the previous evening, Capt. Valarian Razderichin, one of Hooker's aides-de-camp, had reached Butterfield's Falmouth headquarters. Razderichin told the woeful tale of the beating Jackson had inflicted upon Hooker. Butterfield soon dispatched the captain to Sedgwick to report the crisis, and there Razderichin stayed, although Sedgwick sent him as a runner to Butterfield numerous times with messages—most likely Sedgwick's way of keeping the young captain out of his hair.

At about that same time, Hooker dispatched his chief topographical engineer, Brig. Gen. Gouverneur K. Warren, to Sedgwick. At 33, Warren was an obnoxious little creature; but others saw him as promising, the rising star in the Army of the Potomac.[6] The New York native had grown up fewer than 10 miles from the United States Military Academy at West Point. He eventually studied at the Academy, and while there took to the teachings of Dennis Hart Mahan, one of the leading military theorists of the "Old Army."[7] Mahan urged the use of field fortifications rather than the open-field Napoleonic tactics of the day. In 1850, Warren graduated second in his class and went into the engineers, where he served under Capt. Andrew A. Humphreys, a future major general of volunteers. Later, Warren taught mathematics at West Point.[8]

In May 1861, Warren accepted a colonel's commission with the 5th New York Zouaves.[9] Later he was promoted to brigade command in the V Corps, where he served with distinction. On February 4, 1863, Warren joined Hooker's staff as his chief topographical engineer.[10] He and his staff worked tirelessly mapping the region, measuring distances from headquarters to major points in the city and along the Confederate line.

---

6   David M. Jordan, *"Happiness Is Not My Companion": The Life of General G. K. Warren* (Bloomington, IN, 2001), 75.

7   Ibid., 5-6.

8   Warner, *Generals in Blue*, 541-542.

9   Ibid.

10 Jordan, *"Happiness Is Not My Companion,"* 66.

Brigadier General Gouverneur K. Warren, Hooker's chief topographical engineer.

Library of Congress

His staff went to every fordable point on the Rappahannock and Rapidan rivers and took measurements of the water's depth, what the river bottom consisted of, and what branches of the army could cross at each point.[11]

11 W. H. Paine, Notebook, in the Fredericksburg and Spotsylvania National Military Park bound manuscript collection, vol. 408.

"He is a queer mixture," wrote Wainwright of Warren. "I am becoming more than ever convinced that he has a screw loose and is not quite accountable for all his little freaks. . . . "[12] What Warren lacked in social graces, though, he more than made up for in his eye for terrain.

The beady-eyed staff officer reported to Hooker that "General Sedgwick would not have moved at all but for his [Warren's] presence, and that when he did move, it was not with sufficient confidence or ability."[13] As he would demonstrate later in the war, and as historians have lamented ever since, Warren would earn a reputation for overcautious slowness, so it is ironic that his principal task at the time was to prod Sedgwick into action. Hooker also wanted Warren to serve as Sedgwick's guide down the Plank Road to Chancellorsville.

Sedgwick's slowness at this point is difficult to explain. He knew about the previous day's debacle at Chancellorsville. He knew that Hooker still held a position of relative strength in the middle of a precariously separated Confederate army. He knew he was no longer serving as a mere distraction but as an integral component of the army's offensive maneuvers. "Everything in the world depends on the rapidity and promptness of your movement," Butterfield wrote to him shortly after 2:30 a.m. "Push everything."[14]

Nevertheless, Sedgwick decided to make a reconnaissance. With Shaler's men busying themselves searching and clearing the city, Sedgwick turned to the next brigade in line, that of Brig. Gen. Frank Wheaton. Wheaton was not a West Point graduate; rather, the Rhode Island native was commissioned straight into the 1st United States Cavalry in 1855. Wheaton was well connected through marriage: his father-in-law was the ranking general in the Confederacy, Samuel Cooper; his mother-in-law was the sister of Sen. James Murray Mason of the *Trent* affair.[15] In March, while in winter camp, Wheaton and his wife awoke to find their tent on fire after their chimney went up in flames. The Wheatons lost all of their

12 Wainwright, Diary, July 14, 1864, in Nevins, *A Diary of Battle*, 476.

13 Hooker to Bates, April 2, 1877, in the Fredericksburg and Spotsylvania National Military Park bound manuscript collection, vol. 406.

14 *OR* 25, pt. 2, 385.

15 Warner, *Generals in Blue*, 553.

Federal cannon atop Stafford Heights.

Library of Congress

possessions they had with them, and Mrs. Wheaton was so shaken she had to be escorted to Washington in April.[16]

Wheaton swung two regiments from column into line of battle: Lt. Col. Theodore Hamilton's 62nd New York—"Anderson's Zouaves"—and Col. Joseph Kinkead's 102nd Pennsylvania. The regiments pushed across the open plain toward the enemy's line along Marye's Heights.[17] The entire field was obscured by the heavy fog that plagued both armies throughout the spring campaign. "Two regiments moved off toward the hill in line, and they were soon swallowed up in the mist," wrote one Mainer.[18] Slowly but steadily, the men pushed forward up the slight slope until, at 20 yards from the enemy's line along the famous stone wall and Sunken Road, Southern troops unleashed a hail of deadly fire.[19] "Then

---

16 *Pittsburgh (PA) Evening Chronicle*, March 3, 1863, in the Fredericksburg and Spotsylvania National Military Park bound manuscript collection, vol. 362.

17 Raus, *A Generation on the March*, 68.

18 Hyde, *Following the Greek Cross*, 123.

19 *OR* 25, pt. 1, 564.

came the familiar whistling of bullets about us and a crackling fire in the unknown beyond," the soldier wrote. "The sudden lifting of the watery curtain for an instant revealed to us the intrenched line full of men, and our two regiments giving back with heavy loss."[20]

The men from the Empire and Keystone states were put to flight. The historian of the 102nd Pennsylvania recalled that it was "a brief and bloody struggle, too formidable for our inadequate numbers. . . . "[21] In fewer than five minutes, the 102nd Pennsylvania and 62nd New York lost 64 officers and men. The 62nd also lost its color sergeant, and its flag was pierced by at least 30 musket balls. Lieutenant Colonel Hamilton was wounded.[22] "Out of about 150 men in our regiment that made a charge on Sunday morning on the famous stone wall, 70 were either wounded or killed," wrote William Walcott of the 62nd New York, describing the brief and fruitless struggle.

[O]wnley for my Haversack I would have got a very bad wound as the ball st[r]uck me nocked my tin cup in three peases and then passed through my haversack then through my coat pants and everything gave me a wound about [one quarter] of an inch deep in my leg. This happened early in the morning our Regiments being the ownley regiment that made the attack we having no serport we were repulsed.[23]

Sedgwick showed a quick temper as the men came tumbling back. "For God's sake, rally those men," he called to his staff.[24] Major Thomas Hyde and Lt. Col. Ford Kent rode out, drew their sabers, and rallied the men; Sedgwick then pulled his hat over his eyes and turned back toward the city.[25]

The broken Pennsylvanians and New Yorkers did quickly rally. The remaining three regiments of Wheaton's brigade marched up to bolster

20 Hyde, *Following the Greek Cross*, 123.

21 Stewart, *Camp, March, and Battle-Field*, 312.

22 *OR* 25, pt. 1, 617.

23 William P. Walcott to Parents, May 6, 1863, in the Fredericksburg and Spotsylvania National Military Park bound manuscript collection, vol. 356.

24 Hyde, *Following the Greek Cross*, 123.

25 Ibid., 124.

the new front line, about 700 yards from the Confederates. The 102nd Pennsylvania took advantage of a deep cut in the railroad and piled three companies in. To their immediate rear came Capt. Jeremiah McCarthy's 1st Pennsylvania Light Artillery, batteries C and D. These guns fired over the 102nd and quickly drew counterbattery fire from the Rebels, compelling the foot soldiers to pull back behind the long guns.[26]

Wheaton had known that full success with the first two regiments had been a forlorn hope; the commanders were looking for information, not a quick victory. But even that proved of little use: they gleaned only that the enemy was ensconced behind the stone wall and that artillery sat atop Marye's Heights.

Why Sedgwick ordered Wheaton's reconnaissance is baffling. He and his staff already well knew that Confederates had put themselves in a blocking position on the heights. Butterfield and the signal officers, who also had a clear grasp of the tactical situation along the Confederate line, had been sending this word to Sedgwick for days. Butterfield had warned him specifically that there were three regiments in position near the heights.[27] To effectively counter the Confederates, Sedgwick could have assaulted the hill using the balance of Newton's division along with Wheaton's brigade and the brigade of Col. William H. Browne, supporting them all with artillery. The cover of fog would have obscured and aided the attackers. Instead, Sedgwick chose to send in two under-strength regiments, which did little more than inform the enemy that the VI Corps was indeed pushing west.

Sedgwick decided to bring more firepower to bear on the Confederate position, and soon the guns of the VI Corps rolled into battery. A general bombardment rained on the Confederates. From Stafford Heights, 4.5-inch siege rifles and 20-pounder Parrott guns roared to life, battering the Confederates from afar. However, staff officer Halsted thought the artillery did very little but force the Confederates to keep their heads down.[28]

---

26 *OR* 25, pt. 1, 622.

27 *OR* 25, pt. 2, 368.

28 Stoeckel, *Correspondence of John Sedgwick Major-General*, vol. 2, 117.

In the meantime, Sedgwick began to methodically bring the entire VI Corps on line to make an assault. Time was of the essence to Hooker and Butterfield, but apparently not to the overly cautious "Uncle John."

* * *

Lee's "Bad Old Man" should have been ecstatic with the early morning results. Federals had bottle-necked more than two divisions in the city, failed in their light reconnaissance against the Confederate line, and—other than firing artillery blindly into the fog—had done a fantastic job of stymieing their own efforts. To boot, the Federal artillery actually drew reinforcements to Early.

At Banks' Ford, the five regiments of Brig. Gen. Cadmus M. Wilcox's Alabama brigade had been sitting idly throughout the fighting. With little threat of a Federal crossing, Wilcox looked to march to battle, so at dawn he had readied his men to move to Lee's aid near Chancellorsville. However, when Sedgwick opened on Early's men, Wilcox marched to the sound of the closest guns. He arrived with his men on the northern end of Early's battle line. Wilcox began deploying skirmishers in front of Dr. Taylor's home, while he and his staff sought out anyone with knowledge of the situation. Wilcox came upon generals Barksdale and Hays near the Stansbury House. Barksdale informed Wilcox of the situation and shared his concerns about his right flank. Wilcox had been unaware of the situation looming in front of Marye's Heights. Armed with this new information, Wilcox returned to his brigade to ready his men for the impending storm. With the addition of this new brigade, Early had just over 12,000 men manning his line, nearly seven miles long.[29]

Early had positioned the bulk of those men well south of the city, convinced as he had been that the main Federal assault would take place at or near Hamilton's Crossing. Smith's Virginia brigade was on Prospect Hill near the crossing. To Smith's left was Gordon's Georgia brigade. Strung across Deep Run and the Landsdowne Valley was Hoke's North Carolina brigade. On Howison Hill sat the 6th and 9th Louisiana. Telegraph Hill (later known as Lee's Hill) was manned by the 13th and 17th Mississippi. Positioned behind the famed stone wall was the 18th

---

29 *OR* 25, pt. 1, 854-857.

Mississippi, supported by companies C, F, and L of the 21st Mississippi. Atop the crest of Marye's Heights, the vaunted Washington Artillery of New Orleans had placed its guns, supported by the remaining companies of the 21st Mississippi, who ran their line from near Brompton northward across the Plank Road. On Trench Hill, just north of the Marye house, was the rest of Hays' Louisianans. Finally, the line ended with Wilcox's new arrivals near Stansbury and Taylor hills. Pendleton's guns bolstered the line there.

Numerically, the weakest part of the Confederate line was the center, from Howison Hill to Marye's Heights, where perhaps 1,000 Southern soldiers stood ready. The lack of men worried and angered the testy Barksdale, who claimed there were "a million armed Yankees all around him."[30] Topographically, though, Early considered it the strongest stretch of the line because of the natural and artificial fortifications it offered.

Even with Sedgwick's force moving into the city and spreading its line northward, Early still focused the bulk of his forces, some 6,100 men, mainly along Jackson's old line, three to five miles south of the city. The lessons from the previous December, when Meade had broken through the Confederate line in that sector of the battlefield, remained fresh in Early's mind. He had two other good reasons for stacking more men on that portion of his line. If pushed back, he could use Prospect Hill as a pivot point to wheel those men to the south, blocking a Union advance to Spotsylvania Court House or Richmond. The position also protected Early's undersized force from being taken on the right flank and driven north, where they might possibly be crushed against the bend in the Rappahannock River at the far end of the city.

Early had no way to predict when or from where the main Federal attack might come. During the previous few days, Brooks' division had acted aggressively as it expanded the Federal influence in the area around the bridgehead, driving the Confederates back to the rail line at the base of Prospect Hill. On the morning of May 3, Extra Billy Smith had launched three regiments of his brigade into an assault across the open fields south of Deep Run in an effort to drive back the Union skirmish line that had crossed the Richmond, Fredericksburg, & Potomac Railroad. Smith also employed a section of Napoleons from Lt. Col. Snowden Andrews'

---

30 Gallagher, "East of Chancellorsville," 44.

Brigadier General Cadmus Wilcox.

Library of Congress

battalion in support. When the two guns and three regiments proved unequal to the task, Smith brought more guns to bear on the boys in blue. North Carolinians from Robert Hoke's brigade joined in. Union Brig. Gen. Joseph J. Bartlett countered the Confederate moves, receiving support from both Battery A, 1st Maryland Light Artillery (Union) and

Battery A, 1st Massachusetts Light Artillery. Smith failed to fully dislodge Bartlett's brigade, but did succeed in driving the Federals back across the rail line. His "reconnaissance" failed to uncover the enemy's true intentions, though, so the southern end of the field still remained a source of mystery and potential trouble for Early.[31]

Despite all that, the flaws in the Southern line far outweighed its advantages. The entire line lacked depth. Early had one long, thin front that lacked a mobile reserve force. If it broke, all would be lost. The addition of Wilcox, while useful, would do nothing but allow Early to extend his flank nearly to the river. A better use for Wilcox, or for one of Early's brigade's to the south, might have been as a central reserve that would have allowed the Confederates to plug any gaps that might open. Instead, any and all support was more than a dozen miles to the west, and perhaps not available at all: as the morning wore on, Lee would need all the men he had. The Southern commanding general would battle Hooker ferociously in an attempt to re-link with Jackson's corps and drive Hooker into the river.

*   *   *

At around 6:30 a.m., more Union soldiers made their way into town. Gibbon's II Corps division—at least the two full brigades with him; the third was on its way to Banks' Ford—trotted across the new pontoon bridge at the foot of Chatham, reinforcing the men of the VI Corps. Behind Gibbon came two batteries of the 1st Rhode Island Artillery, Capt. William Arnold's Battery A and Lt. T. Frederick Brown's Battery B.[32]

Meanwhile, downriver a few hundred yards at the site of the demolished railroad bridge, where a pontoon bridge had been constructed back in December, Capt. Chauncey Reese and his detachment of United States engineers laid yet another bridge in order to facilitate movement back and forth across the river. "As the VI Corps held the town, there was,

---

31 Wise, *The Long Arm of Lee*, vol. 2, 519-521.

32 Gibbon carried the 1st and 3rd brigade, 2nd division, II Corps into town. These were the brigades of Brig. Gen. Alfred Scully and Col. Norman J. Hall. The 2nd brigade under Brig. Gen. Joshua T. Owen, also known as the Philadelphia Brigade, was on detached duty aiding the artillerists at Banks' Ford on the Rappahannock River.

of course, no opposition to building this bridge," recalled engineer Gilbert Thompson. Confederate artillerists tried taking shots at the engineers floating pontoons into place, but the city's buildings, which sat on a plateau higher than the riverfront, provided useful cover for the engineers. With their view obstructed, the artillerists "lost the range and stopped firing upon them."[33]

Unlike Sedgwick's troops, Gibbon's men knew the streets—hard-earned knowledge from their assault against the heights back in December. Their commander also knew Fredericksburg: during the Peninsula campaign, Gibbon had been stationed in the area while in command of the Iron Brigade.

Once on the city side of the river, Gibbon sought out Sedgwick, still methodically arraying his men for battle. Sedgwick ordered Gibbon to take his men to the northern end of town and attempt to find a way around the Confederate left flank. If such an effort were successful, Sedgwick could sweep Early out of the way to the south and open the road to Chancellorsville without making frontal assaults against the heights.

Gibbon sent orders to his generals on Princess Anne Street to get his brigades moving. In the meantime, he and Warren moved to the northern outskirts of the city on a reconnaissance. What they saw could not have pleased them. Everyone knew about the Rappahannock Canal's millrace, which bisected the open plain on the outskirts of the city and which had proven to be a major inconvenience to assaulting Federals back in December. What Gibbon and Warren had not known was that north of the city the canal presented an even more formidable barrier because it ran in two north-south sluices. At its widest, the canal stretched 51 feet across, and it ran six feet deep.[34] Even as Humphreys' Mississippians hurriedly withdrew from the city, they had taken the time to remove all the planking from two of the bridges spanning the canal, leaving only the runners.[35] If Union soldiers tried to use those bridges, they would have to balance on the runners and cross in single file, making it easy for

---

33 "U.S. Engineer Battalion," *National Tribune*, August 16, 1888, in the Fredericksburg and Spotsylvania National Military Park bound manuscript collection, vol. 415.

34 From a river and canal study consisting of annotated maps in the Fredericksburg and Spotsylvania National Military Park bound manuscript collection, vol. 174.

35 Humphreys, *Recollections of Fredericksburg*.

Modern view of the Rappahannock Canal along Princess Anne Street.

Kristopher D. White

Confederates to mow them down. The resultant bottleneck would slow the entire movement to a crawl.

As the lead elements of Col. Norman J. Hall's brigade arrived on the field, Warren ordered men to remove any planking from the nearest buildings and rebuild the bridge flooring. A detachment of the 19th Massachusetts set to work.[36]

As the ersatz bridge-builders rolled into action, Confederate artillerists on the high ground starting raining shots down on them. Meanwhile, Early began shifting his men in response to the developing Federal movements. The three Creole regiments of Hays' brigade, the 5th, 7th, and 8th Louisiana, rushed to the support of Barksdale's northern flank. Wilcox also shifted men to Taylor Hill and called for artillery support. A section of Lt. Nathan Penick's Pittsylvania Artillery and the four guns of Capt. Joseph Moore's Norfolk Battery took position on

36 *OR* 25, pt. 1, 358-359.

Stansbury Hill and fired into the mass of blue men working on the bridge and moving into the open plain behind.

Gibbon countered by deploying Hazard's Battery on high ground near the stately manor Kenmore and the partially constructed Mary Washington Monument. The elevated position was not as high as the Confederates', but was a far cry better than where the Federal infantry had been operating in the low ground between the two dominating hills. More Southern artillery arrived in the sector, escalating the situation even further. A section of the 4th Company of the Washington Artillery, under Lt. Joseph Norcom, rolled into battery and lobbed shells on the Federals from entrenched redoubts on the heights.

Officers of the 20th Massachusetts jumped from their horses as the shells fell among the ranks.[37] Lying in the field enduring artillery fire frayed the men's nerves. "Pleasant to see a d'd gun brought up to an earthwork deliberately brought to you, to notice your company is exactly in range," future United States Supreme Court Justice Oliver Wendell Holmes, Jr., recalled sarcastically. "1st discharge puff-second puff (as the shell burst) and my knapsack is knocked to pieces."[38] Another shell fell in among him and his men, hitting the young Bay Stater in the heel, forcing him from the field.[39]

It became evident that there was little hope of bridging the canal, and crossing the canal without a bridge was out of the question. Hall, who had had enough nonsense sitting in an open field under artillery fire, ordered his regiments from line into column, then charged across the open field. Rather than rush to the enemy's lines, though, Hall's men rushed through the field and dove for cover behind a stone wall. There they "lay safe & comfortable," according to Capt. Henry Abbott of the 20th Massachusetts, "the shells piling over us." Abbott credited his commander for saving them. "We were exposed to a heavy shell fire for a short time, losing a couple dozen men," Abbott wrote, "but thanks to Col. Hall, who showed wonderful coolness & self possession, where many a man in an

37 Miller, *Harvard's Civil War*, 235.

38 Ibid., 235-236.

39 Ibid., 236.

open space under a heavy fire would have lost his head & destroyed us."[40] Abbott lamented that "we certainly would have given them a roust, if it hadn't been for that cursed canal."[41]

With Hall effectively out of action, Gibbon attempted to move men up closer to the river. Colonel Byron Laflin got the call, leading Brig. Gen. Alfred Sully's brigade. Sully himself had been relieved of command during the campaign for not quelling a near-mutiny days earlier by the 34th New York; Col. Henry Hudson subsequently assumed command of the brigade, but he too was relieved, for intoxication. Now, through a strange twist of fate, it was Col. Laflin of the 34th New York—who had cost Alfred Sully his job—commanding the brigade in combat.

Laflin's men aligned along the River Road, then they too were pinned down. Laflin attempted to find a way out of his tight spot by ordering two companies of the 15th Massachusetts under Capt. Lyman Ellingwood to push west along River Road, but artillery, mixed with Wilcox's fresh Alabamians, turned back their effort. The best the Federal infantry could do was take cover.[42] On the left of Gibbon's division, the 2nd Rhode Island and the 10th and 37th Massachusetts from Col. William Browne's second brigade of Newton's division were shifted from their positions at the edge of the city toward the city cemetery and Kenmore.[43] The 1,300 or so troops were meant to bolster and assist Gibbon, but this was not to be: the Confederate artillery fire raining in from the heights proved to be too much, and the three regiments were forced to take cover and simply endure the shelling.

To break the impasse, a brash young artillery captain, George Adams, rolled his battery into the open plain to the left of Hazard's battery. From its exposed position, Adams' Battery G, 1st Rhode Island Light Artillery, traded shots with the rebel guns on the heights. Although brave, Adams' men were outmatched. (However, the young captain's actions so

---

40 Robert Garth Scott, ed., *Fallen Leaves: The Civil War Letters of Major Henry Livermore Abbott* (Kent, OH, 1991), 174.

41 Ibid.

42 *OR* 25, pt. 1, 353-354.

43 Ibid., 615.

impressed Uncle John that he requested the battery be reassigned to the VI Corps.)[44]

As casualties from the fight staggered to the rear, army surgeons came closer to the front to offer aid. Originally, complained surgeon Edwin Buckman of the 98th Pennsylvania, his supervisor had

> placed us including himself behind the rifle pits, out of the range of shells, bullets or observation and consequently out of the reach of service. We did nothing here and I was not satisfied with the proceeding and was beginning to urge a change when the Surg. of Divis . . . directed several of us to proceed to Fredericksburg to relieve the suffering ones there. . . . We soon arrived . . . and found some surgeons occupying a sand quarry in a very accessible as well as a very protected situation. . . .[45]

Gibbon was bogged down. The door on the federal right had been slammed shut by the quick thinking of Hays and Wilcox. Sedgwick could get no more from his former division, although their presence on the north end of the field would at least tie down Hays' and Wilcox's men.

Sedgwick weighed his options. He could not flank the Confederates: Gibbon was stalled on the river, and Prospect Hill was too far out of the way. Attacking at Prospect Hill meant shifting the entire VI Corps, redeploying its elements on a new battlefront—and, although he did not realize it, striking Early's heaviest concentration of men.

No, he realized, the attack had to come at Marye's Heights and Telegraph Hill.

---

44 Elisha Dyer, *Adjutant General Report of Rhode Island 1861–1865* (Providence, RI, 1893), 393.

45 Edwin Buckman to Mrs. E. D. Buckman, May 9, 1863, in the Fredericksburg and Spotsylvania National Military Park bound manuscript collection, vol. 399.

Chapter Eleven

Across the Old Battlefield

"Sabbath, and a lovelier day never overtook a soldier," wrote Sewell Gray, a 22-year-old captain in the 6th Maine. The sun had burned off the morning fog, revealing a blue sky overhead. The Mainers, hunkered down in the city, could hear the sounds of the artillery battle going on at the north end of the field, where Gibbon was trying to find some way to cross the two branches of the canal. "At 6 we were in line immediately under the enemy's fortifications ready to make the assault. Our batteries are all playing. A terrible battle is raging on the right."[1]

As it became apparent that Gibbon's battle was not opening the way, soldiers began to realize the same thing Sedgwick had already concluded. "Nothing remained but to carry the heights by direct assault," wrote one engineer.[2]

From Fredericksburg, three roads led out of the city toward Marye's Heights, suggesting possible routes of attack. The first, Prussia Street (today's Lafayette Boulevard), did not lead all the way westward; it terminated near the Confederate position at the Sunken Road. The second, Hanover Street, led directly up to and over the Confederate position near the Marye family home of Brompton. The third, the Orange

---

1 Mackowski and White, "From Foxcroft to Fredericksburg," 141.

2 Ibid.

Plank Road (today's William Street), was the route Sedgwick had been ordered to take to get to Hooker. This road, like Hanover Street, led up to and over the Confederate position.

It was obvious to Sedgwick that the main assaults would have to take place on a front about 1,000 yards wide. Men assaulting Marye's Heights would have to move out of the city and deploy from column into line of battle in the face of the enemy. Although a veteran unit could get on line in 30 seconds or less under optimal conditions, the soldiers would still make, for a time, a beautiful target for an artillerist.

The plain from the city to the Confederate lines rose gently over a 900-yard stretch. Most of the ground was open, although fence posts dotted the land, their rails long since taken for firewood and fortifications. At the 600-yard mark, a single leg of the millrace bisected the field. It was 15 feet wide and five feet deep, with three bridges spanning it. Confederate skirmishers had taken up the planks of one of the bridges, but the other two remained in place, inviting passage up toward the heights.

The open attack plain toward Marye's Heights as seen from Federal Hill.

Fredericksburg and Spotsylvania National Military Park

At the 100-yard mark stood Stratton House, a large brick home that sat on the lip of a swale. During the December battle, the swale and Stratton House had both offered protection to Union soldiers stranded in the fields.

Finally, there was the famed stone wall and Sunken Road. Only a small portion of the road was actually sunken, with the stone wall acting as a retaining wall supporting a dirt embankment on the city side of the road. The rest of the wall was free standing, approximately five feet high and two feet thick. The wall was made of Aquia stone, drawn from the same quarry that supplied building material for the United States Capitol.

Along the Sunken Road stood a number of houses. On the eastern side of the road (the city side) sat the Ebert House and store. About 75 yards away, at an opening in the stone wall, stood the Innis House, and 20 yards beyond that the home of Martha Stephens. Stephens was a woman of ill repute who allegedly ran an illegal bar from her home; from the Innis House next door, which she also owned, she allegedly ran a cathouse. About 200 yards south of the Innis House was the three-story Hall House (today the site of the Fredericksburg Battlefield Visitor Center).

On the westward side of the road, at the top of the heights, sat the Marye family home, Brompton, as well as a number of slave cabins that serviced the property. Also atop the hill a square brick wall, six feet high,

The Sunken Road and original portion of the Stone Wall.
The Innis House can be seen in the background.

Fredericksburg and Spotsylvania National Military Park

surrounded the Willis Cemetery, named for Colonel Henry Willis. Inside, 35 headstones dated back as far as 1756.

In December 1862, infantry from North Carolina, South Carolina, Georgia, and Virginia had defended the heights from seven waves of assaults. Not one of Burnside's Union soldiers had touched the wall, nor did any enter the road. "This crest of hills," wrote the London *Times'* correspondent after the battle, "constitutes one of the strongest positions in the world—impregnable to any attack from the front."[3]

The wall had given the Confederates great cover. Most of the casualties they suffered were inflicted as soldiers moved down the face of the heights into the road to reinforce the Georgians originally defending the position. By day's end, some 7,000 Confederates had crammed into the road; they sustained approximately 900 casualties.

Now, in 1863, there were far fewer Confederates. On May 3, the road was filled with the 400 or so men of Col. Thomas Griffin's 18th Mississippi. Their numbers were bolstered by three companies of the 21st Mississippi. Given the length of the road, Griffin was forced to spread his infantry so thin that each man had to cover roughly three yards.[4]

They did have the support of the six guns of the Washington Artillery and two more guns of Parker's Virginia Battery, stationed on Willis Hill.[5] Parker's two 10-pound Parrott guns were on the southern crest of the hill, which put them in position to fire into the valley between Willis and Telegraph hills; sweep the open plain near the railroad, on the south edge of the city; and fire upon any troops attacking Willis Hill from the east and northeast. The six guns of the Washington Artillery, meanwhile, stood ready at the same positions they had held during the first battle of Fredericksburg. The rebel artillerists knew the area so well that any Union soldiers marching across the old battlefield could expect accurately ranged fire.

Colonel James Walton commanded the Washington Artillery. For a time, Walton had ranked E. P. Alexander, Longstreet's First Corps artillery chief, but skill and leadership weighed on the side of Alexander,

---

3 David W. Judd, *The Story of the Thirty-Third N. Y. S. Vols: or Two Years Campaigning in Virginia and Maryland* (Rochester, NY, 1864), 290.

4 Bigelow, *The Campaign of Chancellorsville*, 384-387.

5 *OR* 25, pt. 1, 842-843.

Looking across the open attack plane from the Confederate position atop Willis Hill.

Fredericksburg and Spotsylvania National Military Park

so Walton was relegated to battalion command. He directed Capt. Charles Squires of the 1st Company Washington Artillery to deploy two 3-inch ordnance rifles as close to the military crest of the hill as possible, using the gun emplacements from the first battle. The guns sat about 30 yards in front of the small Willis Hill cemetery. Two more guns, a pair of 12-pound howitzers, were placed near Brompton. According to some Federal accounts, one of these guns took position in an intersection of the Sunken Road near the Innis House. The other gun sat squarely in the middle of the Orange Plank Road.[6]

While not as impregnable as the December defenses had been, Early had made good use of the limited resources at his disposal. "Here was planted the best of his artillery," later wrote the historian of the 33rd New York, "supported by the flower of his infantry under the command of the haughty and supercilious Barksdale, who a few weeks later breathed his

6 Ibid., 842-843, 844, 845-847.

life away on the crimson fields of Gettysburg—abandoned by his own men, without a slave even to bring him a cup of cold water."[7]

Assaulting Telegraph Hill, a little to the south, would pose similar challenges. Telegraph Hill, comparable in height to Big Round Top at Gettysburg, was slightly higher than Willis Hill. There, too, the Federals would have to cross open fields, traverse a branch of Deep Run and the marshy land around it, drive past the Jones House, and make their way up a hill adorned with artillery. Atop Telegraph Hill were the guns of John Fraser's Pulaski Artillery, part of Col. Henry C. Cabell's battalion. Fraser situated on the hill two 10-pound Parrott guns and a 3-inch ordnance rifle, plus a 12-pound howitzer.[8]

At Braehead, the home on Howison Hill, two 10-pound Parrott guns of Carlton's Battery were situated in the front yard, protected by lunettes and supported to the rear by three 12-pound Napoleons of Patterson's Sumter Battery. In reality, the three Napoleons would have served the Confederates better in the position of the 10-pound Parrotts. The shorter-ranged guns would have been closer to the enemy, so that if the hill was assaulted the artillerists could quickly turn to employing double canister against their foes. To the left of Braehead, Confederates placed a 10-pound Parrott gun and a 12-pound howitzer, also of Carlton's Battery.[9]

One Massachusetts officer described the Confederate earthworks as "the meanest description":

> Nothing whatever but rifle pits for the infantry, which you know are trenches a few feet deep, with earth thrown out in front, & which are in fact better suited for an infantry fire, particularly down the slope.... For the artillery, there were epaulements which covered the pieces well

---

7 Judd, *The Story of the Thirty-Third N. Y. S.*, 293.

8 *OR* 25, pt. 1, 842-843, 844, 845-847. The mix of guns harkened back to the days of Sharpsburg, when Confederate artillery consisted of mixed battery after mixed battery. Re-supplying an assortment of guns in a single battery proved to be a huge headache, though, so soon thereafter the Confederates reorganized their entire artillery branch so that batteries were made up of guns of the same make. One advantage to a mixed battery, however, was that the southern artillerist had a mix of long- and short-range ordnance—essentially a gun for any occasion.

9 Sears, *Chancellorsville*, 352.

enough, but they didn't pretend to be works. . . . It is certainly, both for artillery & infantry, the best position that can be imagined.[10]

Whether daunted by the Confederate position or not, the jig was up for Sedgwick. "You will hurry up your column," said orders that arrived at 10:00 a.m. "The enemy's right flank now rests near the Plank Road at Chancellorsville, all exposed. You will attack at once."[11]

Hooker was having a rough time of things on the morning of May 3, and he expected Sedgwick to move in and strike Lee from the rear, relieving pressure on his beleaguered force. As the situation at Chancellorsville teetered back and forth, the flurry of dispatches from Hooker over the course of the morning grew increasingly frantic. "Commanding general desires that you will send the following message . . . to Sedgwick at once. Where is he?"[12]

* * *

Later in the war, the members of VI Corps would be called upon again and again to repeat an innovative attack they first developed on May 3 in front of the daunting Confederate works along Marye's Heights. On November 7, 1863, at Rappahannock Station, they would be called on to batter through Confederate lines and open the way for George Gordon Meade's army to cross the river. On May 10, 1864, Col. Emory Upton would lead a similar battering ram-style attack against Confederates at Doles Salient during the battle of Spotsylvania Court House. Later still, on April 2, 1865, during the siege of Petersburg, it was the VI Corps that finally broke the back of Lee's army, opening the way to Appomattox.

Major General John Newton, who would take credit for the plan, suggested a pair of Federal assaults that would drive up William and Hanover streets, but, rather than array his men in traditional line of battle,

10 Scott, *Fallen Leaves*, 174-175.

11 *OR* 25, pt. 2, 387.

12 Ibid., 388.

Looking down Hanover Street from Federal Hill. One Union assault
column followed this road toward Marye's Heights.

Fredericksburg and Spotsylvania National Military Park

he would put them into two columns, four men abreast. The formation
would allow the men to act as "lances, to pierce [the Confederate] line."[13]

Meanwhile, Sedgwick would order a traditional line of battle to attack
the stone wall. The bulk of Burnham's Light Division would lead that
advance. The idea was to keep Barksdale's men in the road and the
Washington Artillery busy while Newton's assaults went up William and
Hanover streets. If all went well, Newton would turn the northern flank
of Willis Hill, and the Light Division could exploit the breakthrough and
easily carry the road and possibly the heights.

The third prong of the attack, consisting of Albion Howe's division,
would move across the fields in front of Howison Hill toward the
southern end of Willis Hill. Howe's men would step off from the open

13 *National Tribune*, in the Fredericksburg and Spotsylvania National Military Park
bound manuscript collection, vol. 91.

fields just south of the city and wheel to the right. Attacking across the fields would also necessitate an assault against Telegraph Hill so that the Confederates there could not sweep into the vulnerable rear and flank of Howe's men ascending the steepest portion of Willis Hill.

These headlong charges against the Confederate position—particularly at the stone wall—differed significantly from similar charges ordered by Burnside against the same position. Back in December, brigades had lined up in traditional line of battle and assaulted the position with the intent of holding Confederates in place so they could not reinforce the southern end of the line, where the main assaults were taking take place. If the Federals broke through at the stone wall, all the better, but their first assaults were intended mainly as a diversion. Later, Federals kept up pressure there to discourage any Confederate counterattack. Now, in May, the assault formations were more compact and faster-moving, designed specifically to punch through the enemy position.

Along William Street, the northern flanking party prepared itself. Colonel George Spear of the 61st Pennsylvania would lead the assault. Spear was an experienced field officer: he had served as a major with the 23rd Pennsylvania, then transferred into the 61st with a promotion to lieutenant colonel. While with the 61st, Spear was wounded in the neck at Fair Oaks and taken prisoner by Confederates. Following his exchange, Spear was promoted to colonel and assumed command of the regiment.

Along with his own 61st Pennsylvania, Spear would lead three other regiments: the 43rd and 67th New York (also known as the 1st Long Island), with the 82nd Pennsylvania bringing up the rear. Spear knew the weight of the situation, and instead of calling for a meeting with his field and line officers, as might have been customary, he called for a meeting with all of his sergeants. He laid out the plan of attack and told them what he expected of them: even if he fell, they were to carry the assault through.[14]

Up Hanover Street, Col. Thomas Johns would lead the 7th Massachusetts and 36th New York. Both units were from Col. William H. Browne's brigade. The brigade's other three regiments, the 2nd Rhode

---

14 A. T. Brewer, *History Sixty-First Regiment Pennsylvania Volunteers 1861-1865* (Pittsburgh, PA, 1911), 53-55.

Island and the 10th and 37th Massachusetts, were deployed in and around the city cemetery to serve as a bridge between the VI Corps and Gibbon's bogged-down division.

In front of Marye's Heights, the Light Division deployed in a diamond formation, with five companies of the 5th Wisconsin, A, B, F, H, and I, in the lead as heavy skirmishers.[15] The colonel of the 5th Wisconsin, Thomas Allen, expressed unhappiness about his regiment's lead role in the mission, "honorable as it was," although he conceded that with enough support from the other attacks, "We might be successful."[16] Allen was a tough breed of soldier. He had originally served in the 2nd Wisconsin, a unit that had seen action at First Bull Run, and had subsequently been attached to the famed Iron Brigade. He was serving as the 2nd's lieutenant colonel when he transferred into the 5th to take over for Col. Amasa Cobb, who had left to serve in Congress.[17]

Behind the Badgers, a traditional line of battle formed up, with the 6th Maine on the right, the 31st New York in the center, and the 23rd Pennsylvania, "Birney's Zouaves," on the left. Directly behind the main line were the remaining five companies of the 5th Wisconsin.

Although the 23rd was not part of the Light Division, its colonel, John Ely, had volunteered the regiment for this mission.[18] Earlier in the morning, it had gone on an ill-fated reconnaissance of the Sunken Road. The right wing of the regiment, five companies in all, were led to the right end of the Sunken Road to a point near the Hall House. Ely's second in command, Lt. Col. John F. Glenn, advanced his wing to within 10 paces of the wall, nearly point-blank range—when the Confederates opened fire. The 23rd's ill-fated mission had cost it 16 men.[19]

On the left flank of the Light Division's staging area, on the east side of the millrace, were three VI Corps batteries. The six 10-pounder Parrott guns of Lt. William Harn's 3rd New York Light Artillery were deployed

15 Trask, *Fire Within*, 172.

16 Sears, *Chancellorsville*, 352.

17 Trask, *Fire Within*, 170.

18 *OR* 25, pt. 1, 559.

19 Samuel P. Bates, *History of the Pennsylvania Volunteers 1861-65*, Vol. 1 (Harrisburg, PA, 1869), 311-312.

on the north side of the Richmond, Fredericksburg, & Potomac Railroad, near the gas works on the edge of the city. Across the rail bed to the south were the guns of John Newton's divisional artillery under the command of Capt. Jeremiah McCarthy. McCarthy's Pennsylvania battery had come on line following the repulse of Sedgwick's early-morning reconnaissance, and his six rifled pieces were still in position. Although they sat to the left of Harn's guns, due to the nature of the ground, the Pennsylvanians were actually 100 yards closer to the enemy than their Empire State compatriots.[20]

The line of guns was extended farther south by six Napoleons of Battery G, 2nd United States Artillery, commanded by Lt. John H. Butler. They, like the guns of the Pennsylvanians to their right, were 100 yards ahead of those of the New Yorkers even farther up the line.[21]

Howe's division deployed in the open fields south of the rail bed and Hazel Run, keeping his men in a compact formation. They presented a narrow front to the enemy, but because they were three lines deep a few well-placed shots rained down from the heights by the Confederate artillery could devastate them. The lead assault column, commanded by Brig. Gen. Thomas Neill, consisted of the 7th Maine, two battalions of the 21st New Jersey, and the 33rd New York. In the supporting second column were the men of the Vermont Brigade, commanded by Col. Lewis Grant. Grant's line consisted of the 6th Vermont, 26th New Jersey, and the 2nd Vermont. The third column was made up of the 3rd Vermont, 6th Vermont, and the remainder of the 21st New Jersey, all under the command of the 3rd Vermont's Col. Thomas Seaver. Skirmishers from companies A, F, and G of the 77th New York, "The Bemis Heights Regiment," were well advanced in front of the main line, in and around the Jones farm buildings.[22] Earlier in the morning, the 77th had engaged four companies of Confederate skirmishers, two from the 13th Mississippi

---

20 *OR* 25, pt. 1, 563.

21 Ibid.

22 Captain Orrin Rugg to Parents, Fredericksburg and Spotsylvania National Military Park bound manuscript collection, vol. 419.

and two from the 17th Mississippi, around the farm buildings and a line of trenches.[23]

In support of Howe's columns was his divisional artillery, 12 guns of Maj. J. Watts de Peyster. Near the Bowling Green Road were deployed the guns of Capt. Andrew Cowan's 1st New York Light Artillery and Lt. Leonard Martin's Battery F, 5th United States Artillery.[24]

"Bully" Brooks' division, meanwhile, remained in position near the bridgehead. Many of his men had tangled in early-morning skirmishes with Confederates. Joseph Bartlett's brigade, for instance, had moved out across the Bowling Green Road and confronted Smith and Hoke's Confederate brigades. Brooks' artillery support also took part in the exchange. Captain James Rigby's Battery A Maryland Light Artillery (Union) traded shots with a Rebel battery of 12-pound howitzers, which Rigby's men succeeded in driving off—only to find themselves facing their replacements: two 20-pounder Parrott guns. As the heavier guns rolled on line, the smaller howitzers they were replacing showed themselves again, too. At 1,200 yards, though, the concentrated fire from Rigby's guns, as well as the guns of Battery A, 1st Massachusetts Light Artillery and Battery A, 1st New Jersey Light Artillery, managed to silence them.[25]

Bartlett now deployed his men in line of battle roughly along the road, while Col. Henry W. Brown's all-New Jersey brigade extended Bartlett's line near and along the road to the south. Closer to the bridges were deployed the men of David Russell's brigade.

By 10:15 a.m., preparations all along the line were complete. The Federal artillery opened fire. "The siege guns posted on Stafford Heights fired repeatedly on the enemy's works doing good execution," wrote a New Yorker.[26] Surgeon Edwin Buckman said, "These shots come with a crushing force and shock nearly equal to the sharp thunder following close the flash of lightning—every shot being almost exciting enough to make us

---

23 *Advertiser & Register* (Mobile, AL), May 22, 1863.

24 *OR* 25, pt. 1, 611-614.

25 *OR* 25, pt. 1, 596. Rigby reported that he fired 450 shells from this position: 200 Schenkl percussion shells and 250 Schenkl combination shrapnel.

26 Judd, *The Story of the Thirty-Third N. Y. S.*, 294.

jump to our feet."[27] One observer reported that a shell "exploded a rebel caisson at the redoubt near the stonewall, and killed ten horses. After blowing up the caisson it struck two directly behind, and hurled eight others down the steep precipice in the rear into the yawning chasm beneath."[28]

"The firing from artillery is continual," complained one member of Parker's Battery, posted near the southern end of the heights. "If a man raises his head they send a shell at him. A shot passed through the embrasure and the dirt and gravel struck Lt. Brown in the face. He after washing his face in the sponge bucket found that he was not much hurt, but appeared [as] if he was suffering from small pox."[29]

Near 11:00 a.m. Spear and his men of the northern flanking party stepped off from Princess Anne Street, where they unslung their packs to lighten their loads during the charge. They exited the city, passing the Rhode Island and Massachusetts men in the cemetery, and descended down William Street. At the base of the cemetery the ground leveled out, and the column crossed over the bridge of the millrace. Confederate artillery rained on them. They pushed on.

On the far side of the millrace, Williams Street began its steep ascent up Willis Hill. The column pushed upward and onward as the artillery along the crest of the heights kept up a constant fire, aided by small-arms fire from the leftward companies of the 21st Mississippi. As the Federals neared a tannery on the left side of the road, Spear was struck in the head by a shell and killed instantly. His leaderless column wavered, then ground to a halt, the sergeants all but forgetting Spear's order for them to push onward no matter what.

Along Hanover Street, the men of the attacking column stepped off about the same time as their counterparts on William Street. "Col. Johns dismounted; and we moved forward in the charge, our guns uncapped, the order being given to depend on the bayonet alone," wrote a member of the 7th Massachusetts. "[J]ust as we got in motion, the rebel batteries all along

27 Buckman to Mrs. E. D. Buckman, May 9, 1863, in the Fredericksburg and Spotsylvania National Military Park bound manuscript collection, vol. 399.

28 Judd, *The Story of the Thirty-Third N. Y. S.*, 294-295.

29 Sgt. Edward S. Duffy, Diary, May 3, 1863, in the Fredericksburg and Spotsylvania National Military Park bound manuscript collection, vol. 358.

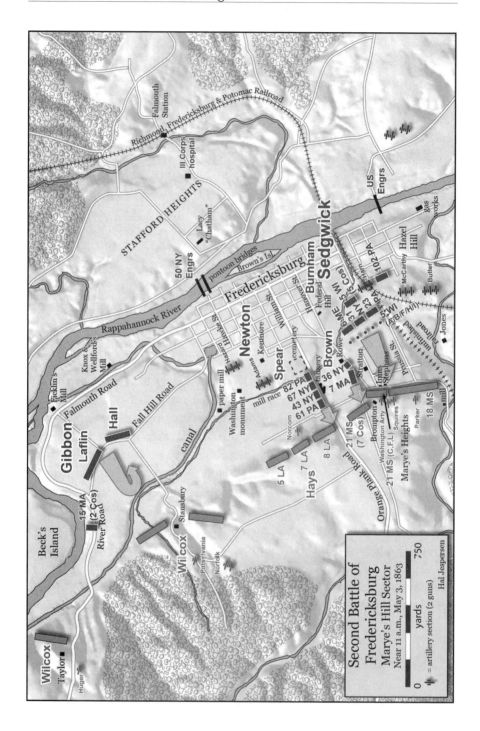

Second Battle of
Fredericksburg
Marye's Hill Sector
Near 11 a.m, May 3, 1863

0   yards   750

= artillery section (2 guns)

Hal Jespersen

the heights opened with shell, and one of the projectiles struck the major [Elihu Faxon] of the 36th New York . . . mortally wounding him, and also disabled some five or six of the men."[30]

The firing picked up as the advance continued. "Though at its exit from the town, this road [Hanover Street] is covered by a few houses, it is fairly under fire all the way," a Federal officer recalled, "and at the ascent of the hill it is a mere gulch, broken and stony, and an awful place for men to be packed in under a plunging fire of grape and canister in addition to musketry fire."[31]

A dip in the road kept the attackers sheltered from much of the small-arms fire that came from the Sunken Road—rifle fire that came from the right-end companies of Humphreys' 21st Mississippi atop the heights and the left-end companies of the 21st Mississippians detached in the road. However, artillery fire poured down as well from Capt. Merritt Miller's 3rd Company of the Washington Artillery.

The Yankees drove hard and fast for the Confederate line. Barksdale asked Pendleton to send more artillery support to aid Griffin's men in the road. None was forthcoming—but more Federals were. When they came out of the swale, they "seemed to rise out of the earth," Humphreys said, "and rushed forward with demonic shouts and yells."[32]

The historian of the 7th Massachusetts described what happened next:

> The column moved in mass by fours at common time, shell and canister cutting through it until we had got within a hundred feet of the stone wall, when Barksdale's brigade of Mississippians poured in a terrific volley from right and left, and checked us for about five minutes. The road or gulch was filled with the dead, wounded, and dying. Col. Johns was down, having been twice severely wounded. . . . [M]ore than fifty men of the leading company. . . were killed and wounded.[33]

In the melee, the Federals began to break. Shouts to retreat mixed with cries to go forward. "[W]e shant get this close again!" someone cried.

30 Hutchinson, *History of the Seventh Massachusetts*, 124-127.

31 *New York Herald*, May 5, 1863.

32 Sears, *Chancellorsville*, 353.

33 Ibid.

But the Hanover Street column was stopped cold as well. Both "lances" were leaderless. Desperately the Yankees sent up a white flag and called for a truce. Confederates all along the line cheered and shouted taunts.

One of Gibbon's men, from where he was pinned down north of the city, watched the carnage that stopped the assaults cold. He expressed the despair of the army: "[W]e gave up hope."[34]

34 Ibid.

Chapter Twelve

Taking the Gibraltar of the South:

The Fall of Marye's Heights

The 6th Maine waited for its turn to head into the fight, Capt. Sewell Gray took time to jot a few more lines in his diary—words that would turn out to be his last: "At 11 we are momentarily expecting the order to storm. God strengthen our arms that we may be victorious. If we fall God strengthen the bereaved."[1]

The order came moments later from the Light Division's commander, Col. Hiram Burnham. As his men lay at the edge of the city, Burnham rode up on horseback and announced, "Boys, I have got a government contract. . . . One thousand Rebels, potted and salted, and got to have 'em in less than five minutes. Forward guide center!"[2]

Colonel Thomas Allen of the 5th Wisconsin, leading the charge, stepped to the front of his men, also looking to inspire confidence. "Perhaps you think you cannot take them; I know you can," he told his men. "When the signal forward is given, you will start at the double quick.

---

1   Mackowski and White, "From Foxcroft to Fredericksburg," 141.

2   Ibid.

You will not fire a gun and you will not stop until you get the order to halt. You will never get that order."[3]

Across the field went the 5th Wisconsin; 10 paces behind followed the 6th Maine, 31st New York, and 23rd Pennsylvania. "We all came to our feet with a tiger," wrote Cpl. Benjamin Thaxter of the 6th Maine.[4] "[N]ow a clear and distinct voice was heard above the roar of battle: 'Forward-March!'" remembered a soldier in the 5th Wisconsin. The soldier went on to say, "The boys arose and ran like deer over the plain, in search of their prey."[5]

Starting on the edge of town, the Light Division had a hundred more yards of distance to cover than the men in either Spear's or Johns' columns. Having to attack across open, pockmarked terrain slowed them too, compared to the smoother approaches the columns had on William and Hanover streets. As a result, when the men—most likely in Johns' column—called for a truce to tend to their wounded, and Col. Thomas Griffin of the 18th Mississippi granted it, the defense along the northern end of the Sunken Road slackened at precisely the time the Light Division poured forward.[6] Colonel Humphreys of the 21st Mississippi therefore thought that the flag of truce had been a "Yankee trick."[7]

In his after-action reports, Early glossed over the matter of the flag of truce, "which was received by [Griffin] improperly." The flag had "barely returned before heavy columns were advanced against the positions. . . . "[8] Barksdale, on the other hand, gave the truce more import:

> Upon the pretext of taking care of their wounded, the enemy asked a flag of truce after the second assault [Johns' column] on Marye's Hill, which was granted by Colonel Griffin, and thus the weakness of our force at

---

3   Trask, *Fire Within*, 172.

4   Benjamin Thaxter, Diary, May 3, 1863, in the Fredericksburg and Spotsylvania National Military Park bound manuscript collection, vol. 69.

5   Letter from soldier in 5th Wisconsin to the *Wisconsin Daily Patriot*, May 20, 1863, in the Fredericksburg and Spotsylvania National Military Park bound manuscript collection, vol. 149.

6   Bigelow, *The Campaign of Chancellorsville*, 384-387.

7   Humphreys, *Recollections of Fredericksburg*.

8   *OR* 25, pt. 1, 842-843.

that point was discovered. It is proper to say that Colonel Griffin, who is a brave and gallant officer, granted this flag of truce without consulting me.[9]

Read in the context of Early's dispatch and other accounts of the battle, it seems unlikely that the Federals had time to discover the weakness of the Confederate position behind the stone wall, somehow communicate that back to Sedgwick, and then get word up to Burnham. Consider that the Light Division started its attack at virtually the same time as the others, and the usefulness of such intelligence becomes even less plausible.

The timing of the flag of truce is also up in the air. One Confederate in the 18th Mississippi claimed that the "cessation of hostilities [was] for an hour or so. . . . "[10] The flag he refers to came about between the second and third assault, while others claim the flag of truce came between the first and second assaults. Apparently enough time elapsed that officers had a chance to order men "to keep down behind our wall and out of sight."[11]

Another Confederate remembered the flag as being "illustrative of Yankee cunning and duplicity": "The bearer of the flag was, as we were subsequently informed, a officer of high rank in the disguise of a subaltern—a shrewd, Keen, observant fellow who made his eyes do their full duty during their interview."[12]

The final nail comes from Barksdale himself. The continuation of his report reads like a Lost Cause paean:

It will thus be seen that Marye's Hill was defended by but one small regiment, three companies, and four pieces of artillery. A more heroic struggle was never made by a mere handful of men against overwhelming odds. According to the enemy's own accounts, many of this noble little

9 Ibid., 840.

10 C. E. Holmes, "Confederate Boy's Recollection of War," *National Tribune*, in the Fredericksburg and Spotsylvania National Military Park bound manuscript collection, vol. 455.

11 Ibid.

12 Jones, *The Civil War Memoirs of Captain William J. Seymour*, 52.

Brigadier General William Barksdale.

Library of Congress

band resisted to the death with clubbed guns even after his vast hordes swept over and around the walls.[13]

Barksdale's case was better served by making more of the flag of truce than it deserved. That way, he could claim that his men were defeated not because they were not ready but because of Federal perfidy.[14]

In any event, because of the pause offered by the flag of truce, Griffin's men in the Sunken Road were startled to see the Light Division sweeping across the plain. "We all allowed that the whole Army of the Potomac were coming, you'uns kept up such a wicked yelling," one Confederate later recalled.[15]

Uphill the Federals charged, with muskets uncapped, under fire from artillerists at the top of the heights and the two howitzers in the Sunken Road. Confederate infantry opened up as well. The Light Division faced opposition of a different sort, too: partially exposed remains of dead soldiers from the previous December's attacks, uncovered by winter weather, reached dead limbs up from the earth, desiccated lips pulled back from teeth in ghastly expressions.[16]

"Across the 'slaughter pen' we went with a terrific yell," wrote Adj. Charles A. Clark of the 6th Maine.[17] "Artillery and musketry poured a fire upon us which seemed to make the whole atmosphere hot and lurid. Men fell on every hand," Cpl. Wainwright Cushing said:

[G]rape-shot and shrapnel and bullets tore through our ranks, while officers and men were dropping on every hand. It was a race with death, but with all this terrible tension we were under we kept our formation, the lines closing up as they were thinned by the firing. A little in front of the first rifle-pit was a board fence and it seemed to me that bullets were splintering every square foot of it as we came near. How anyone should

13 Ibid.

14 *OR* 25, pt. 1, 842-843, 844, 845-847.

15 Charles A. Clark, "Campaigning with the Sixth Maine," in Iowa, Military Order of the Loyal Legions of the United States, *Sketches and Incidents* (Des Moines, IA, 1897), 47.

16 Alfred Randolph to S. G. Randolph, April 20, 1864, in the Fredericksburg and Spotsylvania National Military Park bound manuscript collection, vol. 387.

17 Gray, Diary, 15.

escape being struck in the hail of lead seemed to me a wonder. We went over the fence, under it, and through it.[18]

Private C. E. Holmes of the 18th Mississippi, stationed in the Sunken Road, later said his rifle—"on account of the gun having been fired so often"—became hot to the touch. "My ramrod stuck in the barrel," he said. "I had driven it against this stone fence in order to get the bullet down, but I could not remove my ramrod. The Yankees were very thick, about 1,000 within 20 feet of where I stood. . . . I had no time to lose, so I fired into them ramrod and all. . . . "[19]

Burnham, urging the Federal assault forward, was unhorsed by the burst of an artillery shell, leaving him with a slight head wound—but onward surged his men, past the fairgrounds, over the slight swale that had offered protection for so many Federals back in December, and around the few homes that still dotted the landscape. The withering fire began to take its toll on them, and although the Mainers and Wisconsinites pressed onward, the New Yorkers and Pennsylvanians sought cover—or, "ran like very sheep" in the less-charitable assessment of a member of the 5th Wisconsin. He accused the New Yorkers, charged with protecting their left flank, with running in disorder and throwing themselves on the ground as if dead.[20]

As Burnham's men closed on the stone wall, a group of men from the 7th Massachusetts, who had sought refuge from the enemy fire along Hanover Street, peered through a small wooden fence. From their vantage point near the Sarah Sisson Store, the Bay Staters saw how thin Griffin's line actually was. The 7th's second in command, Lt. Col. Franklin P. Harlow, quickly grasped the situation. Fighting off pain from a gut wound, he tried to rally his men. "Soon out of the confusion rings the

18 Wainwright Cushing, "Description of the Ensuing Charge," vol. 3 of *War Papers: Read Before the Commandery of the State of Maine, Military Order of the Loyal Legions of the United States* (Portland, ME, 1908), 46.

19 C. E. Holmes, "Confederate Boy's Recollection of War," *National Tribune*, in the Fredericksburg and Spotsylvania National Military Park bound manuscript collection, vol. 455

20 James S. Anderson to Parents, May 25, 1863, in the Fredericksburg and Spotsylvania National Military Park bound manuscript collection (no bound volume).

clarion shout of Lt. Col. Harlow 'Forward, forward boys!" a soldier recalled.[21]

"Now commenced an exciting race between the gallant men of the 6th Maine, 5th Wisconsin, and our regiment [the 31st NY] to see which should get their colors in first," wrote a regimental drummer boy.[22]

Harlow's men surged forward. "[T]he old Seventh struggled through and over the stone wall, bleeding at every step," wrote the Massachusetts soldier. "Turning to the right, we rushed over the rebel redoubt, capturing two pieces of artillery which had occupied the same position the previous December."[23]

Along William Street, the flagging assault column of the dead Colonel Spear rallied as well, thanks to the leadership of Col. Alexander Shaler. The column lurched forward and made its way up the road and heights. As the mixed column crested the hill, the men made their way north, clearing the redoubts along the heights (today part of the campus of the University of Mary Washington).

When Spears had led the initial assault, the Confederate guns along the heights, under Lieutenant Norcom, were busily blasting away at Gibbon's men, but they quickly turned their guns on the assault column, creating an artillery crossfire. Now, with Shaler reviving the assault, the Louisianans were in a bad position: because of the rolling terrain of the hill and the fortifications, including Landry's redoubt, the artillerists were taken in the flank. Norcom's men escaped capture by mere moments, some of them cutting the artillery horses from the limber chests and riding them to safety.[24] Norcom's two howitzers, left behind, fell to the Union swarm. For his actions, Alexander Shaler was later awarded the Medal of Honor.

But it was the lead regiments of Burnham's Light Division that broke the line first, swarming past the Innis and Stephens houses and up and over

---

21 Hutchinson, *History of the Seventh Massachusetts*, 125-127.

22 John Ahern, newspaper article, "Local Affairs," in the Fredericksburg and Spotsylvania National Military Park bound manuscript collection, vol. 143.

23 Hutchinson, *History of the Seventh Massachusetts*, 126.

24 Noel G. Harrison, *A Walking Tour of Civil War Sites on the North (Main) Campus of Mary Washington College*, in the Fredericksburg and Spotsylvania National Military Park bound manuscript collection, vol. 173. This brochure was written in the 1980s in draft version only.

the stone wall, into the Sunken Road. "There was a hand-to-hand conflict at this point of short duration, and the enemy was routed," recalled Clark. "It is not true that bayonets were never crossed during the war, they were used at the stone wall by our men, and after the battle it was found by actual account that forty of the rebels had been bayoneted here." Clubbed muskets were also used freely. One attacker "bayoneted two adversaries, and then brained a third with the butt of his musket."[25] The badgers from Wisconsin and woodsmen from Maine were unleashing all the pent-up rage that had festered in the Army of the Potomac since December over Fredericksburg and Marye's Heights.

A member of the 5th Wisconsin described the rush for the wall:

> Maddened at the loss of many a dear friend, who had been on the battle-field since the commencement of the rebellion, our boys rushed on. . . . Far in advance of the line of skirmishers, Col. Allen could be seen, with his sword in one hand, and his revolver in the other, leading the way for his men. The wall was reached and Colonel Allen was the first to mount the parapet. He had a number of narrow escapes, his clothing being riddled by bullets.[26]

"When the works were fairly won, a rebel fired at one of our men but his cap snapped," wrote Capt. Evan R. Jones of the 5th Wisconsin, "whereupon the Badger . . . coolly loaded his musket and deliberately shot his enemy." Some of the soldier's fellow privates objected to what they considered murder. "His ready reply was, 'He would have shot me if his darned old cap had been good for anything.'"[27]

As the hand-to-hand carnage mounted, Colonel Griffin of the 18th Mississippi sought to end it. From his position just south of the Stephens House, the colonel threw his arms in the air and bellowed, "Don't murder

25 Mundy, *No Rich Men's Sons*, 116-117.

26 Letter from soldier in the 5th Wisconsin to the *Wisconsin Daily Patriot*, May 20, 1863, in the Fredericksburg and Spotsylvania National Military Park bound manuscript collection, vol. 149.

27 Captain Evan R. Jones, *Personal Recollections of the American War*, in the Fredericksburg and Spotsylvania National Military Park bound manuscript collection, vol. 353, 12.

In the hours following the battle, photographer Andrew Russell captured
one of the most iconic images from the war: the dead of the
18th Mississippi lining the Sunken Road.

Library of Congress

my men, I will surrender!"[28] Griffin and a handful of men surrendered, but
others scrambled up the heights in search of safety behind the guns of the
Washington Artillery.

From below, meanwhile, more Federals approached the road. The
23rd Pennsylvania approached the wall to the left of the 6th Maine. The
Pennsylvanians had not fared as well in the charge because of flanking fire
from the south end of Willis Hill and, for a time, from Howison Hill.
Canister poured among the men, stopping them cold. "The rebs opened a
severe fire as they neared the stone wall and one of the men wounded was
Charley Smallwood of Co. G.," recalled the regimental historian. "To get
out of range of fire, he crawled over to a house that stood on the edge of the

28 C. E. Holmes, "Confederate Boy's Recollection of War," *National Tribune*, in the
Fredericksburg and Spotsylvania National Military Park bound manuscript collection,
vol. 455.

road, it being occupied by Confederate sharpshooters, he was taken prisoner and turned over to the trenches in the Sunken Road. . . . Here he was left until . . . our line swept into the Sunken Road, the Johnnies broke and he found he was among his own people."[29]

Using the railroad cut on the south end of the city, a company of the 102nd Pennsylvania made its way to the southern end of the Sunken Road and fired into the flank of Griffin's men.[30] The road was now an untenable position for the Confederates. The howitzers in the road had been overrun, and the artillery on top of the heights was now of no use because the guns could not be depressed far enough to hit anything; even if the artillerists could depress their pieces, they would hit their own men if they fired, intermingled as they were with the swarming Federals.

As it was, those artillerists were soon in for an unpleasant surprise of their own. Once the 5th Wisconsin and 6th Maine had cleared the road of Confederates, they surged toward a saddle in the heights that separated Brompton to the north from the Willis Cemetery to the south. When the Federals reached the top, they were directly in the rear of Confederate gunners who were preoccupied by other Federals running at them straight up the hill. Recalled one artillerist:

> About 10 the Yanks of Sedgwick's Corps suddenly charged our position. We poured canister into them from our works & drove them back in great confusion when much to our astonishment we were fired on in the rear by the 6th Maine who had run over the infantry on our left in front of the Marye's House came on our rear while we were busy with those in our front & took us at our position. Our last gun was fired when 6 or 8 yanks were in the entrance. It blew them to atoms. They also took Lt. Brown with 2 guns of Parker's Battery & 1 gun of the 3rd, Capt. Miller succeeded in getting off 1 gun & the limber of the other gun.[31]

---

29 Survivors Association, *History of the Twenty Third Pennsylvania Volunteer Infantry Birney's Zouaves: Three Months and Three Years Service in the Civil War 1861-1865* (Philadelphia, PA, 1903-1904), 142.

30 OR 25, pt. 1, 622.

31 John Coski, "In the Field and on the Town with the Washington Artillery," David A. Woodbury, ed., in *Treasures from the Archives: Select Holdings From the Museum of the Confederacy* (Campbell, CA, 1996), 117.

Scars of battle are still evident even today on the walls of the
Willis Cemetery atop Marye's Heights.

Kristopher D. White

Gunners took refuge behind the brick wall of the Willis Cemetery, along with survivors from the 21st and 18th Mississippi who escaped the carnage in the road. Private C. E. Holmes, one of those Mississippians, sped past the Washington Artillery as their pieces fell to the Yankee horde. Atop the heights he ran into his friend, Tommy Thompson, and the pair ducked into a nearby ice house on the Marye property. "We saw it was covered with cornstalks, fodder, etc. . . . and thought it a good place to hide," he recalled:

> I said 'Jump in.' He said 'No! You jump in first and I will follow.' About that time the Yankees, who were advancing in column, turned loose and their bullets whistled thru the top of the ice house . . . so I jumped into an ice house full of water. I did not want to drown like a rat in a barrel, so I made an effort to get out. . . . I succeeded in drawing myself up to the door, and as my head came to the top, saw a half dozen or more Yankees with their guns leveled on me.[32]

There was little the Confederates could do to stem the tide. Wilcox, for instance, attempted to send a regiment, the 10th Alabama, from Taylor's Hill, but it was unable to reach the front before the heights fell. Colonel Humphreys, meanwhile, attempted to change his regiment's front so that instead of facing the city it faced southward along Marye's Heights, in the hope of sweeping fire along the crest of the heights toward Brompton. However, as soon as Humphreys' men pulled out of their earthworks they received enfilading fire from Adams' Battery, which had been sparring with Norcom's section of the Washington Artillery earlier in the day. Humphreys was forced to pull off the heights and find another way to assist—or to at least save his regiment to fight another day.[33]

Atop Willis Hill, the Confederates tried to make a quick getaway with their pieces, and one unit even took the body of a fallen officer. "Lieut. Frederick Habersham had been killed at his section," recalled one gunner. "His comrades determined to have his body, and lashed it to the trail of a

---

32 C. E. Holmes, "Confederate Boy's Recollection of War," *National Tribune*, in the Fredericksburg and Spotsylvania National Military Park bound manuscript collection, vol. 455.

33 Humphreys, *Recollections of Fredericksburg*, n.p.

gun, and there it hung, firmly bound, a sight not often witnessed, while the battery, already late in retiring, was at a gallop in escape from the pursuing enemy. It was accomplished handsomely, and the brave fellow received his interment by the hands of loving wife and friends at his home in Savannah."[34]

Not all batteries were so lucky. "Without firing a shot, our line pushed ahead with wild and indescribable frenzy, swarmed over the last and strongest redoubts and fortifications on the summit, and captured 7 guns of the famous Washington Artillery and numerous prisoners," remembered Clark.[35]

Clark's friend, Capt. Sewell Gray of Company A, did not fare so well. Coming over the stone wall by the Innis house, Gray took a blast of canister to the chest. He died instantly. "If we fall, God strengthen the bereaved," he had written moments before the assault started. He left behind his new bride, Dicea, whom he had married less than two months earlier at Easter.

* * *

The situation for the Confederates quickly went from bad to worse. Howe's assault, the southernmost prong of Sedgwick's attack, came across the plain toward Willis and Telegraph hills. "On the first Sabbath in May, God called upon this regiment to ascend Marye's Heights and worship him, not with psalm and thanksgiving, but with the musket," recalled a member of the 77th New York.[36]

"The lines started over the plain at double quick in splendid style, the rebels opening at the same time all their batteries on the heights, pouring a terrible fire on the advancing lines," said Col. Lewis Grant, "but on they went, driving the rebels before them."[37]

---

34 G. Moxley Sorrel, *Recollections of a Confederate Staff Officer* (New York, NY, 1905), 158.

35 Gray, Diary, n.d., 48.

36 Robert F. Morrow, Jr., *77th New York Volunteers: "Sojering" in the VI Corps* (Shippensburg, PA, 2004), 76.

37 *OR* 25, pt. 1, 602-603.

Captain Sewell Gray, Company A, 6th Maine Infantry.

Lawrence Hjalmarson

"All at once our brigade was ordered up and we started on a double-quick on a charge to take the forts and batteries that we could not take before," wrote Henry Taylor of the 21st New Jersey.[38] The Garden Staters, along with the 7th Maine, the 33rd New York, and half of the 77th New York, swung to the north, putting them in position to hit Willis Hill

38 Henry Taylor, Diary, May 3, 1863, in the Fredericksburg and Spotsylvania National Military Park bound manuscript collection, vol. 73.

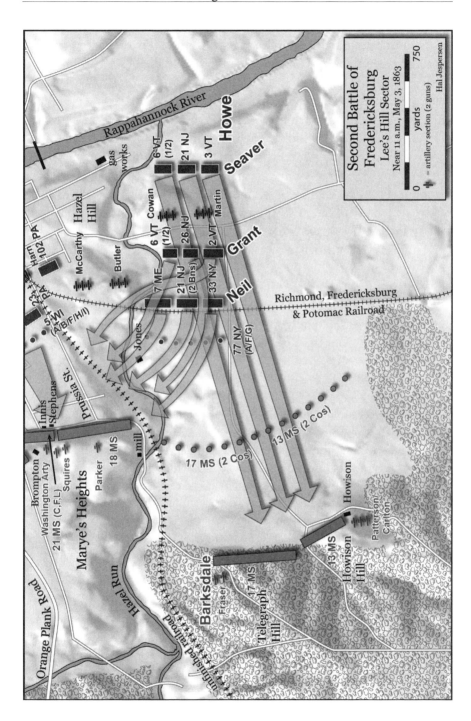

Second Battle of
Fredericksburg
Lee's Hill Sector
Near 11 a.m, May 3, 1863

0   yards   750

= artillery section (2 guns)

Hal Jespersen

on its southern flank. "Death-dealing shells plow our ranks, but still the advancing columns press on ward," wrote one soldier.[39]

Deployed as skirmishers, the 77th New York led the way across the plain below the heights—which subjected them to converging and plunging artillery fire from Willis, Howison, and Telegraph hills.[40] Lieutenant Colonel Windsor French did his best to move his men in the open, while attempting to conceal their true destination. French had his skirmish line move at common time, then quick time, then back to common, all the while moving his men on the oblique from right to left.[41] The right half of French's skirmish line then turned toward Willis Hill, leading the way for approximately half of the division.

Thomas Neill's first line of troops crossed Hazel Run, as did the bulk of Lewis Grant's second wave.[42] Next the line reached an unfinished railroad cut that ran into the city from the west. As the line of blue dove in, Confederates on the left, most likely men of the 18th Mississippi pulling out of the Sunken Road, fired down the length of the cut, felling a number of men from the 77th and 33rd New York. Still the line pushed on.[43] Wrote one New Yorker with the 33rd:

Quickly descending to the ravine at the left, they double-quick through the underbrush and obstructions of every description, cheered on and led forward by the Colonel, Lt. Col, Major, and Adjutant. The rebel gunners see them coming through the thicket and depressing their guns, rain down a tempest of canister. . . . The old flag, which waved in triumph at Golden's Farm, Williamsburg, and Antietam, goes down. A second color-bearer seizes the banner and raises it on high, but a bullet quickly lays him low. Another grasps the standard, until six have been shot down, when Sgt. Vandecar rushed forward, hoists the tattered banner on his musket, and the regiment presses forward. As they emerge from the woods to the opening, they are saluted with a rapid fire from the rebel

39 Howard Coffin, *Full Duty: Vermonters in the Civil War* (Woodstock, VT, 1993), 171.

40 Morrow, *77th New York Volunteers*, 77-78. By this point the entire 77th New York was deployed as skirmishers, covering the entirety of the massed division front.

41 Morrow, *77th New York Volunteers*, 77-78.

42 *OR* 25, pt. 1, 602.

43 Morrow, *77th New York Volunteers*, 77-78.

Postwar image of Hazel Run.

Fredericksburg and Spotsylvania National Military Park

infantry supports, but unmindful of the deluge of iron hail, they push on, clamber up . . . sweep over the parapet, and capture a thirty-two pounder at a bound.[44]

But even as the 33rd New York crested the top of Marye's Heights, the men were "met by a galling fire from two lines of battle which the enemy formed within one hundred yards of us," one of their lieutenants wrote. "[W]e met with the strongest kind of reception, in the shape of bullets, that this regiment has had accorded to them during the past two years. It was a perfect storm of the 'leaden messengers of death.'"[45] The 21st New

---

44 Judd, *The Story of the Thirty-Third N. Y. S.*, 297.

45 L. C. Mix, Rochester, *Rochester (NY) Daily Union and Advertiser*, May 13, 1863, in the Fredericksburg and Spotsylvania National Military Park bound manuscript collection, vol. 216.

Jersey met a similar reception: "[A]s we went up over the hill they did just pour it into us."[46]

However, numbers and the resulting momentum were on the Northern side. "At them went our boys, loading and firing as fast as they could," a captain with the 33rd New York said. "A storm of bullets swept the hill, thinning our ranks terribly, but our brave boys stood it like heroes, and many a rebel bit the dust."[47] In less than 30 minutes, said the Jerseyman from the 21st, Henry Taylor, "we had gained the top of the hill capturing one brass piece meant for our benefit. . . . "[48]

Since the Light Division was already mopping up the last of the resistance, the 33rd and the 21st turned about and made their way for Barksdale's command post on Telegraph Hill instead. "Instead of holding the heights which we had ought to have done, we were pushed on after them to a piece of woods where the dead were covering the ground," wrote Taylor. "It was a hard day and a bloody one. The old troops that have been out since the beginning of the war said it was the hardest fight that they ever saw."[49]

Grant's brigade, meanwhile, was also making its way toward Telegraph Hill. Far in front of Grant's line was the left half of the 77th New York's skirmish line. "Over the plain we went under a heavy fire of musketry, grape, and canister & shell," recalled Capt. Orrin Rugg. "I could see them tear the ground all around me and could hear the grape & canister whizzing all around me."[50] According to one man in the 2nd Vermont, "The Rebels opened on us from every piece they had, from a 24 pounder to a pocket pistol."[51] Grant's Vermonters continued onward, but his single regiment of Garden State troops, the 26th New Jersey, buckled

---

46 Henry Taylor, Diary, May 3, 1863, in the Fredericksburg and Spotsylvania National Military Park bound volume collection, vol. 73.

47 H. J. Gifford to W. Seward, Esq., May 7, 1863, New York State Military Museum and Veterans Research Center http:// dmna.ny.gov/ historic/reghist/ civil/infantry/ 33rdInf/33rdInfCWN.htm (accessed June 27, 2012).

48 Taylor, Diary, n.d.

49 Ibid.

50 Orrin Rugg to Parents, May 11, 1863, in the Fredericksburg and Spotsylvania National Military Park bound manuscript collection, vol. 318.

51 Howard Coffin, *Full Duty*, 172.

under the pressure—with their colonel, Andrew J. Morrison, leading the skedaddle. "[W]hen about half way across the large field and near to some hay and tobacco barns the Jersey boys: 'which by the way were under a pretty lively cannonading from the rebels' broke and ran for the barn," wrote Hiram H. Tilley of the 2nd Vermont. "[T]his left the fighting for our regiment. [W]e charged across the open field to the foot of the Heights where we had to cross 'as best we could' a wide ditch partly full of muddy water after which 'under a heavy fire of muskets' we charged up the Heights. . . . "[52]

The collapse of the 26th New Jersey created a problem for Grant because it cut off the 2nd Vermont, positioned on their left. "By the right flank," the quick-thinking Grant barked, and his Green Mountain Boys, conditioned by drill, complied; the order quickly shifted the 2nd Vermont from a battle line to a column of fours. As the Vermonters made their way past the disarrayed New Jerseyans, they redeployed and made for the north end of Telegraph Hill, rather than the south end of Willis Hill as their comrades had.

Meanwhile, Grant left one of his officers, Lt. Frank Butterfield, to assist the 26th's second in command, Lt. Col. Edward Martindale, in rallying the men from the Garden State. "A shell exploded beneath the Lieutenant Colonel's horse, nearly lifting him from his saddle," recalled Sgt. Maj. Amos J. Cummings, "but his only reply was 'Forward, men—act like Jerseymen!'"[53] Some of the men, "braver than the rest," joined in and "fought like heroes," a Vermonter later said.[54]

Most of Howe's first two lines crested Willis Hill nearly simultaneously, perhaps five minutes behind the men of the Light Division. It was a heroic feat for the men of the 2nd Division, forced as they were to climb the steepest part of the precipice. On the hillcrest, Parker's battery kept things hot for the advancing Federals, too. "I must say that their artillery men was gritty," one Federal later admitted. "They

---

52 Hiram H. Tilley to Father and Mother, May 6, 1863, in the Fredericksburg and Spotsylvania National Military Park bound manuscript collection, vol. 323.

53 Alan A. Siegel, *For the Glory of the Union: Myth, Reality, and the Media in Civil War New Jersey* (Madison, NJ, 1984), 165.

54 Emil Rosenblatt, *Anti-Rebel: The Civil War Letters of Wilbur Fisk* (Croton-on-Hudson, NY, 1983), 79.

did not abandon their guns until our men had shot nearly all of them down. . . . "[55]

As the men of the 77th New York made their way up the heights, they overtook many of the retreating men of the 18th Mississippi, who had been doing what they could to work their way around the base of Willis Hill. After the 77th's skirmishing with the Mississippians earlier in the day, they found the chance to revenge themselves ripe: the right wing of the 77th managed to capture 50 of the Mississippians, including their lieutenant colonel, William Luse, plus two captains, and Cpl. Michael Lamey came away with the 18th's regimental colors.[56] Within minutes, the New Yorkers added one mountain howitzer, one Napoleon, and two limber chests to their spoils of war.[57] "Colonel French and General Neill riding up the hill to see who would reach the cannon first; and I see the flash of Colonel French's sword as he tapped the cannon first," a New Yorker recalled. Neill told French to "write your name on it! You have won it! It is yours!"[58] Accolades for the 77th abounded: "Noble Seventy-Seventh, you have covered yourself with glory!" Howe told them.[59]

The New Yorkers took time to realign. They rallied on the colors and made the final push up over the heights, closely followed by the men of the 7th Maine and 33rd New York. Elements of the 21st New Jersey and half of the 6th Vermont appeared within moments. "Up now, my brave boys and give it to them," Grant shouted, and the line surged forward.[60]

"[O]nward and upward over one after another of the enemy's works Fredericksburg is ours," wrote a member of the 6th Vermont.[61] Other units poured onto the heights as well. "[W]e had to double-quick clear

55 William Stowe to Parents, May 10, 1863, in the Fredericksburg and Spotsylvania National Military Park bound volume collection, vol. 47.

56 *OR* 25, pt. 1, 611; Morrow, *77th New York Volunteers*, 79.

57 *OR* 25, pt. 1, 610.

58 Morrow, *77th New York Volunteers*, 79-80.

59 Edward H. Fuller, *Battles of the Seventy-Seventh New York State Volunteers, Third Brigade, Sixth Corps, Second Division. Mustered in, November 23, 1861. Mustered out, June 27, 1865. By one of the boys* (Gloversville, NY, 1901), 120.

60 Rosenblatt, *Anti-Rebel*, 79.

61 Coffin, *Full Duty*, 172.

round to the place where the assaulting column had got up," wrote Capt. Henry Abbott of the 20th Massachusetts, one of the units that had been pinned down in Gibbon's failed assault, "and the double-quick up the heights, & then deploying, sweep across the plateau, our skirmishers driving the rebels like sheep."[62]

As the first two waves of Howe's division helped mop up the resistance on Willis Hill, Howe's third column, under Colonel Seaver, deviated from course and made a beeline for Telegraph Hill. Any success on Willis Hill would be short-lived if Confederates could still use the artillery platform on Telegraph Hill to rain fire down on the victorious Federals.

Seaver's men pushed across the muddy plain with bayonets fixed. Confederate gunners—artillerists under Patterson, Fraser, and Carlton—met them with barrels of shot and shell, while the men of the thin line of Confederate infantry holding the earthworks steeled themselves for the pending clash. In front, Company B of the 13th Mississippi, the Wayne Rifles, were out on the skirmish line and were forced to withdraw as quickly as possible, with the Federals only yards behind them.[63] One Confederate remembered that "shell, grape and bullet [were] sweeping around us."[64] The skirmishers dove into the trenches—with the 3rd Vermont hot behind them, then the 4th Vermont, then the 21st New Jersey.

After extracting themselves from the traffic jam on the plain, the 2nd Vermont caught up with the portion of the 77th New York that had made its way toward Telegraph Hill. The two units seized a rifle pit at the northern base of Telegraph Hill, with two companies of the Vermonters mixing in with the skirmish line of the five New York companies. The two units then began to work their way to the top.[65] "[U]p the hill we

---

62 Scott, *Fallen Leaves*, 174.

63 Crute, *Lee's Intrepid Army*, 74-75.

64 *Advertiser & Register* (Mobile, AL), May 22, 1863, in Fredericksburg and Spotsylvania bound manuscript collection, vol. 63.

65 G. G. Benedict, *Vermont in the Civil War. A History of the Part Taken by the Vermont Soldiers and Sailors in the War for the Union, 1861-5*, 2 vols. (Burlington, VT, 1886), vol. 1, 365-366.

went together yelling like mad men and all the time a sharp fire going on, the rebs retreating as we advanced," one man later recalled.[66]

Telegraph Hill is steep on the south, north, and east sides, making the avenues of advance limited for an attacker. "At the right there was a deep ravine . . . filled with brush and felled trees," wrote Wilbur Fisk of the 2nd Vermont. "The rebs had set fire to the brush on top of the hill, and the hot, suffocating smoke drifted into our faces. . . . "[67]

Atop the hill, the fight was short and deadly—the hardest fight the Vermonters had ever participated in, Fisk opined. "During this fight a brave little fellow just to my right was shot through the neck. The ball cut his jugular vein," he wrote. "He was told that he could not live and asked if he had any word that he wanted to send to his friends. 'Tell them,' says he, 'that I was a good soldier,' and truly he had been one."[68]

Amidst the disarray, the Federals did what they could to patch together a battle line to make a final push up the hill. The skirmishers of the 2nd Vermont and 77th New York were still just in front of the patchwork battle line. The 7th Maine was on the right, with the 33rd New York to their left; the remaining eight companies of the 2nd Vermont continued the battle line, which terminated with elements of the 26th New Jersey.

The Mississippians tried to buy time for the artillerists to get off the line, but just then survivors from the 18th Mississippi, having mere moments previously made their escape from the New Yorkers at the base of Willis Hill, stumbled their way into the action on Telegraph Hill. Members of the 13th and the 18th became entangled under pressure from Seaver's Federals. From his headquarters, Barksdale rode into the fray to do what he could to untangle the mess.

Some help was at hand for the harried Mississippian. Unlimbering on a ridge behind Telegraph Hill and to the right of the Telegraph Road were the guns of Capt. J. B. Richardson's 2nd Company of the Washington Artillery. Richardson had been ordered on May 1 to the Hamilton's Crossing sector with a section of Napoleons from his company under Lt.

---

66 Orrin Rugg to Parents, May 11, 1863, in Fredericksburg and Spotsylvania bound manuscript collection, vol. 318.

67 Rosenblatt, *Anti-Rebel*, 79.

68 Ibid., 80.

John Britton, as well as a section of the 4th Company under Lt. H. I. Battle, who also had two Napoleons. On the morning of May 3, Richardson requested to take his guns to the Marye's Heights sector to help staunch the Union threat. Colonel James Walton ordered Richardson into battery along the Telegraph Road at about the time Willis Hill was falling to Burnham and Howe. That put Richardson's four guns in position to unlimber and fire onto the blue masses atop Willis Hill.[69]

Below Richardson's guns, the 13th and 17th Mississippi were in a state of disarray, to say nothing of the mob that was the 18th Mississippi, which, at the moment, was swamping the 13th. As the 13th tried to rally around Barksdale, more Federals made their way to the works: the 33rd New York, followed by the 7th Maine, which had assaulted Marye's Heights, then turned about and made its way down Willis Hill. "Quickly descending to the ravine at the left, they double-quick through underbrush and obstructions of every description," wrote the regimental historian. "The Rebel gunners see them coming through the thicket, and depressing their guns, rain down a tempest of canister."[70] Although they lost six color-bearers in the process, the men of the 33rd resisted the artillery assault and made their way across the narrow valley to help secure the lower line of works.[71]

With no infantry support—and with Col. James Walbridge's 2nd Vermont and Col. Robert Taylor's 33rd New York pushing from the front—Richardson had seen enough. Having done all he could, the captain began pulling his guns off the line one by one. However, Federal small-arms fire managed to kill the wheel driver of one of the Napoleons in Battle's section. One of the horses was killed, too, making it impossible to pull the brass piece off the field; thus, the Confederates were forced to yield yet another field gun to the enemy.[72]

Also arriving by now were men of the 5th Vermont. The 5th had been held in a reserve position, lending support to Martin's and Cowan's guns. Now unleashed, they followed the 3rd and the 4th to the top of Telegraph

---

69 Coski, *In the Field and on the Town*, 118-119.

70 Judd, *The Story of the Thirty-Third N. Y. S.*, 297.

71 Ibid.

72 Coski, *In the Field and on the Town*, 119.

Hill.[73] Artillery support, too, was close at hand.[74] Cowan's guns battered Confederate gunners with counter-battery fire, but due to faulty ammunition did not do the damage the young captain wanted.[75] Martin's battery had also been firing on the heights, but then joined the fray more directly, following the 5th Vermont to the crest of the hill. Martin placed his rifled pieces in the Rebel works just moments after they fell, and his gunners harried Confederate infantry and artillery as they withdrew.[76] The last knuckle of Confederate resistance had fallen. "Yankee cheers rent the air," said a soldier from the Bay State.[77]

Barksdale turned his horse from the front and led the retreat two miles to the rear.[78] "I reckon now the people of the Southern Confederacy are satisfied that Barksdale's brigade and the Washington Artillery can't whip the whole Yankee army," one Southern artillerist complained.[79]

Telegraph Hill was now in Union hands. The heights behind Fredericksburg finally belonged to the Army of the Potomac. In less than 30 minutes, the VI Corps had captured its objective, sent Early reeling back, and kicked in the door to Chancellorsville.

* * *

In his official report of the battle, Early had little to say—he devoted only 85 words to it.

> All his efforts to attack the left of my right line were thwarted, and one attack on Marye's Hill was repulsed. The enemy, however, sent a flag of truce to Colonel Thomas Griffin, of the Eighteenth Mississippi

---

73 Benedict, *Vermont in the Civil War*, 365-367.

74 Ibid.

75 *OR* 25, pt. 1, 612.

76 Ibid., 613.

77 Charles Brewster to Mary Brewster, May 10, 1863, in Fredericksburg and Spotsylvania bound manuscript collection.

78 *Advertiser & Register* (Mobile, AL), May 22, 1863, in Fredericksburg and Spotsylvania bound manuscript collection, vol. 63.

79 Danny Davis, "Return to Fredericksburg," in *America's Civil War* (September 1992), 37.

Regiment, who occupied the works at the foot of Marye's Hill with his own and the Twenty-First Mississippi Regiment, which was received by him improperly, and it had barely returned before the heavy columns were advanced against the positions, and the trenches were carried, and the hill taken.[80]

Early's division lost few men, though. The brunt of the attack was absorbed by Barksdale and the Washington Artillery.

According to official after action reports, the artillerists lost 45 men and six guns: one 3-inch ordnance rifle, three Napoleons, two 12-pounder howitzers, and 29 horses.[81] Parker's section lost two 10-pounder Parrott guns, 27 men, and 28 horses.

Barksdale lost 226 killed or wounded and 350 captured—among them, Colonel Griffin and Lieutenant Colonel Luse of the 18th Mississippi, along with their flag. "A large quantity of prisoners have been taken," wrote a New Jersey private. "Some are clothed half decently, others . . . haven't hardly enough clothes on to wad a gun. . . . They are saucy and sour, but admit that fighting Joe completely got them this time."[82]

"Our success was glorious," agreed Clark, but, he added, "we had paid for it dearly."[83]

The Light Division alone sustained 798 casualties. Howe's division suffered roughly 600, and the two assaulting columns on William and Hanover streets roughly 400 total. It is worth noting that exact casualty figures for the battle are difficult to calculate because many of the units were engaged later on May 3 and 4. One shocked corporal summed it up most aptly: "The wounded are almost innumerable."[84]

"We did not think that it was to be such a bloody day for us," said a New Jerseyman.

80 *OR* 25, pt. 1, 1001-1002.

81 Ibid.

82 E. P. Ackerman, "Wreaths of Smoke from the Battle Field," *Newark (NJ) Daily Advertiser*, May 6, 1863, in Fredericksburg and Spotsylvania bound manuscript collection, vol. 193.

83 Gray, Diary, 46.

84 Cpl. Joseph K. Taylor, "Civil War Letters," in the Fredericksburg and Spotsylvania National Military Park bound manuscript collection, vol. 112.

Although short, the battle was hard-fought on both sides, resulting in heavy losses in relation to the number of men engaged. "It was a trip to hell boys but we made it," Colonel Allen said afterward.[85]

Sadly, the Chancellorsville journey of the VI Corps was just getting started.

85 Trask, *Fire Within*, 174.

Chapter Thirteen

Forcing Sedgwick's Hand:

Wilcox's Delaying Action

A Butternut rider rode hell-bent-for leather toward the Chancellorsville crossroads. His message harkened back to the days of revolution when Revere and Dawes made the midnight ride. This particular message was a bit different: *Sedgwick is coming! Sedgwick is coming!*

Robert E. Lee, sitting astride his white horse, Traveller, occupied ground that, only hours earlier, had served as Fighting Joe Hooker's headquarters. With the Chancellorsville mansion in flames, its residents safely evacuated by occupying Federals, Lee surveyed his cheering men. Captured in postwar iconography, this would become known as "His Supreme Moment." Indeed, Chancellorsville would become known as "Lee's Greatest Victory." Superlatives came easily enough, but the victory did not.

Lee's outnumbered and outgunned army had outmaneuvered and outfought Hooker's vastly superior Army of the Potomac. Following Jackson's surprise flank attack, which left the Federals rocking on their heels but also left the Confederate army divided and vulnerable, Hooker bungled by giving up key high ground at Hazel Grove, allowing the Confederates to reunite with hardly a shot exchanged. Jeb Stuart, in command in place of the wounded Jackson, rejoined his men with Lee's forces at around 7:45 a.m., and together they battered at Hooker's position around the crossroads. For five hours, the battle ebbed and flowed in a contest that only Antietam had matched for bloodiness.

The Federals, trading shots from Fairview with the Confederates, held their own, but ammunition began to run low. Due to problems in the chain of command, new ammunition failed to flow to the front. One by one, Federal artillery pieces fell silent at Fairview, the crossroads, and Hooker's headquarters at the Chancellor house.

The Confederates also managed to exploit a gap in the Federal line, created by Brig. Gen. Joseph W. Revere, grandson of Paul Revere. Revere pulled his brigade out of line without orders, ostensibly to "reform" in the rear, and the North Carolinians of Dorsey Pender's brigade poured through the opening. The entire Federal line began to fold.

To add injury to insult, Hooker himself was knocked senseless by an artillery shell that smashed into the porch of the Chancellor house, where he had been watching the debacle unfold. The shell hit a pillar Hooker was standing next to, which split in two and smashed into the general, knocking him to the ground—many thought he was dead.

"But I soon revived," Hooker later wrote, "and to correct the misapprehension, I insisted on being lifted upon my horse. . . ."[1] He rode to the rear, to the Bullock House, where nausea and lightheadedness overcame him. He dismounted, vomited, and lay on a blanket spread on the ground. A shot of brandy revived him. "Scarcely was I off the blanket when a solid shot, fired by the enemy at Hazel Grove, struck in the very center of that blanket, where I had a moment before been lying, and tore up the earth in a savage way."[2]

No doubt the incident left Hooker shaken, but the extent of his injury has been the source of much speculation by postwar historians, most of whom propagate accounts that portray him in a daze. For instance, Capt. William Candler, one of Hooker's staff officers, said, "For the remainder of the day he was wandering, and was unable to get any ideas into his head."[3] I Corps division commander Abner Doubleday said Hooker "suffered great pain and was in a comatose condition for most of the time.

---

1   Bates, "Hooker's Comments on Chancellorsville," 220-221.

2   Ibid.

3   Sears, *Chancellorsville*, 338.

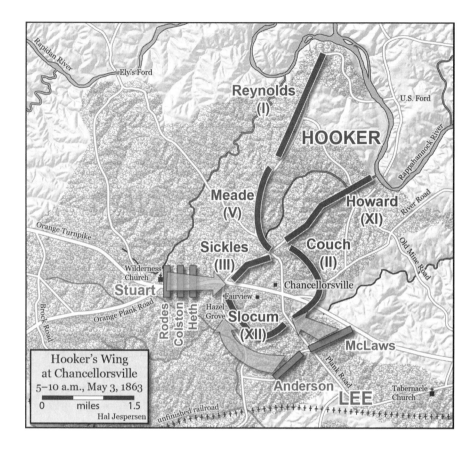

Hooker's Wing
at Chancellorsville
5–10 a.m., May 3, 1863

0   miles   1.5

Hal Jespersen

His mind was not clear, and they had to wake him up to communicate with him."[4] Even Hooker himself provided fuel for the fire, apparently crying out in anguish, "I wish to God someone would put a bullet through my head," although whether he was despairing over his wound or the death of his friend, Maj. Gen. Hiram G. Berry of Maine, seems unclear.[5]

An emphasis on an addle-brained Hooker neglects other accounts, such as George Gordon Meade's, who stressed that "Hooker never lost his head." Newspapermen on the scene reported that Hooker's injury was not serious, that he was stunned but unhurt, that his "reaction to his wound

---

4   Ibid.

5   Ruth L. Silliker, ed., *Rebel Yell & the Yankee Hurrah*, 82.

was more one of weariness than anything else."[6] An old colleague pointed out that night that "the General was as communicative with me as in the old Peninsular days."[7]

If Hooker was senseless, then is it a wonder the Federals lost at Chancellorsville? Could a speedier John Sedgwick have alleviated the crisis had his corps appeared on the scene at the moment of Hooker's injury? Or was Hooker of sound mind and capable of command but lost the battle because of actual ineptitude? Was he just out-generaled? The stakes of interpretation are enormous.

A clear consensus seems to hold that Hooker was dazed at least for the short term, but refused—despite being nearly unable even to speak—to relinquish command to II Corps commander Darius Couch, his most senior officer. He apparently met with Couch at 9:30 a.m., then called him back around 10:00 a.m. Couch was already trying to manage the deteriorating situation around the intersection when Hooker issued orders to "draw in the front and make some new dispositions." In effect, Couch was "simply acting as executive officer to General Hooker in fulfilling his instructions"—in other words, Hooker turned Couch into an extremely high-ranking staff officer.[8]

As Couch returned to the line, he met Meade, who was elated at the prospect of Couch in command because he thought Couch would take the fight to the Confederates. It was not so, Couch informed him, much to Meade's chagrin. Couch nonetheless ably evacuated the line around Chancellorsville and pulled the Union army back to a new position, about a mile north of the crossroads, behind fortifications being constructed by the 50th New York Engineers (under orders from Hooker). Hooker looked to anchor both flanks on the river, then dig in and hide until Sedgwick's 23,000 men came to save his own nearly 75,000.

Even as Hooker withdrew the Army of the Potomac, turtle-like, into a more protected defensive huddle, Robert E. Lee rode into the Chancellorsville clearing. He was at the zenith of his power. Major Charles Marshall described the exhilarating scene:

---

6   Hebert, *Fighting Joe Hooker*, 224.

7   Nevins, *A Diary of Battle*, 197.

8   *OR* 25, pt. 1, 307.

The fierce soldiers with their faces blackened with smoke of battle, the wounded crawling with feeble limbs from fury of the devouring flames, all seemed possessed with common impulse. One long unbroken cheer, in which the feeble cry of those who lay helpless on the earth blended with the strong voices of those who still fought, rose high above the roar of battle, and hailed the presence of the victorious chief. He sat in the full realization of all that soldiers dream of—triumph; and as I looked upon him, in the complete fruition of the success which his genius, courage, and confidence in his army had won, I thought that it must have been from such a scene that men in ancient times rose to the dignity of gods.[9]

At the time, no one would have imagined that this iconic moment represented the crowning achievement of the Army of Northern Virginia. In the next few hours, Lee and his men would begin the slow, gradual descent toward surrender at Appomattox.

All of that lay in the future, however. For the moment, Lee sought to refocus his army. His soldiers needed to get back into order, resupply quickly, and turn toward Hooker's new line to deliver the killing blow. Lee had perhaps 35,000 men ready to throw at 75,000 men, now behind a newly fortified line.

The Chihuahua had the Rottweiler in the corner. Could Lee pull more magic out of his hat and crush Hooker's army, or did Hooker finally have Lee right where he wanted him?

*   *   *

As Lee steeled his men for the task before them, the rider from Early's command galloped onto the field. It was around 12:30 p.m. A sense of urgency erupted among the men of Lee's staff, but Lee remained cool, calm, and calculating. He understood the situation at Fredericksburg, was fully aware of the flaws in the Southern line. He knew Early's men had been living on borrowed time. With Hooker under control, Lee had the luxury of turning his attention toward the eastern front.

---

9 Ernest B. Furgurson, *Chancellorsville 1863: The Souls of the Brave* (New York, NY, 1993), 250.

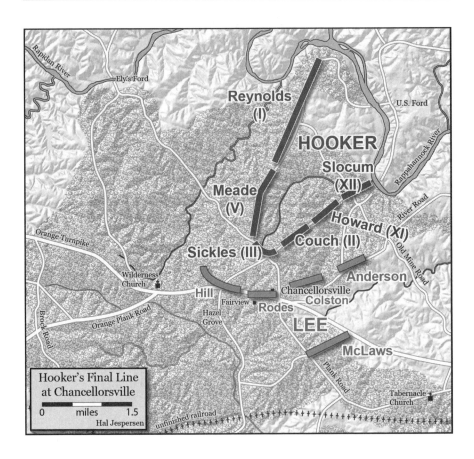

"Now what are you telling me about Major Sedgwick?" Lee asked the courier.[10] Lee had known Sedgwick from the days of the Old Army, and hadn't broken the habit of referring to the younger officer by his former rank.

The messenger, William Owen, known as "Brother William" because he was the chaplain of the 17th Mississippi, told a tale of woe from the Fredericksburg front.[11] When the chaplain finished, Lee calmly said, "I am very much obliged to you; the major is a nice gentleman; I don't think he would hurt us very badly, but we are going to see about him at once." In fact, another of Early's staffers, Lt. A. L. Pitzer, had ridden to Lee as the

10 Stiles, *Four Years Under Marse Robert*, 178.

11 Ibid.

Heights were falling to warn him. Lee responded by dispatching the division of Lafayette McLaws to "make a special call" upon Sedgwick.[12] More reinforcements would follow.

Once more Lee looked to slam the trap shut and turn the tables on Hooker. The closer Sedgwick came to Chancellorsville, the farther away he would be from the protection of the river. If Early had followed orders and swung his men south of Fredericksburg, they would be in position to then march north and west and come in behind Sedgwick's force. By splitting his army again, Lee risked a counterattack from the Army of the Potomac, but he had every reason to believe that the bedraggled Hooker was not going anywhere.

And indeed, Early had followed the orders laid out by Lee. Showing grace under fire, the Southern forces around Fredericksburg pulled back in the face of a determined, albeit slow, enemy.

Old Jube had arrived on the scene as his lines crumbled and fell away from Fredericksburg. Quickly realizing the gravity of the situation, he mobilized the artillery and infantry he could muster on hand into line of battle to delay the Federals as best they could. Another of Early's important advantages was that he commanded veteran combatants who did not flee pell-mell in panic toward Lee's position at Chancellorsville; instead, they withdrew southwesterly along the Telegraph Road as ordered. Scattered units, such as Harry Hays' three regiments north of the stone wall, took a circuitous route to meet up with the rest of the withdrawing division.[13]

William Barksdale also got his scattered brigade into a fighting formation. "Our center has been pierced, that's all, we will be alright in a little while," declared an upbeat Barksdale, who oversaw the withdrawal from Telegraph Hill.[14] Despite the collapse of his line, the politician-turned-general had the situation well in hand and, like Early, looked to establish a new defensive line.

Behind Telegraph Hill, the ground leveled considerably. Upon the plateau, Barksdale organized his defense. Along with the two regiments of

12 Ibid.

13 *OR* 25, pt. 1, 856.

14 William Martin Owen, *In Camp and Battle with the Washington Artillery* (Baton Rouge, LA, 1999), 218-219.

Hays' brigade overseen by Col. William Monaghan, the 13th and 17th Mississippi formed a line facing northeast. One of Barksdale's staff officers also reined in what was left of Humphreys' 21st Mississippi, which had been forced to take a roundabout way across the back side of Marye's Heights, then across the railroad cut and Hazel Run before finally climbing Telegraph Hill.

For a time, the formation enjoyed covering fire provided by Carlton's and Fraser's guns.[15] As the line withdrew, however, it left no infantry support for the artillery, so Carlton and Fraser limbered up and extricated themselves, rejoining their infantry counterparts near the Leach Farm about a half-mile down the Telegraph Road. More support began to coalesce on this new, meager defensive line.

With Barksdale's covering line established, Early looked to redeploy the bulk of his division across the Telegraph Road near the Cox House (Lee's winter headquarters), about two miles southwest of the city. The ever-aggressive John B. Gordon double-timed three regiments from his Georgia brigade to the new line; more support arrived as Hays' three regiments finally found their way around the battlefield.

Early readied his men for another fight, but it was not forthcoming. Puzzled, he rode from the Cox House north toward the Orange Plank Road to see what was up. As he pushed forward, he quickly ascertained that his men were in little danger: Sedgwick apparently had no interest in following up his victory at Marye's Heights. It was a lucky draw for Early, "who had passed heavy columns up the Plank road through Fredericksburg. . . ."[16]

Sedgwick had orders to push west as quickly as possible to relieve his beleaguered commander. After getting the units of Newton and the Light Division sorted out, which took long enough to raise Sedgwick's temper, the VI Corps set out—cautiously.

Sedgwick's sloth-like speed was, ironically enough, the result of a deluge of messages telling him to hurry up. He had received a slew of messages to that effect since before dawn from Dan Butterfield, Cyrus Comstock, Rufus Ingalls, and other officers. They asked about the

---

15 *OR* 25, pt. 1, 840.

16 Ibid., 1,001.

progress of the corps, told of the opportunity that waited ahead near the crossroads if he moved quickly, and inquired after Sedgwick.[17] Messages also arrived conveying mixed tales about the progress of the battle: one minute, success seemed inevitable; the next, doom loomed over all. Sedgwick had no way of knowing what he might be marching into.[18]

To make matters even worse, the road to Chancellorsville was anything but clear.

*　*　*

Brigadier General Cadmus Wilcox's brigade was not really attached to Early's forces at Fredericksburg. He had moved to the battlefield of his own accord in response to the sound of guns, but as the battle progressed he and his men saw little action. They were in a perfect blocking position, though: they allowed Gibbon neither to gain the River Road leading west nor flank Early and Barksdale from the heights.

Now, with Early's withdrawal, Wilcox stood essentially alone. But if anyone was up to such a task, it was the 38-year-old North Carolinian, a stalwart in the Army of Northern Virginia. Wilcox had attended the University of Tennessee and was an 1846 graduate of West Point.[19] While serving in Mexico, he received a brevet promotion for gallantry at Chapultepec. In the interwar years, he served as a groomsman for future Union general Ulysses S. Grant (James Longstreet served as Grant's best man).[20] Wilcox also taught tactics for five years at West Point and wrote a manual on the subject for rifle and infantry.[21] When the war came, Wilcox went with his native South and was commissioned colonel of the 9th Alabama. He served at First Manassas, and in October 1861 he was promoted to brigadier general and assumed brigade command. He served with distinction on the Peninsula but performed poorly at Second Manassas.

17 OR 25, pt. 2, 380-392.

18 Ibid.

19 Warner, *Generals in Gray*, 337.

20 Furgurson, *Chancellorsville 1863*, 273.

21 Tagg, *The Generals of Gettysburg*, 310.

With the exception of his dress (he wore a straw hat and short coat), Wilcox was a thoroughly professional soldier. His officers and men dubbed him "Old Billy Fixin'."[22] Due to the lack of promotion within the Army of Northern Virginia, Wilcox requested a transfer out, which Lee denied.[23] Following the first battle of Fredericksburg, Wilcox oversaw the construction of zigzag trenches, which improved the fields of fire and helped protect against enemy flanking maneuvers.[24]

Now Wilcox was in for the fight of his life. He was about to prove why he deserved to command a division over Maj. Gen. George E. Pickett, who had been promoted before him.

As Barksdale's men were being driven back from Marye's Heights, Wilcox looked to help out in any way possible. When he first arrived, he led the 10th Alabama around the rear of the heights, toward the sounds of the guns, but en route he came upon Harry Hays, who was pulling his three regiments off the heights. Wilcox asked Hays to join with his command and take the fight to the enemy, but Hays demurred, citing instructions from Early, who had ordered him to the Cox House line. Thwarted but undaunted, Wilcox countermarched the 10th Alabama and rejoined his brigade.

Wilcox could have joined Early in retreat, or he could have taken the River Road toward Chancellorsville and Lee's men, but instead he took it upon himself to slow Sedgwick's advance by pitting his 1,800 men against Sedgwick's entire corps.

First, Wilcox anchored the left end of his brigade near the Stansbury House and ran his line diagonally toward the Orange Plank Road; beyond, the right of the line terminated some 500 or 600 yards in front of the George Guest House. Wilcox then deployed a line of skirmishers across his brigade front.[25] Four artillery pieces of the Pittsylvania Artillery were placed on the right end of the line, one section forward of the line, the

22 Ibid.

23 Ibid., 311.

24 Joseph T. Glatthaar, *General Lee's Army: From Victory to Collapse* (New York, NY, 2008), 253.

25 *OR* 25, pt. 1, 856-857.

second behind it.[26] "This held the enemy in check for some time," Wilcox wrote. "At length they deployed skirmishers to the front and began to advance. This was slow and delayed by frequent halts, they seemed reluctant to advance."[27]

On Wilcox's left, Gibbon had pushed across the canals and up Stansbury Hill, engaging Wilcox on the left before the new line was fully established. (Gibbon may have also engaged the three regiments of Hays' brigade as well, although existing reports are unclear.) In all, Gibbon's skirmish line under Capt. George Ryerson bagged 103 Confederates before its advance was cut short by orders from Sedgwick, who called upon Gibbon to march into Fredericksburg and join the pursuit west.[28]

Howe's division had also continued its battle westward. After clearing Telegraph Hill and assisting in the capture of Willis Hill, a portion of Howe's division kept on pushing the Rebels. The 3rd and 4th Vermont of Grant's brigade moved forward in a heavy skirmish formation.[29] The Pittsylvania Artillery, situated on Wilcox's right, opened on them and ground their advance to a halt. Then the Federal skirmishers jerked forward, only to halt again. "I never got into a place where the air was as full of lead as it was for the short time after we got on top of those heights," wrote one Vermonter.[30]

Artillery support for the VI Corps men reached Brompton and went into action, engaging the Confederate artillery at about 800 yards. Lieutenant William Harn's 3rd New York Light Artillery and Capt. William McCartney's Battery A, 1st Massachusetts Light Artillery pounded away at Wilcox's men and guns.[31] The artillery fire, mixed with the movement of Federal skirmishers, compelled Wilcox to withdraw his line toward Taylor's Hill and the River Road.[32] For now, the road to

26 Ibid., 884, 856-857.

27 Ibid., 856-857.

28 Ibid., 351, 358-359.

29 Ibid., 603.

30 Edward J. Feidner, ed., *"Dear Wife": The Civil War Letters of Chester K. Leach* (Burlington, VT, 2002), 144.

31 *OR* 25, pt. 1, 564-565.

32 Ibid., 857.

Chancellorsville lay open. Ever so slowly, Sedgwick's force made its way out the Plank Road toward the Guest house.

As Sedgwick crept forward, Gibbon was under specific orders from Butterfield to stay in Fredericksburg itself. Gibbon's men would police the city, tend to the wounded, protect the pontoon bridges, and round up any discarded equipment.[33] "The whole town was vacated and the houses all open," wrote surgeon Edwin Buckner of the 98th Pennsylvania, who did a walk-through once the fighting ended. "[V]ery few citizens showed themselves after the fighting was over—the three sieges to which the place has been subjected has marked most of the houses with holes from shot, shell and bullets—some are extensively riddled—others marked with but a single hole or mark of a shell."[34] His walk also took him to Marye's Heights and the infamous stone wall and Sunken Road that ran along the

Confederate earthworks atop Marye's Heights.

Library of Congress

33 *OR* 25, pt. 2, 412-413.

34 Edwin Buckman to Mrs. E. D. Buckman, May 9, 1863, in the Fredericksburg and Spotsylvania National Military Park bound manuscript collection, vol. 399.

heights' base. "[N]o stronger fortification could be made and well had the rebels manned it, as the dead bodies left there show full well," he recalled. "The foot way was full of them."[35]

By 12:30 p.m., Sedgwick had made little headway. Two miles out of the city, with the head of the column near the Guest house, the corps ground to a halt yet again. Sedgwick set up headquarters in the house, a two-and-a-half-story home of brick and wood surrounded by 453 acres of sprawling farm. There may have been as many as five outbuildings.[36] Mr. Guest met the general, who promptly informed his host that the Federals were "after Cadmus [Wilcox] . . . and were going to pick him up."[37]

Sedgwick's mood seemed to be turning, at least a little. His men's spirits were high. Although fatigued by the overnight march, the early battle, and now the heat of the day, the Federals had just captured the heights and seven pieces of artillery and were now breaking into open country.[38] "We were wild with delight," a New Jersey private wrote.[39]

Sedgwick used the opportunity to call up fresh troops, those of the 1st Division under "Bully" Brooks. Brooks' men had successfully pushed Early's skirmishers back to a rail bed on the late evening of May 2, and they had repulsed a half-hearted attack from Billy Smith's men and skirmishers from Hoke's brigade on the morning of May 3. The artillery attached to Bully's division—four batteries in all—had bombarded Howison Hill, Hoke's men, and Pendleton's guns along the Confederate line.[40] But their action had been minor compared to the work done by the rest of VI Corps, so Sedgwick called on them to lead the march west. However, that meant that Brooks' men had to withdraw to the Bowling Green Road, march north into the city, west along the Orange Plank

---

35 Ibid.

36 Harrison, *Chancellorsville Battlefield Sites*, 195.

37 Ibid.

38 Ibid.

39 Siegel, *For the Glory of the Union*, 166.

40 *OR*. 25, pt. 1, 563.

Road, overtake the head of the column, and make for Hooker.[41] Newton would follow, then Howe.

While he waited, Sedgwick attempted to reopen communications with Federal headquarters via Banks' Ford. Roving Confederates captured several of Sedgwick's messengers, but word did eventually get through, and work on a new telegraph line began in midafternoon. Sedgwick tried, too, to round up a local guide to lead the way west, but to no avail.

It would take Brooks nearly two hours to reach Sedgwick at the Guest house—two hours in which Sedgwick's frustrations grew once again. Those two hours also gave McLaws the opportunity to move east from Chancellorsville, Wilcox to get reorganized, and Early to position himself to get back into the fight.

When Brooks finally got rolling west, he had a fight all his own waiting for him.

41 Ibid., 567.

Chapter Fourteen

Fighting in the Churchyard:

The Battle of Salem Church

Between Marye's Heights and the Wilderness, 10 miles to the west, the countryside of Spotsylvania County rolled lazily from one long ridgeline to the next, with wide valleys of farmland between. Several small streams cut deep ravines toward the Rappahannock to the north. Along with the farmhouses that dotted the roadside were a church and a schoolhouse. There was a tollhouse, too, for travelers using the turnpike.

As Sedgwick crawled westward, he got farther and farther away from Federal signal stations until, finally, the head of his column was out of sight. Butterfield, back at headquarters in Falmouth, lost touch. By the time Sedgwick paused at the Guest house, restoring communications became a priority.

To the north of the army's position, at the northern apex of a bend in the Rappahannock, lay Banks' Ford. Because it was about three and a half miles from Fredericksburg—about a third of the way between the city and Chancellorsville—the ford had been one of Hooker's objectives throughout the campaign. If captured, the ford would provide shortened lines for communication, resupply, and reinforcement between the army and Falmouth. However, Confederates maintained a grip on the ford. Even when Wilcox had moved toward Fredericksburg in response to the sounds of the morning fight, he left at the ford dismounted troopers from Maj. C. R. Collins' 15th Virginia Cavalry and Cobb's section of the Pittsylvania Artillery.

Another of Banks' Ford's advantages was that it offered two crossing points.[1] The first, established in 1817, boasted a ferry by 1855. The second, a little upstream, was established in 1860.[2] That same year, William Scott established a sawmill on the northern bank of the ford, in Stafford County.[3] There were at least two buildings in the complex. The timber was cut at the mill, then floated downriver to the Rappahannock Canal to circumvent the falls.[4] Because of Scott's presence, people sometimes referred to the crossing as Scott's Ford.

The south bank of the ford rose approximately 125 feet from the river. During the winter of 1862-63, Confederates strengthened the position even further with heavy fortifications. During the failed "Mud March" of January 1863, Ambrose Burnside made a run at the ford, but the terrain, fortifications, and excellent fields of fire—not to mention the mud—made it impossible for him to make a lodgment on the south bank.

Time and again during the early phases of the Chancellorsville campaign, Federals passed in the vicinity of Banks' Ford. With the changing tactical situation of May 3, they now, finally, had their chance to take it.

The 19th Maine of John Gibbon's division was stationed on the north bank of the ford, assigned to guard the telegraph line between Hooker's position at Chancellorsville and Butterfield's at Falmouth. For support, Brig. Gen. Henry J. Hunt, Hooker's chief of artillery, deployed part of the artillery reserve on the ford's northern bank: four 4.5-inch siege rifles, four 12-pounder Napoleons, twenty-eight 3-inch ordnance rifles, and two more unspecified sections in reserve (most likely four more 3-inch ordnance rifles). In all, Hunt had 48 guns arrayed for battle.[5]

(Hunt had ended up at Banks' Ford after an ongoing squabble with the commanding general had left him stripped of tactical control of the artillery. Sadly, Hunt's talents would have better served Hooker at

1   Harrison, *Chancellorsville Battlefield Sites*, 199.

2   Ibid.

3   Ibid.

4   Ibid.

5   *OR* 25, pt. 1, 248-249.

Chancellorsville, where a lack of artillery ammunition at the crossroads and Fairview led to the collapse of the line.)

Arriving as additional support for the guns was the Philadelphia Brigade of Gibbon's division.[6]

Meanwhile, across the river, the meager Confederate force in the trenches totaled fewer than 150 men. They would have stood little chance if an assault had come, but as it was, when Sedgwick's advance had forced Wilcox to withdraw back to the River Road, the troopers and artillerists rejoined the brigade, leaving the ford—finally—undefended.

With no opposition, the 50th New York Engineers set to work laying bridges.[7] It was nearly 3:00 p.m. on May 3. Their bridging material had been at the ford since 7:00 a.m. on May 1.

As work progressed, Hunt dispatched an aide, Maj. Alexander Doull, to the far side of the river. Doull swam across on his horse, then set out in search of the missing VI Corps.[8] At the same time, Sedgwick sent an aide toward the ford.[9] When the aide failed to return, he sent a second. Marauding Confederates bagged both of them. A third aide finally made it through. Communication was reestablished.

The reestablished link gave the engineers incentive to finish their bridge at a feverish pace, wrapping up by 4:00 p.m. The Philadelphia Brigade moved across the ford to secure the right bank. By then, the sounds of battle were reverberating through the river valley.[10]

*   *   *

It had been nearly four hours since Sedgwick's men had swept Marye's Heights, yet they were still seven miles from their objective. Sedgwick was ten and a half hours behind schedule. Hooker had wanted the VI Corps at Chancellorsville at dawn, but at the rate of advance it was making he would have been lucky to have it there by nightfall.

6   Ibid.

7   Ibid., 215.

8   Ibid., 248.

9   Ibid.

10 Ibid., 248-249.

At 1:00 p.m., Butterfield received a message from Warren, who informed the chief of staff on behalf of Sedgwick that

> [w]e have advanced with Newton's division on the Plank road as far as the Guest's house. The heights were splendidly carried at 11 A.M. by Newton. Howe immediately afterward carried the heights to the south of Hazel Run. We have been waiting to get his division behind us before advancing. . . . Brooks' division were kept by the enemy's fire in position on our left, and after the heights were carried he had 3 miles to march and join us.[11]

As soon as Brooks arrived on the scene about 3:00 p.m. to lead the march westward, two cannon shots boomed at him. Lieutenant James Cobb's section of the Pittsylvania Artillery, stationed about 800 yards in front of Brooks' position, lobbed a pair of shells that hit Capt. James Rigby's Battery A, 1st Maryland Light Artillery (Union). Captain Theodore Read, the assistant adjutant general of Brooks' division, was severely wounded and Sgt. John Wormsley of Rigby's battery was killed, as was one of the battery's horses.[12] The rest of Brooks' men scrambled to prepare for battle.[13]

Biding his time along the River Road, Wilcox had been eyeing an opportunity to slow Sedgwick's column. Bolstered by a few reinforcements from Maj. C. R. Collins' 15th Virginia Cavalry and Cobb's section of the Pittsylvania Artillery from Banks' Ford, he had set off for a ridgeline six miles west of the city: Salem Heights, the highest point between Fredericksburg and Chancellorsville. Union signalmen could not see past the heights, and so would not know about the surprise "Billy Fixin'" was fixin' to spring.

Near 3:00 p.m., word reached Wilcox that the bulk of McLaws' division was marching hard to his relief. Troops from Richard Anderson's division—specifically, the all-Virginia brigade of "Little Billy" Mahone—would be coming, too. Wilcox just needed to buy them the time they would need to get on the field and deploy.

---

11 *OR* 25, pt. 2, 393.

12 *OR* 25 pt. 1, 567-568; Sears, *Chancellorsville*, 378.

13 Sears, *Chancellorsville*, 378.

As an early-warning system, Wilcox arrayed the 50 or so dismounted troopers from the 15th Virginia Cavalry in a skirmish line across the turnpike just to the rear of Idlewild, a two-and-a-half story, Gothic Revival brick farmhouse on the south side of the road.[14] The 222-acre farm, owned by 30-year-old William Dowman, included a woodlot that the cavalrymen used to screen their numbers from the approaching Federals.[15] On the north side of the road, beside the tollhouse, Lt. James Cobb unlimbered his section of the Pittsylvania Artillery.[16]

A half-mile behind the skirmish line waited the rest of Wilcox's brigade, deployed into line of battle. There, Wilcox also stationed the guns of Capt. Joseph Moore's Norfolk Battery.[17] When pressed heavily in front, Wilcox would have the ability to pull back to Salem Heights, still another half-mile to the rear. By the time that happened, Wilcox hoped, McLaws' division would be on the field, hidden by the terrain and in a position to surprise any Union forces too hot on Wilcox's heels.

And now the Federals were coming. In response to Cobb's artillery fire, Brooks threw forward the six companies of the 2nd New Jersey under Col. Samuel Buck as skirmishers.[18] The New Jersey men, outfitted with longer-range Springfield rifles than the dismounted Virginians, and outnumbering them, too, pushed back the troopers.[19] Falling back past Wilcox's line at the tollhouse, the 15th Virginia made for the protection of Salem Heights. As the cavalrymen passed rearward through the infantry's front, Wilcox deployed a new line of skirmishers from the infantry.[20]

Brooks also deployed his artillery. Battery D of the 2nd U.S. Artillery under Lt. Edward Williston set two sections of Napoleons to the left of the Plank Road and one section in the road itself. Rigby's Maryland guns set up to the right of the road, as did the six 10-pounder Parrott guns of Lt.

---

14 *OR* 25, pt. 1, 857.

15 Ibid., 857; Harrison, *Chancellorsville Battlefield Sites*, 187.

16 *OR* 25, pt. 1, 857, 884.

17 Ibid., 884-885.

18 Joseph Bilby, *Three Rousing Cheers: A History of the Fifteenth New Jersey from Flemington to Appomattox* (Hightstown, NJ, 1993), 62; OR 25, pt. 1, 567.

19 Bilby, *Three Rousing Cheers*, 69.

20 *OR* 25, pt. 1, 857.

Augustin Parson's Battery A, 1st New Jersey Light Artillery.[21] "The enemy then threw shells to the right and left of the church, through the woods, endeavoring to reach our infantry," Wilcox wrote.[22]

Cobb was wounded in the arm by a piece of shrapnel. Unable to command his guns in the face of the coming threat, he instead withdrew them to Salem Heights.[23] Wilcox began giving ground, as well. The guns of Joseph Moore's Virginia Battery appeared, attempting to cover the withdrawal, but failed somehow to find a proper position from which to fire.[24] With Federals bearing down on him in force, Wilcox had to leave his wounded behind.

*   *   *

Salem Heights represented one of best defensive positions on the Fredericksburg or Chancellorsville battlefields.

The ridge was named for the Salem Baptist Church, referred to in many war accounts as either the "brick church" or the "red brick church."[25] Constructed in 1844, Salem Church was modest compared to the churches of downtown Fredericksburg and, for that matter, to many of the area's most stately homes.[26] Made of simple red brick, it stood two stories high and measured 38 by 42 feet.[27] At the outbreak of the war, 77 congregants belonged to the church, including 57 white members and 20 African-Americans.[28] Two western doorways allowed access to the main floor of the sanctuary. On the south side of the church, a third door led to the overhead slave gallery. Six windows on the northern and southern

21 Bilby, *Three Rousing Cheers*, 67; National Archives of the United States, record group 156: Records of the Office of the Chief of Ordnance—"Summary Statements of Quarterly Returns of Ordnance and Ordnance Stores on Hand in Regular and Volunteer Army Organizations, 1862-1867, 1870-1876."

22 *OR* 25, pt. 1, 855-857.

23 Ibid., 857.

24 Ibid., 857, 884-885.

25 Ibid., 857.

26 Harrison, *Chancellorsville Battlefield Sites*, 161.

27 Furgurson, *Chancellorsville 1863*, 274.

28 Harrison, *Chancellorsville Battlefield Sites*, 161.

Salem Church today.

Kristopher D. White

walls provided a bounty of natural light, and a large window on the eastern wall, behind the pulpit, kept the chaplain amply illuminated. During the first battle of Fredericksburg, the church housed many refugees from the bedraggled city.

About 60 yards southeast of the church stood a dilapidated one-and-a-half-story log schoolhouse. Confederate riflemen positioned themselves in both the schoolhouse and the church in preparation for the coming battle.

On the western side of Salem Heights ran a line of earthworks, cut during the winter of 1862-63 by Pickett's Virginia division. The eastern side of the ridge boasted hedgerows very reminiscent of the bocage hedgerows of later American battles in Normandy, France. Such hedgerows normally served as thick barriers to delineate property lines, and were thick enough to keep cattle in without having to build a traditional fence.[29]

Confederates also made use of Jones Woods, which ran on both sides of the Orange Plank Road. At the western edge of the wood line, 200 yards from the church (near the modern site of a McDonalds), sat the modest William Perry homestead. Perry's 20 acres made a perfect setting for Confederate artillery.[30] East of the woods, about a quarter mile from Salem Church, sat Maple Grove, the home of William S. Williams.[31] Another quarter mile to the east of Maple Grove sat the George Farish

A postwar view of Jones Woods along the north side of the turnpike.

Fredericksburg and Spotsylvania National Military Park

29 Ibid., 167-170.

30 Ibid., 164-166.

31 Ibid., 173-176.

house (the modern-day site of the Belk department store at the Spotsylvania Mall).[32]

While the crest of the hill offered many areas for Confederates to conceal themselves, the eastern approaches were for the most part open.

As Wilcox withdrew his men to the new position, word arrived that McLaws' division was approaching from the west. Wilcox informed the messenger to go back to the column and tell them to deploy behind the cover of the heights.[33] The newly arrived division started to come on line near the Perry house, out of sight of the VI Corps' long guns.

As McLaws deployed, Wilcox directed a company of his 9th Alabama into the church and another into the schoolhouse. The rest of the 9th moved about 75 yards behind the church and took a reserve position. Wilcox deployed the 8th Alabama on the right of the line south of the Plank Road; to its left was the 10th Alabama. North of the road was the 11th Alabama, with its right anchored on the road; to its left was the 14th Alabama. The five regiments numbered nearly 1,700 fighters. The Alabamians used Pickett's old earthworks as well as the bocage hedgerows for cover. As a commander, Wilcox could have done little better for a defensive line. It lacked only close artillery support.

"Then for perhaps twenty minutes shells came crashing and howling through the woods, hunting for our positions," wrote an Alabamian, "but we were hugging the ground closely. . . ."[34]

On the Union side, by 3:45 p.m. the balance of Brooks' division was coming onto the battlefield, using the Plank Road as the axis of advance. On the north side of the road, swinging from column into line, was Col. Henry Brown's fine New Jersey Brigade. The brigade had once been commanded by Brig. Gen. Philip Kearny, a one-armed, no-nonsense general who whipped the New Jersey men into excellent fighting shape, becoming one of the finest brigades in the Army of the Potomac. Brown had commanded the 3rd New Jersey before his promotion.

Although a veteran officer, Brown's deployment of the brigade on the open plain in front of Salem Heights was scattered and susceptible to being

---

32 Ibid., 171-172.

33 *OR* 25, pt. 1, 857-858.

34 Baquet, "Salem Church" in, *History of the First Brigade*, 242.

flanked. For starters, the six companies of the 2nd New Jersey were still deployed to the front under Colonel Buck. On the north side of the road, Brown placed the 1st New Jersey, with its left on the Plank Road; the rest of the 3rd New Jersey deployed to the right of the 1st.[35] Brown placed the two regiments under the 1st's colonel, Mark Collet.[36] On the south side of the road, with its right resting on it, was the 23rd New Jersey.

Another of the brigade's regiments, the 15th New Jersey, was still trying to make its way to the front after having been left behind in Fredericksburg to tend to the division's wounded from the Marye's Heights battle. The final regiment, the 4th New Jersey, was in the rear of the column guarding the division's wagon trains. The absence of the two regiments left the New Jersey brigade woefully undermanned as it marched into battle.

Adding to Brown's concerns was the fact that the six companies of the 2nd New Jersey did not cover the front of the attacking column, so Brown was forced to deploy two companies of the 3rd New Jersey to strengthen the skirmish line, weakening his right flank. To bolster Brown's weakened line, Brooks sent forward the men of the 95th and 119th Pennsylvania from David Russell's brigade.[37] The two-regiment demi-brigade was under the command of the 95th's Col. Gustavus Town.[38]

On the south side of the road, to the left of the 23rd New Jersey, deployed the bulk of Brig. Gen. Joseph J. Bartlett's brigade: the 121st New York, the 96th Pennsylvania, and the 5th Maine. Bartlett was a New Yorker by birth and a lawyer by trade. The Binghamton resident answered his country's call in 1861 and was appointed major of the 27th New York. The 27th fought at First Bull Run, and when Bartlett's commanding officer, Col. Henry Slocum, was wounded, the young major assumed command of the regiment and performed well.[39] On the Peninsula, he was elevated to brigade command and performed admirably in that capacity, too. He could be haughty at times, yet was down-to-earth

35 *OR* 25, pt. 1, 570-571.

36 Ibid.

37 Ibid., 568.

38 Ibid., 580-581.

39 Warner, *Generals in Blue*, 23-24.

enough to enjoy games of baseball with the enlisted men. Apparently, the general was quite a ball player.[40]

As Bartlett brought his men into formation, he took operational control of the 23rd New Jersey positioned to the right of his brigade. Directly behind the 23rd was Bartlett's 16th New York. Thus, when Brooks stepped off, there were essentially three different brigade commanders on the field, and some of the units were not reporting to their own commander. Brooks hardly worried about it, though; as patchwork as his force was, he had only Wilcox's brigade to sweep away—or so he thought.

*   *   *

It was nearly 5:00 p.m. by the time the men of Brooks' command strode forward up the gentle slope toward Salem Heights. The 23rd New Jersey and 121st New York headed directly for the church itself; Bartlett's men drove for the high ground south of the road. "Artillery fire ceased," a Confederate noted, "and now, bravely, with banners flying, infantry lines come forward, their alignment perfect."[41]

For the members of the 121st, it would be their first true taste of combat. Their regimental commander was one of the best and brightest rising stars in the United States Army, Col. Emory Upton. The Batavia, New York, native was born on August 27th, 1839.[42] For a time he attended Oberlin College in Ohio, but disliked the liberal college curriculum.[43] The young pupil traded Oberlin for an appointment to West Point, where he graduated in May 1861, ranking eighth.[44]

Upton was made first lieutenant in the 5th United States Artillery, but prior to Bull Run succeeded in becoming an aide on Brig. Gen. Daniel Tyler's staff. Upton served well as a staff officer and is credited with firing

---

40 Tagg, *The Generals of Gettysburg*, 108-109.

41 Baquet, "Salem Church," 242.

42 Warner, *Generals in Blue*, 519.

43 Stephen E. Ambrose, *Upton and the Army* (Baton Rouge, LA, 1993), 7.

44 Warner, *Generals in Blue*, 519.

A 1960s view looking toward Salem Heights from the Federal vantage point.

Fredericksburg and Spotsylvania National Military Park

the first shot at Blackburn's Ford.[45] Later, he was promoted to captain and led a battery and divisional artillery in the VI Corps. In late 1862, Upton was appointed colonel of the new 121st New York. The unit took a quick liking to their colonel, but the honeymoon phase was brief. Upton treated the men of the regiment as if they were cadets at West Point and instilled iron discipline, which drove some lesser officers to resign their commissions.[46]

The young colonel was described as having "a light mustache, high cheek bones, thin face, and a strong, square jaw. He had a small mouth and thin, usually closed lips, which made his mouth look even smaller. His deep blue, deep-set eyes 'seemed to be searching all the time.'"[47] Upton's biographer, Stephen Ambrose, described the man as being "single minded in his purpose." According to Ambrose, "He never drank, smoked, or

45 Ambrose, *Upton and the Army*, 17.

46 Ibid., 20-21.

47 Ibid., 20.

cursed, and seldom laughed. He was asocial to the point of being acutely uncomfortable in the presence of civilians."[48]

Regardless of what the men under his command thought, Upton was every inch a soldier and one of the finest combat leaders to come out of the Army of the Potomac. He always led from the front. By the time of Salem Heights, the 121st New York was known as "Upton's Regulars," and the discipline he had instilled in the men would prove invaluable in the coming minutes.

As the New Yorkers advanced to the church and school, the Confederate skirmish line opened fire. A small woodlot of approximately 300 yards' depth bordered the eastern side of the church, and Bartlett's line on the south side of the Plank Road drove for it.[49] "The woods were thick with harsh, unyielding undergrowth, with little large timber," Bartlett recalled. "It afforded no protection to our troops from the showers of bullets which were rapidly thinning our ranks, but retarded their advance so much that nothing but the most unflinching bravery could make them withstand their fearful loss while overcoming so many natural obstacles."[50]

Frustrated by the Confederate resistance, Upton ordered the 121st to fix bayonets and move forward at the double-quick, charging the Confederates and driving them back.[51] The Federals "made a slight halt," Wilcox recalled; "then, giving three cheers, they came with a rush, driving our skirmishers rapidly before them."[52]

With 50 yards of woods still ahead of them, the 121st New York was hit with "a heavy fire of musketry" from the 8th and 10th Alabama, concealed in the earthworks scratched out over the winter by Pickett's

48 Ibid., 3.

49 *OR* 25, pt. 1, 589.

50 Ibid., 581.

51 Isaac O. Best, *History of the 121st New York State Infantry* (Chicago, IL, 1921), 69.

52 *OR* 25, pt. 1, 858.

Colonel Emory Upton, 121st New York.

Library of Congress

men.[53] However, as Upton later recalled, "The fire was received without creating the slightest confusion."[54] The New Yorkers pushed on.

"The enemy returns our fire, first by volley and then promiscuously." an Alabamian said. "For a few moments everywhere along the line the enemy are staggered, but do not retreat. The battle for a time seems

53 Best, *History of the 121st New York*, 69.

54 Ibid.

hanging in the balance, and then the momentum of the attack is such as to break our lines."[55]

With assistance from the 96th Pennsylvania on their left, the New Yorkers first managed to clear Wilcox's Alabamians from the school and church. However, more Southerners sprang forward "as one man, and, with the rapidity of lightning, restore[d] the continuity of our line, breaking the lines of our enemy with its deadly fire and forcing him to give way...."[56]

"Suddenly as if by magic, a line of men rose up and delivered their fire almost in our faces," a member of Upton's regiment recalled.[57] Wilcox's men were well entrenched and their fire so great, another New Yorker said, that "we were unable to get at them on the account of their strong works, while they could fire upon us in open field."[58] From that open position near the church, the Pennsylvanians, New Yorkers, and New Jersey boys battled it out with the Alabamians. In rapid succession, the 121st lost six color-bearers. Said an Alabamian: "The slaughter of the advancing line of the enemy is terrible...."[59]

"The struggle became furious...." wrote one Confederate. "It sounded like a large cane break on fire and a thunder storm with repeated claps, one clap following the other."[60]

The aggressive Upton sought to drive into the Confederate works, but could not do so without support on his right. The 23rd New Jersey, known as the "Yahoos," were having a rough time advancing. They, too, were entering their first major combat and, to add to their problems, their right flank was exposed, since it lay on the open road. Upton sent his second in command to coordinate with the 23rd's leader, Col. E. Burd

55 Baquet, "Salem Church," 243.

56 *OR* 25, pt. 1, 858.

57 Best, *History of the 121st New York*, 69.

58 William Remmel to Parents, May 5, 1863, in the Fredericksburg and Spotsylvania National Military Park bound manuscript collection, vol. 357.

59 Baquet, "Salem Church," 243.

60 John L. G. Wood to his Aunt, May 10, 1863, in the Fredericksburg and Spotsylvania National Military Park bound manuscript collection, vol. 291.

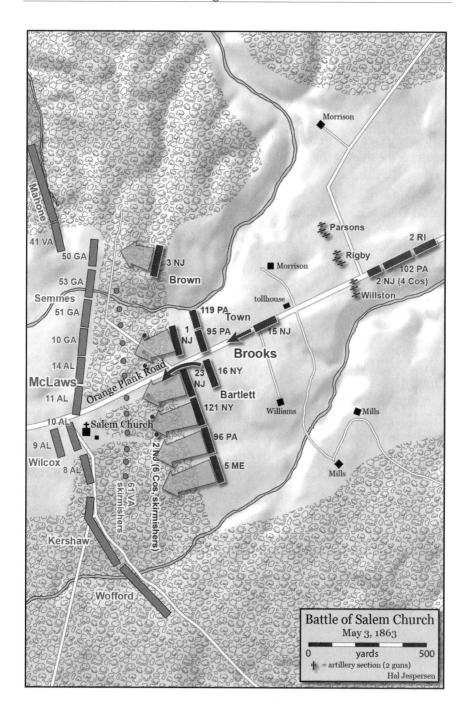

Battle of Salem Church
May 3, 1863

0   yards   500

🎵 = artillery section (2 guns)

Hal Jespersen

Grubb, but Grubb could not get his men moving to support the New Yorkers and Pennsylvanians to their left.

Following the 23rd into action was Col. Joel Seaver's 16th New York. The 16th swung to the right of the 23rd and then around them, using the open road to advance toward the heights. The 16th, entering their final battle, were a two-year regiment set to go home in a matter of weeks. After the battle, their comrades in the 121st would go out of their way to point out that the short-timers did their full duty in the face of the enemy.[61]

As the soldiers of the 16th New York pushed up the exposed road, they were subjected to a hellacious fire from their front and exposed right flank because they had failed to link with any of Brown's New Jersey units on the north side of the road. Yet although the 10th and 14th Alabama laid into them, still the New Yorkers did their best to advance. "Never was the Sixteenth put into a hotter fight," recalled the regimental historian, Newton Martin Curtis. The 16th carried 410 men into action on May 3 and sustained 154 casualties attempting to take Salem Heights.[62]

Aiding the wounded men of the 16th New York was Reverend Francis B. Hall. Hall was described as a ripe scholar, a good sermonizer, a zealous parish worker, and one who would perform the duties of a chaplain in an acceptable manner.[63] The unarmed chaplain followed the men of his regiment into battle. As men fell up and down the line, he did what he could for their bodies and spirits. When Confederates finally drove the 16th from the field, Hall made it off with his flock. For his actions in the face of the enemy, Hall was awarded the Medal of Honor—the only noncombatant chaplain so distinguished.[64]

The two New York regiments, along with their New Jersey counterparts, clung near the crest of the hill. A haze of smoke hung over the ridge—not just the normal acrid smoke of gunpowder, but black, billowing smoke from the underbrush of Jones Woods, which had caught fire from the flash of discharging rifles.

---

61 Best, *History of the 121st New York*, 64.

62 Newton Martin Curtis, *From Bull Run to Chancellorsville: The Story of the Sixteenth New York Infantry together with Personal Reminiscences* (New York, NY, 1906), 249.

63 Ibid., 266.

64 Ibid., 266-267.

The 96th Pennsylvania and the 5th Maine, both to the left of the 121st New York, should have been working their way around the flank of Wilcox's men to sweep them from the ridge. Instead, as they reached a spot about 30 yards from the edge of the woodlot, they were met with a crushing fire. "[S]uddenly I saw two lines of battle of the 'Rebs' rise to their feet," recalled Capt. Jacob Haas of the 96th Pennsylvania. "I ordered my men to put in a volley, which they did with fine effect I think. . . . At any rate it saved us in some measure for had they got their 1st volley on us I think somebody would have been hurt. And then the circus commenced."[65]

* * *

Lafayette McLaws was a bear of a man, with a finely coiffed beard and wavy ringlets in his long hair. Like his corps commander, fellow Peach State native James Longstreet, McLaws was a West Point graduate of the class of 1842, ranking 48 of 62.[66] His low standing in his class was not a true indicator of what was to come. He served well in Mexico and in the Mormon War.

While in the antebellum army, he married and, through that union, was related to President Zachary Taylor as well as future Confederates Richard Taylor and Jefferson Davis. It was also during his time in the Old Army that McLaws was injured in a firearm accident that left the otherwise healthy officer with a mangled, nearly useless left hand, which he ever after tried to keep hidden.[67]

When war broke out between the states, McLaws went with the Confederacy and was appointed colonel of the 10th Georgia. He rose quickly through the ranks and, by the siege of Yorktown, was at the head of a division. After Lee reorganized the army, McLaws found his division within Longstreet's corps. In the field, McLaws could wield a division with precision, but had to be closely supervised because he was not

---

65 David A. Ward, *Amidst A Tempest of Shot and Shell: A History of the Ninety-Sixth Pennsylvania Volunteers* (New Haven, CT, 1988), 282.

66 Warner, *Generals in Gray*, 204; Tagg, *The Generals of Gettysburg*, 210.

67 Tagg, *The Generals of Gettysburg*, 209.

Major General Lafayette McLaws.

Museum of the Confederacy

especially creative. Despite that, he was an outstanding leader of men when thrust into a combat role.

During the Chancellorsville campaign, McLaws' division had already seen three solid days of combat. It had led the assault down the Plank Road on May 1, kept Hooker's attention through vigorous demonstrations on May 2, and squeezed the Federal left in a series of assaults earlier that morning of May 3. McLaws had then marched his 6,500 men six miles eastward and, under Wilcox's guidance, straight into position on the backslope of Salem Heights.

McLaws deployed the Georgia brigade of Brig. Gen. Paul J. Semmes to Wilcox's left. Semmes' men took position under a hail of gunfire. "The 50th Ga. Regiment doubled quick into the fight without having time to form a line," a member of the 53rd Georgia said.[68] The two regiments sustained their heaviest casualties of the fight just moving into position.[69]

To Semmes' left, McLaws deployed the men of Mahone's brigade, and Mahone deployed the men of the 61st Virginia forward as skirmishers.[70]

To the right of Wilcox, whose line continued across the Plank Road and terminated 150 yards south of the schoolhouse, McLaws placed the men of Brig. Gen. Joseph B. Kershaw, and beyond them, at the extreme right, the men of Brig. Gen. William T. Wofford. These were the men that the 96th Pennsylvania and 5th Maine ran into, quite by surprise, when they tried to flank Wilcox.

With the addition of the four relatively fresh Confederate brigades, the entire tactical situation had changed. Brooks' division, which had outnumbered Wilcox by nearly three to one, was now outnumbered by more than two to one. The Federal advance on the south side of the road was stopped cold.

On the north side of the road, the Federals fared no better. The 1st and 3rd New Jersey drove forward at the double-quick toward the 11th and

---

68 John L. G. Wood to Aunt, May 10, 1863, in the Fredericksburg and Spotsylvania National Military Park bound manuscript collection, vol. 291.

69 *Macon (GA) Telegraph*, May 26, 1863, in the Fredericksburg and Spotsylvania National Military Park bound manuscript collection, vol. 290.

70 Both Mahone's and Wilcox's brigades were part of Maj. Gen. Richard Anderson's division. Since McLaws was the senior officer on the field, he had operational control over all Confederate units.

Brigadier General William "Little Billy" Mahone.

Museum of the Confederacy

14th Alabama when a volley suddenly ripped through their right flank. Semmes' Georgia brigade, posted in a strong position, ran on a slight oblique rather than a true north-south line in order to take advantage of cover along the fence row and in the trenches. Lieutenant Colonel William Henry of the 1st New Jersey described the enemy as "strongly posted behind brush, fence, and intrenchments in a wood on the right and left of the road, from which position a destructive musketry fire was kept up on us."[71]

During the fight, the 3rd New Jersey lost contact with the 1st and drifted north, exposing both units to fire from three sides. Colonel Brown did what he could to encourage the men and obtain reinforcements, but none seemed readily available.[72] The demi-brigade of Colonel Town had not stepped off with the assault; instead, his Pennsylvanians lay in the field far to the rear of the Jersey boys.

Relief came from Sedgwick himself. Moving closer to the action, "Uncle John" spied a regiment trying to make its way to the battlefield: the men of Col. William Penrose's 15th New Jersey. The unit had been tasked earlier in the day with collecting the wounded from the Sunken Road.[73] Now Sedgwick ordered them into action, directing them to the front, past the prone Pennsylvanians. "Suddenly we encountered soldiers lying at rest along the road," remembered Lewis Van Blarcom of the 15th New Jersey, "and soon after marching by in four ranks, we filed to the right from the road into an open field, and marching a short distance, we heard the order 'left face, forward march.' and we marched in a line of battle toward the woods."[74] Brown then directed them to the brigade's right flank.[75] At the urging of the veterans of the 3rd New Jersey, Penrose's men dropped their knapsacks to cover their comrades' withdrawal.

The Garden State men entered "a thick pine woods" to their front and received scattered skirmish fire, followed by a Confederate volley.[76] "The [15th] regiment halted, and without any general order to fire the four hundred and fifty rifles of the 15th responded with a deafening roar to the

71 *OR* 25, pt. 1, 576.

72 Alanson A. Haines, *History of the Fifteenth Regiment New Jersey Volunteers* (New York, NY, 1883), 53-55.

73 Ibid., 52-53.

74 Newspaper memoir of Capt. Lewis Van Blarcom, 15th New Jersey, in the Fredericksburg and Spotsylvania National Military Park bound manuscript collection, vol. 109.

75 Bilby, *Three Rousing Cheers*, 66.

76 Marshall B. Stull, 15th New Jersey, *Sussex (NJ) Register*, May 22, 1863.

rebel volley," one of them recalled.[77] In the melee, Penrose tried to order his men to fire by file, but the noise of the battle drowned the colonel's orders, so the 15th fired wildly into the overwhelming Confederate numbers.[78]

The Jersey boys retired to a small wooded hollow a few hundred yards to the rear.[79] There, the major of the 3rd, J. W. H. Stickney, allowed his men a brief respite from the action.

As the 3rd pulled back, a bullet struck Brown in the thigh. He was taken from the field, and command devolved on Colonel Buck of the 2nd New Jersey, who had been commanding the skirmish line to the front, whose members were just 50 yards from the Confederates, picking off enemy officers as best they could.[80]

Not only did the Confederates hold a remarkably strong position, but the terrain itself continued to work against the Federals. Because they were forced to fire uphill, and the Southerners were in trenches and behind hedgerows, much of the Federal fire flew harmlessly over the heads of the front-line Confederates.

With the repulse of the 3rd New Jersey, the Confederates Wilcox and Semmes could sense the whole Federal line wavering.

Semmes was a fine specimen of a soldier. He was 48 years old and, although he had served in the prewar militia, was a banker and plantation owner by trade. When his country called, Semmes joined with the 2nd Georgia and was appointed its colonel.[81] His brother, Raphael Semmes, captain of the raider CSS Alabama, was arguably the most famous naval officer to fight for the Confederacy.

Time and again, Paul Semmes performed admirably in battle—and always suitably dressed for the occasion, too, with "polished boots, spotless linen, elegant uniform a brilliant red sash around his waist and shoulders and a red turban on his head[.] [W]hen the fight began he took position in front of his brigade so as to be seen by every man in it if

77 Newspaper memoir of Lewis Van Blarcom, 15th New Jersey.

78 Bilby, *Three Rousing Cheers*, 66.

79 Ibid.

80 Ibid., 66-67.

81 Tagg, *The Generals of Gettysburg*, 216.

Brigadier General Paul J. Semmes.

Fredericksburg and Spotsylvania National Military Park

possible. Pelides did not shine brighter in his martial array or inspire more courage in his followers or more terror to his enemies."[82]

Semmes was near the right end of his brigade line, held by Lt. Col. Willis C. Holt's 10th Georgia. Holt's men had seen action near the crossroads of Chancellorsville on the morning of May 3, when they had bagged nearly the entire 27th Connecticut. Leaving one company behind to guard the spoils of war, Holt's nine remaining companies came on line with the rest of Semmes' brigade. "Scarcely had we got into position," Holt recalled, "when the enemy fired upon us at a distance of not exceeding one hundred yards, which was returned by us in such a manner as to completely break their lines."[83]

Wilcox seized the opportunity and ordered his men forward in a counterattack. Not to be outdone, Semmes followed suit. "[S]eeing the brigade immediately upon my right (Gen. Wilcox's) charging," Holt said, "I communicated it to Gen. Semmes, who ordered us to charge, when every man and officer in my regiment leaped the fence and dashed forward at the enemy with a yell, cutting them down as they advanced and completely routing them. . . ."[84] Two full brigades were rushing down Salem Heights. "The Yanks were surprised to find this line too stubborn to be moved," recalled Frederick West of the 51st Georgia, "and holding their position unmoved did not long stand the conflict, wavered and broke. Then one of those wild shouts so terrible to the Yankees was heard along our lines and the Rebel lines charged upon them. They could not stand this and fled before us in the wildest confusion."[85]

Holt stated afterward that "Gen. Semmes was with us in the charge and, as usual, was in the front ranks. 'No officer or man, with any pride, could skulk behind and see his General display such courage as General Semmes displayed in this charge.'"[86]

82 Andrew Jackson McBride, Memoir, in the Fredericksburg and Spotsylvania National Military Park bound manuscript collection, vol. 126.

83 OR 25, pt. 1, 838.

84 Ibid.

85 Frederick G. West to Miss Maggie, May 18, 1863, in the Fredericksburg and Spotsylvania National Military Park bound manuscript collection, vol. 128.

86 OR 25, pt. 1, 838. The 10th had arguably its best day on May 3: it captured 124 men and collected 159 guns, 81 bayonets, and four cartridge boxes. "Thus in one day this

Federals on both sides of the road fell back. Some men ran for their lives, others fought in small pockets around determined officers. Upton stuck to the heights as long as he could. Lieutenant Adam Rice of the 121st New York claimed that the young colonel was the bravest man he ever saw.[87] Even as others in the 121st broke in confusion, Upton hung on until an officer from Bartlett's staff rode forward with an order and an inquiry, "Damn you, don't you know enough to fall back?"[88]

Upton finally relented and withdrew his men, "leaving the extreme point to which they have gotten beyond the church distinctly marked with their dead and wounded lying in a line. . . ." an Alabamian noted. "The carnage was awful."[89] Out of 453 men engaged, Upton would lose 276 of them—the most casualties suffered by any Northern unit in the fight.[90]

The "Yahoos" of the 23rd New Jersey pulled out, as did the 16th New York, both pursued by elements of the 10th and 11th Alabama. Confederates captured earlier in Salem Church and held captive there were unexpectedly freed, and the detachment guarding them from the 23rd New Jersey ended up as prisoners instead. "So hotly was the ground contested that at one time during the fight [Federals] were at one end of the church and our[s] were at the other," an Alabamian recalled. "We had literally converted the House of God into a charnel house and had pushed aside the Book of Life and were using the instruments of death."[91]

By this time, Colonel Upton had been unhorsed. The colonel found Bartlett's staff nearby and ordered an aide to relinquish his horse. Upton

---

regiment with a force of two hundred and thirty men, captured more than double their number of prisoners, and I have no doubt killed and wounded more than their own number," by Lt. Col. Holt's calculation.

87 Adam C. Rice, "Letters and Diaries," in the Fredericksburg and Spotsylvania National Military Park bound manuscript collection, vol. 357.

88 Best, *History of the 121st New York*, 70.

89 Baquet, "Salem Church," 244.

90 Phillip W. Parsons, *The Union Sixth Army Corps in the Chancellorsville Campaign: A Study of the Engagements of Second Fredericksburg, Salem Church and Bank's Ford, May 3-4, 1863* (Jefferson, NC, 2010), 109. Upton's brother Henry served as a lieutenant in the 121st New York. He fell with a wound to his right shoulder and lung. Henry survived the wound but due to complications was discharged from the army in February 1864.

91 Baquet, "Salem Church," 276.

Brigadier General Joseph Bartlett.

Library of Congress

took to the new charger and rode for the Federal artillery line to the rear. There, the young officer urged the battery commander to push his smoothbore guns closer to the battle line in hopes of stemming the rebel counterattack.[92]

Major William Lessig of the 96th Pennsylvania did what he could to get his men out of harm's way. As his men fell back toward the Federal

92 *Rochester (NY) Daily Union and Advertiser*, May 11, 1863.

artillery line, the major and two of his companies came across the Williams house. Inside, the men took "featherbeds and mattresses off the beds . . . [and] made a perfect fort of it. . . ."[93]

Alabamans in the 8th and 9th, meanwhile, pressed the 96th Pennsylvania to perform "a great skeedipper."[94] The "right wing broke and fell back," one of the Pennsylvanians wrote in his diary, and that was all she wrote for Bartlett's men on the south side of the road.[95]

On the north side of the road, a dangerous gap had formed between the 1st and 15th New Jersey, and Semmes' Georgians targeted it. Town's Union demi-brigade, which had stayed out of the action thus far, drove for the gap as well. The two groups clashed. The 95th and 119th Pennsylvania roared with volley after volley, but the Confederates still came on. Colonel Town, a prewar printer who had been with the 95th Pennsylvania since August of 1861, fell dead, as did his second in command, Lt. Col. Elisha Hall.[96] Town's demi-brigade broke and headed for the rear. So, too, did the men of the 1st New Jersey, but as they did their Colonel Collet was gunned down.

Even at the far end of the Federal line, where the 5th Maine still toiled in the woods, Confederate power was overwhelming. There, too, it took a direct order carried by one of Bartlett's staffers to withdraw the men in the face of an unwinnable fight. "For God's sake, Colonel, get your men out of this as quickly as possible, for you are nearly surrounded," he yelled.[97]

"[T]he Rebels had thier [sic] own way and were advancing with a rush waving thier [sic] old red rag of a battle flag and yelling like demons," said a Bay Stater in Newton's division, which helped cover the retreat.

93 Ward, *Amidst A Tempest of Shot and Shell.*

94 Bilby, *Three Rousing Cheers*, 67.

95 Luckenbill, Diary, May 3, 1863.

96 Roger D. Hunt, *Colonels in Blue: Union Army Colonels of the Civil War: The Mid-Atlantic States Pennsylvania, New Jersey, Maryland, Delaware, and The District of Columbia* (Mechanicsburg, PA, 2007), 166.

97 Parsons, *The Union Sixth Army Corps*, 102.

The Union line, recalled Francis Morse of the 121st New York, had been "blown away."[98]

* * *

As the Federal position crumbled, the men of the 15th New Jersey, sent to relieve the 3rd New Jersey, found themselves unable to extricate themselves. Colonel Penrose even urged his men to charge the enemy—a command they wholly ignored.[99] Many of the men were struggling with their firearms. The Enfield muskets they carried had begun fouling in the heat of battle. Men had to slam rounds home by pounding the ramrod with rocks or against trees. Others picked up rifles from their dead and wounded comrades of the 3rd New Jersey, who had carried Springfield muskets.[100] They tried slugging it out with the Confederates until the men of the 3rd came out of the safety of their hollow to aid those who had intended to save them.

The 3rd and 15th New Jersey were the last units on the field, and they were about to be surrounded. The 15th New Jersey's color sergeant, David E. Hicks, hoisted the colors high and waved them defiantly in the face of the enemy. As he did, a bullet struck him in the head, spattering his brains over his comrades.[101] In the ensuing struggle, the next consecutive color-bearer of the 15th New Jersey, Cpl. Samuel Rubadeau, lost the flag to the Confederates.

More Pennsylvanians made their way forward to support the stranded Jersey men. The 102nd Pennsylvania, from Frank Wheaton's brigade, dashed forward into "dense volumes of sulphurous smoke. . . ."[102] They too were met by a storm of lead. Wheaton sent the 2nd Rhode Island and 37th Massachusetts to help. "We advanced across a field to the brow of a hill and opened fire. Here our men began to fall, and the Rebels still

---

98 G. Cilella Salvatore, *The 121st New York Infantry Regiment: A Thesis*, in the Fredericksburg and Spotsylvania National Military Park bound manuscript collection, vol. 258.

99 Ibid., 68.

100 Bilby, *Three Rousing Cheers, 69*.

101 Ibid.

102 Stewart, *Camp, March, and Battlefield*, 316.

advanced," wrote Elisha Hunt Rhodes of the 2nd Rhode Island. "Forward is the word again, and with a yell we rushed on the Rebel lines which broke and fled for the woods."[103] In the counterattack, the 2nd Rhode Island's colonel, Horatio Rogers, recaptured the lost New Jersey flag.

Many of the New Jersey men had survived close calls with death. A pistol saved the life of George Henderson when a bullet hit the cylinder; the plate on George Beaver's cartridge box stopped a rebel bullet from piercing his side; Cpl. William Dugan was saved by a breastplate of iron body armor he wore into battle.[104] The harrowing day was not yet over for them, though. When the 15th retreated, they took position in front of the 139th Pennsylvania, who were laying down cover fire. As the Keystone State boys fired, many did so into the backs of the New Jersey men, killing Pvt. William Tharp of Company E.[105]

It took the action of Rigby's, Williston's, and Parson's guns to halt the Confederate counterattack. The Georgians came within 100 yards. "They opened fire on us a battery of artillery nearly enfilading our lines from right to left—opened upon us with grapeshot," said a Georgia private who lived through the maelstrom. "Our friends were fighting behind us and shooting into our ranks and it was evident we could not remain in this position of unsupported advance, and fell back to our place in line."[106]

Sedgwick himself had directed the artillery fire. It was the fastest he had moved all day.

*   *   *

When the Union line collapsed, Bully Brooks had been close to the front, and onrushing Alabama troops set their eyes on capturing the division commander. Brooks and his aide, Lt. Daniel Wheeler, spurred their horses back toward friendly lines.[107] Upon reaching the cover of

103 Robert Hunt Rhodes, ed. *All for the Union: The Civil War Diary and Letters of Elisha Hunt Rhodes* (New York, NY, 1991), 106.

104 Bilby, *Three Rousing Cheers*, 70-71.

105 Ibid., 69.

106 Frederick G. West to Miss Maggie, May 18, 1863, in the Fredericksburg and Spotsylvania National Military Park bound manuscript collection, vol. 128.

107 Bilby, *Three Rousing Cheers*, 67.

Federal guns, Brooks remarked to Wheeler, "Twenty Five years in the army Mr. Wheeler, and ruined at last."[108]

Brooks, who would eventually be ruined not by his repulse at Salem Church in May 1863 but by his part in the December 1862 cabal to unseat Ambrose Burnside, had lost some 1,500 casualties. Through the skillful use of terrain and maneuver, the Confederates sustained fewer than 700 casualties. The fight had lasted just over an hour.

"This action was the most disastrous of the trip," said Surgeon Edwin Buckman of the 98th Pennsylvania.[109]

By 6:00 p.m., both sides were settling into positions to out-stare each other for the night. Daylight was fading, as was "Uncle John" Sedgwick's hearty confidence. His road to Chancellorsville was blocked, so he went on the defensive, placing a ringed defense to the north of the Plank Road, protecting his new line of retreat: Banks' Ford.

Lee was now fully in the driver's seat; it was up to him to decide whom he would pitch into first. Would it be Sedgwick or Hooker?

108 Ibid.

109 Edwin Buckman to Mrs. E. D. Buckman, May 9, 1863, in the Fredericksburg and Spotsylvania National Military Park bound manuscript collection, vol. 399.

Chapter Fifteen

With Their Backs to the River

A full moon rose over the smoldering battlefield that evening. The din of battle, clearly heard miles to the east at Chancellorsville, had been replaced by the night sounds of insects—and the moans of thousands of wounded. Litter bearers crisscrossed the battlefield, their lanterns clanking and casting eerie shadows as they swayed from the handles of the litters. The Salem Church cemetery was scattered with dozens of new dead.

Not far from where the members of the 95th Pennsylvania had gone to ground, the corpse of one of their comrades, "a brave young fellow," as described by a member of the regiment, lay on the top rail of a fence. He had been scrambling over during their retreat and "was shot dead just as he reached the top most rail. . . ."

[T]here he fell, and remained equipoised in death, to the surprise and horror of all around; after we had fallen back, and during the night, a gentle breeze rocked the corpse to and fro in its aerial position, the moon shed a halo about the head and face of this "somebody's darling," and a rebel picket made the scene more hideous by the flash of his rifle, which seemed to come from beneath the dead soldier.[1]

Confederates scavenged among the fallen. "Shoes, that were so much needed, were among the spoils," wrote a member of the 8th Alabama.[2] He found a fellow Alabamian from Company A, a big Irishman named "Old Robinson," sitting on the ground beside a badly wounded Federal officer, quietly smoking a pipe.

"What are you doing?" the first Alabamian asked.

"I'm waitin' on this man here," Old Robinson replied. "He's got a bit of a job to do. I took him for a dead one, and was after pulling the boots off of him, when he said he was dyin', and asked me to wait till he was dead. And, faith, he's very slow about it!"[3]

Salem Church, used earlier in the day as a riflemen's position and then a prison, now served as a hospital. Its brick walls bore pockmark wounds from the battle. "Here hundreds of wounded of both armies were brought for surgical attention," wrote Col. Robert McMillian of the 24th Georgia:

> The sight inside the building, for horror, was perhaps, never equaled within so limited a space, every available foot was crowded with wounded and bleeding soldiers. The floor, the benches, even the chancel and pulpit were all packed almost to suffocation with them. The amputated limbs were piled in every corner almost as high as a man could reach; blood flowed in streams along the aisle and out the doors; screams and groans were heard on all sides, while the surgeons, with their assistants, worked with knives, saws, sutures, and bandages.[4]

1 G. Norton Galloway, Memoir, *The Ninety-Fifth Pennsylvania Volunteers*, in the Fredericksburg and Spotsylvania National Military Park bound manuscript collection, vol. 141.

2 Baquet, "After Cadmus," *History of the First Brigade*, 246.

3 Ibid.

4 C. C. Sanders, "Chancellorsville," in *Southern Historical Society Papers*, 52 vols. (Richmond, VA, 1901), vol. 38, 170-172.

Overflow spilled out into the churchyard.[5] Among the wounded men strewn across the ground was Pvt. Josiah Crispin of the 23rd New Jersey, who was befriended in his final moments of life by Lt. Rufus Jones of the 9th Alabama, who later recounted Crispin's story:

> After the battle was over I was passing over the ground which was held a few minutes before by the Union forces, when my attention was attracted by a groan from a man I thought was dead. I went to him and turned him over and found that he was still alive. I drew my flask from my pocket and I poured some of the contents down his throat. When he soon revived and asked me in a weak voice if I was going to kill him. I spoke to him kindly and asked him if I could do anything more for him by opening his coat. I saw that he was mortally wounded and would soon die as a Minie ball had pierced his left breast, just below the nipple, in the region of his heart. . . . I spread down a blanket and fixed his knapsack under his head so as to give him temporary ease of pain. I filled his canteen with water from my own and started to leave him for the purpose of sending our ambulance corps to have him sent to our hospital. When he called me back and looking up in my face remarked that war was a cruel, cruel, thing. I saw that he was sinking fast and I raised his head upon my knee and gave him a strong drink of brandy and water. He thanked me very kindly and with tears coursing down his cheek exclaimed, "My dear sister, Mary, I will never see you again and you will wait in vain for my return. Oh my god! Why did I leave my happy home? I know that death has laid his heavy hand upon me, but I am thankful that I am not afraid to go." He then put his hand into his breast pocket and took out his diary handing it to me saying, "Take this, my kind friend, and read it if you choose. It is the idle thought of a poor soldier while far away from those he loved and then send it to my sister Mary. You will find her address on the inside of this poor diary of mine. Give me your hand. And may God bless you for the kindness you have shown to an enemy." I raised his head, but his soul had taken its flight from this battlefield to where all is peace and the clash of arms are never heard. I have passed through much and witness many sad scenes but none have left such an impression upon my memory as the death of this brave soldier. I had him buried with several others in the immediate vicinity of the stately old church, Salem Church (whose name will grace the pages of

5 Ibid.

our country's history for future generations to come). A small and rude pen of rails marks his last resting place. . . . I will return to my regiment near Fredericksburg and anything I can do for you, to his grave, or body, will cheerfully be done.[6]

Jones' letter to Mary Crispin is made more poignant by the fact that Jones wrote it while incarcerated in a Federal prisoner of war camp at Johnson's Island on Sandusky Bay in Ohio.

Daniel M. Holt, a surgeon with Upton's 121st New York, was on the field tending to the wounded when he got himself turned around in the gloom. Trying to find his lines, he and his small party of medical attendants ended up bumping instead into members of Kershaw's brigade. "I am very sorry you have fallen into the hands of the Rebels this time, and there is no help for you!" an officer told him, as Holt later recalled. "Federal army be damned! and you too!!" Confederates put Holt and his medical team under guard and led them to Salem Church in the rear. There, they spent the night working alongside Confederate surgeons in a frenzied attempt to save the lives of men of both sides.[7] One of those Confederate surgeons was George R. C. Todd, the brother of the first lady of the United States, Mary Todd Lincoln. (George referred to Mary as a "poor weak-minded woman. . . .")[8]

"The night was inexpressibly gloomy," wrote Sedgwick's adjutant, Lt. Col. Martin McMahon. "Fires were not allowed to be lighted, and there was not even the excitement of a picket alarm to relieve the singular stillness."[9]

---

6 Rufus Jones to Mary Crispin, October 13, 1863, in the Fredericksburg and Spotsylvania National Military Park bound manuscript collection. Jones was captured at Gettysburg in July 1863. He was sent to Johnson's Island, from which he escaped in January of 1864.

7 Dr. Daniel Holt, "In Captivity," in *Civil War Times Illustrated* (August 1979), 35.

8 Ibid., 36-38. It should be noted that Holt and other captured Union medical personnel were treated very well. Both sides exhibited a great deal of respect toward the much-needed physicians. Holt stated that General Lee himself visited Salem Church on four separate occasions to see to the wounded and conversed with Holt each time. The general expressed the grave state of affairs in the southern medical departments, often referring to the lack of supplies needed to help the wounded men.

9 Ibid., 35-38.

A group of veterans gathered outside Salem Church.

Fredericksburg and Spotsylvania National Military Park

At Sedgwick's headquarters, with the dead of the day's fighting strewn across the landscape before him, the VI Corps commander looked agitated. The repulse of his movement toward Chancellorsville left him with few choices. He could try another push in the morning, although he had no idea how many Confederates waited for him, and he had lost any element of surprise. He could move back toward Fredericksburg, but he was already getting worrisome reports that Barksdale's men were back there somewhere, harrying his rear. Or he could hunker down and wait for Hooker to come to his rescue. The irony was hard to miss: Hooker had been waiting for rescue from Sedgwick, and Sedgwick now waited for rescue from Hooker.

It appeared, though, that Hooker was going nowhere. His new position north of the Chancellorsville intersection was strong, and he intended to wait there for an attack by Lee—although why he assumed an outnumbered Lee would attack the fortified Federal position is unclear, unless one perhaps takes into account Hooker's head wound from earlier in the day.[10]

A dispatch from Warren complicated matters. The engineer had used the crossing at Banks' Ford to return to Hooker's headquarters, arriving there around 11:00 p.m. "I find everything snug here," he wrote to Sedgwick, outlining what he understood Hooker's plans to be. "General Hooker wishes [the Confederates] to attack him tomorrow, if they will," Warren wrote. "He does not desire you to attack again in force unless he attacks at the same time."[11]

Warren sent the message after midnight, but it did not reach Sedgwick for nearly seven hours, and by then Sedgwick's situation had changed significantly. By that point, much of the rest of Warren's dispatch seemed particularly unimportant to Sedgwick, especially because Hooker had not issued a single order to Sedgwick directing the VI Corps' movements:

> He says you are too far away to direct. Look well to the safety of your corps, and keep up your communications . . . at Banks' Ford and Fredericksburg. You can go either place, if you think best. To cross at Banks' Ford would bring you in supporting distance of the main body and would be better than falling back to Fredericksburg.[12]

Hooker's complete abdication of his responsibilities toward the largest corps in his army seems hard to explain away, although Hooker spent his postwar career laying much of the blame for Chancellorsville at Sedgwick's feet. While criticism of Sedgwick's glacial pace is certainly justified, the army commander's neglect of the VI Corps suggests Hooker was far more culpable.

With no direction from his commander, and no option standing out as obviously best, Sedgwick decided to rearrange his line into a tighter defensive perimeter around Banks' and Scott's fords. The line, which ran for nearly three miles, started near a bend in the Rappahannock River about a mile and a half north of the tollhouse. From the river, the line ran south across the Plank Road, where it turned back north and again

---

10 And yet the supremely confident Lee planned to do precisely that.

11 *OR* 25, pt. 1, 396.

12 Ibid.

anchored near another bend in the Rappahannock. Sedgwick ordered the divisions of Burnham and Newton to face west, joined by Wheaton's brigade from Brooks' division. Near the tollgate, Russell's brigade faced west a little, too, but also bent toward the south, joining with the New Jersey Brigade, now under Col. Samuel Buck. Finally, the brigades of Thomas Neill and Lewis Grant made up the element of the VI Corps facing eastward.

There were inherent weaknesses in the line, though. Because of the terrain, and lacking an adequate number of men, neither flank was actually anchored on the river, which could offer Confederates the chance to slip through and drive toward the Federal rear and Banks' Ford. The terrain posed another problem: the rolling nature of the fields offered high hills and low valleys. The high hills would offer positions of strong defense for the Federal infantry, but the low valleys would hamper the use of artillery because the big guns could not depress their muzzles enough to cover some points. On the left flank, where the valleys and paucity of men made it impossible to form a contiguous line, the line had considerable gaps.

The greatest weakness in the line, though, was Sedgwick's lack of reserves, made all the more acute because no one knew whether Hooker would ever send help. Brigade commanders each did what they could to keep a regiment off the line, in case of disaster.

The true backbone of Sedgwick's line was the guns of Tompkins' VI Corps artillery, which covered the open fields of advance to the west. The long reach of Hunt's reserve guns at the ford also afforded Sedgwick potential cover. From Stafford Heights across the river from Fredericksburg, more of Hunt's guns watched the backs of Gibbon's men.

Sedgwick also had the important advantage of interior lines. The VI Corps controlled portions of the River Road, providing an easy avenue for men to move to and from the river and back and forth between the right and left flanks. It also held the Orange Plank Road, which provided open fields of fire and another way to move men from flank to flank. By holding the Orange Plank Road, Sedgwick sat on the direct line between Chancellorsville and Fredericksburg, separating McLaws' division from Early's, which had started making grumbling noises in the VI Corps' rear. Coordinating an attack across the enemy's front would be a major headache and liability for the Confederates, to say the least.

From the dispositions of the VI Corps, it was obvious to anyone with any military knowledge that Sedgwick had no idea when or where his enemies might come from. The best he could do was make sure his closest exit, Banks' Ford, was secure. If he had to get north of the river quickly, he could.

With all that weighing on him, Sedgwick felt Hooker's lack of communication keenly. "From time to time he dictated a dispatch to General Hooker," wrote McMahon. "He would walk a few paces apart and listen; then returning to lie down again in the damp grass with his saddle for a pillow and try to sleep."[13]

Even as "Uncle John" attempted in vain to get even a little sleep, as restless as it might be, his men were settling into their new positions.

*   *   *

During the battle for Salem Heights, Lee's Bad Old Man had been out of the fight, even though his division sat only three miles from the battlefield. Even there, it posed a threat, had Sedgwick attempted to maneuver around McLaws' right flank. But Sedgwick did not make the attempt, so Early's men sat dormant, giving them additional time to catch their collective breath.

Late in the day, as the fighting around Salem Church quieted, Early's men made their presence known on the Telegraph Road by haranguing a Federal battery trying to catch up with Sedgwick's column after spending the day broken down in the city. The battery escaped to safety only after getting uncomfortably close to Early's men. "The approaching darkness rendered objects very indistinct," Early explained, "and we therefore watched the approaching piece until it got within a few hundred yards of us, when the drivers suddenly discovered who we were, wheeled rapidly, and dashed to the rear."[14]

---

13 Martin T. McMahon, "The Sixth Army Corps," *United States Service Magazine*, vol. V, 211. While in the field, or angry, it was common for Sedgwick to sleep under the stars. Staff office Martin T. McMahon recalled one instance of Sedgwick sleeping outside. "Once our quartermaster had spread a tent and the general lay down before it. When he went to sleep, I saw a shower coming up and ordered a soldier to put a tent fly over him; he woke up in about 10 minutes and said 'Who spread that?' I told him. 'Tell them to take it away.' I said, 'It's going to rain.' 'Never mind; it will cool me off.' He then lay down during the rain." Also, on the last night of Sedgwick's life, he slept beside a hay bale under the stars. Styple, *Generals in Bronze*, 83-85.

14 *OR* 25, pt. 1, 1,001-1,003.

A modern view of the battle-scarred Salem Church.

Kristopher D. White

Because only a few Confederate units had been embroiled in the morning's action on Marye's Heights, Early still had 6,100 men who had done little more than skirmish or maneuver. His was still the freshest division in the Army of Northern Virginia, and he intended to get it back into the battle. Early sent word to Lee and McLaws that he intended to attack in the morning to retake Marye's Heights and drive Sedgwick into the river.

Lee's spirits must have lifted at Early's dispatch. "I very much regret the possession of Fredericksburg by the enemy," the commander had written to his Bad Old Man earlier that afternoon, suggesting that he combine with McLaws for a coordinated attack. "I think you would demolish them. See if you cannot unite with him, and together destroy him."[15] Ever the audacious gambler, Lee appreciated a soldier willing to take the fight to the enemy in the spirit of Napoleon or Jackson. He sent word to McLaws, ordering him to aid in the assaults. "Communicate with [Early], and arrange the junction, if necessary and practicable," he wrote. "It is necessary that you beat the enemy, and I hope you will do it."[16]

Even with the combined strength of Early's and McLaws' divisions—plus Mahone's and Wilcox's brigades—Lee realized that the match would be unfavorable to his commanders in numbers, but he also recognized that the Federals seemed to have lost their fighting spirit. A determined assault from two veteran divisions could break Sedgwick.

Early prepared his men for battle. His largest brigade, John Brown Gordon's, would have the honor of retaking Marye's Heights, supported by "Extra Billy" Smith's Virginia brigade and Barksdale's Mississippi brigade, still attached to Early. Hays' and Hoke's brigades would attack north across Hazel Run and, after Marye's Heights fell, try to link with elements of McLaws' division to make the final assault on the Federals of the Greek Cross.

Near 7:00 a.m., Old Jube put his men into motion. He rode to Hoke and Hays to inform them of their orders and finalize their dispositions, then turned onto the Telegraph Road to lead Gordon up to Fredericksburg. However, when he reached the position assigned to the

15 *OR* 25, pt. 2, 769-770.

16 Ibid.

six Georgia regiments, there was no one there. Gordon, in his zeal, had launched the attack ahead of schedule. "Whether it was my fault or the fault of the wording of the order itself, I am not able to say; but there was a serious misunderstanding about it," Gordon later said.[17]

In prepping his men for the attack, Gordon had told his men, "I don't want you to holler. Wait until you get up close to the heights. Let every man raise a yell and take those heights. . . ."[18] The men answered Gordon's announcement with "a prolonged and thrilling shout, and moved briskly to the attack."[19]

Gordon's men first swept over Telegraph Hill—which, to their surprise, had been left unoccupied by the Federals. However, several local women, on a mission of mercy, were combing the hilltop for any remaining wounded soldiers.

Beyond, around Hazel Run, Gordon's men hit their first opposition. Members of the 33rd New York, "while regaling ourselves upon coffee, hard tack and pork," saw Gordon's movement and pushed forward in an effort to slow the Confederate advance.[20] "The Regiment was thrown forward as a forlorn hope, trusting that by desperate fighting we might hold the enemy in check," wrote Capt. James McNair.[21]

"We gained the heights as quickly as possible," wrote one of McNair's privates, W. L. Ingraham, "and there found ourselves face to face with the same foe we had driven from the same spot the day previous."[22] Ingraham complained that "instead of fortifying and holding those heights, gained with so much loss" the previous day, they had "pressed on in an insane

---

17 Gordon, *Reminiscences of the Civil War*, 100.

18 Mills Lane, ed. *"Dear Mother: Don't grieve about me. If I get killed, I'll only be dead."*: *Letters from Georgia Soldiers in the Civil War* (Savannah, GA, 1977), 233.

19 Gordon, *Reminiscences of the Civil War*, 100.

20 George A. Gale to unknown correspondent, May 9, 1863, source unknown.

21 Henry Wells Hand, ed. *Centennial History of the Town of Nunda?: With a Preliminary Recital of the Winning of Western New York, from the Fort Builders Age to the Last Conquest by Our Revolutionary Forefathers?* (Rochester, NY, 1908), 499.???

22 W. L. Ingraham to the *Democrat and American*, May 24, 1863, New York State Military Museum and Veterans Research Center, http://dmna.ny.gov/historic/reghist/civil/infantry/33rdInf/33rdInfCWN.htm (accessed June 12, 2012).

attempt to form a junction with Hooker."[23] Now he and his comrades were paying the price of that oversight. Ingraham took a bullet in his right side, directly over his bowels.

"You may ask if it went through me," he later wrote to his hometown newspaper, which had reported him dead after the battle:

> The wonder is that it did not. It was sent with force enough to go through three human bodies if nothing intervened to prevent. But through a kind Providence, my life was saved in this way. The ball, in the first place, passed through two thicknesses of my leather belt, then through my knit woolen blouse, and through my military jacket, and struck directly at the left end of my right hand vest pocket. I happened to have in that pocket—and the wonder is that they were all in the spot where the ball struck—a couple of brass buttons, a bone button, a couple of steel pens, and a leather string. These stopped the ball, and saved my life. The brass buttons were bent out of all shape, the bone button was broken into minute fragments, the pens were broken and bent into small pieces, and the leather string jammed and cut into two parts. . . .

The blow knocked me senseless, and the next thing I knew, two fellows in grey clothes were rolling me over, and exploring my wounds and my pockets at the same time. They asked me if I was able to walk. I told them I should hardly think so. They picked me up, saying that a half dead man was better than no prisoner. I while protested, but they hung to me, and after a [while] had me within their lines. One of their physicians examined me, and gave me treatment in the kindest manner.[24]

Meanwhile on the battlefield, the rest of Ingraham's compatriots fell back; Gordon's men, hot behind them, splashed chest-deep through Hazel Run and up the opposite slope of Willis Hill—quickly reclaiming Marye's Heights in the process. Most of Gibbon's division had already fallen back into the city to guard the bridges, and the token holding force he had left atop the heights withdrew without any more fight. Gordon, atop a fresh horse he had found riderless on the battlefield, celebrated the victory by christening his new steed "Marye." "[S]he proved to be the most superb

23 Ibid.

24 Ibid.

battlehorse that it was my fortune to mount during the war," he later reminisced.[25]

At the base of the heights, Barksdale's four Mississippi regiments retook the famous stone wall, severing the tenuous connection between Sedgwick and his rear guard. Barksdale wanted to push onward, but Early called him off: "[d]esist from the attack on the town and . . . dispose of [your] brigade so as to resist any advance from that direction."[26]

In the city, Gibbon still held the streets, supported by Hunt's guns on Stafford Heights, but he stood little chance of re-linking with the VI Corps by way of the Orange Plank Road. "[T]o our surprise, the rebels appeared in sight back of the town, rapidly filled up the entrenchments from which they were driven the day before," said one member of the 49th New York, stationed in the city. "We were in their power for a sudden charge would have taken us all prisoner."[27]

Gibbon looked for guidance. The highest-ranking officer nearby was Dan Butterfield. Butterfield sent orders to pull up the bridge that had been laid at the site of the old railroad bridge at the south end of town, but he ordered that the bridge below Chatham be left alone. Soon thereafter, though, a message came from Hooker directly, countermanding Butterfield's order and directing that both bridges stay in place. He also ordered Gibbon to keep his toe-hold on the city. "General Hooker wishes you kept at Fredericksburg," read the new orders from Butterfield.[28] Gibbon tried to keep at least a portion of Early's men fixed on him and not on Sedgwick.

When Confederates reappeared on the heights, the defense of the approaches to the city fell to Col. Norman J. Hall's brigade, which had been assigned to collect the dead from the May 3 battlefield. With roughly a mile and half of ground to cover, the spontaneous new assignment initially looked as if it might be too much for Hall's undersized brigade to handle. However, when elements of Smith's and Barksdale's brigades

25 Gordon, *Reminiscences of the Civil War*, 101.

26 Early, *Jubal Early's Memoirs*, 225.

27 John Michel Priest, *Turn Them Out To Die Like a Mule: The Civil War Letters of John N. Henry, 49th New York, 1861-1865* (Leesburg, VA, 1995), 221-222.

28 *OR* 25, pt. 2, 397.

A soldier stands guard over the grave and uncompleted monument to Mary Ball Washington on the outskirts of Fredericksburg.

Fredericksburg and Spotsylvania National Military Park

probed toward the city, they were "coolly, and handsomely repulsed and driven to their cover with some loss."[29] The battle-hardened 20th Massachusetts and 42nd New York—"The Tammany Hall Regiment"—held their ground. Still, if the Confederates advanced in force, Hall knew there was little he would be able to do. He mustered all the men he could find—including some 225 stragglers of the VI Corps—and deployed the bulk of his brigade in a skirmish line surrounding the north, west, and south sides of the city, with at least 25 feet between each man.[30] The only true mobile reserve he had were three companies of the 19th Massachusetts under Maj. Edmund Rice.[31]

29 *OR* 25, pt. 1, 359.

30 Scott, *Fallen Leaves*, 175.

31 Ibid.

From the Lacy House, Gibbon sent out Capt. William Plumer's 1st Company of Massachusetts Sharpshooters, also known as Andrew's Sharpshooters. Hall ordered the men "to occupy some buildings across the street south of the [city] cemetery," said marksman Luke Emerson Bicknell.[32] The deployment was easier said than done. "When I reached the street [William Street]," Bicknell said,

> I found that it was continuously swept by fire which made the surface fairly boil and [made] the air blue as twilight. Nine out of ten would have fallen in crossing the street; so I commenced drilling holes through the brick wall of the cemetery. Firing from the top of the wall was out of the question until we had the enemy quieted down, for a ramrod held above the wall was hit again and again, and a hat pushed up was riddled in a moment.[33]

The open space between the heights and city were a no-man's-land. Both sides seemed more than happy to exchange fire from a distance without venturing into the open fields or roads. Gibbon's division in the city was poised to do what it could to help Sedgwick's exposed corps, but his men proved to be little threat to the Confederates.

Butterfield grew more nervous. From the north side of the river, his spotters had a good view of what was happening. "Forces engaging Gibbon in front of Fredericksburg seem to imperil our communication with Sedgwick. . . ." he telegraphed Hooker. "I judge Sedgwick was waiting to here [sic] from you. It is important that he should get Warren's dispatch. Gibbon just advised me that deserter reports Longstreet's force in direction of Bowling Green."[34] While there was no way to confirm such a report, Butterfield well knew the railroad was, indeed, running up to Hamilton's Crossing, so rumors of Longstreet's arrival were certainly plausible. It is even possible that Gibbon mistook Gordon's initial approach over Telegraph Hill as the arrival of Longstreet's troops—mistaking one Georgian for the other—coming as the butternuts

---

32 Alden C. Ellis, *The Massachusetts Andrew Sharpshooters* (Jefferson, NC, 2012), 54.

33 *OR* 25, pt. 2, 397.

34 Ibid., 404.

did from a direction in which there were not supposed to be any Confederates.

Gordon represented the immediate threat, though. The victory at Willis Hill was not enough to quench his thirst for battle, new as he was to his brigadier's duties. He aggressively pushed his men to the west, supported by Smith's brigade, aiming his 2,500 men for a break in the Union lines near Taylor and Stansbury hills. As he did so, Federal artillery from Howe's position began pounding his men, and he pulled back to the cover of Willis Hill. Smith came up on Gordon's right and unwisely struck out toward Thomas Neill's brigade, but he too received a crushing fire from combined infantry and artillery units. Stubbornly the Virginians held on in an exposed position near Stansbury Hill. It turned into "a sharp fight," and losses quickly mounted.[35] The 58th Virginia became detached from the brigade and managed to have a quarter of its men captured along with their battle flag. "They were thus captured by their own misconduct, the enemy sending to take possession of them, which I could not prevent without bringing on a heavy engagement," Early wrote.[36]

His decision to avoid a heavy engagement stemmed from his realization that McLaws had no intention of joining the assault. By this time, it was almost 11:00 a.m., and he had heard no guns at all from Salem Heights, although he knew the clamor made by his own men certainly must have been audible. Near Hazel Run, Early called off Hoke and Hays from attacking—and he fumed.

*   *   *

At Chancellorsville, Lee eyed Hooker's position, wondering what "Mr. F. J." Hooker was up to. In a way, it was Antietam all over again: Lee stood on blood-soaked landscape after a particularly savage battle, vastly outnumbered by the bruised Union army before him, defying his enemy by waiting him out. Who had the stronger nerves? In Maryland, an intimidated McClellan had refused to move, allowing Lee to finally slip away—and the Union commander's stationary shell shock had lasted so

35 Ibid., 409.

36 Early, *Jubal Early's Memoirs*, 226.

long that Lincoln finally removed him from command. Now, Lee resolved to stare down Hooker in like fashion.

He must have believed that Hooker still had at least some capacity for aggression, else he might have ventured eastward toward Salem Church earlier than he did. He stayed put throughout May 3 and into May 4, however, knowing that if Hooker did make a move, the full brunt of battle would fall on the shoulders of Jeb Stuart, the cavalryman- turned-infantry corps commander now leading Jackson's men on the field. May 3 had been Stuart's finest day of the war, directing assaults that eventually collapsed the Union line. As capable as Stuart was, though, Lee saw no reason to press their luck and put Stuart in a position from which he would have to fend off Hooker's giant, wounded, angry army should the Federals make a push. Lee could only hope that Early could make quick work of Sedgwick, then move to aid the rest of the army at the crossroads.

There is little wonder that, in postwar years, supporters invested so much energy into propping up Lee's legacy. So much did, in fact, rest on him and his corps commanders, and without them the Army of Northern Virginia suffered a serious leadership vacuum. Longstreet was just starting to make his way north from Suffolk. Jackson, wounded during the battle, was just beginning an ambulance trip south to Guinea Station to take a train to a hospital in Richmond.[37] Stuart, promoted to take command of the Second Corps following the fall of Jackson and the wounding of A. P. Hill, left even the cavalry wing without an experienced commander. It harkened back to the days of the Peninsula campaign: when Lee took over, the command structure was unwieldy, and orders had to be issued to individual divisions. Once more, without Longstreet and Jackson, the command structure fell flat.

---

37 Following the amputation of Jackson's arm, Jackson's doctors determined that he should be taken to Richmond, Virginia, where he could recuperate in an actual hospital. Jackson was taken on May 4, 1863, 27 miles south to Guinea Station, Virginia, the location of the Confederate railhead. A number of his staff officers arrived ahead of the general's ambulance wagon. They were informed the tracks south, closer to Richmond, had been severed by Jackson's West Point roommate, Brig. Gen. George Stoneman. Stoneman, commanding the Federal raid on and around Richmond, cut the rail lines. Jackson was forced to stay at a nearby plantation office, owned by Thomas Coleman Chandler. On May 7, the tracks were restored, but that same day Jackson was diagnosed with pneumonia and could not be moved. Over the next three days, his condition worsened, and on May 10, he died, never making it to Richmond. Chris Mackowski and Kristopher White, *The Last Days of Stonewall Jackson*, 2nd ed. (Sacramento, CA, 2013).

At the moment, the piece of the puzzle giving Lee the most trouble was, surprisingly, the stalwart Lafayette McLaws. Without his corps commander, Longstreet, a fellow Georgian, McLaws had seemed lost, perhaps apprehensive, during the current campaign. On the morning of May 4, Sedgwick's consolidated position and the superiority of Tompkins' artillery had paralyzed him into inaction.

Fortunately for Lee, Hooker seemed just as frozen, and so the Confederate commander thinned his own ranks even further in an attempt to move things along on the Salem Church front. Just after 8:00 a.m., in answer to a request from McLaws, Lee dispatched the remaining three brigades of Anderson, 4,000 men, to fill the gap between Early and McLaws. By linking the two wings with three more brigades, Lee brought the numbers there up to almost a 1-to-1 ratio.

Anderson made his way to the coming battlefield, but it took a great deal of time to get into position because Sedgwick held nearly a mile of the Orange Plank Road, obstructing Anderson's direct line of march. To get to his assigned position, Anderson had to take back roads and then cut across country. Once his men came to Hazel Run, they had to ascend and descend hills and valleys and deal with rocky terrain and thick underbrush. They finally started filing into position around 11:00 a.m.

Lee arrived at Salem Church shortly thereafter.

Chapter Sixteen

A Fighting Withdrawal:

The Battle of Banks' Ford

On the morning of May 4, as Lee arrived on the Salem Heights battlefield to prepare his hodgepodge "corps" for battle, Sedgwick looked for some sort of direction—any kind of direction at all—from higher up.

It had been a long night full of silence from headquarters. Sedgwick had sent three messages to Hooker, but as of 6:00 a.m. he had received no orders and no reply aside from the unofficial note from Warren. "I am anxious to hear from General Hooker," he wrote to Butterfield. "There is a strong force in front of me, strongly posted. I cannot attack with any hope of dislodging them until I know something definite as to the position of their main body and ours. I have sent two or three messengers to Banks' Ford, but none have returned, nor have I heard from the general since yesterday."[1]

When a message from Hooker finally did arrive around 8:30 a.m., it did little to relieve Sedgwick. "The general commanding desires that you telegraph to him your exact position," it said. "What information have you respecting the force of the enemy in front and rear? What is your strength? Is there any danger of a force coming up in your rear and cutting

---

1 *OR* 25, pt. 2, 402.

off communications? Can you sustain yourself acting separately or in cooperation with us?"[2]

Sedgwick had to be disconcerted by the communiqué. Not only were there no instructions, the commanding general apparently had little clue as to where Sedgwick was or what he should do with the left wing of the army. Sedgwick sent word back to Hooker that it "depends upon the condition and position of your force whether I can sustain myself here." He would have been even more befuddled had he seen a dispatch Butterfield had sent him at 8:00 a.m. (By this point, the delay in relaying orders would have been comical—if it was not also becoming very problematic.) "The general . . . desires that if any portion of your force is available, and can be spared, they be moved. . . ." Butterfield wrote. "He is under the impression that you have three brigades in reserve, and thinks perhaps two of them might be disposed as above."[3]

Clearly, neither Sedgwick nor Hooker had any idea what was happening on the other's front, and neither entertained the thought of advancing without support from the other. "My position is bad," Sedgwick lamented in a later note to Hooker, indicating that it would be hard to defend because his men were stretched thin. "Can you help me strongly if I am attacked?"[4] Gun shy from the previous evening's drubbing, Sedgwick was even more worried because he believed the enemy had been reinforced during the night.[5]

Rumors of Longstreet's arrival—untrue—fueled his paranoia, and intelligence reports from Thaddeus Lowe's balloon overestimated Early's force by almost a factor of two.[6]

By the time Gordon launched his impotent midmorning assault, Sedgwick expected the worst and interpreted the attack in that light: "The enemy are pressing me hard," he wrote at 11:00 a.m. "The enemy threatens

2   Ibid., 402-403.

3   Ibid., 404.

4   Ibid., 408.

5   Ibid., 402.

6   Ibid., 409.

An Edwin Forbes sketch of the fighting at Banks Ford. In the right foreground is Falmouth, Virginia. Federal gunners are firing from this position in support of Sedgwick's men in the far distance, represented by a ball of smoke.

Library of Congress

me strongly on two fronts," he added 15 minutes later.[7] He had even begun taking position to cross the Rappahannock "whenever necessary."[8]

Hooker believed Lee intended "to make the attempt to pierce our center," but as the morning wore on and no attack came, Hooker started to reevaluate his options. It seems he still could not find the nerve to make a direct assault, but he started to eye a possible movement around Lee's army in a Jackson-like flanking maneuver. Do not cross the river at Banks' Ford, he ordered Sedgwick. "If it is practicable for you to maintain a position south side Rappahannock, near Banks' Ford, you will do so," the order read. "It is very important that we retain position at Banks' Ford."[9] A subsequent order said "the position of your corps on the south bank of the Rappahannock will be as favorable as the general could desire. It is for

7 Ibid.

8 Ibid., 407.

9 Ibid., 408.

Major General Richard Anderson.

*Fredericksburg and Spotsylvania
National Military Park*

this reason he desires that your troops may not cross the Rappahannock."[10]

A forward thrust somewhere along his Chancellorsville line would have crushed Stuart's meager force; even with Anderson still on the scene, Hooker would have enjoyed better than a two-to-one advantage against the Confederates. Even on the evening of May 3, he had boasted to Charles Wainwright that he would give Lee one more day to attack him, "and 'then if he does not,' said Hooker, 'let him look out.'"[11] But by morning, he was already hedging. "I felt [Chancellorsville] could be carried only at a frightful loss," he later tried to explain.[12] Shaken by his two near-death experiences on May 3, dazed from his concussion, humbled by Jackson's surprise attack, Hooker was in no condition for a battle of nerves with Lee. Rather than use his army for attack, he considered maneuvering away, suggesting he had lost confidence in his army as well as himself.

Such was an unfair assessment of the fighting qualities of the Army of the Potomac. Hooker had been outmaneuvered and outgeneraled. And now that an opportunity for redemption had presented itself, Hooker was proving unequal to the task.

*   *   *

10 Ibid.

11 Nevins, *A Diary of Battle*, 193-194.

12 Sears, *Chancellorsville*, 399.

Hours elapsed. Lee arrived at Salem Church around 11:00 a.m. and discovered that the Union positions in front of Anderson had been poorly reconnoitered . McLaws' sluggishness had already set the commanding general in a mood, and the lack of information about the Federal dispositions only made it worse. "[T]he old man seemed to be feeling so real wicked," artillerist Porter Alexander said.[13]

Lee directed the intelligence-gathering himself. As the picture along the west-facing front of the Federal horseshoe became clearer to him, Lee understood the extent of the gap between McLaws' and Early's divisions. He filled in the space in his line with the brigades of Ambrose Wright, Carnot Posey, and Edward Perry from Richard Anderson's First Corps division. In the meantime, he also tried to sort out the communication snafus between Early and McLaws; each, it turned out, had been expecting the other to start the attack. McLaws was the senior officer on the field, thus he should have taken the reins of the attack and coordinated between his men and the men of Early's division—yet this fact apparently did not occur to the burly Georgian.

The army commander was not the only one whose nerves were on end. Private William Judkins of the 22nd Georgia saw comrades so unnerved by the previous day's fight that one of them shot himself in the foot. "Major Walden of our regiment told him that it should have been through his heart. He cursed the fellow for a coward," Judkins wrote. A member of his own Company G "swallowed some tobacco to make himself sick, which it did, so he could get out of the fight. . . . He came very near being court-martialed for it."[14]

Resigned to the reality that the underprepared McLaws was not as aggressive as he should be, Lee turned to Early and Anderson's men to deliver an assault on the left of Sedgwick's position. If Early, supported by Anderson, could drive in Howe's VI Corps division, the Federals would be forced to either fight backed against the Rappahannock or be driven west into the waiting arms of McLaws.

Coordinating divisions from two separate corps proved more difficult than expected, compounded by the length of the communication line

13 Gary W. Gallagher, *Fighting for the Confederacy*, 213.

14 Judkins, Memoir, 51.

linking all the units. While the Confederates settled into their places, Federal gunners took shots at them. "I have indeed respect for that artillery!" one of Wilcox's men wrote.

> We had no works worth mentioning, could not advance because the line was not complete, and retreat was out of the question, so we had to stay. Never, I think, did a party of men hug the ground so close as we did. Everybody was as quiet as death. One might have heard a pin drop, I think, but for the unearthly whizzing of the enemy's missiles, and in the latter part the groans of the wounded.[15]

The Federals watched the Confederate deployments with edgy interest. "Movements of heavy columns of the enemy were plainly visible all the morning," wrote a Vermonter:

> Our lines were so extended that we could not be well supported. We were aware of our precarious situation, and only waited for the night in which to evacuate unless reinforcements come for us. We anxiously hoped they might come, and woe would have been to the rebels had but a single corps come to our relief. [W]e waited on our arms the bursting of the storm which seemed inevitable. Closely did we watch the declining sun and the movements of the hosts opposed to us.[16]

It was not until nearly 6:00 p.m. that Alexander finally set things in motion—three cannon shots, fired in rapid succession, signaled the start of the assault—and a race began against fading daylight. "About an hour before dark they fired a signal gun and they piled in on us from three sides as thick as bees around a hive," wrote a Vermonter.[17] "The whole hillside was alive with men," added a Mainer. "A magnificent sight."[18]

15 Fred Reipschlager, *Register and Advertiser* (Mobile, AL), June 3, 1863, in the Fredericksburg and Spotsylvania National Military Park bound manuscript collection, vol. 63.

16 Letter to *Vermont Watchman and State Journal*, May 22, 1863, in the Fredericksburg and Spotsylvania National Military Park bound manuscript collection, vol. 149.

17 Robert Pratt to Brother Sid, May 13, 1863, in the Fredericksburg and Spotsylvania National Military Park bound manuscript collection, vol. 323.

18 Hyde, *Following the Greek Cross*, 75.

Gordon's Georgia brigade stepped off from Marye's Heights, marching northwest, driving in much of the skirmish line in Howe's front. Gordon's men then engaged Howe's forward line, consisting of Thomas Neill's brigade, bolstered by the 4th and 5th Vermont from Grant's Vermont brigade. The balls flew thick as hailstones, said a member of the 21st New Jersey. "I no more expected to get out of that place alive that I expected to fly," he remembered.[19] His colonel, Gilliam Van Houten, was not so lucky. Neill himself met with misfortune, too. As his men started to give way, the general's horse was hit and Neill was thrown to the ground. Neill survived, but confusion reigned supreme. "I rode into . . . battery smoke and barely escaped being blown to pieces by one of our own shells," recalled Maj. Thomas Hyde of the 7th Maine.[20]

Hoke and Hays, meanwhile, moved in a more northerly direction toward the Orange Plank Road. "It was a splendid sight to see the rapid and orderly advance of these two brigades," Early said.[21] A member of Hays' 9th Louisiana remembered it a little differently, saying his regiment went at the Federals like a pack of hunting dogs, "not at a double quick but as hard as they could run squalling & hollering as loud as they could." The Yanks, he said, "got up and dusted."[22]

"The column in our front (7th, 8th, and 9th Louisiana) advanced within four rods of us, their dirty flag waving, and on they come," remembered one Vermonter. "[Confederate] batteries are at work at the highest speed, the men lie close to the ground calm but determined."[23]

After crossing the road, though, Robert Hoke was struck in the shoulder and severely wounded. Leaderless, the North Carolinians drifted into Hays' men. Colonel Isaac Avery of the 6th North Carolina assumed brigade command and got the Tar Heels back in order, but not before they unleashed a volley into their Creole counterparts.

19 John J. Toffey to Parents, May 9, 1863, in the Fredericksburg and Spotsylvania National Military Park bound manuscript collection, vol. 46.

20 Hyde, *Following the Greek Cross or Memoirs of the Sixth Army Corps*, 75.

21 Early, *Early's Memoirs, 229.*

22 Sears, *Chancellorsville*, 414.

23 Letter to *Vermont Watchman and State Journal*, May 22, 1863, in the Fredericksburg and Spotsylvania National Military Park bound manuscript collection.

Colonel Lewis Grant.

Fredericksburg and Spotsylvania National Military Park

Hays' men took even more of a shellacking as they moved toward the Federals. Their line of march exposed the brigade's left flank to the men of the Vermont brigade. "[O]n they came like an avalanche to all appearances as though all would be swept before them," recalled one Green Mountain

Brigadier General Thomas Neill.

Fredericksburg and Spotsylvania National Military Park

Brigadier General Robert F. Hoke.

*Fredericksburg and Spotsylvania
National Military Park*

Boy.[24] Grant's men opened with "[a] wall of fire on three sides. The air was fairly hissing with round shot, grape, canister, and minie balls."[25] Across the Rappahannock, Federal shells fell in the ranks of the 9th Louisiana; one shell alone dropped 17 men killed and wounded.[26]

"We were partly secluded from sight by the unevenness of the land," another Vermonter explained. "In an instant at the word, we sprung to our feet with bayonets fixed and charged. We soon dispersed them and took many prisoners. . . . Their colors were only saved by being torn from the staff and put in the pocket of one long-legged chap, who made good use of his legs."[27]

Hays' stunned men careened into Neill's line; the chaos unexpectedly overwhelmed the 20th New York, which broke and ran under the pressure. A largely German regiment from New York City, the 20th would earn the ignoble nickname—shared by the men of Howard's XI Corps, who were likewise largely German and who had broken under Jackson's surprise flank attack—as "the Flying Dutchmen."

24 Erastus Scott to Father, May 18, 1863, in the Fredericksburg and Spotsylvania National Military Park bound manuscript collection, vol. 285.

25 Henry E. Handerson, *Yankee in Gray: The Civil War Memoirs of Henry E. Handerson: with a selection of his wartime letters* (Cleveland, OH, 1962), 102.

26 Jones, *The Civil War Memoirs of Captain William J. Seymour*, 55.

27 Letter to *Vermont Watchman and State Journal*, May 22, 1863, in the Fredericksburg and Spotsylvania National Military Park bound manuscript collection, vol. 149.

Colonel Isaac Avery, 6th North Carolina.

Fredericksburg and Spotsylvania National Military Park

The fleeing New Yorkers posed a problem for Rigby's artillerists. By running across the front of the Maryland battery, the New Yorkers blocked its field of fire. "They frightened my horses," Rigby added, "and created so much confusion I could do nothing."[28] With Confederates close on their heels, the artillerists were forced to limber and head for the rear. "We retreated in the best order possible, turning and firing on the enemy at every opportunity," recounted a retreating officer of the 7th Maine.[29]

Early's assault became a victim of its own success, though. "[O]wing to the rapidity of our charge, the brigade became inextricably confused," explained a lieutenant with the 9th Louisiana. "One half the men were so broken down by previous hard marching as to be unable to keep up with the rest. . . . No support was near us, and fresh bodies of the enemy flanking us on the right."[30]

Along Anderson's front, the men of Wright and Posey stepped off from their positions along Hazel Run. In the tangled undergrowth and growing darkness, they, like Hoke's brigade, drifted out of position and were unable to stay connected with Early. Wright's and Posey's men drifted to left, and in doing so cut off Perry's Floridians, diluting the punch of all three brigades. As they got closer to the Union lines, concentrated artillery and small arms fire shredded them. In their own confused entanglement, they could do little to respond, although their presence at least kept Brooks tied down so he could not reinforce other parts of the beleaguered Federal line.

Darkness began taking hold of the battlefield. Fog rolled off the river, mingling with the smoke of battle. "Uncle John" worried about the fate of his men. The men themselves worried, too. "General, it looks as if the Sixth Corps is going to close its career today," a young officer had said to him just a little while earlier.

"It has somewhat that appearance," Sedgwick replied.

"Then if the Sixth Corps goes out of existence today, I hope it will be with a blaze of glory that will light the history of this war for all time."

---

28 *OR* 25, pt. 1, 597.

29 Selden Connor to unknown correspondent, May 10, 1863, in Selden Connor Papers, Brown University, "Connor, Selden, Virgil R. Connor, and Lot M. 1812-1883 Morrill."

30 Handerson, *Yankee in Gray*, 102.

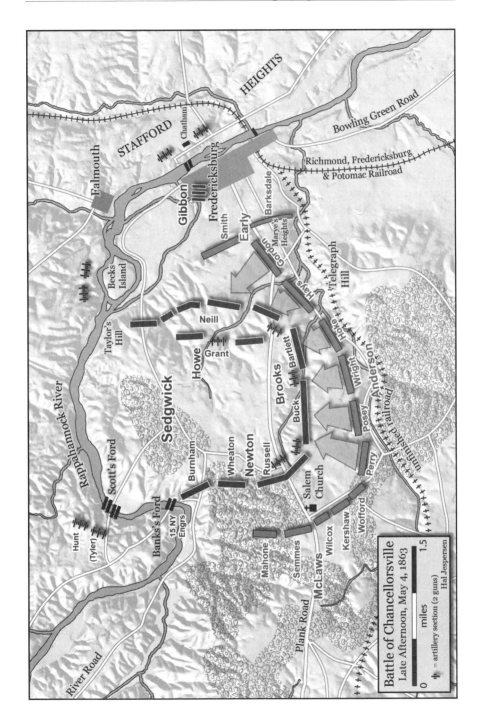

Battle of Chancellorsville
Late Afternoon, May 4, 1863

0 miles 1.5

⊬ = artillery section (2 guns)

Hal Jespersen

Sedgwick smiled. "I will tell you a secret," he said; "there will be no surrendering."[31]

He had not said there would be "no retreating," however, and as the Confederates squeezed him, Sedgwick dispatched Newton to the ford to lay out a new defensive line. There, Newton found a surprisingly sober Henry Benham. The two engineers laid out a line that would protect the line of retreat, covered by Hunt's guns, now commanded by Brig. Gen. Robert O. Tyler. They also began to oversee the evacuation of wounded soldiers and the surgeons who tended them.

At the front, using their interior lines, the 31st New York, 98th Pennsylvania, and Battery G, 2nd United States Artillery shifted from the Federal right flank to the beleaguered left. The 31st moved in to help the 4th Vermont, which was being pushed closer to the river. "Our brigade formed the first line of battle, and a short distance in the rear were the Vermonters formed in line to support us," wrote Capt. George Gale of the 31st. When the Confederates advanced in double rows of battle, "[t]heir first line seemed to melt away as if by magic, before our fire, but their second soon came up to the work, and we found there was work before us. By this time their right and left, had succeeded in gaining a position where they could pour a cross fire into us, which they did. We were now forced to fall back, and, having done so, we formed our line on that of the Vermonters."[32]

Grant then countered, advancing his entire brigade into Early's mass of gray. "At every discharge the grape could be heard rattling against the trees like throwing a handful of pebbles against the side of a building," wrote Wilbur Fisk of the 2nd Vermont. "No enemy could stand such a fire, and they were soon driven back."[33] The charge of the Vermonters took the last steam out of the Confederate advance.

But by this time Sedgwick had had enough. He began pulling the VI Corps back for withdrawal across the river.

---

31 Martin T. McMahon, *Proceedings of the Reunion Society of Vermont Officers 1864-1868* (Burlington, VT, 1885), 24.

32 George A. Gale to Mother and Sister, May 9, 1863, New York State Military Museum and Veterans Research Center, http://dmna.ny.gov/historic/reghist/civil/infantry/33rdInf/33rdInfCWN.htm (accessed April 9, 2012).

33 Fisk, *Hard Marching Every Day*, 84.

Lee ordered McLaws to pursue and not allow the Union men to cross the river and escape. "Genls Anderson & Early drove the enemy handsomely from the positions on Dowman's Hill beyond the Plank road. . . ." he wrote. "We can't find any of the enemy south of the Plank road. But if we let them alone until morning we will find them again intrenched, so I wish to push them over the river tonight."[34] It was the first and only night attack Lee ever ordered.

McLaws received the order near 10:00 p.m. "At the signal forward we all moved at once," wrote a member of Wofford's brigade, charged with part of the pursuit. "The Yankees fought well at first, but when they found we were on three sides of them they made tracks for the river."[35] Wilcox's brigade, too, joined in the pursuit, but the Confederates could do little more than grope ahead in the deepening gloom through the thick woods. Skirmishes broke out in the dark. "We still moved forward—pressing them at every point until 1 o'clock at night—capturing many prisoners," Wofford's man wrote. "We pushed forward as far as we thought prudent in the night."[36]

Artillerists tried to support the advance, but in the dark they guessed their shots as much as aimed them. Federal artillerists responded in kind. "[T]hey fired rappidly with both artillery and small arms, but were routed in great confusion," wrote Isaiah Fogelman of the 8th Louisiana. "They rallied four times. The 4th line of battle checked our charge."[37]

For another Louisianan, Thomas Benton Reed of the 9th, the day's engagement had been his first major fight, but it was the advance through the dark wood that would leave the most lasting impression. "We were going through a piece of woods and I stopped to load my gun," he wrote. "The Yankees were shelling us and the shells were bursting and pounding in those large tree tops, and just as I got my gun loaded a piece of shell

34 Clifford Dowdy, *The Wartime Papers of Robert E. Lee* (Cambridge, MA, 1987), 454-455.

35 William Montgomery to unknown correspondent, May 7, 1863, in the Fredericksburg and Spotsylvania National Military Park bound manuscript collection, vol. 29.

36 Ibid.

37 Isaiah Fogelman, Diary, 20, in the Fredericksburg and Spotsylvania National Military Park bound manuscript collection, vol. 113-06.

struck a man just in front of me and tore his head all in pieces and his blood and brains spattered all over me."[38]

Reed would get another shock the next morning when he discovered that one of his brothers had been killed in the fight. "oh! such a night as this one was," Reed lamented. "I had come to Virginia to be with my brothers and now they were both dead. One was buried and the other—oh! the horrors of war . . . !

> The ball had pierced his right cheek, just under his right eye, and had come out at the back of his head. I suppose when the ball struck him he threw his right hand to his face and held his gun in his left hand—at least this is the way he was lying when we found him. It seemed that he had not made a struggle.[39]

Both sides groped at each other through the dark, firing as much at shadows as at each other. Federals felt the squeeze as much from their own diminishing ammunition as from the steady Confederate pressure. Members of the 49th New York, for instance, reported firing 60 rounds each before finally running out.[40] As they did, some of them slipped away from the line to a house a short distance to the rear, where they tended to their wounded. Then, "it being dark and being relieved, they fell back."[41]

Word never made it to their skirmishers out front, though, who found themselves cut off. "[W]e could see nothing to fire at but the flash of the enemy's gun," wrote one member of the regiment in a letter to his hometown newspaper. "Slowly but surely they were advancing in large numbers, we could hear the cracking of dry sticks under their feet which told [us] plainly that . . . if they advanced we must surely be taken for they

38 Thomas Benton Reed, *A Private in Gray* (New York, NY, 2012), 30.

39 Ibid., 31-32.

40 A. W. Brazee, letter to the *Jamestown (NY) Journal*, May 13, 1863, in the Fredericksburg and Spotsylvania National Military Park bound manuscript collection, vol. 395.

41 Ibid.

must have had at least a regiment in front of our skirmishers. . . . We could hear the commands of their officers and of course they could hear ours."[42]

Faced with such odds, the New Yorkers resorted to trickery. A wily captain huddled with the men in a few squads, then ordered, over-loudly, "Battalion, halt!"

"We've got them now—reinforcements are at hand!" one of his privates shouted.

"Battalion," the captain commanded, "ready, aim fire!"

Every member of the squad fired "at the word," but the order immediately followed to cease firing. "Boys," said the captain, "if they advance, give them a volley; reserve your full fire till you can make it count, then give them h—l."

"[T]his little plan of strategy seemed to have the desired effect for the enemy instead of advancing, fell back," the New Yorker wrote. "[A]s soon as the word could be passed along the line, we did the same thing, . . ."[43]

Nonetheless, all along the constricting Federal line, Confederates exerted slow but inexorable pressure. Sedgwick sent word to Hooker urgently asking for instructions. "My army is hemmed in upon the slope. " he wrote. "If I had only this army to care for, I would withdraw it tonight. Do your operations require that I should jeopardize it by retaining it here? An immediate reply is indispensable, or I may feel obliged to withdraw."[44]

Word finally returned near 2:00 a.m.: "Withdraw. Cover the river, and prevent any force crossing."[45]

Sedgwick had his men moving almost immediately. Engineers had covered the planks with sod to muffle noise, and soldiers tried to cross quietly. "One little circumstance shows the caution we took not to attract the attention of the enemy. . . . [W]e were ordered to take our cups from

---

42 Letter from 49th New York to the *Jamestown (NY) Journal*, May 22, 1863, in the Fredericksburg and Spotsylvania National Military Park bound manuscript collection, vol. 395.

43 Ibid.

44 *OR* 25, pt. 2, 412.

45 Ibid., 418.

the outside of our haversacks and place them inside. . . ." wrote a Vermonter, Henry H. Houghton.[46]

Yet the Confederates knew what was up, even through the fog. Artillerists under Alexander's orders started lobbing shells in the direction of the bridges. The first shot "had the desired effect as it struck the line moving on the bridge and we could distinctly hear the horses tramping on the wood bridge in wild confusion," wrote James Phillips of the 12th Virginia. Satisfied, Alexander asked his men to "put another in the same place." "[A]nd so the guns opened on them and played havoc with them," Phillips continued. "Teams & men were knocked over in the river and were drowned. They finally got over the river before daybreak."[47]

Once over, reported Pennsylvania surgeon Edwin Buckman, they "rested in the ravines and woods beyond until morning when we moved a couple of miles and encamped in the woods two nights and days during which time it rained a good deal making the camp most abominably muddy."[48]

If Hooker had had his way, though, Sedgwick might have stayed on the south bank after all. A second message came from him countermanding the first and ordering Sedgwick to stay. Hooker had changed his mind and issued the second order only 15 minutes later, but the communications problems that had plagued the entire campaign played a hand in delaying the second order by two hours. By that point, already part way across and now under fire, Sedgwick had no intention of turning back. "Uncle John" was uncertain about the size of the Confederate force besieging him, uncertain whether he could hold his hemmed-in line along the river, and uncertain whether Hooker would actually even aid the VI Corps. The march across the Rappahannock continued.

Not that it continued in good order, necessarily. "We stood the fire and so did they for our batteries did pour in the [grape] and canister to

46 Henry H. Houghton, Memoir, in the Fredericksburg and Spotsylvania National Military Park bound manuscript collection, vol. 53.

47 James E. Phillips, Memoir, in the Fredericksburg and Spotsylvania National Military Park bound manuscript collection, vol. 118.

48 Edwin Buckman to Mrs. E. D. Buckman, May 9, 1863, in the Fredericksburg and Spotsylvania National Military Park bound manuscript collection, vol. 399.

them and mowed them down awful but they drove us back near to the pontoons where we remained on skirmish and in line of battle," recalled Henry Taylor of the 21st New Jersey.[49]

As the night slipped toward morning and Confederate pressure continued, order among the Federals began to deteriorate. By the time the 102nd Pennsylvania—one of the last units to cross—reached the bridge, confusion abounded. Confederate troops could be heard closing in, and the regiment seems to have disintegrated in the darkness. Some of the Pennsylvanians managed to escape, but more than a hundred were taken prisoner. Captain Orlando M. Loomis of Company I, together with several other paroled prisoners, later claimed that the regiment's flag was "torn from its staff, tied around some stones, and thrown into the river to prevent the enemy from taking it."[50]

The 21st New Jersey claimed to be the last rear-guard regiment on the hostile side of the river. "We undertook to swim or ford the Rappahannock but came near being drowned and gave up," Henry Taylor wrote, "but we concluded to go up to the pontoons, and it was well we did for the bridges were up but they came over for us, the Rebs shelling and firing on us. After crossing we fell back in the woods from the river. The Rebs commenced to shell us; they drove us out and we fell back farther."[51]

By then, though, it was all smoke and thunder. Sedgwick had effected a successful crossing. The Army of the Potomac's VI Corps sat safely on the north side of the river.

49 Henry Taylor, Diary, May 4, 1863, in the Fredericksburg and Spotsylvania National Military Park bound manuscript collection, vol. 73.

50 Richard Sauers, *Advance the Colors: Pennsylvania Civil War Battle Flags*, 2 vols. (Harrisburg, PA, 1991), vol. 2, 342-345. This flag was recovered from the Rappahannock and is today on display at Soldiers & Sailors Memorial Hall and Museum in Pittsburgh, Pennsylvania.

51 Henry Taylor, Diary, May 4, 1863, in the Fredericksburg and Spotsylvania National Military Park bound manuscript collection, vol. 73.

Banks' Ford on the Rappahannock River in the postwar years.

Fredericksburg and Spotsylvania National Military Park

Chapter Seventeen

"We might have gained a great victory."

As the late-night hours of May 4 dissolved into the early morning hours of May 5, Fighting Joe Hooker called his corps commanders together at Chancellorsville. Sedgwick, of course, was still trapped along the Rappahannock to the east, but Hooker had summoned Butterfield from Falmouth, and he invited Warren to sit in, as well. His messenger could not find XII Corps commander Henry Slocum, but the rest of the generals assembled. The moon, just past full, hung high over Hooker's large tent.

Should the army stay on its current front and fight it out, Hooker asked, or should the army retreat in the face of an inferior enemy? He invited the generals to discuss the question, then he and Butterfield excused themselves.

Warren proposed to stay and fight, as did Meade and Reynolds—neither of whom had seen much action thus far, and so had huge numbers of fresh men at their disposal. Reynolds, having cast his vote, lay down on a cot for a nap and asked Meade to wake him when the deliberations concluded. Howard, who had created much of the mess they were in by the inattention that had permitted Jackson's surprise flank attack, and so had a reputation to rehabilitate, also wanted to stay and fight. Meade added that the absent Slocum, he knew, also wanted to advance.

Major General Henry Slocum.

Fredericksburg and Spotsylvania National Military Park

Couch, with the caution of a McClellanite, seemed to favor retreat, although he was somewhat noncommittal about it. Later, he would claim that it was because he did not trust Hooker's leadership. The pugnacious Sickles, somewhat surprisingly, opted for retreat as well. As a political general, whom few in the room respected or cared to hear from, he based his decision on political rather than military reasons, and he could already read which way Hooker's wind was blowing.

Hooker reentered, listened to the summary of the discussion, and concluded that the four-to-two decision to stay and fight meant that the army should retreat. "What was the point of calling us together at this time of night when he intended to retreat anyhow?" groused Reynolds.[1] A befuddled Slocum arrived just as the party was breaking up.

And so the Chancellorsville campaign came to a close. Gibbon withdrew his division and all the wounded he could out of the city of Fredericksburg, while Hooker withdrew his army across the Rappahannock.

"We marched, we fought, we failed," wrote one Indiana soldier. "We were not defeated but we did not defeat."

Brigadier General Alpheus Williams was more pointed in his conclusion: "We have lost physically and numerically, but still more morally . . . by universal want of confidence in the commanding officer."[2]

*　*　*

In its May 23 issue, *Harper's Weekly* featured an engraving of the 6th Maine standing atop Marye's Heights, its banner triumphantly planted in the Confederate works, a battle-worn Star-Spangled Banner with tattered edges unfurled over piles of defeated Rebels.[3]

"Every one sees that our corps has not only done its whole duty, but has achieved the only success obtained," wrote Sedgwick in a June 3 letter to his sister.[4] Sadly, the full-page image in *Harper*'s notwithstanding, there was little truth in Sedgwick's statement.

To his credit, his crossing of the Rappahannock and the diversion he provided worked to perfection in the earliest days of the campaign. The VI

1　Bigelow, *The Campaign of Chancellorsville*, 420.

2　Williams, *From the Cannon's Mouth*, 204.

3　It should be noted that the Light Division was a short-lived experiment. As the Army of the Potomac moved north in pursuit of Lee during the Gettysburg campaign, the Union high command disbanded the Light Division on June 11, 1863.

4　Sedgwick to Emily Sedgwick Welch, June 3, 1863, in Stoeckel, ed., *Correspondence of John Sedgwick Major-General*, vol. 1, 131.

The 6th Maine victorious atop Marye's Heights from the
May 23, 1863, edition of *Harper's Weekly*.

Library of Congress

Corps' presence kept Lee off balance and unsure of the Federal army's intentions. Lee realized almost too late that Sedgwick's presence south of the beleaguered city was merely a feint, and had Hooker not paused at Chancellorsville on April 30 the campaign might have turned out very differently.

After Lee once turned his attention away, Sedgwick still had the opportunity to re-attract it, but because of poor communications and his own lack of assertiveness, Sedgwick failed to launch the diversionary attacks ordered by Hooker. He likewise failed, on May 2, to take advantage of Robert Chilton's bungled orders and capture the Confederate line on Marye's Heights when Early had temporarily evacuated the position.

When ordered to relieve Hooker, Sedgwick moved at a pace so slow it could almost have been measured in geological time. The Gibraltar of Virginia—Marye's Heights—intimidated him so much that he wasted precious hours methodically arranging his men for their assaults even though he had a vastly superior force. Once he had captured the Heights, he held them for only 20 hours before nervous orders from a nervous Butterfield allowed Gordon's single brigade to recapture them with very little resistance, effectively splitting the VI Corps from Gibbon's division in the city, isolating both units and leaving each with only a single line of retreat.

After that initial victory at Marye's Heights, Sedgwick failed to follow up by pressing on with all haste to Chancellorsville. While prudent to wait for his freshest division to take the lead, the movement cost precious time when time was of the essence. By the time the opening salvos of the fight at Salem Heights were fired at 3:25 that Sunday afternoon, the VI Corps had moved barely four-and-a-half miles out of the city. By the time Brooks assaulted the heights near 5:30 p.m., he was outmanned and outgunned. After Sedgwick pulled the VI Corps back into a long defensive line along the Rappahannock, he was unable to hold it and was essentially spooked back across the river.

* * *

Hindsight provides a perspective on the situation that Sedgwick did not always have, making it easier to point out his list of failures during the campaign. Likewise, that hindsight makes it possible to examine the forces beyond his control and consider the opportunities he created for his commander at Chancellorsville.

Throughout the entire campaign, Joe Hooker played his cards close to his vest and shared his battle plan with very few people. Couch was an exception, as the army's second in command, but none of the army's corps commanders knew Hooker's vision at the opening of the campaign. In modern parlance, it is called "commander's intent"; officers articulate it to their subordinates so that if someone gets knocked out of action, others can still carry out the plan. If the head injury Hooker suffered did not qualify as an example of getting knocked out—literally—few things would.

Only George Stoneman, commander of the cavalry corps, had a clear idea of his role in operations: to wreak as much havoc behind Confederate lines as possible. But the ineffective Stoneman proved to be a bust in that role. For his poor performance, he would quickly be relieved of command.

Sedgwick, in command of the entire left wing of the army, knew that his men were to function as a diversionary force, but he knew little else; and he soon learned how impossible it would be to coordinate efforts between his wing and Hooker's. The 25-mile line of communication proved highly unreliable, subject to long delays, garbled transmissions, and obstructed views. That Hooker and Butterfield failed to find a rhythm between themselves complicated matters for everyone, with particularly grievous results for Sedgwick. Time and again Butterfield dropped the ball: when asked for orders, many times he would not issue them; and when he did, they went against orders Hooker had already sent. The sloppy staff work in the Federal high command muddied the waters for all Hooker's subordinates.

Much could be and has been said about Hooker's failure to use his much larger army to better advantage on May 3 and 4. That was particularly true on May 4, when the men of the Greek Cross drew Lee's attention to Salem Church, leaving a sparsely defended Confederate position under the command of a general inexperienced at leading infantry. It would have taken a superhuman effort for Stuart to hold on at Chancellorsville long enough for Lee to disengage the forces near Salem Church, march them west, and redeploy them for battle. Yet although his most battle-tested corps commanders urged the Union commanding general to attack, Hooker, concussed, would not pull the trigger.

Brigadier General George Stoneman from the
May 23, 1863, edition of *Harper's Weekly*.

Fredericksburg and Spotsylvania National Military Park

It was the Army of the Potomac's best opportunity since Antietam to destroy the Army of Northern Virginia—and Hooker left the opportunity sitting there on the field, unexploited, as he slipped to the safety of the north bank of the river.

*   *   *

By the second week in May, letters had already reached homes, newspapers, and politicians in the North and the South. They told tales of heroism and horror from the bloody fields of Virginia. They told tales of loss.

"It is difficult to realize in the time of an action, the extreme peril one's life is in," wrote soldier-turned-correspondent Wilbur Fisk. "Death there seems of less consequence than anywhere else, one gets so used to it. . . . But when the excitement is over and we go back to camp and see so many comrades whose society was our pleasure, missing, we feel very keenly the loss we have sustained."[5]

While grief always remained personal, another dark cloud hung over the army as a whole. Letters home still reflected a high fighting spirit, but they reflected something darker, too: many of the men were beginning to lose faith in Old Joe. "[W]e might have gained a great victory, but we lacked the leader and are again looking for some one worthy of the army whose energies no defeat can tame," wrote one Federal.[6]

"This army has done some terrible fighting in the past few days," lamented a soldier in the 5th Maine,

but the results are far different from what I expected they would be. Hooker handled his men as well as ever any army were handled. (I have no doubt from what I can learn that the cowardly conduct of the 11th Corps was the cause of the disaster.) What is to be done now I do not know. I see no way but to raise more men. We must not give up the ship. This rebellion *must be crushed*, if it takes *every* man of the North to do it. Let the recruits come forward and fill up this army, and we will try them *again* and *again*, if need be, until we succeed.[7]

Indeed, Hooker had his defenders. "I hope the people will be mild in their judgments of Hooker, and above all I hope he will not be

---

5   Fisk, *Hard Marching Every Day*, 80.

6   Josiah M. Favill, Memoir, in the Fredericksburg and Spotsylvania National Military Park bound manuscript collection, vol. 266.

7   Newspaper article, May 25, 1863, *Eastern Argus*, in the Fredericksburg and Spotsylvania National Military Park bound manuscript collection, vol. 257.

superceded," wrote a Vermonter. "I cannot believe it was a fault of his, and he has certainly shown his bravery and good generalship."[8]

But overwhelmingly, the buzz against Hooker was negative. "There is a great deal of talking in the camp, and I see the press is beginning to attack Hooker," wrote Meade to his wife. "I think these last operations have shaken the confidence of the army in Hooker's judgment, particularly among the superior officers."[9] Alpheus Williams was typical. "People at home fancy this war is waged for the Union and for a stable and united government, but it is a mistake," the general officer wrote, outspoken in his post-campaign disgruntledness. "It is carried on exclusively to make heroes of charlatans and braggarts!"[10]

In particular, Hooker was taking quite a bit of heat from his corps commanders. Couch, Slocum, and Reynolds, in particular, all wanted rid of him. Slocum went so far as to suggest they petition the President; but, lacking the support of the others and perhaps remembering the fallout from the coup against Burnside, the XII Corps commander backed off. Couch was so thoroughly disgusted with Hooker, though, that he was even willing to leave his beloved II Corps: he requested a transfer and was reassigned to command the backwater Department of the Susquehanna.[11]

Knowing the corps commanders' minds might have been of interest to Lincoln, torn as he already was about what to do with the army commander. The cabinet and Congress were split, as well. In the weeks following the battle, political leaders came into the army's camp. Governors, congressmen, and senators all heard similar stories from officers and men from their own states: Fighting Joe was a problem.

---

8 *Vermont Watchman and State Journal*, May 22, 1863, in the Fredericksburg and Spotsylvania National Military Park bound manuscript collection, vol. 149.

9 Meade, *Life and Letters of George Gordon Meade*, vol. 1, 373.

10 Quaife, *From the Cannon's Mouth*, 203.

11 Later in the year, Slocum would find himself in the unfortunate position of having to serve under Hooker again in the western theater. Only a compromise brokered by Lincoln kept the peace, and Slocum was essentially given an independent command. Hooker was later passed over for promotion in favor of the less senior but also less politically ambitious O. O. Howard (talk about adding insult to injury!), and Hooker resigned in protest. Slocum, meanwhile, rose to command of the newly formed XX Corps, which consisted of his former XII Corps and Howard's old XI Corps. In 1864, Slocum rose to command of the Army of Georgia.

Lincoln had come to the same conclusion, if for no other reason than because of Hooker's ongoing clashes with him and General in Chief Henry Halleck. The Joint Committee on the Conduct of the War went so far as to investigate the allegations of Hooker's rumored drunkenness on the battlefield. The findings showed that there was no possible way the general had been impaired by spirits.

Hooker squirmed under the attention and tried to divert it by shifting blame—principally onto Stoneman, Howard, and Sedgwick. "It would be unbecoming in me to express an opinion," Hooker later blustered, "although the Army have given me abundant reason to believe, and so has the country, that they attach no part of the failure to my conduct."[12]

Stoneman, of course, did deserve the blame heaped on him. His raid, one of Hooker's best ideas of the campaign, had been dismally executed. The disruptions he caused were so minor, so easily fixed, and so far away from the front that they had virtually no impact on the battle.[13] "If Lee had been severed from his base of supplies," Hooker predicted, "I certainly should not have retired across the River before giving him an old fashioned struggle for ascendency."[14]

Howard, too, deserved blame—and he got plenty. The failure of his line on May 2 did lead to a panicked rout. But the disarray has been over-exaggerated in subsequent years, in service to the legends that have grown up around Jackson and Lee. And it was Hooker's withdrawal from Hazel Grove at dawn on May 3 that allowed the vulnerable wings of the separated Confederate army to reunite without a fight. That, more than Howard's collapse, put Hooker in an ultimately untenable position at Chancellorsville—and only then because Hooker's spat with Hunt left a gap in communications that imperiled the Federal artillery. Often

---

12 Meade, *Life and Letters of George Gordon Meade*, vol. 1, 373.

13 One could easily argue that the most significant effect of Stoneman's Raid was the delay it caused in getting the wounded Jackson to Richmond for treatment. However, the pneumonia from which Jackson suffered was so far advanced that it is impossible to truly speculate what effect, if any, his inability to get to Richmond had on his ultimate death. The pneumonia was so severe that it is just as likely that Jackson could have gotten to Richmond without incident but still died, so blaming his death on the fact that he was stranded at Guinea Station would be as simplistic as it would be convenient.

14 Hooker to Bates, April 7, 1877, in the Fredericksburg and Spotsylvania National Military Park bound manuscript collection, vol. 406.

Major General Oliver Otis Howard.

Fredericksburg and Spotsylvania National Military Park

forgotten, too, is that Howard's defense on May 2 was formulated in response to assumptions Hooker made about Jackson's marching column. "Lee is in full retreat toward Gordonsville," Hooker had told Howard, "and I have sent out Sickles to capture his artillery."[15] By sending Sickles out to "capture his artillery," Hooker created a gap in his lines, thus

---

15 Couch, "Chancellorsville Campaign," 163.

isolating his numerically smallest corps from the rest of the Army of the Potomac.

Despite the XI Corps' collapse at Chancellorsville, and again two months later at Gettysburg, Howard was given important positions of leadership in Sherman's western army and in the postwar Freedmen's Bureau, and over a long career would eventually rise to important commands in the West, most notably in a difficult campaign against the Nez Perce. He would also found Howard University in Washington, D.C.

John Sedgwick, given the most difficult job of all Hooker's corps commanders, received much of the blame, as well, and his sluggish performance certainly deserved criticism. Hooker accused him of "being slow and afraid to fight; also of disobeying orders directly," which was a flagrantly trumped-up charge.[16] However, Sedgwick's capture of Marye's Heights remained the only bright spot of the entire campaign, earning him a degree of protection that was bolstered by the respect and admiration of the men in his corps. Sedgwick's performance at Chancellorsville, in contrast to Hooker's, had somehow made the VI Corps commander untouchable.

"I have received nothing but congratulations for the splendid conduct of my corps except the General," Sedgwick wrote to his sister, "and he dare not come out boldly and accuse me or my corps of any want of skill in handling or bad behavior on the part of the men. I will not attempt to say where the fault lay. It will someday be exposed."[17]

Sedgwick's death in 1864 at the battle of Spotsylvania Court House made him the highest-ranking Union general killed during the war. It also gave "Uncle John" a martyr's status that made it harder to criticize him. "Sedgwick was a fine man—a man you could be fond of," admitted his replacement, Maj. Gen. Horatio Wright. "He was a good soldier, but not a great soldier, such as some of his friends would like to make you believe."[18] Yet Sedgwick got his own monument in 1887 to mark the place where he fell, as well as an ornate equestrian monument, dedicated in 1913, on the Gettysburg battlefield. More importantly, his ironic last words made for

16 Nevins, *A Diary of Battle*, 213.

17 Sedgwick to Emily Sedgwick Welch, n.d., in Stoeckel, ed., *Correspondence of John Sedgwick Major-General*, vol. 2, 109.

18 Horatio Wright on John Sedgwick, in Styple, *Generals in Bronze*, 210.

Veterans surround the monument to John Sedgwick on the
Spotsylvania Court House Battlefield.

Fredericksburg and Spotsylvania National Military Park

the kind of sublime story Civil War fans love: he boasted that Confederate sharpshooters could not hit the broad side of an elephant—seconds before they shot him in the head. That anecdote has stood as a far more enduring legacy than anything anyone remembers about his performance at Chancellorsville.

Nonetheless, criticism of Sedgwick would become a common theme in Hooker's attempts to explain away Chancellorsville—a process that began with a 1:30 a.m. dispatch sent to Lincoln on May 4. "I do not despair of success," Hooker claimed. "If Sedgwick could have gotten up, there could have been but one result."[19] In his postwar writings, Hooker went so far as to attack Sedgwick for his role in the Federal pursuit of Lee's army following the victory at Gettysburg. "If Genl. Meade had understood Genl. Sedgwick's true character," Hooker wrote, "he would never have sent that officer in pursuit of a retiring enemy."[20]

19 *OR* 25, pt. 2, 378.

20 Hooker to Bates, April 2, 1877, in the Fredericksburg and Spotsylvania National Military Park bound manuscript collection.

Looking back on Chancellorsville, Hooker lamented that he did not place Reynolds in charge of the left wing, and went so far as to say that he regarded Reynolds "as the ablest officer under me. . . ."[21] No doubt Reynolds would have been a better selection, not for any lack of skill in Sedgwick, but rather because Sedgwick was just rejoining the army after recovering from three serious wounds, and he had never before commanded a corps, let alone a wing of an army. Reynolds, on the other hand, had led the I Corps in action and knew his subordinates' strengths and weaknesses.

Hooker's postwar memory lapses became more and more convenient. For instance, he complained, "The heights around Fredericksburg were occupied by a small number of the enemy, but in front of the walls of Marye's Heights, as you well know, [is] a formidable stonewall with earth embankments. General Sedgwick ought to have known from his service with General Sumner the 13th of December the year previous."[22] Had Hooker completely forgotten that Sedgwick had not been present at First Fredericksburg? It seems a hard thing for Hooker to have forgotten, since he was the one who promoted Sedgwick to command of the VI Corps in early 1863.

Hooker also seems to have forgotten, although they remained in the written record, his orders to Sedgwick to take the Plank Road west to Chancellorsville. This most direct route from Fredericksburg ran through the heart of Marye's Heights. "I could not think, that he would select that point in preference to all others for his point of attack," Hooker groused. "If he had gone up Deep River [Deep Run], I still think that the position could easily have been turned, without the loss of the time required to form his columns for assault."[23] At the time, though, a flanking maneuver at Deep Run would have been almost out of the question: had Brooks turned his division north and up the Confederate line, there would have been 6,100 Confederates directly in his rear.

Hooker's attempts at justification became less and less connected to the truth as postwar years unfolded. He claimed that he had wanted to pull

21 Bates, "Hooker's Comments on Chancellorsville," 222.

22 Hooker to Bates, April 2, 1877, letters of Joe Hooker, in the Fredericksburg and Spotsylvania National Military Park bound manuscript collection, vol. 406.

23 Ibid.

his army out of Chancellorsville and re-cross the river at Banks' Ford to do battle there, but could not because Sedgwick had pulled out against orders.[24] Given that Sedgwick hardly had room to maneuver the VI Corps on the south bank of the Rappahannock at Banks' Ford, there would have been no way the entire Army of the Potomac could have operated there effectively. Lee had hemmed Sedgwick into a salient on three sides, and Confederate artillery on the heights above the plain of Banks' Ford lobbed shells at the Federals with impunity. Hooker's farcical ploy was just more of the blame game: because Hooker never had the chance to redeploy to Banks' Ford and fight, he could, through conjecture, blame Sedgwick for his own shortcomings.

The men of the Greek Cross fired back their own barbs in defense of their corps commander. The response of VI Corps adjutant Col. Martin T. McMahon was typical: "Any man who says that the failure could in any degree be attributed to Sedgwick, insults every soldier in his command and dishonors the memory of the dead."[25]

Eight days after the campaign ended, staff officer R. F. Halsted wrote, "How different everything might, nay, would have been if we had had the cooperation's of even a small part of the immense force with Fighting Joe Hooker! Why did he not keep Lee occupied so that he would not have dared turn his back to Chancellorsville, to fall upon us?"[26] It was a legitimate question. "What was Hooker there for?" Halsted asked. "To entrench himself, with six corps under his command and expect and even order one single corps to march right through the enemy, to 'crush and destroy,' were the words of his order to the General [Sedgwick]. . . [?]"[27]

As May moved into June, and the clashes between Lincoln and Hooker continued, the president, who had lost faith in the general's ability, tightened the reins on Hooker. Hooker chafed. On June 27, he finally said, "I beg to be understood, respectfully, but firmly, that I am unable to comply with this condition with the means at my disposal, and

---

24 Ibid.

25 Martin T. McMahon, *General John Sedgwick: Address Delivered Before the Vermont Officers' Reunion Society* (Rutland, VT, 1880), 24.

26 Halsted to Miss Sedgwick, May 13, 1863, in Stoeckel, ed., *Correspondence of John Sedgwick Major-General*, vol. 2, 124-125.

27 Ibid., 125.

earnestly request that I may at once be relieved from the position I occupy."[28] Lincoln obliged the next day, appointing V Corps commander George Gordon Meade to take Hooker's place. Hooker was reassigned to the West, and Meade thereafter felt the sting from bitter Hooker supporters such as Sickles and Butterfield, who did much to sabotage Meade's position.

Conveniently, Hooker never wrote an official report on the battle of Chancellorsville, and in subsequent years, as he tried to rehabilitate his image, his story varied on many points, shifting from audience to audience. Hooker chose to emphasize, instead, the victory he scored at Chattanooga on November 24, 1863—the so-called "Battle Above the Clouds" at Lookout Mountain—even going so far as to commission James Walker to create a 13x30-foot painting that put Hooker front and center in the action.[29]

What writings Hooker did leave behind concerning Chancellorsville fell to Pennsylvania historian Samuel Bates, who referred to himself as Hooker's "Literary Executor."[30] Bates had the opportunity in October 1876 to visit the battlefields of Fredericksburg, Chancellorsville, and Antietam with Fighting Joe. Bates used what he learned on those visits, coupled with Hooker's papers, to tell Hooker's side of the story—not so much as an outsider looking in, but more as a wide-eyed college student hanging on every word of the worldly professor who was leading him astray. In 1882, Bates wrote a full-length battle study, that defended Hooker and made excuses for him while at the same time blaming others, just as Hooker himself had once done.

Despite the trials and tribulations the Army of the Potomac had gone through, the army Hooker left behind still had a great deal of fight left in it

---

28 *OR* 27, pt. 1, 60.

29 Even that seemed to fail. The *New York Times*, in its review of the piece on October 17, 1874, said: "The figures in the foreground are somewhat stiffly drawn, and the pose of the Major General and his white horse is decidedly too much after the Napoleonic model. The proprietor of the picture, is, however, as we know, fully satisfied with it, and as he was a somewhat prominent actor in the scene it represents, he surely ought to be a competent judge. But viewing it as a work of art, and such we presume it claims to be, we think it entitled to be termed respectable, but nothing more." The painting now hangs on permanent display atop Lookout Mountain at the Chickamauga and Chattanooga National Military Park visitor center.

30 Bates, "Hooker's Comments on Chancellorsville," 215.

after Chancellorsville. Meade, the proud V Corps commander, summed up the feelings of much of the army. "I don't know what to make of the political condition of the country," Meade wrote. "One thing I do know, I have been long enough in the war to want to give them one thorough good licking before any peace is made. And to accomplish this, I will go through a great deal."[31]

*   *   *

For Confederates, the march away from the battle at Salem Church had a much different tenor. Rain started to fall on May 5, but it did little to dampen the Southerners' mood as they marched, "splashing through the mud in wild, tumultuous spirits, singing, shouting, jesting, heedless of soaking rags, drenched to the skin, and burning again to mingle in the wild revelry of battle."[32] Only Marse Robert seemed nonplussed, having missed his opportunity to, at the very least, crush Hooker's largest corps—and perhaps more. "I . . . was more depressed than after Fredericksburg," Lee recounted; "our loss was severe, and again we had gained not an inch of ground and the enemy could not be pursued."[33]

Lee left Early and Barksdale to keep an eye on Banks' Ford, where Sedgwick's bridges still offered the Federals a chance to recross should they so choose. One of the Rhode Islanders sent to take up the bridges, Elisha Hunt Rhodes, noted that the Confederates "had complete command" of the Federal side of the river. "We were powerless to do anything. . . ." Rhodes said. "After dark we got some long ropes and going down a ravine to the river we would make it fast to a boat. The men stationed around a bend in the ravine would then pull, and as the boat would grate upon the gravel and rocks the Rebels would fire a volley. But we kept on, and daylight showed all the boats safe up on the hills. . . ."[34]

Lee, meanwhile, had still intended to strike a blow at Hooker, unaware that Mr. F. J. had begun his own withdrawal across the river.

---

31 Meade, *The Life and Letters of George Gordon Meade*, vol. 1, 354.

32 Ralph Happel, *Salem Church Embattled* (Washington, DC, 1980), 50.

33 Lee, quoted by John Sedden, July 1, 1863, in *Southern Historical Society Papers*, 4 (1877), 153-154.

34 Rhodes, *All for the Union*, 107-108.

"Preparations were made to assail the enemy's works at daylight on the 6th," Lee wrote in his report of the battle, "but on advancing our skirmishers it was found that under the cover of the storm and darkness of the night he had retreated over the river."

As noted earlier, Lee's regret was that although Chancellorsville marked the Army of Northern Virginia's greatest battlefield victory yet, it had lost out on destroying, at the least, a large portion of Hooker's army. Andrew Hero of the Washington Artillery proudly wrote on May 14 that "[a]gain I have passed through the terrible ordeal of one of those sanguinary conflicts by the aid of which we hope to achieve the independence of the Confederacy and still the end of this crusade seems to be as far distant as ever. Though we gave them a firstrate drubbing yet the victory was not as complete as it was expected to have been. . . ."[35]

*   *   *

Some of Lee's subordinates seemed more intent on using Chancellorsville, and Second Fredericksburg/Salem Church in particular, as an opportunity to take potshots at each other. Barksdale and Early, each notoriously hotheaded, went at each other with fervor over who was to blame for the temporary loss of Fredericksburg and Marye's Heights.

It started when Lee's Bad Old Man took issue with some of the accounts he read in The *Richmond Enquirer* about his men at Second Fredericksburg. He wrote to the paper and asked them to correct the false information. *His* men did not lose Marye's Heights, he corrected, implying that Barksdale belonged to someone else's corps. "I will state that my division did not lose Marye's Hill, but one of my brigades [Gordon's, formerly Lawton's] recaptured it. . . ."[36]

Early's recriminations did not sit well with Barksdale, who retorted in the paper that "[m]y brigade needs no defense at my hands. Its reputation, won upon many battle-fields, is well established. This communication is

35 Andrew Hero to Father, May 14, 1863, in the Fredericksburg and Spotsylvania National Military Park bound manuscript collection, vol. 28.

36 Gary W. Gallagher, *Lee & His Army in Confederate History* (Chapel Hill, NC, 2001), 240.

not written for that purpose, but to correct erroneous impressions which Gen. Early's publication was calculated to make."[37]

The only aspect of the fall of Marye's Heights the two could agree upon was that Col. Thomas Griffin was the man to blame. He accepted the flag of truce from the Yankees without permission from either Barksdale or Early.[38]

The war of words continued into the early portion of the Gettysburg campaign before Lee finally put a stop to the nonsense. Barksdale's death on July 3, 1863, at the Hummelbaugh Farm on the Gettysburg battlefield cooled the debate even more, as might be expected, although some line officers from both commands still fired shots at one another in postwar correspondence and articles.

Barksdale's men had every reason to hold their heads high. Although they lost the Sunken Road and Marye's Heights, they represented themselves well against overwhelming odds. Even after the fall of Barksdale at Gettysburg, the brigade was capably led by the colonel of the 21st Mississippi, Benjamin Humphreys. It served well through the end of the war. The fact that Gordon retook the heights for the South, and that Sedgwick got bottled up and was forced back across the river, ensured that any stigma associated with the short-term loss of Marye's Heights would soon be forgotten.

Likewise, Jubal Early had many fine days ahead. His division fought well at Gettysburg, sweeping the "Flying Dutchmen" of the XI Corps from the battlefield on July 1, 1863. His men were also integral to Lee's battles in the Wilderness and at Spotsylvania Court House in the spring of 1864. He ascended to command Jackson's old Second Corps. Early's toughest times would come later in the summer and fall of 1864 in the Shenandoah Valley against "Little Phil" Sheridan, which would eventually cost Early command of the Second Corps. Still, by the end of the war, Early was one of the most respected officers to come out of the Army of Northern Virginia, and his old division had amassed an impressive collection of battle honors.

---

37 William Barksdale to *Richmond (VA) Enquirer*, May 13, 1863, in the Fredericksburg and Spotsylvania National Military Park bound manuscript collection, vol. 137.

38 *OR* 25, pt. 1, 1,001; *OR* 25, pt. 1, 840.

Cadmus Wilcox and his Alabama brigade deserve special note, as well. They had their finest day of the war on May 3, 1863. "Wilcox is entitled to especial praise for the judgment and bravery displayed in the advance of General Sedgwick towards Chancellorsville, and for the gallant and successful stand at Salem Church," Lee reported.[39] One of Wilcox's men summed it up more succinctly: "Wilcox had out-generaled Sedgwick."[40] Following Gettysburg, Wilcox, a rising star in the army, finally received a division and his major general's stars.

Most incredibly, perhaps, is that the tarnish of the Chancellorsville campaign did not stick to the Union VI Corps. The men had earned few battlefield accolades prior to Chancellorsville because of their relative newness to the army. Once called into action, though, they fought three battles within 36 hours: Marye's Heights, Salem Heights, and Banks' Ford. In the course of these they sustained 4,590 casualties, the highest number among Hooker's army. "It had been baptized in blood," said a New Yorker, "and amid wonderful achievements of heroism, every member of the noble corps felt an exulting pride in his relation to it, and regarded his badge as a mark of great honor."[41]

The *coup de main* tactics the men of the VI Corps employed at Marye's Heights were used to important, successful effect later in the war at Rappahannock Station, Spotsylvania Court House, and Petersburg, and by the end of the war they had earned one of the most respectable war records in the Army of the Potomac. "Over all these scenes," wrote one New Yorker, "the Greek Cross waved proudly on the banners of the corps, while its veteran legions wrought deeds which linked that badge with an unfading glory and renown."[42]

*   *   *

39 Dowdy, *The Wartime Papers of Robert E. Lee*, 470.

40 Baquet, *History of the First New Jersey Brigade*, 240.

41 Stevens, *Three Years in the Sixth Corps*, 215.

42 William F. Fox, *Regimental Losses in the Civil War, 1861-1865* (Albany, NY, 1889), 79.

Yet the glory did fade—and it began to fade as early as May 10, 1863, at 3:15 in the afternoon. The death of Stonewall Jackson that afternoon recast the entire narrative of Chancellorsville.

The counterbalance of tragedy provided "Lee's Greatest Victory" with a qualifier: Lee won, but at the cost of Jackson. In postwar years, that became especially significant, because Chancellorsville proved to be Lee's last offensive victory of the war. Lee, it turned out, could not win without his "right arm." Thus, Jackson's martyrdom became a central tenet in the Lost Cause mythology, which meant that stories of Chancellorsville tended to focus on *that particular* story, largely to the exclusion of all others.

The first monument on the battlefield, a quartz boulder placed by veterans as early as 1876, marked the area where Jackson was wounded. A more formal monument was erected in 1888. In 1903, James Power Smith, a former member of Jackson's staff, placed granite markers around the area's battlefields, including one where Lee and Jackson bivouacked on the night of May 1 before Jackson started his flank attack; he placed another at Guinea Station to mark the location of Jackson's death.

The building where Jackson died became the focus of preservation efforts, and was eventually turned into the Stonewall Jackson Shrine by a ladies' preservation organization from Richmond. It was turned over to

Veterans gather at the Stonewall Jackson Monument on the Chancellorsville Battlefield.

Fredericksburg and Spotsylvania National Military Park

the National Park Service (NPS) in 1937. That same year, the NPS installed a marker of its own at the bivouac site and planted a pair of cedar trees there in tribute to the Confederate leaders. Along with the bivouac site, land preservation in the park centered on other Jackson-specific sites, such as the wounding site and the route of the flank march.

In line with the NPS philosophy at the time, the Chancellorsville Battlefield Visitor Center was constructed in 1963 as close as possible to the most important event of the battle: the wounding site.

Non-Jackson-related property historically received lower priority. For instance, it was not until the mid-seventies that the land at the Chancellorsville crossroads was preserved, yet there is little doubt that the artillery duel between the Federals at Fairview and the Confederates at Hazel Grove determined the outcome of the battle. Property occupied by Lafayette McLaws—the only place on the battlefield where fighting occurred on all three days—did not get preserved until the mid-nineties, in an effort led not by the NPS but a private preservation group. Massive swaths of property associated with the first day's fighting also went unprotected for decades and was the subject of intense legal wrangling in the late nineties and throughout the aughts.

And, of course, the entire Salem Church battlefield fell victim to the onslaught of commercial development before anyone could do much of anything to save it.

It stands to reason that postwar Southern memory coalesced as it did: Second Fredericksburg was an outright Confederate loss, regardless of where blame rested, and Salem Church, while a Confederate victory, was disorganized and disappointing. The relative dearth of Confederate accounts along the "forgotten front" suggests intentional forgetting.[43]

Not surprisingly, therefore, many visitors to the Chancellorsville battlefield come ignorant of the scope and savagery of the fighting on May 3, knowing little about the fighting to the east, at Salem Church. A mention of Fredericksburg conjures images only of December, not May. Second Fredericksburg and Salem Heights took place after Jackson's wounding, after all. Somehow, as the story often goes, Jackson gets

---

43 And it also explains why parts of this narrative may have felt Union-heavy to some readers.

MONUMENT TO 23RD REGT. N. J. VOLS. SALEM CHURCH.

A newly constructed 23rd New Jersey monument on the Salem Church
Battlefield. Because of the expansion of modern-day
Virginia Route 3, the steps no longer exist.

Fredericksburg and Spotsylvania National Military Park

wounded and then suddenly Lee scores his greatest victory. No one quite seems to know how that happened, or why—and some do not even care.

The prominence of the Jackson narrative, more than anything, has inflicted the most casualties on John Sedgwick's VI Corps, whose role in the campaign has largely been forgotten. During the May 3 fight at the crossroads and the fighting at Second Fredericksburg and Salem Heights, the Army of the Potomac and the Army of Northern Virginia amassed a staggering 21,357 casualties, second only to the one-day butcher's bill of Antietam.[44] Sadly, the men who fought and fell that day will always be overshadowed by the fall of one man the night before.

Still, John Sedgwick, John Gibbon, Jubal Early, William Barksdale, Cadmus Wilcox, and the thousands of men under their commands fought heroically under trying conditions. The loss of their stories predicated the loss of the fields on which they fought their battles—which has, in turn, made it even harder to remember their stories.

That gives Meade's once-prophetic words criticizing Hooker's secretive nature an extra resonance. He had worried that "important plans may be frustrated by subordinates, from their ignorance of how much depended on their share of work."[45] The same may explain why the battlefields of Second Fredericksburg and Salem Church have essentially vanished: history has largely forgotten just how much depended on their share of work.

44 Sears, *Chancellorsville*, 389.

45 Meade, *The Life and Letters of George Gordon Meade*, vol. 1, 367.

Appendix A

Orders of Battle: Chancellorsville
April 27 – May 6, 1863

Key: k = killed; mw = mortally wounded; w = wounded; c = captured; r = relieved

Army of the Potomac (Union)
Maj. Gen. Joseph Hooker

Chief of Artillery: Brig. Gen. Henry Hunt
Chief Signal Officer: Capt. Samuel Cushing
Chief Topographical Engineer: Brig. Gen. Gouverneur Warren

Headquarters Guard: Oneida (New York) Cavalry: Capt. Daniel Mann

Ordnance Detachment: Lt. John Edie

Train Guard: 4th New Jersey Infantry (7 companies): Col. William Birney
Capt. Robert Johnston

Provost Guard: Brig. Gen. Marsena Patrick
93rd New York Infantry: Col. John S. Crocker
6th Pennsylvania Cavalry (2 companies: E and I): Capt. James Starr
8th United States Infantry (6 companies: A, B, C, D, F, and G): Capt. E. W. H. Read

Detachment Regular Cavalry: Lt. Tattnall Paulding

Patrick's Brigade: Col. William Rogers
21st New York Infantry: Lt. Col. Chester Sternberg
23rd New York Infantry: Col. Henry Hoffman
35th New York Infantry: Col. John G. Todd
80th New York Infantry (20th Militia): Col. Theodore B. Gates
12th Ohio Independent Light Artillery: Capt. Aaron C. Johnson
Maryland Light Artillery, Battery B: Capt. Alonzo Snow

Engineer Brigade: Brig. Gen. Henry Benham
15th New York Engineers: Col. Clinton G. Colgate
50th New York Engineers: Col. Charles B. Stuart
Battalion United States Engineers: Capt. Chauncey B. Reese

Artillery Reserve: Brig. Gen. Robert O. Tyler
1st Connecticut Heavy Artillery, Battery B: Lt. Albert Brooker
1st Connecticut Heavy Artillery, Battery M: Capt. Franklin A. Pratt
5th New York Independent Light Artillery: Capt. Elijah D. Taft
15th New York Independent Light Artillery: Capt. Patrick Hart
29th New York Independent Light Artillery: Lt. Gustav von Blucher
30th New York Independent Light Artillery: Capt. Adolph Voegelee
32nd New York Independent Light Artillery: Lt. George Gaston
1st United States Artillery, Battery K: Lt. Lorenzo Thomas, Jr.
3rd United States Artillery, Battery C: Lt. Henry Meinell
4th United States Artillery, Battery G: Lt. Marcus P. Miller
5th United States Artillery, Battery K: Lt. David H. Kinzie
32nd Massachusetts Infantry (one company: C): Capt. Josiah C. Fuller

I Corps
Maj. Gen. John Reynolds

Chief of Artillery: Col. Charles Wainwright
Headquarters Escort: 1st Maine Cavalry, Company L: Capt. Constantine Taylor

First Division
Brig. Gen. James Wadsworth

First Brigade: Col. Walter Phelps, Jr.
22nd New York: Maj. Thomas J. Strong
24th New York: Col. Samuel R. Beardsley
30th New York: Col. William M. Searing
84th New York (14th Militia): Col. Edward B. Fowler

Second Brigade: Brig. Gen. Lysander Cutler
7th Indiana: Lt. Col. Ira G. Grover
76th New York (Cortland County Regiment): Col. William P. Wainwright
95th New York (Warren Rifles): Col. George H. Biddle
147th New York (Oswego Regiment): Col. John G. Butler
56th Pennsylvania: Col. William Hofmann

Third Brigade: Brig. Gen. Gabriel Paul
22nd New Jersey: Col. Abraham G. Demarest
29th New Jersey: Col. William R. Taylor
30th New Jersey: Col. John J. Cladek
31st New Jersey: Lt. Col. Robert R. Honeyman
137th Pennsylvania: Col. Joseph B. Kiddoo

Fourth Brigade (Iron Brigade): Brig. Gen. Solomon "Long Sol" Meredith
19th Indiana: Col. Samuel J. Williams
24th Michigan: Col. Henry A. Morrow
2nd Wisconsin: Col. Lucius Fairchild
6th Wisconsin: Col. Edward S. Bragg
7th Wisconsin: Col. William W. Robinson

Divisional Artillery: Capt. John A. Reynolds
1st New Hampshire Light Artillery: Capt. Frederick Edgell
1st New York Light Artillery, Battery L: Capt. John A. Reynolds
4th United States Artillery, Battery B: Lt. James Stewart

Second Division
Brig. Gen. John Robinson

First Brigade: Col. Adrian Root
16th Maine: Col. Charles W. Tilden
94th New York (Belle Jefferson Rifles): Capt. Samuel A. Moffett
104th New York (Wadsworth Guards): Col. Gilbert G. Prey
107th Pennsylvania: Col. Thomas F. McCoy

Second Brigade: Brig. Gen. Henry Baxter
12th Massachusetts (Webster Regiment): Col. James L. Bates
26th New York: Lt. Col. Gilbert S. Jennings
90th Pennsylvania: Col. Peter Lyle
136th Pennsylvania: Col. Thomas M. Bayne

Third Brigade: Col. Samuel Leonard
13th Massachusetts: Lt. Col. N. Walter Batchelder
83rd New York (9th Militia): Lt. Col. Joseph A. Moesch
97th New York: Col. Charles Wheelock
11th Pennsylvania: Col. Richard Coulter
88th Pennsylvania (Cameron Light Guards): Lt. Col. Louis Wagner

Divisional Artillery: Capt. Dunbar Ransom
2nd Maine Artillery, Battery B: Capt. James A. Hall
5th Maine Artillery, Battery E: Capt. George F. Leppien (w); Lt. Edmund Kirby (mw);
Lt. Greenleaf T. Stevens

1st Pennsylvania Independent Light Artillery, Battery C: Capt. James Thompson
5th United States Artillery, Battery C: Capt. Dunbar R. Ransom

Third Division
Maj. Gen. Abner Doubleday

First Brigade: Brig. Gen. Thomas Rowley
121st Pennsylvania: Col. Chapman Biddle
135th Pennsylvania: Col. James R. Porter
142nd Pennsylvania: Col. Robert P. Cummins
151st Pennsylvania (School Teacher Regiment): Col. Harrison Allen

Second Brigade (Bucktail Brigade): Col. Roy Stone
143rd Pennsylvania: Col. Edmund L. Dana
149th Pennsylvania (Second Bucktails): Lt. Col. Walton Dwight
150th Pennsylvania (Third Bucktails): Col. Langhorne Wister

Divisional Artillery: Maj. Ezra Matthews
1st Pennsylvania Light Artillery, Battery B: Capt. James H. Cooper
1st Pennsylvania Light Artillery, Battery F: Lt. R. Bruce Ricketts
1st Pennsylvania Light Artillery, Battery G: Capt. Frank P. Amsden

II Corps
Maj. Gen. Darius Couch

Chief of Artillery: Lt. Col. Charles H. Morgan
Headquarters Escort: 6th New York Cavalry (2 companies: D and K):
Capt. Riley Johnson

First Division
Maj. Gen. Winfield Scott Hancock

First Brigade: Brig. Gen. John Caldwell
61st New York (Clinton Guards): Col. Nelson A. Miles (w); Lt. Col. K. Oscar Broady
66th New York (Governor's Guard) (attached): Col. Orlando Morris
148th Pennsylvania: Col. James A. Beaver (w); Maj. George A. Fairlamb

Second Brigade (Irish Brigade): Brig. Gen. Thomas Meagher
28th Massachusetts: Col. Richard Byrnes
63rd New York (Third Regiment Irish Volunteers): Lt. Col. Richard C. Bentley
69th New York (First Regiment Irish Brigade): Capt. James E. McGee
116th Pennsylvania (battalion, 4 companies): Maj. St. Clair A. Mulholland

Third Brigade: Brig. Gen. Samuel Zook
52nd New York (Sigel Rifles): Col. Paul Frank
Lt. Col. Charles G. Freudenberg
57th New York (Zook's Voltigerus): Lt. Col. Alford B. Chapman
140th Pennsylvania: Col. Richard P. Roberts

Fourth Brigade: Col. John Brooke
27th Connecticut: Col. Richard S. Bostwick (c)
2nd Delaware: Lt. Col. David L. Stricker
64th New York: Col. Daniel G. Bingham
53rd Pennsylvania: Lt. Col. Richards McMichael
145th Pennsylvania: Col. Hiram L. Brown

Fifth Brigade (attached): Col. Edward Cross
5th New Hampshire: Lt. Col. Charles Hapgood
81st Pennsylvania: Col. H. Boyd McKeen (w)
88th New York: Col. Patrick Kelly

Divisional Artillery: Capt. Rufus Pettit
1st New York Light Artillery, Battery B: Capt. Rufus D. Pettit
4th United States Artillery, Battery C: Lt. Evan Thomas

Second Division
Brig. Gen. John Gibbon

First Brigade: (1) Brig. Gen. Alfred Sully; (2) Col. Henry Hudson;
(3) Col. Byron Laflin
19th Maine: Col. Francis Heath
15th Massachusetts: Maj. George C. Joslin
1st Minnesota: Lt. Col. William Colvill, Jr.
34th New York: Col. Byron Laflin
Lt. Col. John Beverly
82nd New York (2nd Militia): Col. Henry W. Hudson
Lt. Col. James Huston

Second Brigade (Philadelphia Brigade): Brig. Gen. Joshua T. Owen
69th Pennsylvania: Col. Dennis O'Kane
71st Pennsylvania: Col. Richard P. Smith
72nd Pennsylvania: Col. De Witt C. Baxter
106th Pennsylvania: Col. Turner G. Morehead

Third Brigade: Col. Norman Hall
19th Massachusetts: Lt. Col. Arthur F. Devereux
20th Massachusetts (Harvard Regiment): Lt. Col. George N. Macy?
7th Michigan: Capt. Amos E. Steele, Jr.

49th New York: Col. James E. Mallon
59th New York: Lt. Col. Max A. Thoman
127th Pennsylvania: Col. William W. Jennings

Divisional Artillery
1st Rhode Island Light Artillery, Battery A: Capt. William A. Arnold
1st Rhode Island Light Artillery, Battery B: Lt. T. Frederick Brown

Sharpshooters: 1st Company Massachusetts: Capt. William Plumer

Third Division
Maj. Gen. William "Blinky" French

First Brigade: Col. Samuel Carroll
14th Indiana: Col. John Coons
24th New Jersey: Col. William B. Robertson
28th New Jersey: Lt. Col. John A. Wildrick (c); Maj. Samuel K. Wilson
4th Ohio: Lt. Col. Leonard W. Carpenter
8th Ohio: Lt. Col. Franklin Sawyer
7th West Virginia: Col. Joseph Snider
Lt. Col. Jonathan H. Lockwood

Second Brigade: Brig. Gen. William Hays (c); Col. Charles Powers
14th Connecticut: Maj. Theodore G. Ellis
12th New Jersey: Col. J. Howard Willets (w); Maj. John T. Hill
108th New York: Col. Charles J. Powers
Lt. Col. Francis E. Pierce
130th Pennsylvania: Col. Levi Maish (w); Maj. Joseph S. Jenkins

Third Brigade: (1) Col. John MacGregor; (2) Col. Charles Albright
1st Delaware: Col. Thomas A. Smyth
4th New York: Lt. Col. William Jameson
132nd Pennsylvania: Col. Charles Albright
Lt. Col. Joseph E. Shreve

Divisional Artillery
1st New York Light Artillery, Battery G: Lt. Nelson Ames
1st Rhode Island Light Artillery, Battery G: Capt. George W. Adams

II Corps Reserve Artillery
1st United States Artillery, Battery I: Lt. Edmund Kirby (mw)
4th United States Artillery, Battery A: Lt. Alonzo H. Cushing

III Corps
Maj. Gen. Daniel Sickles

Chief of Artillery: Capt. George Randolph

First Division
Brig. Gen. David Birney

First Brigade: (1) Brig. Gen. Charles Graham; (2) Col. Charles Egan
57th Pennsylvania: Col. Peter Sides
63rd Pennsylvania: Lt. Col. William S. Kirkwood (mw); Capt. James F. Ryan
68th Pennsylvania: Col. Andrew H. Tippin
105th Pennsylvania (Wildcat Regiment): Col. Amor A. McKnight (k);
Lt. Col. Calvin A. Craig
114th Pennsylvania (Collis Zouaves): Col. Charles H. T. Collis (r);
Lt. Col. Frederick F. Cavada
141st Pennsylvania: Col. Henry J. Madill

Second Brigade: Brig. Gen. J. H. Hobart Ward
20th Indiana: Col. John Wheeler
3rd Maine: Col. Moses B. Lakeman
4th Maine: Col. Elijah Walker
38th New York: Col. P. Regis de Trobriand
40th New York (Mozart Regiment): Col. Thomas W. Egan
99th Pennsylvania: Col. Asher S. Leidy

Third Brigade: Col. Samuel Hayman
17th Maine: Col. Thomas A. Roberts; Lt. Col. Charles B. Merrill
3rd Michigan: Col. Byron R. Pierce (w); Lt. Col. Edwin S. Pierce
5th Michigan: Lt. Col. Edward T. Sherlock (k); Maj. John Pulford
1st New York: Lt. Col. Francis L. Leland
37th New York: Lt. Col. Gilbert Riordan

Divisional Artillery: Capt. Judson Clark
New Jersey Light Artillery, Battery B: Lt. Robert Sims
1st Rhode Island Light Artillery, Battery E: Lt. Pardon S. Jastram
3rd United States Artillery (2 batteries: F and K): Lt. John G. Turnbull

Second Division
Maj. Gen. Hiram Berry (k); Brig. Gen. Joseph Carr

First Brigade: (1) Brig. Gen. Joseph Carr; (2) Col. William Blaisdell
1st Massachusetts: Col. Napoleon B. McLaughlen
11th Massachusetts: Col. William Blaisdell; Lt. Col. Porter D. Tripp

16th Massachusetts: Lt. Col. Waldo Merriam
11th New Jersey: Col. Robert McAllister
26th Pennsylvania: Col. Benjamin C. Tilghman (w); Maj. Robert L. Bodine

Second Brigade (Excelsior Brigade): (1) Brig. Gen. Joseph Revere;
(2) Col. J. Egbert Farnum
70th New York: Col. J. Egbert Farnum; Lt. Col. Thomas Holt
71st New York: Col. Henry L. Potter
72nd New York: Col. William Stevens (k); Maj. John Leonard
73rd New York: Maj. Michael W. Burns
74th New York: Lt. Col. William H. Lounsbury (w); Capt. Henry M. Alles (w);
Capt. Francis E. Tyler
120th New York: Lt. Col. Cornelius D. Westbrook

Third Brigade: Brig. Gen. Gershom Mott (w); Col. William Sewell
5th New Jersey: Col. William J. Sewell
Maj. Ashbel W. Angel (w); Capt. Virgil M. Healy
6th New Jersey: Col. George C. Burling (w); Lt. Col. Stephen R. Gilkyson
7th New Jersey: Col. Louis R. Francine; Lt. Col. Francis Price
8th New Jersey: Col. John Ramsey (w); Capt. John G. Langston
2nd New York: Col. Sidney W. Park (w); Lt. Col. William A. Olmsted
115th Pennsylvania: Col. Francis A. Lancaster (k); Maj. John P. Dunne

Divisional Artillery: Capt. Thomas Osborn
1st New York Light Artillery, Battery D: Lt. George B. Winslow
New York Light Artillery, 4th Battery: Lt. George F. Barstow;
Lt. William T. McLean
1st United States Artillery, Battery H: Lt. Justin E. Dimick (mw);
Lt. James A. Sanderson
4th United States Artillery, Battery K: Francis W. Seeley

Third Division
Maj. Gen. Amiel Whipple (mw); Brig. Gen. Charles Graham

First Brigade: Col. Emlen Franklin
86th New York: Lt. Col. Barna J. Chapin (k); Capt. Jacob H. Lansing
124th New York (Orange Blossoms): Col. Augustus Van Horne Ellis
122nd Pennsylvania: Lt. Col. Edward McGovern

Second Brigade: Col. Samuel Bowman
12th New Hampshire: Col. Joseph H. Potter (w); Lt. Col. John Marsh (w);
Maj. Moses Savage (w)
84th Pennsylvania: Lt. Col. Milton Opp
110th Pennsylvania: Col. James Crowther (k); Maj. David M. Jones (w, c)

Third Brigade: Col. Hiram Berdan
1st United States Sharpshooters: Lt. Col. Casper Trepp
2nd United States Sharpshooters: Maj. Homer R. Stoughton

Divisional Artillery: Capt. Albert von Puttkammer;
Capt. James Huntington
10th New York Independent Light Artillery: Lt. Samuel Lewis
11th New York Independent Light Artillery: Lt. John E. Burton
1st Ohio Light Artillery, Battery H: Capt. James F. Huntington

V Corps
Maj. Gen. George Gordon Meade

Chief of Artillery: Capt. Stephen Weed
Headquarters Escort: 17th Pennsylvania Cavalry (Squadron):
Capt. William Thompson

First Division
Brig. Gen. Charles Griffin

First Brigade: Brig. Gen. James Barnes
2nd Maine: Col. George Varney
18th Massachusetts: Col. Joseph Hayes
22nd Massachusetts: Col. William S. Tilton
1st Michigan: Col. Ira C. Abbott
13th New York (battalion, 2 companies): Capt. William Downey
25th New York: Col. Charles A. Johnson
118th Pennsylvania: Col. Charles M. Prevost
2nd Co. Massachusetts Sharpshooters: Lt. Robert Smith

Second Brigade: (1) Col. James McQuade; (2) Col. Jacob Sweitzer
9th Massachusetts: Col. Patrick R. Gurney
32nd Massachusetts: Lt. Col. Luther Stephenson
4th Michigan: Col. Harrison Jeffords
14th New York: Lt. Col. Thomas M. Davies
62nd Pennsylvania: Col. Jacob B. Sweitzer; Lt. Col. James C. Hull

Third Brigade: Col. Thomas B. W. Stockton
20th Maine: Lt. Col. Joshua Chamberlain
16th Michigan: Lt. Col. Norval Welch
12th New York: Capt. William Huson
17th New York: Lt. Col. Nelson Bartram
44th New York: Col. James C. Rice

83rd Pennsylvania: Col. Strong Vincent
Brady's company, Michigan Sharpshooters

Divisional Artillery: Capt. Augustus Martin
Massachusetts Light Artillery, Battery C: Capt. Augustus P. Martin
Massachusetts Light Artillery, 5th Battery E: Capt. Charles A. Phillips
1st Rhode Island Light Artillery, Battery C: Capt. Richard Waterman
5th United States Artillery, Battery D: Lt. Charles E. Hazlett

Second Division
Maj. Gen. George "Tardy George" Sykes

First Brigade: Brig. Gen. Romeyn Ayres
3rd United States Infantry (6 companies: B, C, F, G, I, and K):
Capt. John D. Wilkins
4th United States Infantry (4 companies: C, F, H, and K): Capt. Hiram Dryer
12th United States Infantry (8 companies: A, B, C, D, and G (1st Battalion);
A, C, and D (2nd Battalion)): Maj. Richard S. Smith
14th United States Infantry (8 companies: A, B, D, E, F, and G (1st Battalion);
F and G (2nd Battalion)): Capt. Jonathan B. Hager; Maj. Grotius R. Giddings

Second Brigade: Col. Sidney Burbank
2nd United States Infantry: (5 companies: B, C, F, I, and K):
Capt. Salem S. Marsh (k); Capt. Samuel A. McKee
6th United States Infantry: (5 companies: D, F, G, H, and I): Capt. Levi Bootes
7th United States Infantry: (4 companies: A, B, E, and I): Capt. David P. Hancock
10th United States Infantry: (4 companies: D, G, H, and K): Lt. Edward G. Bush
11th United States Infantry: (8 companies: B, C, D, E, F, and G (1st Battalion);
C and D (2nd Battalion)): Maj. DeLancey Floyd-Jones
17th United States Infantry (7 companies: A, C, D, G, and H (1st Battalion);
A and B (2nd Battalion)): Maj. George Andrews (w)

Third Brigade: Col. Patrick O'Rorke
5th New York: Col. Cleveland Winslow
140th New York: Lt. Col. Louis Ernst
146th New York: Col. Kenner Garrard

Divisional Artillery: Capt. Stephen Weed
1st Ohio Light Artillery, Battery L: Capt. Frank C. Gibbs
5th United States Artillery, Battery I: Lt. Malbone F. Watson

Third Division
Brig. Gen. Andrew Humphreys

First Brigade: Brig. Gen. Erastus Tyler
91st Pennsylvania: Col. Edgar M. Gregory (w); Lt. Col. Joseph H. Sinex
126th Pennsylvania: Lt. Col. David W. Rowe (w)
129th Pennsylvania: Col. Jacob G. Frick
134th Pennsylvania: Col. Edward O'Brien

Second Brigade: Col. Peter Allabach
123rd Pennsylvania: Col. John B. Clark
131st Pennsylvania: Maj. Robert W. Patton
133rd Pennsylvania: Col. Franklin B. Speakman
155th Pennsylvania: Lt. Col. John H. Cain

Divisional Artillery: Capt. Alanson Randol
1st New York Light Artillery, Battery C: Capt. Almont Barnes
1st United States Artillery, Batteries E-G: Capt. Alanson M. Randol

VI Corps
Maj. Gen. John Sedgwick

Chief of Artillery: Col. Charles Tompkins
Headquarters Escort: Maj. Hugh Janeway
1st New Jersey Cavalry, Company L: Lt. Voorhees Dye
1st Pennsylvania Cavalry, Company H: Capt. William S. Craft
Provost Guard: 4th New Jersey Infantry (3 companies: A, C, and H):
Capt. Charles Ewing

First Division
Brig. Gen. William T. H. Brooks

First Brigade: Col. Henry Brown (w); Col. Samuel Buck (w); Col. William Penrose
1st New Jersey: Col. Mark W. Collet (k); Lt. Col. William Henry, Jr.
2nd New Jersey: Col. Samuel L. Buck; Lt. Col. Charles Wiebecke
3rd New Jersey: Maj. J. W. H. Stickney
15th New Jersey: Col. William H. Penrose; Lt. Col. Edward L. Campbell
23rd New Jersey: Col. E. Burd Grubb

Second Brigade: Brig. Gen. Joseph Bartlett
5th Maine: Col. Clark S. Edwards
16th New York: Col. Joel J. Seaver
27th New York: Col. Alexander D. Adams

121st New York: Col. Emory Upton
96th Pennsylvania: Maj. William H. Lessig

Third Brigade: Brig. Gen. David Russell
18th New York: Col. George R. Myers
32nd New York: Col. Francis E. Pinto
49th Pennsylvania: Lt. Col. Thomas M. Hulings
95th Pennsylvania: Col. Gustavus W. Town (k); Lt. Col. Elisha Hall (k);
Capt. Theodore H. McCalla
119th Pennsylvania: Col. Peter C. Ellmaker

Divisional Artillery: Maj. John Tompkins
Massachusetts Light Artillery, Battery A: Capt. William H. McCartney
New Jersey Light Artillery, Battery A: Lt. Augustin N. Parsons
Maryland Light Artillery, Battery A: Capt. James H. Rigby
2nd United States Artillery, Battery D: Lt. Edward B. Williston

Second Division
Brig. Gen. Albion Howe

Second Brigade: Col. Lewis Grant
2nd Vermont: Col. James H. Walbridge
3rd Vermont: Col. Thomas O. Seaver; Lt. Col. Samuel E. Pingree
4th Vermont: Col. Charles B. Stoughton
5th Vermont: Lt. Col. John R. Lewis
6th Vermont: Col. Elisha L. Barney
26th New Jersey: Col. Andrew J. Morrison; Lt. Col. Edward Martindale

Third Brigade: Brig. Gen. Thomas Neill
7th Maine: Lt. Col. Selden Connor
21st New Jersey: Col. Gilliam Van Houten (mw); Lt. Col. Isaac S. Mettler
20th New York: Col. Ernst von Vegesack (w)
33rd New York: Col. Robert F. Taylor
49th New York: Col. Daniel B. Bidwell
77th New York: Lt. Col. Windsor B. French

Divisional Artillery: Maj. J. Watts de Peyster
1st New York Independent Light Artillery: Capt. Andrew Cowan
5th United States Artillery, Battery F: Lt. Leonard Martin

Third Division
Maj. Gen. John Newton

First Brigade: Col. Alexander Shaler
65th New York: Lt. Col. Joseph E. Hamblin
67th New York: Col. Nelson Cross
122nd New York: Col. Silas Titus
23rd Pennsylvania: Col. John Ely
82nd Pennsylvania: Maj. Isaac C. Bassett

Second Brigade: Col. William Browne (w); Col. Henry Eustis
7th Massachusetts: Col. Thomas D. Johns (w); Lt. Col. Franklin P. Harlow
10th Massachusetts: Lt. Col. Joseph B. Parsons
37th Massachusetts: Col. Oliver Edwards
36th New York: Lt. Col. James J. Walsh
2nd Rhode Island: Col. Horatio Rogers, Jr.

Third Brigade: Brig. Gen. Frank Wheaton
62nd New York: Lt. Col. Theodore Hamilton (w)
93rd Pennsylvania: Capt. John S. Long
98th Pennsylvania: Col. John F. Ballier (w); Lt. Col. George Wynkoop
102nd Pennsylvania: Col. Joseph M. Kinkead
139th Pennsylvania: Col. Frederick H. Collier

Divisional Artillery: Capt. Jeremiah McCarthy
1st Pennsylvania Light Artillery, Batteries C and D: Capt. Jeremiah McCarthy
2nd United States Artillery, Battery G: Lt. John H. Butler

Light Division
Col. Hiram Burnham

6th Maine: Lt. Col. Benjamin F. Harris
31st New York: Col. Frank Jones
43rd New York: Col. Benjamin F. Baker
61st Pennsylvania: Col. George C. Spear (k); Maj. George W. Dawson
5th Wisconsin: Col. Thomas S. Allen
3rd New York Independent Light Artillery: Lt. William A. Harn

XI Corps
Maj. Gen. Oliver Otis Howard

Chief of Artillery: Lt. Col. Louis Schirmer
Headquarters Escort: 1st Indiana Cavalry (2 companies: I and K):
Capt. Abram Sharra

Provost Guard: 8th New York (1 company): Lieutenant Herman Rosenkranz

First Division
Brig. Gen. Charles Devens, Jr. (w); Brig. Gen. Nathaniel McLean

First Brigade: Col. Leopold von Gilsa
41st New York: Maj. Detleo von Einsiedel
45th New York: Col. George von Amsberg
54th New York: Lt. Col. Charles Ashby (c); Maj. Stephen Kovacs
153rd Pennsylvania: Col. Charles Glanz (c); Lt. Col. Jacob Dachrodt

Second Brigade: (1) Brig. Gen. Nathaniel McLean; (2) Col. John Lee
17th Connecticut: Col. William H. Noble (w); Maj. Allen G. Brady
25th Ohio: Col. William P. Richardson (w); Maj. Jeremiah Williams
55th Ohio: Col. John Lee; Lt. Col. Charles B. Gambee
75th Ohio: Col. Robert Reily (k); Capt. Benjamin Morgan
107th Ohio: Col. Seraphim Meyer (w, c); Lt. Col. Charles Mueller

Divisional Artillery
13th New York Light Artillery: Capt. Julius Dieckmann

Second Division
Brig. Gen. Adolph von Steinwehr

First Brigade: Col. Adolphus Buschbeck
29th New York: Lt. Col. Louis Hartmann (w); Maj. Alex. von Schluembach
154th New York: Col. Patrick H. Jones (w); Lt. Col. Henry C. Loomis
27th Pennsylvania: Lt. Col. Lorenz Cantador
73rd Pennsylvania: Lt. Col. William Moore (w)

Second Brigade: Brig. Gen. Francis Barlow
33rd Massachusetts: Col. Adin B. Underwood
134th New York: Col. Charles R. Coster
136th New York: Col. James Wood, Jr.
73rd Ohio: Col. Orland Smith

Divisional Artillery
1st New York Light Artillery, Battery I: Capt. Michael Wiedrich

Third Division
Maj. Gen. Carl Schurz

Unattached: 82nd Ohio Infantry: Col. James S. Robinson

First Brigade: Brig. Gen. Alexander Schimmelfennig
82nd Illinois: Col. Frederick Hecker (w); Maj. Ferdinand H. Rolshausen (w);
Capt. Jacob Lasalle
68th New York: Col. Gotthilf Bourry
157th New York: Col. Philip P. Brown, Jr.
61st Ohio: Col. Stephen J. McGroarty
74th Pennsylvania: Lt. Col. Adolph von Hartung

Second Brigade: Col. Wladimir Krzyzanowski
58th New York: Capt. Frederick Braun (mw); Capt. Emil Koenig
119th New York: Col. Elias Peissner (k); Lt. Col. John T. Lockman
75th Pennsylvania: Col. Francis Mahler
26th Wisconsin: Col. William H. Jacobs

Divisional Artillery
1st Ohio Light Artillery, Battery I: Capt. Hubert "Leather Breeches" Dilger

XI Corps Reserve Artillery: Lieutenant Col. Louis Schirmer
2nd New York Light Artillery: Capt. Hermann Jahn
1st Ohio Light Artillery, Battery K: Capt. William L. DeBeck
1st West Virginia Light Artillery, Battery C: Capt. Wallace Hill

XII Corps
Maj. Gen. Henry Slocum

Chief of Artillery: Capt. Clermont Best
Provost Guard: 10th Maine (3 companies): Capt. John D. Beardsley

First Division
Brig. Gen. Alpheus Williams

First Brigade: Brig. Gen. Joseph Knipe
5th Connecticut: Col. Warren W. Packer (c); Lt. Col. James A. Bette;
Maj. David F. Lane
28th New York: Lt. Col. Elliott W. Cook (c); Maj. Theophilus Fitzgerald

46th Pennsylvania: Maj. Cyrus Strous (mw); Capt. Edward L. Witman
128th Pennsylvania: Col. Joseph A. Mathews (c); Maj. Cephas W. Dyer

Second Brigade: Col. Samuel Ross (w)
20th Connecticut: Lt. Col. William B. Wooster (c); Maj. Philo. B. Buckingham
3rd Maryland: Lt. Col. Gilbert P. Robinson
123rd New York: Col. Archibald L. McDougall
145th New York: Col. E. Livingston Price (w); Capt. George W. Reid

Third Brigade: Brig. Gen. Thomas Ruger
27th Indiana: Col. Silas Colgrove
2nd Massachusetts: Col. Samuel M. Quincy
13th New Jersey: Col. Ezra A. Carman; Maj. John Grimes (w);
Capt. George A. Beardsley
107th New York: Col. Alexander S. Diven
3rd Wisconsin: Col. William Hawley

Divisional Artillery: Capt. Robert Fitzhugh
1st New York Light Artillery, Battery K: Lt. Edward L. Bailey
1st New York Light Artillery, Battery M: Lt. Charles E. Winegar (c);
Lt. John D. Woodbury
4th United States Artillery, Battery F: Lt. Franklin B. Crosby (k);
Lt. Edward D. Muhlenberg

Second Division: Brig. Gen. John White Geary
First Brigade: Col. Charles Candy
5th Ohio: Lt. Col. Robert L. Kilpatrick (w); Maj. Henry E. Symmes
7th Ohio: Col. William R. Creighton
29th Ohio: Lt. Col. Thomas Clark
66th Ohio: Lt. Col. Eugene Powell
28th Pennsylvania: Maj. Lansford F. Chapman (k); Capt. Conrad U. Meyer
147th Pennsylvania: Lt. Col. Ario Pardee, Jr.

Second Brigade: Brig. Gen. Thomas Kane
29th Pennsylvania: Lt. Col. William Rickards, Jr.
109th Pennsylvania: Col. Henry J. Stainrook (k); Capt. John Young, Jr.
111th Pennsylvania: Col. George A. Cobham, Jr.
124th Pennsylvania: Lt. Col. Simon Litzenberg
125th Pennsylvania: Col. Jacob Higgins

Third Brigade: Brig. Gen. George "Pap" Greene
60th New York: Lt. Col. John C. O. Redington
78th New York: Maj. Henry R. Stagg; Capt. William H. Randall
102nd New York: Col. James C. Lane
137th New York: Col. David Ireland
149th New York: Maj. Abel G. Cook (w); Capt. Oliver T. May;
Lt. Col. Koert S. Van Voorhis

Divisional Artillery: Capt. Joseph Knap
1st Pennsylvania Light Artillery, Battery E (Knap's): Lt. Charles A. Atwell (w);
Lt. James D. McGill
1st Pennsylvania Light Artillery, Battery F (Hampton): Capt. Robert B. Hampton (mw);
Lt. James P. Fleming

Cavalry Corps
Brig. Gen. George Stoneman

First Division
Brig. Gen. Alfred Pleasonton

First Brigade: Col. Benjamin Davis
8th Illinois Cavalry: Lt. Col. David R. Clendenin
3rd Indiana Cavalry: Col. George H. Chapman
8th New York Cavalry: Lt. Col. William Markell
9th New York Cavalry: Col. William Sackett

Second Brigade: Col. Thomas Devin
1st Michigan Cavalry (1 company: L): Lt. John K. Truax
6th New York Cavalry: Lt. Col. Duncan McVicar (k); Capt. William E. Beardsley
8th Pennsylvania Cavalry: Maj. Pennock Huey
17th Pennsylvania Cavalry: Col. Josiah Kellogg

Divisional Artillery
6th New York Independent Artillery: Lt. Joseph W. Martin

Second Division
Brig. Gen. William Averell

First Brigade: Col. Horace Sargent
1st Massachusetts Cavalry: Lt. Col. Greely S. Curtis
4th New York Cavalry: Col. Louis P. Di Cesnola
6th Ohio Cavalry: Maj. Benjamin C. Stanhope
1st Rhode Island Cavalry: Lt. Col. John L. Thompson

Second Brigade: Col. John McIntosh
3rd Pennsylvania Cavalry: Lt. Col. Edward S. Jones
4th Pennsylvania Cavalry: Lt. Col. William E. Doster
16th Pennsylvania Cavalry: Lt. Col. Lorenzo D. Rogers

Divisional Artillery
2nd United States Artillery, Battery A, Capt. John C. Tidball

Third Division
Brig. Gen. David McM. Gregg

First Brigade: Col. Judson Kilpatrick
1st Maine Cavalry: Col. Calvin S. Douty
2nd New York Cavalry: Lt. Col. Henry E. Davies, Jr.
10th New York Cavalry: Lt. Col. William Irvine

Second Brigade: Col. Percy Wyndham
12th Illinois Cavalry: Lt. Col. Hasbrouck Davis
1st Maryland Cavalry: Lt. Col. James M. Deems
1st New Jersey Cavalry: Lt. Col. Virgil Brodrick
1st Pennsylvania Cavalry: Col. John P. Taylor

Reserve Cavalry Brigade: Brig. Gen. John Buford
6th Pennsylvania Cavalry: Maj. Robert Morris, Jr.
1st United States Cavalry: Capt. R. S. C. Lord
2nd United States Cavalry: Maj. Charles Whiting
5th United States Cavalry: Capt. James Harrison
6th United States Cavalry: Capt. George C. Cram

Horse Artillery: Capt. James Robertson
2nd United States Horse Artillery, Batteries B and L: Lt. Albert O. Vincent
2nd United States Horse Artillery, Battery M: Lt. Robert Clarke
4th United States Horse Artillery, Battery E: Lt. Samuel S. Elder

*   *   *

Army of Northern Virginia (Confederate)
Gen. Robert E. Lee

First Corps
Lt. Gen. James "Pete" Longstreet (detached duty, Suffolk, VA)
First Corps commanded by Robert E. Lee during battle

McLaws' Division
Maj. Gen. Lafayette McLaws

Wofford's Brigade: Brig. Gen. William Wofford
16th Georgia (Sallie Twiggs Regiment): Col. Goode Bryan
18th Georgia (Savannah Volunteer Guards): Col. S. Z. Ruff
24th Georgia: Col. Robert McMillan
Cobb's Georgia Legion: Lt. Col. Luther Glenn
Phillips' Georgia Legion: Lt. Col. E. S. Barclay, Jr.

Semmes' Brigade: Brig. Gen. Paul Semmes
10th Georgia: Lt. Col. Willis C. Holt
50th Georgia: Lt. Col. Francis Kearse
51st Georgia: Col. W. M. Slaughter (mw); Lt. Col. Edward Ball (w)
53rd Georgia: Col. James Simms

Kershaw's Brigade: Brig. Gen. Joseph Kershaw
2nd South Carolina (2nd Palmetto Regiment): Col. John D. Kennedy
3rd South Carolina: Maj. Robert C. Maffett
7th South Carolina (Enfield Rifles): Col. Elbert Bland
8th South Carolina: Col. John W. Henagan
15th South Carolina: Lt. Col. Joseph F. Gist
3rd South Carolina Battalion (Laurens Battalion): Lt. Col. William G. Rice

Barksdale's Brigade: Brig. Gen. William Barksdale
13th Mississippi: Col. J. W. Carter
17th Mississippi: Col. W. D. Holder
18th Mississippi: Col. Thomas Griffin (c)
21st Mississippi: Col. Benjamin G. Humphreys

Cabell's Battalion: Col. Henry Cabell
Carlton's Troup Artillery (Georgia) Battery: Capt. Henry Carlton
Fraser's Pulaski (Georgia) Battery: Capt. John Fraser
1st Company Richmond Howitzers, McCarthy's (Virginia) Battery:
Capt. Edward McCarthy
Manly's North Carolina Battery: Capt. Basil Manly

Anderson's Division
Maj. Gen. Richard Anderson

Wilcox's Brigade: Brig. Gen. Cadmus Wilcox
8th Alabama: Col. Y. L. Royston (w); Lt. Col. H. A. Herbert
9th Alabama: Maj. J. H. J. Williams
10th Alabama: Col. William H. Forney
11th Alabama: Col. J. C. C. Sanders
14th Alabama: Col. L. Pinckard (w)

Wright's Brigade: Brig. Gen. Ambrose "Rans" Wright
3rd Georgia: Maj. John F. Jones (w); Capt. Charles Andrews
22nd Georgia: Lt. Col. Joseph Wasden
48th Georgia: Lt. Col. Reuben W. Carswell
2nd Georgia Battalion: Maj. George Ross

Mahone's Brigade: Brig. Gen. William "Little Billy" Mahone
6th Virginia: Col. George T. Rogers
12th Virginia: Lt. Col. Edward M. Field
16th Virginia: Lt. Col. R. O. Whitehead
41st Virginia: Col. William Allen Parham
61st Virginia: Col. Virginius D. Groner

Posey's Brigade: Brig. Gen. Carnot Posey
12th Mississippi: Lt. Col. Merry B. Harris (w); Maj. Samuel B. Thomas
16th Mississippi: Col. Samuel E. Baker
19th Mississippi: Col. Nathaniel H. Harris
48th Mississippi: Col. Joseph M. Jayne (w)

Perry's Brigade: Brig. Gen. Edward Perry
2nd Florida: Maj. Walton R. Moore (w)
5th Florida: Maj. Benjamin Davis (w)
8th Florida: Col. David Lang

Garnett's Artillery Battalion: Lt. Col. John Garnett; Maj. Robert Hardaway
Grandy's Norfolk (Virginia) Blues Battery: Capt. C. R. Grandy
Lewis' Pittsylvania (Virginia) Battery: Lt. Nathan Penick
Maurin's Donaldsonville (Louisiana) Battery: Capt. Victor Maurin
Moore's Norfolk (Virginia) Battery: Capt. Joseph Moore

First Corps Artillery Reserve
Alexander's Battalion: Col. Edward Porter Alexander
Eubank's Bath (Virginia) Battery: Lt. Osmond Taylor
Jordan's Bedford (Virginia) Battery: Capt. Tyler Jordan
Moody's Madison (Louisiana) Battery: Capt. George Moody
Parker's Richmond (Virginia) Battery: Capt. William Parker
Brooks Artillery (Rhett's Battery) (South Carolina): Capt. A. B. Rhett
Woolfolk's Ashland (Virginia) Battery: Capt. Pichegru Woolfolk, Jr.
Washington (Louisiana) Artillery Battalion: Col. James Walton
Squires' First Company: Capt. Charles Squires (c); Lt. C. H. C. Brown
Richardson's Second Company: Capt. John Richardson
Miller's Third Company: Capt. Merritt Miller
Eshleman's Fourth Company: Capt. Benjamin Eshleman

Second Corps
(1) Lieutenant Gen. Thomas "Stonewall" Jackson (mw);
(2) Maj. Gen. Ambrose Powell Hill (w); (3) Brig. Gen. Robert Rodes;
(4) Maj. Gen. J. E. B. Stuart

A. P. Hill's Light Division
(1) Maj. Gen. Ambrose Powell Hill; (2) Brig. Gen. Henry Heth (w);
(3) Brig. Gen. William Dorsey Pender (w); (4) Brig. Gen. James Archer

Heth's Brigade: (1) Brig. Gen. Henry Heth; (2) Col. John Brockenbrough
40th Virginia: Col. J. M. Brockenbrough; Lt. Col. Fleet Cox (w);
Capt. T. E. Betts

47th Virginia: Col. Robert M. Mayo
55th Virginia: Col. Francis Mallory (k); Lt. Col. William S. Christian (w);
Maj. Andrew D. Saunders (k); Lt. R. L. Williams; Maj. Evan Rice
22nd Virginia Battalion (2nd Battalion): Lt. Col. Edward P. Tayloe

Thomas' Brigade: Brig. Gen. Edward Thomas
14th Georgia: Col. R. W. Folsom.
35th Georgia: Capt. John Duke
45th Georgia: Lt. Col. W. L. Grice
49th Georgia: Maj. S. T. Player

Lane's Brigade: Brig. Gen. James Lane
7th North Carolina (State Troops): Col. Edward G. Haywood (w);
Lt. Col. Junius Hill (k); Maj. William L. Davidson (w); Capt. N. A. Pool
18th North Carolina: Col. Thomas J. Purdie (k); Lt. Col. Forney George (w);
Maj. John D. Barry
28th North Carolina: Col. S. D. Lowe; Capt. Edward F. Lovill
33rd North Carolina: Col. Clark M. Avery (w); Capt. Joseph H. Saunders
37th North Carolina: Col. William M. Barbour (w)

McGowan's Brigade: (1) Brig. Gen. Samuel McGowan (w);
(2) Col. O. E. Edwards (mw); (3) Col. A. Perrin; (4) Col. D. H. Hamilton
1st South Carolina (Provisional Army): Col. D. H. Hamilton; Capt. W. P. Shooter
1st South Carolina Rifles (Orr's Rifles): Col. James M. Perrin (mw);
Lt. Col. F. E. Harrison
12th South Carolina: Col. John L. Miller
13th South Carolina: Col. O. E. Edwards; Lt. Col. B. T. Brockman
14th South Carolina: Col. Abner Perrin

Archer's (Fifth) Brigade: (1) Brig. Gen. James Archer; (2) Col. Birkett Fry
13th Alabama: Col. B. D. Fry
5th Alabama Battalion: Capt. S. D. Stewart (k); Capt. A. N. Porter
1st Tennessee (Provisional Army): Lt. Col. Newton J. George
7th Tennessee: Lt. Col. John A. Fite (w)
14th Tennessee: Col. William McComb (w); Capt. R. C. Wilson

Pender's Brigade: Brig. Gen. William Dorsey Pender
13th North Carolina: Col. A. M. Scales (w); Lt. Col. J. H. Hyman
16th North Carolina: Col. John S. McElroy (w); Lt. Col. William A. Stowe (w)
22nd North Carolina: Lt. Col. Christopher C. Cole (k); Maj. Laben Odell (k);
Capt. George Graves
34th North Carolina: Col. William L. J. Lowrance
38th North Carolina: Col. William J. Hoke

Walker's Battalion Artillery: Col. Reuben L. Walker; Maj. William Pegram
Brunson's Pee Dee (South Carolina) Battery: Capt. Ervin Brunson
Crenshaw's Virginia Battery: Lt. John Chamberlayne
Davidson's Letcher (Virginia) Battery: Capt. Greenlee Davidson (mw);
Lt. Thomas Brander
McGraw's Purcell (Virginia) Battery: Lt. Joseph McGraw
Marye's Fredericksburg (Virginia) Battery: Capt. Edward Marye

D. H. Hill's Division
(1) Brig. Gen. Robert E. Rodes; (2) Brig. Gen. Stephen D. Ramseur

Rodes' Brigade: (1) Brig. Gen. Robert E. Rodes; (2) Col. Edward A. O'Neal (w);
(3) Col. Josephus M. Hall
3rd Alabama: Capt. M. F. Bonham
5th Alabama: Col. Josephus M. Hall; Lt. Col. E. Lafayette Hobson (w);
Capt. W. T. Renfro (mw); Capt. T. M. Riley
6th Alabama (Rifle Regiment): Col. James N. Lightfoot
12th Alabama: Col. Samuel B. Pickens
26th Alabama: Col. E. A. O'Neal; Lt. Col. John S. Garvin (w); Lt. Miles J. Taylor

Colquitt's Brigade: Brig. Gen. Alfred Colquitt
6th Georgia: Col. John T. Lofton
19th Georgia: Col. Andrew J. Hutchins
23rd Georgia: Col. Emory F. Best
27th Georgia: Col. Charles T. Zachry
28th Georgia: Col. Tully Graybill

Ramseur's Brigade: (1) Brig. Gen. Stephen Ramseur (w); (2) Col. Francis Parker
2nd North Carolina (State Troops): Col. William R. Cox (w)
4th North Carolina (State Troops): Col. Bryan Grimes
14th North Carolina: Col. R. Tyler Bennett
30th North Carolina: Col. Francis M. Parker

Doles' Brigade: Brig. Gen. George Doles
4th Georgia: Col. Philip Cook (w); Lt. Col. D. R. E. Winn
12th Georgia: Col. Edward Willis
21st Georgia: Col. John T. Mercer
44th Georgia: Col. John B. Estes

Iverson's Brigade: Brig. Gen. Alfred Iverson
5th North Carolina (State Troops): Col. Thomas M. Garrett (w);
Lt. Col. John W. Lea (w); Maj. William J. Hill (w); Capt. S. B. West
12th North Carolina: Maj. D. P. Rowe (mw);
Lt. Col. R. D. Johnston, of the 23rd North Carolina

20th North Carolina: Col. T. F. Toon; Lt. Col. N. Slough
23rd North Carolina: Col. D. H. Christie

Carter's Artillery Battalion: Lt. Col. Thomas Carter
Reese's Jeff Davis Alabama Battery: Capt. William Reese
Carter's King William (Virginia) Battery: Capt. William Carter
Fry's Orange (Virginia) Battery: Capt. Charles Fry
Page's Morris Louisa (Virginia) Battery: Capt. R. C. M. Page

Early's Division
Maj. Gen. Jubal "Old Jube" Early

Gordon's Brigade: Brig. Gen. John Gordon
13th Georgia (Barlow Light Infantry): Col. James Smith
26th Georgia: Col. Edmund Atkinson
31st Georgia: Col. Clement Evans
38th Georgia: Col. James Mathews
60th Georgia: Col. William Stiles
61st Georgia: Col. John Lamar

Hoke's Brigade: (1) Brig. Gen. Robert Hoke (w); (2) Col. Isaac Avery
6th North Carolina (State Troops): Col. Isaac Avery; Maj. Samuel Tate
21st North Carolina: Lt. Col. William Rankin; Col. William Kirkland
54th North Carolina: Col. James McDowell (mw); Lt. Col. Kenneth Murchison
57th North Carolina: Col. Archibald Goodwin (w)
1st Battalion North Carolina Sharpshooters: Maj. R. W. Wharton

Smith's Brigade: Brig. Gen. William "Extra Billy" Smith
13th Virginia: Lt. Col. James Terrill
49th Virginia: Lt. Col. Jonathan Gibson
52nd Virginia: Col. Michael Harman
58th Virginia: Col. Francis Board

Hays' Brigade: Brig. Gen. Harry Hays
5th Louisiana: Col. Henry Forno
6th Louisiana: Col. William Monaghan
7th Louisiana (Pelican Regiment): Col. Davidson Penn (c)
8th Louisiana: Col. Trevanion Lewis (c)
9th Louisiana: Col. Leroy Stafford (c)

Andrews' Artillery Battalion: Lieutenant Col. R. Snowden Andrews
Brown's Fourth Maryland Chesapeake Battery: Capt. W. D. Brown
Carpenter's Alleghany (Virginia) Battery: Capt. Joseph Carpenter
Dement's First Maryland Battery: Capt. William Dement
Raine's Lee (Virginia) Battery: Capt. Charles Raine

Trimble's Division
Brig. Gen. Raleigh Colston

Paxton's Brigade (Stonewall Brigade): (1) Brig. Gen. Elisha "Bull" Paxton (k);
(2) Col. John Funk
2nd Virginia: Col. J. Q. A. Nadenbousch (w); Lt. Col. Raleigh T. Colston
4th Virginia: Maj. William Terry
5th Virginia: Col. J. H. S. Funk; Lt. Col. Hazael J. Williams
27th Virginia: Col. James Edmondson (w); Lt. Col. Daniel Shriver
33rd Virginia: Col. Abraham Spengler

Jones' Brigade: (1) Brig. Gen. John R. Jones; (2) Col. Thomas S. Garnett (mw);
(3) Col. A. S. Vandeventer
21st Virginia: Capt. John B. Moseley
42nd Virginia: Lt. Col. R. W. Withers
44th Virginia: Maj. Norvell Cobb (w); Capt. Thomas R. Bucker
48th Virginia: Col. Thomas S. Garnett; Maj. Oscar White
50th Virginia: Col. A. S. Vandeventer; Maj. Lynville Perkins; Capt. Frank W. Kelly

Colston's (Third) Brigade: (1) Col. Edward T. H. Warren (w);
(2) Col. Titus V. Williams (w); (3) Lt. Col. S. T. Walker; (4) Lt. Col. S. D. Thruston;
(5) Lt. Col. H. A. Brown
1st North Carolina (State Troops): Col. John A. McDowell (w);
Capt. Jarrette Harrell (w); Capt. Louis Latham
3rd North Carolina (State Troops): Lt. Col. S. D. Thruston (w); Maj. William Parsley
10th Virginia: Col. E. T. H. Warren; Lt. Col. Samuel Walker (k);
Maj. Joshua Stover (mw); Capt. A. H. Smals
23rd Virginia: Lt. Col. Simeon T. Walton
37th Virginia: Col. Titus V. Williams

Nicholls' Brigade: (1) Brig. Gen. Francis T. Nicholls (w); (2) Col. Jesse M. Williams
1st Louisiana: Capt. Edward D. Willett
2nd Louisiana (Louisiana Zouaves): Col. J. M. Williams; Lt. Col. Ross Burke
10th Louisiana: Lt. Col. John M. Legett (k)
14th Louisiana (1st Regiment Polish Brigade): Lt. Col. David Zable
15th Louisiana (2nd Regiment Polish Brigade): Capt. William C. Michie

Jones' Artillery Battalion: Lt. Col. Hilary Jones
Carrington's Charlottesville Battery: Capt. James McD. Carrington
Garber's Staunton (Virginia) Battery: Lt. Alexander Fultz
Latimer's Courtney (Virginia) Battery: Capt. W. A. Tanner
Thompson's Louisiana Guard Battery: Capt. Charles Thompson

Second Corps Artillery Reserve: Col. Stapleton Andrews
Brown's Artillery Battalion: Col. J. Thompson Brown

Brooke's Warrenton (Virginia) Battery: Capt. James Brooke
Dance's Powhatten (Virginia) Battery: Capt. Willis Dance
Graham's 1st Rockbridge (Virginia) Battery: Capt. Archibald Graham
Hupp's Salem (Virginia) Battery: Capt. Abraham Graham
Watson's Richmond Howitzers, 2nd Company: Capt. David Watson
Smith's Richmond Howitzers, 3rd Company: Capt. Benjamin Smith, Jr.

McIntosh's Artillery Battalion: Maj. D. G. McIntosh
Hurt's Alabama Battery: Capt. William Hurt
Johnson's Richmond Battery: Capt. Marmaduke Johnson
Lusk's 2nd Rockbridge (Virginia) Battery: Capt. John Lusk
Wooding's Danville (Virginia) Battery: Capt. George Wooding

Army Reserve Artillery: Brig. Gen. William Pendleton
Cutts' Sumter (Georgia) Artillery Battalion: Lt. Col. A. S. Cutts
Ross' Sumter (Georgia) Battalion, Battery A: Capt. Hugh Ross
Patterson's Sumter (Georgia) Battalion, Battery B: Capt. George Patterson

Nelson's Artillery Battalion: Lt. Col. William Nelson
Kirkpatrick's Amherst (Virginia) Battery: Capt. T. J. Kirkpatrick
Massie's Fluvanna (Virginia) Battery: Capt. John Massie
Milledge's Georgia Battery: Capt. John Milledge, Jr.

Cavalry Division
Maj. Gen. J. E. B. Stuart

First Brigade: Brig. Gen. Wade Hampton
1st North Carolina Cavalry (9th Volunteers)
1st South Carolina Cavalry
2nd South Carolina Cavalry
Cobb's Georgia Legion (9th Cavalry)
Phillips' Georgia Legion (Cavalry)

Second Brigade: Brig. Gen. Fitzhugh Lee
1st Virginia Cavalry: Col. James Drake
2nd Virginia Cavalry: Col. Thomas Munford
3rd Virginia Cavalry: Col. Thomas H. Owen
4th Virginia Cavalry: Col. Williams C. Wickham

Third Brigade: Brig. Gen. W. H. F. "Rooney" Lee
2nd North Carolina Cavalry: Maj. C. M. Andrews
5th Virginia Cavalry: Col. Thomas Rosser
9th Virginia Cavalry: Col. Richard L. T. Beale

10th Virginia Cavalry: Col. J. Lucius Davis
13th Virginia Cavalry: Col. John R. Chambliss, Jr.
15th Virginia Cavalry: Lt. Col. John Critcher

Fourth Brigade: Brig. Gen. William "Grumble" Jones
1st Maryland Battalion (CSA Cavalry): Maj. Ridgely Brown
6th Virginia Cavalry: Lt. Col. John Green
7th Virginia Cavalry: Lt. Col. Thomas Marshall
11th Virginia Cavalry: Col. Lunsford L. Lomax
12th Virginia Cavalry: Col. A. W. Harman
34th Virginia Battalion (Cavalry): Lt. Col. V. A. Witcher
35th Virginia Battalion (Cavalry, "Comanches"): Lt. Col. Elijah V. White

Stuart Horse Artillery: Maj. R. F. Beckham
Lynchburg (Virginia) Beauregard's Battery: Capt. M. N. Moorman
1st Stuart Horse Artillery: Capt. James Breathed
2nd Stuart Horse Artillery: Capt. William M. McGregor
Washington (South Carolina) Battery: Capt. James F. Hart

Appendix B

The Chancellorsville Campaign
by the Numbers

All statistics are based on both the *Official Records of the War of the Rebellion* (Series I, vol. 25, part 1); and *The Campaign of Chancellorsville: A Strategic and Tactical Study*, by John Bigelow, Jr.

The Army of the Potomac		
Organization	*Present for Duty*	*Killed, Wounded, and Missing*
I Corps	16,908	299
II Corps	16,893	1,193
III Corps	18,721	4,119
V Corps	15,824	700
VI Corps	23,667	4,610
XI Corps	12,977	2,412
XII Corps	13,450	2,824
Artillery Reserve	1,610	0
Cavalry Corps	11,541	389
Provost Guard	2,217	0
Totals	**133,868**	**17,278**

The Army of Northern Virginia

Organization	Present for Duty	Killed, Wounded, and Missing
First Corps	17,755	3,326
Second Corps	38,199	9,381
Artillery Reserve	480	3
Cavalry Division	2,500	111
Totals	60,892	12,821

I Corps Losses at Fitzhugh's Crossing April 29 - May 2, 1863

Organization	Killed	Wounded	Missing	Total
7th Indiana	14	-	5	19
19th Indiana	1	3	1	5
12th Massachusetts	-	1	-	1
13th Massachusetts	2	1	-	3
24th Michigan	4	20	-	24
22nd New Jersey	-	6	-	6
29th New Jersey	1	3	-	4
1st New York Light, Artillery, Battery L	-	8	-	8
22nd New York	-	10	-	10
24th New York	-	1	-	1
30th New York	-	1	-	1

I Corps Losses at Fitzhugh's Crossing April 29 - May 2, 1863 (continued)			
Organization	Killed	Wounded	Missing	Total
76th New York	-	1	-	1
83rd New York	-	1	-	1
84th New York	-	23	-	23
95th New York	-	2	5	7
147th New York	-	6	-	6
56th Pennsylvania	2	8	-	10
90th Pennsylvania	1	7	-	8
107th Pennsylvania	-	1	-	1
135th Pennsylvania	-	1	-	1
136th Pennsylvania	-	6	-	6
2nd Wisconsin	-	5	1	6
6th Wisconsin	3	13	-	16
7th Wisconsin	3	5	1	9
4th U.S. Artillery, Battery B	-	1	-	1
Totals	18	138	8	164

VI Corps Losses at Franklin's Crossing April 29 - May 2, 1863

Organization	Killed	Wounded	Missing	Total
31st New York	1	9	-	10
49th Pennsylvania	-	3	-	3
95th Pennsylvania	-	3	-	3
119th Pennsylvania	1	3	-	4
Totals	**2**	**18**	**-**	**20**

Engineer Brigade Losses at Fitzhugh's Crossing, United States Ford, and Banks' Ford April 29 - May 4, 1863

Organization	Killed	Wounded	Missing	Total
15th New York Engineers	1	-	-	1
50th New York Engineers	-	6	1	7
United States Engineer Battalion	-	-	-	-
Totals	**1**	**6**	**1**	**8**

Losses in Gibbon's Division and Sedgwick's Corps at Second Fredericksburg, Salem Church, and Banks' Ford May 3-4, 1863

Organization	Killed	Wounded	Missing	Total
Gibbon's Division				
Sully's Brigade	-	16	4	20

Losses in Gibbon's Division and Sedgwick's Corps at Second Fredericksburg, Salem Church, and Banks' Ford May 3-4, 1863 (continued)				
Organization	*Killed*	*Wounded*	*Missing*	*Total*
Hall's Brigade	3	56	8	67
Artillery Brigade	5	18	-	23
Totals	8	90	12	110
Howe's Division				
Grant's Brigade	39	295	97	431
Neill's Brigade	52	394	404	850
Artillery Brigade	-	8	1	9
Totals	91	697	502	1,290
Newton's Division				
Shaler's Brigade	7	86	67	160
Browne's Brigade	42	248	22	342
Wheaton's Brigade	48	237	200	485
Artillery Brigade	1	4	18	23
Totals	**98**	**605**	**307**	**1,010**
Light Division	93	395	310	798
Total VI Army Corps	**485**	**2,620**	**1,485**	**4,590***

* Losses slightly vary between the *Official Records* and Bigelow's exhaustive study because Bigelow was privileged to more updated information at the time he wrote his study.

Losses in Early's, McLaws', and Anderson's Divisions at Second Fredericksburg, Salem Church, and Banks' Ford May 3-4, 1863				
Organization	*Killed*	*Wounded*	*Missing*	*Total*
Early's Division				
Hays' Brigade	63	306	369	738
Smith's Brigade	11	75	86	172
Gordon's Brigade	16	144	160	320
Hoke's Brigade	35	194	229	458
Totals	125	719	844	1,688
McLaws' Division**				
Wofford's Brigade	71	414	490	975
Semmes' Brigade	85	482	567	1,134
Kershaw's Brigade	11	89	100	200
Barksdale's Brigade	45	181	226	452
Totals	212	1,166	1,383	2,761
Anderson's Division***				
Mahone's Brigade	20	129	149	298
Perry's Brigade	20	87	107	211
Wilcox's Brigade	55	384	439	878
Posey's Brigade	36	176	212	424
Wright's Brigade	25	248	273	546
Totals	**156**	**1,024**	**1,180**	**2,357**

** Losses, with the exception of Barksdale's brigade, include actions around the Chancellorsville Crossroad from May 1-3, 1863.

*** Losses also include actions around the Chancellorsville Crossroad from May 1-3, 1863.

Appendix C

The Road Well Traveled: The Postwar History of Fredericksburg's Sunken Road

Just as development swallowed the Salem Church battlefield beginning in the late 1970s, the Second Fredericksburg battlefield fell victim to a similar fate decades earlier. In the decades following the Civil War, the city of Fredericksburg came out from behind its sheltered position along the banks of the Rappahannock River and crept westward toward Marye's Heights. By the 1920s, most of the open killing fields had morphed into friendly neighborhoods, and the infamous Sunken Road—where Confederate defenders had once repulsed waves of Northern attacks and where, later, the Union Sixth Corps finally broke through—fell victim to another invasion: the automobile.

The Sunken Road, known in 1862-63 as the Telegraph Road, was the Interstate 95 of its day. The road led from the United States capital of Washington, D.C., south 50 miles to Fredericksburg; from there, it continued its journey south to the Confederacy's capital of Richmond.

Here in Fredericksburg, along a front a few hundred yards long, Confederate infantry held the road in force during the first and the second battles of Fredericksburg. Union repulses during the first battle cost nearly 5,000 lives. During the second battle, the Union army took the wall at a far lower cost—1,500 casualties.

Following the war, the Telegraph Road along Fredericksburg's outskirts remained an active city street. Travelers moving between Washington and Richmond would cross the old battlefield along its most famous sector.

Those approaching from the north would be the first to encounter the portion of the road that was actually sunken. Below the Marye Family home of

Brompton, the dirt road sat nearly five feet below the surround terrain. To the left and right, two stone retaining walls held the earth back from tumbling in on the roadway. This sunken portion only ran for some 35 yards, terminating at the intersection with Mercer Street.

On the south side of the intersection near the Innis House, the wall started anew, although there it was a free-standing wall, not a retaining wall. This portion of the wall was likely constructed to keep travelers out of the yards of the local inhabitants, or in the case of Martha Stephens, as a way to funnel travelers into the illegal bar that she ran from her home. The wall ran approximately to where Willis Hill/Telegraph Road started its westward turn, approximately 220 yards from the Innis House.

In the years after the battle, most of the original stone wall was removed from Fredericksburg. Some used the free-standing wall in construction projects, while others wanted to take a piece of history home with them, picking up pieces of the wall as they passed through the battlefield on their way to their next destinations.

With the advent of automobiles, the road was eventually paved. Two-way traffic kept the thoroughfare busy, although the road continued to offer easy access to anyone who wanted to visit the battlefield.

When the National Park Service built the Fredericksburg Battlefield Visitor Center in 1936, workers raised the building on the most prominent part of the battlefield as was the custom of the day. The action in front of the Stone Wall and along the Sunken Road remained the most famous part of the battle of Fredericksburg—remembered as such, in part, because the Telegraph Road passed right through that sector, keeping it fresh in everyone's minds. Therefore, it seemed only natural that the Civilian Conservation Corps (CCC) construct the new visitor center near the Sunken Road.

As part of their work on the battlefield, the CCC built a new stone wall along the southernmost stretch of the Sunken Road, which runs in front of the National Cemetery and the cemetery caretaker's cottage. While the wall ended up being much smaller than the original, it looked more a wall made from field stone rather than the quarried stone the original wall had been actually made of. Today, the three contrasting walls each tell their own tale and show the evolution of the wall and how it was interpreted over the years.

As more visitors came to the battlefield, the NPS grew more and more concerned about safety. Battlefield visitors frequently wandered into the busy roadway in an attempt to see monuments or as they tried to conjure visions of the rapidly disappearing open fields. On several occasions, the NPS petitioned the City of Fredericksburg to shut the road down to traffic, but the requests fell on deaf city council ears.

In 1972, the city finally approved a compromise, making the road a one-way street, with traffic flowing from north to south. Eleven thousand cars still passed along the road every week, though, and drivers frequently ignored the posted 25-mile-per-hour speed limit. In attempt to further curb speeding, the road was narrowed from 18 feet across to 10 feet.

With the opening of a local bypass known as the Blue and Gray Parkway in the mid 1990s, traffic along the Sunken Road decreased precipitously—by some 80 percent. Finally, in May of 2001, the city gave its permission to close the road, although it took more than three more years for that to finally happen.

In August 2004, with the road closed to traffic and its management turned over to the NPS, the park service set forth an ambitious two million dollar renovation plan for both the road and exhibits within the visitor center ($580,000 was earmarked for the road and surrounding landscape). Contractors stripped the pavement from the roadbed and laid down a clay base, with a layer of gravel atop it. Although the road was dirt only at the time of the battle, the rocky base today prevents the road from turning into a quagmire during heavy rainstorms. They also re-widened the roadbed from 10 feet back to its original 18.

The original stone wall remains much as it did during the battles, still acting as a retaining wall. The second stretch of the wall, which once ran past the Innis House until souvenir hunters stripped it away, was replaced by the NPS between 2004-2005. Utilizing digitized photographs and archeological digs, the park service was able to determine the footprint of the original wall. It placed this rebuilt wall within three to four inches of the original. Pennsylvania sandstone replaces the original Aquia Stone that once formed the formidable barrier.

However, photographs also showed the condition of the stones in and around the time of battle. When the new wall was completed, park service officials weren't happy with how "pretty" the wall was, and had the stonemasons tear down the wall and batter the stones to create more of a wartime appearance.

The archeological work also uncovered a multitude of bullets. Federal artillery shells remained buried in the earth near the base of the original wall. One dig came across the trash pit of Martha Stephens: more than 500 pounds of oyster shells and champagne bottles were found in the pit, along with the leg of a rather risqué doll.

On Memorial Day in 2005, the NPS finally reopened the road to the public, with a small ribbon-cutting ceremony. Guest speakers, including authors George Rable and Frank O'Reilly, gave talks and led tours of the reclaimed battleground. Today, visitors can safely stroll in and along the road, climb to the top of Marye's Heights, and appreciate the once-battle torn roadway that now leads only to history.

For further reading on the refurbishment of the road, we recommend Joan M. Zenzen, *At the Crossroads of Preservation and Development: A History of Fredericksburg and Spotsylvania National Military Park.*

Appendix D

Medal of Honor Recipients at the Battles of Second Fredericksburg, Salem Church, and Banks' Ford

All Medal of Honor citations were collected by the staff of the Fredericksburg and Spotsylvania National Military Park. These citations may be accessed in its bound manuscript collection or at either the Fredericksburg or Chancellorsville Battlefield Visitor Center.

Cpl. Edward Brown, Jr., 62nd New York Infantry, Co. G—At Salem Heights: "Severely wounded while carrying the colors, he continued at his post, under fire, until ordered to the rear." (May 3-4, 1863)

Lt. Franklin George Butterfield, 6th Vermont Infantry, Co. C.—At Salem Heights: "Took command of the skirmish line and covered the movements of his regiment out of a precarious position." (May 4, 1863)

Lt. Charles Amory Clark, 6th Maine Infantry, Co. A—At Brooks (Banks') Ford: "Having voluntarily taken command of his regiment in the absences of its commander, at great personal risk and with remarkable presences of mind and fertility of resources, led the command down an exceedingly precipitous embankment to the Rappahannock River and by his gallantry, coolness, and good judgment in the face of the enemy saved the command from capture or destruction." (May 4, 1863)

Sgt. Robert John Coffey, 4th Vermont Infantry, Co. K—At Banks' Ford: "Single-handedly captured two officers and five privates of the 8th Louisiana Regiment (C.S.A.)." (May 4, 1863)

Sgt. Maj. Amos Jay Cummings, 26th New Jersey Infantry—At Salem Heights: "Rendered great assistance in the heat of the action in rescuing a part of the field batteries from an extremely dangerous and exposed position." (May 4, 1863)

Maj. John Curtis Gilmore, 16th New York Infantry—At Salem Heights: "Seized the colors of his regiment and gallantly rallied his men under a very severe fire." (May 3, 1863)

Col. Lewis Addison Grant, 5th Vermont Infantry—At Salem Heights: "Personal gallantry and intrepidity displayed in the management of his brigade and in leading it in the assault in which he was wounded." (May 3, 1863)

Chaplain Francis Bloodgood Hall, 16th New York Infantry—At Salem Heights: "Voluntarily exposed himself to a heavy fire during the thickest of the fight and carried wounded men to the rear for treatment and attendance." (May 3, 1863) Hall was the second of only three chaplains to earn the Medal of Honor during the war and the only one to earn the honor while performing his duties on the battlefield under fire while unarmed.

Sgt. Ephraim Harrington, 2nd Vermont Infantry, Co. G—At Fredericksburg: "Carried the colors to the top of the heights and almost to the muzzle of the enemy's guns." (May 3, 1863)

Pvt. James Holehouse, 7th Massachusetts Infantry, Co. B—At Marye's Heights: "With one companion voluntarily and with conspicuous daring advanced beyond his regiment, which had been broken in the assault, and halted beneath the crest. Following the example of these two men, the colors were brought to the summit, the regiment was advanced and the position held." (May 3, 1863)

Pvt. James Hezikiah Luther, 7th Massachusetts Infantry, Co. D—At Fredericksburg: "Among the first to jump into the enemy's rifle pits, he himself captured and brought out three prisoners." (May 3, 1863)

Cpl. Lowell Mason Maxham, 7th Massachusetts Infantry, Co. F—At Fredericksburg: "Though severely wounded and in the face of a deadly fire from the enemy at short range, he rushed bravely forward and was among the first to enter the enemy's works on the crest of Marye's Heights and helped to plant his regimental colors there." (May 3, 1863)

Cpl. Peter McAdams, 98th Pennsylvania Infantry, Co. A—At Salem Heights: "Went 250 yards in front of his regiment toward the position of the enemy and under fire brought within the lines a wounded and unconscious comrade." (May 3, 1863)

Cpl. John P. McVeane, 49th New York Infantry, Co. D.—At Fredericksburg Heights (Salem Heights): "Shot a Confederate color-bearer and seized the flag; also approached, alone, a barn between the lines and demanded and received the surrender of a number of the enemy within." McVeane, who also spelled his named "McVean," was killed on May 10, 1864, at Spotsylvania. His remains (if they were recovered) were not identified. He was awarded the Medal of Honor posthumously on September 21, 1870. (May 4, 1863)

Col. Alexander Shaler, 65th New York Infantry—At Marye's Heights: "At a most critical moment, the head of the charging column being about to be crushed by a severe fire of the enemy's artillery and infantry, he pushed forward with a supporting column, pierced the enemy's works, and turned their flank." (May 3, 1863)

Capt. Forrester L. Taylor, 23rd New Jersey Infantry, Co. H—At Chancellorsville (Banks' Ford): "At great risk voluntarily saved the lives of and brought from the battlefield two wounded comrades." (May 3, 1863)

Lt. William G. Tracy, 122nd New York Infantry, Co. I—At Chancellorsville: "Having been sent outside the lines to obtain certain information of great importance and having succeeded in his mission, was surprised upon his return by a large force of the enemy, regaining the Union lines only after greatly imperiling his life." (May 2, 1863) Tracy was on detached duty with Maj. Gen. Henry Slocum's XII Corps.

Lt. Daniel Davis Wheeler, 4th Vermont Infantry, Co. G—At Salem Heights: "Distinguished bravery in action where he was wounded and had a horse shot under him." (May 3, 1863) Wheeler, who eventually rose to the rank of brigadier general, returned to the Fredericksburg area after the war, married a local woman, and after his death was buried in the Fredericksburg city cemetery.

Appendix E

Whatever Happened To . . . ?

Immediately following the Chancellorsville Campaign, **Major General Joseph Hooker** looked to lay the blame at the feet of others, particularly George Stoneman, John Sedgwick, and Oliver O. Howard. The finger-pointing partially paralyzed the Army of the Potomac. Politicians made their way in and out of camp, and the entire army was abuzz. Hooker's accusations leveled at high-ranking officers, mixed with his farcical proclamations that he'd been so close to victory, became too much for his corps commanders. Major General Henry Slocum, along with major generals John Reynolds and Darius Couch, informed senators, governors, and President Lincoln that Hooker was not fit to command the army—although each went out of his way to say he was not the man for the job either. Well aware of the storm around him, Hooker had few allies to depend upon, and even the president shut him off. Lincoln stripped Hooker of much of his power by closing the direct line of communication between them, which made Hooker report to general of the armies, Maj. Gen. Henry Halleck. Hooker and Halleck loathed one another.

With his power in question, Hooker was forced to yield the initiative in the east to Robert E. Lee and the Army of Northern Virginia. Lee did not hesitate, and on June 3, 1863, began moving his army west and north. In the meantime, unwilling to enter another battle under Hooker, Darius Couch asked to be relieved of command. Slocum, Sedgwick, and Reynolds, meanwhile, kept pushing for Hooker's removal. As all this controversy raged, the Army of the Potomac shrank as enlistments expired for many veteran two-year regiments and even fresh nine-month regiments.

The internal woe reached a head on June 27. In a series of messages between Halleck and Hooker, the two generals argued over the use and defense of the Federal stronghold at Harpers Ferry, in western Virginia. Hooker wanted the post abandoned and the men added to the ranks of his army (depleted as it had been by enlistment expirations). Halleck refused to relent. Hooker offered his resignation, and to his surprise Lincoln accepted it. On June 28, just days before the battle of Gettysburg, Hooker was notified of the change and replaced by Maj.

Gen. George Meade, who had not pushed for Hooker's removal or had even vied for the command in the first place. A stunned Hooker spent the next few months out of the war.

Hooker was either too valuable or too dangerous to keep in the capital city for long, however. In September 1863, as a response to the Union defeat at Chickamauga, the XI Corps and XII Corps were transferred from the Army of the Potomac to the Western Theater, and Hooker was given command of both. Hooker and his new command performed well during Maj. Gen. Ulysses S. Grant's effort to break the Confederate siege of Chattanooga, Tennessee, particularly at the battle of Lookout Mountain on November 24. Grant, however, had little use for Fightin' Joe, whose reputation had soured relations between them.

In 1864, the XI Corps and XII Corps were converted into the XX Corps as part of the Army of the Cumberland. They fought hard and well under Hooker all the way to the gates of Atlanta, Georgia, where Hooker's Civil War service came to a rather abrupt end. Major General James McPherson, the much-beloved and respected commander of the Army of the Tennessee, was killed in action on July 22, 1864. Hooker stood to advance into the position, but Maj. Gen. William T. Sherman held Hooker in deep contempt. In a cold calculated move, the commander of all Union troops in the Western Theater promoted Oliver O. Howard—the man Hooker blamed the most for his defeat at Chancellorsville—to replace McPherson. This slap was too much for Hooker, who tendered his resignation for a second time in 13 months.

Hooker remained in the army, but was thrust into backwater departmental commands. His most notable service following the Atlanta Campaign came in May 1865, when he oversaw the funeral procession and first burial of Abraham Lincoln. He married in October of that year, but within weeks his health took a turn for the worse when he suffered a stroke while attending a reception for Ulysses S. Grant. The stroke partially paralyzed the right side of his body. He suffered another stroke in 1867. Hooker attributed both strokes to his Chancellorsville wound.

In July 1868, Hooker's wife passed away. He never remarried and the couple had no children. He officially retired from the U.S. Army and became active in postwar veteran reunions, doing all he could to "clear" his name from the blemish that was Chancellorsville. He traveled to the fields of his former glory days and wrote extensively to historian Samuel Bates. His health also became more of a concern. He walked with a cane and visibly shook; servants had to cut his meat at meals.

Joseph Hooker died on October 31, 1879. He was laid in state in New York's City Hall. His body was taken to Cincinnati, Ohio, where he was buried. Attendees/ pallbearers at his funeral included former Union generals Butterfield, Hancock, and Doubleday, as well as prominent civilians Charles Tiffany of the famed Tiffany Company, and John Jacob Astor, who would later die on the *Titanic*.

Major General John Sedgwick ("Uncle John") was none too happy with Joe Hooker, who had accused Sedgwick and his VI Corps of being afraid to fight and that Sedgwick had disobeyed direct orders. Sedgwick had it out with him over what he called "a pack of lies." Although cooler heads prevailed, it was clear to the men of VI Corps that they were branded men in Hooker's eyes.

In July, Sedgwick's VI Corps was the last infantry corps to arrive on the field at Gettysburg late on the second day and saw very little action. Meade spread VI Corps units from the base of Little Round Top on the army's left to Rock Creek and Powers Hill on the army's extreme right. Without a concentrated command, there was little for Sedgwick to do but maintain a headquarters and spend most of July 2 and 3 as a spectator. He took the lead, however, in the pursuit of Lee back into Virginia.

Like the rest of the army, Sedgwick and his men saw limited action until November 1863, when Meade tasked the V Corps and VI Corps with forcing a crossing of the Rappahannock River near modern-day Remington, Virginia. His corps captured nearly 1,700 Confederates, eight battle flags, and four pieces of artillery, but little else was accomplished. During the subsequent Mine Run campaign, the VI Corps again saw limited action.

After spending the winter near Culpeper, Virginia, Sedgwick entered into his final campaign. On May 3, 1864, the Army of the Potomac marched again into the Wilderness in the opening movement of what would become known as the Overland Campaign. When battle erupted on May 5, Sedgwick's VI Corps fought just north of Saunder's Field. It was a mixed performance by all involved. On May 8, the corps made its way south to Spotsylvania Court House, where late in the day the men assaulted Laurel Hill but failed to take the position. The next morning, Sedgwick was near an artillery battery along Brock Road when an enemy sharpshooter put a bullet through his head. He was the most senior-ranking Northern officer to fall in the war. He was buried in Cornwall Hallow, Connecticut.

John F. Reynolds enjoyed an even shorter post-Chancellorsville career than did John Sedgwick. After the close of the campaign, Reynolds retained command of his beloved I Corps. There was little to fault in his operations during the campaign because his corps saw such limited action. He found plenty of fault with his commander, however, and thus worked with Slocum, Sedgwick, and Couch to oust Hooker. Since then, rumors have swirled that President Lincoln offered Reynolds command of the Army of the Potomac, though no hard evidence of this exists.

Reynolds made his way north to Gettysburg with the rest of the army in June. When he heard the news of Hooker's removal, Reynolds called upon his friend and one-time subordinate George Meade to congratulate and confer with him. Meade gave Reynolds command of what the new army commander termed the Left Wing of the Army of the Potomac: Reynolds' I Corps, Brig. Gen. John Buford's 1st Cavalry Division, and the III Corps and XI Corps (which Meade may have regarded as his least trustworthy units). Just two days later, Buford's horsemen engaged the lead elements of Lee's army three miles west of Gettysburg. Reynolds rode ahead to assess the situation and called his I Corps into action. While overseeing the deployment of the Iron Brigade, a Confederate bullet caught him in the back of the head and he died instantly. His body was evacuated from the field and carried to Baltimore, Philadelphia, and then finally his hometown of Lancaster, Pennsylvania, where he was laid to rest on July 4, 1863—less than 50 miles away from the spot where he had been killed. Reynolds was the highest-ranking officer to fall at the battle of Gettysburg.

If there was a mainstay in the II Corps, it was **Brig. Gen. John Gibbon**. At Gettysburg, part of his division helped repulse James Longstreet's assault along the Emmitsburg Road on July 2 and Pickett's Charge on July 3, 1863, where Gibbon was wounded a second time. Between the end of the Gettysburg Campaign and the opening of the Overland Campaign, Gibbon oversaw draft departments in Philadelphia and Cleveland. Back in charge of his division in the Wilderness in May 1864, Gibbon battled A. P. Hill's and Longstreet's men along the Orange Plank Road. Days later, his men fought at the Bloody Angle at Spotsylvania on May 12, and then again over the same ground on May 18.

At the battle of Ream's Station outside Petersburg on August 25, 1864, the II Corps performed poorly, and corps commander Maj. Gen. Winfield Scott Hancock leveled the blame at Gibbon. A rift formed between the two friends that never fully healed. Shortly thereafter, Grant promoted Gibbon to major general of volunteers and gave him command of the XXIV Corps in the Army of the James, a command he held until the close of hostilities. At Appomattox, Gibbon was appointed as one of the commissioners who received the Confederate surrender.

Gibbon stayed in the U.S. Army after the war, serving on the Plains during the Indian Wars of the 1870s and 1880s. His 7th U.S. Infantry marched to the relief of Maj. Marcus Reno's three companies, besieged during the battle of the Little Big Horn in 1876. Gibbon later led a successful campaign against the Nez Perce, and in 1885 was promoted to brigadier general in the Regular Army. He retired in 1891, and died in Baltimore, Maryland, in 1896. He was interred in Arlington National Cemetery.

In an effort to maintain the momentum garnered by his stunning victory at Chancellorsville and relieve pressure against Confederate Vicksburg, **Robert E. Lee** led his army north into Pennsylvania. The invasion met with defeat in early July at Gettysburg and was fortunate to execute a successful withdrawal back into Virginia. Lee did what he could to keep his army in fighting shape, but dwindling supplies and manpower (most of Longstreet's First Corps was transferred to Georgia in the fall of 1863) posed severe challenges. The winter of 1863-64 was hard on Lee and his men.

In the spring of 1864, a new adversary entered the Eastern Theater in the form of Lt. Gen. Ulysses S. Grant. With Lee's army as his goal, Grant battered the Confederates at every turn beginning in early May in the Wilderness. The determined Union commander battled and maneuvered his way south to the James River and then to Petersburg, where both sides settled into a quasi-siege. Other than limited offensive operations and thrusts into the Shenandoah Valley, Lee had lost the initiative. The siege lasted until early April 1865, when Grant finally broke Lee's line and chased the broken Army of Northern Virginia to Appomattox Court House, where "the Old Gray Fox" surrendered.

After Appomattox Lee embraced peace and urged others to do so as well. He accepted the presidency of Washington College in Lexington, Virginia (today's Washington and Lee University). While in Lexington, Lee gathered papers to write a memoir on his participation in the war. Unfortunately, he was not able to finish his memoir. On September 28, 1870, Lee suffered a stroke and his condition steadily deteriorated. He died the following month on October 12, just five years after he surrendered his famed army. He is buried in a family tomb beneath the college chapel at Washington and Lee.

Jubal A. Early's actions at Second Fredericksburg and Banks' Ford earned Robert E. Lee's unwavering respect and admiration. Lee's "Bad Old Man" maintained his place at the head of his Second Corps division as the army approached Gettysburg. He arrived along the Harrisburg Road on July 1 and launched an audacious and overwhelming assault that helped fold the Federal right flank in less than an hour.

Controversy engulfed the next phase of battle when Lee asked Early's commanding officer, Lt. Gen. Richard Ewell, to finish the attack and carry the heights south of town "if practicable." Ewell's two divisions on the field had already seen a great deal of action. Major General Robert Rodes' division had sustained heavy losses and was in no condition to forge ahead, but Early, whose division was still relatively fresh, refused to take the lead on the assault. Precious minutes ticked by as the various officers in charge debated the issue. When word arrived from Early's least trustworthy brigade commander, William "Extra Billy" Smith, that Union soldiers had been spotted east of town, Smith's and John Gordon's brigades deployed to meet the threat. As quickly as the Federals had arrived, however, they also vanished. The result of this confusion was that no major Confederate attack against Cemetery Hill or Culp's Hill was undertaken. Many Southerners and especially Early—who was looking to excuse his own culpability—blamed Ewell for the eventual Confederate loss at Gettysburg.

Early continued in command of his division. He and his men performed extremely well in the Wilderness in May of 1864. During the battle of Spotsylvania Court House, Lee temporarily elevated Old Jube to command the Third Corps when A. P. Hill fell ill, a position in which Early excelled. By the end of May, Early found himself leading the Second Corps when Lee removed General Ewell from command. That summer, Lee dispatched the Second Corps to the Shenandoah Valley, where Early moved his small "army" all the way to the gates of Washington, D.C. Unable to take the heavily fortified city, Early turned back and raised havoc in the Valley. Grant grew tired of Early's Shenandoah antics and by the end of the summer called upon a newly formed army under Maj. Gen. Philip Sheridan to dispatch Early. Sheridan defeated Early in three major battles (Third Winchester, Fisher's Hill, and Cedar Creek), and by the end of October the Union controlled Virginia's vital breadbasket.

While the bulk of his survivors rejoined Lee in the trenches around Petersburg, Early took to campaigning in southwestern Virginia. In March of 1865, Union Brig. Gen. George A. Custer all but destroyed what was left of Early's force at Waynesboro, Virginia. By April, Lee's army was on the verge of surrender and Early was on his way to Mexico. The unrepentant "Bad Old Man" made a circuitous journey north on a ship to Canada, where he stayed for some time. While there, he penned a short memoir of his 1864 exploits and corresponded with Robert E. Lee.

Early eventually returned to Virginia, where he became the first president of the Southern Historical Society. In that capacity, the "Lost Cause" writings of the 1870s-1890s took hold. Early enshrined the memories of Lee and Stonewall Jackson while he dueled in words with anyone who spoke ill of them or him. His bitter personal battle with James Longstreet succeeded in turning him (and Ewell) into scapegoats for Lee's failure at Gettysburg. Many veterans who differed with Early's views refused to voice their opinions until after his death in 1894. Early is buried in Lynchburg, Virginia.

In the weeks following Chancellorsville, the headstrong **Brig. Gen. William Barksdale** and the equally difficult Jubal Early turned from fighting Yankees to fighting one another. Each blamed the other for the failure to hold the line on May 3 against Sedgwick's and Gibbon's assault. In reality, it had been a no-win scenario for either commander. Still, the two traded barbs in the Richmond papers. Early, who blamed Barksdale's men for failing to hold the Sunken Road, demonstrated a vicious tongue that would show itself all too often during the postwar years. Barksdale gave as good as he got, firing back blow for blow. With the Gettysburg Campaign on the horizon, Lee himself finally had to step in and put an end to the infighting.

Barksdale led his brigade of Mississippians to Gettysburg with the rest of the army where, on July 2, his men made a grand charge toward the Peach Orchard. The Union line was held by Dan Sickles' III Corps, which was stretched thin as Longstreet slowly but steadily released brigade after brigade to break through Meade's attenuated left flank. Once Barksdale's brigade was released about 6:00 p.m., it crossed 600 yards in a matter of a few minutes. Sitting atop his horse, Barksdale rode in the lead with his hat in hand, waving his men on to victory. The Mississippians broke through along the Emmitsburg Road and drove deep into the Union line on lower Cemetery Ridge until a Federal counterattack coupled with Southern exhaustion and casualties drove them back. One of the losses was Barksdale himself, who had been mortally wounded earlier in the charge and eventually captured. Barksdale was taken to the Hummelbaugh farm along the Taneytown Road, where he died the next day. He was buried in Jackson, Mississippi.

Brigadier General Cadmus M. Wilcox performed perhaps the greatest delaying action of the Civil War on the afternoon of May 3, 1863. His accomplishment allowed Lee to dispatch reinforcements eastward from the Chancellorsville crossroads to stem the Federal tide moving west from Fredericksburg. Wilcox went on to Gettysburg, where his men saw limited action on July 2 in Biesecker Woods before participating in a failed assault against lower Cemetery Ridge. On July 3, Wilcox was tasked with supporting Pickett's right flank, but by the time his brigade moved out the charge had already failed.

Following Gettysburg, Lee promoted Wilcox to major general and put him in command of a division, which Wilcox led well during the fighting at the Wilderness, Spotsylvania, Cold Harbor, and during the siege of Petersburg. On April 2, 1865, when Grant's attack crushed Lee's lines around Petersburg, Wilcox and his men bought valuable time defending Fort Gregg, which in turn gave Lee a few precious hours to withdraw the Confederate army.

Following the war, Wilcox settled in Washington, D.C. President Grover Cleveland appointed him to head the railroad division of the Land Office. Wilcox never married, but instead cared for his brother's widow and children. He died in Washington, D.C., on December 2, 1890, where he is buried.

Bibliography

Newspapers

Albany (NY) Evening Journal
Daily Eastern Argus (Portland, ME)
Weekly Recorder (Fayetteville, NY)
Fredericksburg (VA) Daily Star
The Herald
Jamestown (NY) Journal
London *Times*
Macon (GA) Telegraph
Advertiser and Register (Mobile, AL)
National Tribune
New York Times
New York Tribune
Newark (NJ) Daily Advertiser
Pittsburgh (PA) Evening Chronicle
Rochester (NY) Daily Union & Advertiser
Southern Enterprise (Greenville, SC)
Sussex (NJ) Register

Journals and Periodicals

Civil War Times Illustrated
Fredericksburg History and Biography
The Fredericksburg Times
Southern Historical Society Papers
Vermont Watchman and State Journal

Manuscript Collections

Fredericksburg and Spotsylvania National Military Park bound manuscript collection. *This collection encompasses nearly 600 bound volumes of papers. These papers have been collected from repositories all over the United States. Sources from which the papers, letters, diaries, etc., in this book were aggregated included, but were not limited to:*

Boston Public Library, Boston, MA
Brown University, Providence, RI
Civil War Library and Museum, Philadelphia, PA
Duke University, Durham, NC
Georgia Department of Archives and History, Atlanta, GA
Gettysburg National Military Park, Gettysburg, PA
Gilder Lehrman Library, New York, NY
Harvard University, Cambridge, MA
Huntingdon Library, San Marino, CA
Library of Congress, Washington, D.C.
Louisiana State University, Baton Rouge, LA
Maine State Historical Society, Bangor, ME
Military Order of the Loyal Legions of the United States Collection
Mississippi Department of Archives and History, Jackson, MS
Museum of the Confederacy, Richmond, VA
National Archives of the United States, Washington, D.C.
New Jersey State Archives, Trenton, NJ
New York State Archives, Albany, NY
New York State Military Museum and Veterans Research Center, Albany, NY
New York State Library, Albany, NY
North Carolina Department of Archives and History, Raleigh, NC
North Carolina State University, Raleigh, NC
Norwich University, Northfield, VT
Pennsylvania State Archives, Harrisburg, PA
Soldiers and Sailors Hall Memorial Hall and Museum, Pittsburgh, PA
State Historical Society of Wisconsin, Madison, WI
United States Military Academy at West Point, West Point, NY
United States Army Military History Institute, Carlisle, PA
University of Georgia, Athens, GA
University of North Carolina at Chapel Hill, Chapel Hill, NC

University of Pittsburgh, Pittsburgh, PA
University of South Carolina, Columbia, SC
University of Vermont, Burlington, VT
University of Virginia, Charlottesville, VA
Virginia State Archives, Richmond, VA
Virginia State Library, Richmond, VA
Western Reserve Historical Society, Cleveland, OH
Yale University, New Haven, CT

Primary Sources

Adams, Charles F. *A Cycle of Adams Letters, 1861-1865.* 2 vols. Ed. Worthington Chauncy Ford. Boston, MA: Houghton Mifflin, 1920.

Angle, Paul M. *Abraham Lincoln's Letter to Major General Joseph Hooker Dated January 26, 1863: A Facsimile Reproduction of the Letter with Explanatory Text by Paul M. Angle.* Chicago, IL: The Caxton Club, 1942.

Allen, Randall and Bohannon, Keith S. eds., *Campaigning with "Old Stonewall": Confederate Captain Ujanirtus Allen's Letters to His Wife.* Baton Rouge, LA: The Louisiana State University Press, 1998.

Baquet, Camille. *History of the First New Jersey Brigade, New Jersey Volunteers: From 1861 to 1865 Compiled Under the Authorization of Kearny's First New Jersey Brigade Society.* Princeton, NJ: MacCrellish and Quigley State Printers, 1910.

Bates, Samuel P. *History of the Pennsylvania Volunteers 1861-65,* Vol. 1. Harrisburg, PA: B. Singerly, State Printer, 1869.

Bauer, K. Jack, ed. *Soldiering: The Civil War Diary of Rice C. Bull.* Ed. K. Jack Bauer. Novato, CA: Presidio Press, 1995.

Best, Isaac O. *History of the 121st New York State Infantry.* Chicago, IL: Lt. Jas. H. Smith, 1921.

Bicknell, George W. *History of the Fifth Regiment of the Maine Volunteers: Comprising Brief Descriptions of its Marches Engagements, and General Services from the Date of its Muster in, June 24, 1861 to the time of its Muster Out, July 27, 1864.* Portland, ME: H. L. Davis, 1871.

Brewer, A.T. *History Sixty-First Regiment Pennsylvania Volunteers 1861-1865.* Pittsburgh, PA: Art Engraving & Printing, Co., 1911.

Brown, Joseph M.. *Historical Sketch of the Sixteenth Regiment, N. Y. Volunteer Infantry: From April 1861 to May 1863.* Albany, NY: Unknown, 1886.

Congressional Committee on the Conduct of the War. *Report of the Congressional Committee on the Operations of the Army of the Potomac: Causes of its Inactions and Ill Success. Its Several Campaigns. Why McClellan was Removed. The Battle of Fredericksburg. The Removal of Burnside.* New York, NY: The Tribune Association, 1863.

Coski, John. "In the Field and on the Town with the Washington Artillery." *Treasures from the Archives: Select Holdings From the Museum of the Confederacy.* Ed. David A. Woodbury. Campbell, CA: Regimental Studies, Inc., 1996.

Couch, Darius N. "Chancellorsville Campaign." *Battles and Leaders of the Civil War.* 4 vols. New York, NY: Castle Books, 1956.

Curtis, Newton Martin. *From Bull Run to Chancellorsville: The Story of the Sixteenth New York Infantry together with Personal Reminiscences.* New York, NY: Knickerbocker Press, 1906.

Cushing, Wainwright. "Description of the Ensuing Charge." Vol. 3 of *War Papers: Read Before the Commandery of the State of Maine, Military Order of the Loyal Legions of the United States.* Portland, ME: Lefavor-Tower Company, 1908.

Dawes, Rufus Robinson. *Service with the Sixth Wisconsin Volunteers.* Marietta, OH: E. R. Alderman and Sons, 1890.

Dowdy, Clifford, ed. *The Wartime Papers of Robert E. Lee.* Cambridge, MA: Da Capo Press, 1987.

Dyer, Elisha. *Adjutant General Report of Rhode Island 1861-1865.* Providence, RI: Providence Press Company, 1893.

Early, Jubal Anderson. *Jubal Early's Memoirs: Autobiographical Sketch and Narrative of the War Between the States.* Baltimore, MD: The Nautical & Aviation Publishing Company of America, 1989.

Feidner, Edward J., ed. *"Dear Wife": The Civil War Letters of Chester K. Leach.* Burlington, VT: University of Vermont, 2002.

Fisk, Wilbur. *Hard Marching Every Day: The Civil War Letters of Wilbur Fisk 1861-1865.* Ed. Ruth Rosenblatt and Emil Rosenblatt. Lawrence, KS: University Press of Kansas, 1994.

Fuller, Edward H. *Battles of the Seventy-Seventh New York State Volunteers, Third Brigade, Sixth Corps, Second Division. Mustered in, November 23, 1861. Mustered Out, June 27, 1865. By one of the Boys.* Gloversville, NY: N. P., 1901.

Gallagher, Gary W., ed. *Fighting for the Confederacy: The Personal Recollections of General Edward Porter Alexander.* Chapel Hill: University of North Carolina Press, 1989.

Gordon, John B. *Reminiscences of the Civil War.* Dayton, OH: Morningside, 1985.

Haines, Alanson A. *History of the Fifteenth Regiment New Jersey Volunteers.* New York, NY: Jenkins & Thomas, 1883.

Hall, H. Seymour. *Fredericksburg and Chancellorsville: In the Military Order of the Loyal Legions of the United States: War Talks in Kansas.* Kansas City, MO, 1906.

Handerson, Henry E. *Yankee in Gray: The Civil War Memoirs of Henry E. Handerson: with a selection of his war time letters.* Cleveland, OH: Press of Western Reserve, 1962.

Holt, Daniel. "In Captivity." *Civil War Times Illustrated*, August 1979, 34-39.

Holt, David. *A Mississippi Rebel in the Army of Northern Virginia*. Baton Rouge, LA: Louisiana State University Press, 1995.

Howard, Oliver Otis. *Autobiography of Oliver Otis Howard: Major General United States Army*. 2 vols. New York: The Baker and Taylor Company, 1908.

Hutchinson, Nelson V. *History of the Seventh Massachusetts Volunteer Infantry in the War of the Rebellion of the Southern States Against Constitutional Authority, 1861-1865*. Taunton, MA: Regimental Association, 1890.

Hyde, Thomas W. *Following the Greek Cross or Memoirs of the Sixth Army Corps*. Boston, MA: Houghton, Mifflin & Company, 1894.

Jackson, Huntington W. "Sedgwick at Fredericksburg and Salem Heights." *Battles and Leaders of the Civil War*. 4 vols. New York, NY: Castle Publishing, 1956.

Jackson, Mary Anna. *Memoirs of Stonewall Jackson: By his Widow Mary Anna Jackson*. Louisville, KY: The Prentice Press, 1895.

Jones, Terry L., ed. *The Civil War Memoirs of Captain William J. Seymour: Reminiscences of a Louisiana Tiger*. Baton Rouge, LA: The University of Louisiana Press, 1991.

Judd, David W. *The Story of the Thirty-Third N. Y. S. Vols: or Two Years Campaigning in Virginia and Maryland*. Rochester, NY: Benton & Andrews, 1864.

Lane, Mills, ed. *"Dear Mother: Don't grieve about me. If I get killed, I'll only be dead.": Letters from Georgia Soldiers in the Civil War*. Savannah, GA: Beehive Press, 1977.

Lowe, Jeffrey, ed. *Letters to Amanda: The Civil War Letters of Marion Hill Fitzpatrick, Army of Northern Virginia*. New York, NY: Mercer University Press, 2003.

Malles, Ed, ed. *Bridge Building in Wartime: Colonel Wesley Brainerd's Memoirs of the 50th New York Volunteer Engineers*. Knoxville, TN: The University of Tennessee Press, 1997.

Markle, Donald E., ed., *The Telegraph Goes to War: The Personal Diary of David Homer Bates, Lincoln's Telegraph Operator*. Hamilton, NY: Schroder Publications, 2003.

McMahon, Martin T. *General John Sedgwick: Address Delivered Before the Vermont Officers Reunion Society*. Rutland, VT: Tuttle & Company, 1880.

——. *Proceedings of the Reunion Society of Vermont Officers 1864-1868*. Burlington, VT: Burlington Free Press Association, 1885.

——. "The Sixth Army Corps." *United States Service Magazine*. Vol. V.

McClellan, George B. *The Civil War Papers of George B. McClellan: Selected Correspondence 1860-1865*. Ed. Stephen W. Sears. Cambridge, MA: Ticknor & Fields, 1989.

Meade, George Gordon. *The Life and Letters of George Gordon Meade: Major General United States Army*. 2 vols. Ed. George Gordon Meade, Jr. New York, NY: Charles Scribner's & Sons, 1913.

Nevins, Allan, ed. *A Diary of Battle: The Personal Journals of Colonel Charles S. Wainwright, 1861-1865.* New York, NY: Da Capo Press, 1998.

Owen, William Martin. *In Camp and Battle with the Washington Artillery.* Baton Rouge, LA: Louisiana State University Press, 1999.

Patrick, Marsena Rudolph. *Inside Lincoln's Army: The Diary of General Marsena Rudolph Patrick, Provost Marshal General, Army of the Potomac.* Ed. David E. Sparks. New York: Thomas Yoseloff, 1964.

Pinto, Francis E. *History of the 32nd Regiment, New York Volunteers in the Civil War, 1861-1863 and Personal Recollections During that Period.* Bethesda, MD: University Publications of America, 1992.

Priest, John Michel. *Turn Them Out To Die Like A Mule: The Civil War Letters of John N. Henry, 49th New York, 1861-1865.* Leesburg, VA: Gauley Mount Press, 1995.

Reed, Thomas Benton. *A Private in Gray.* New York, NY: Create Space Independent Publishing, 2012.

Rhodes, Robert Hunt, ed. *All for the Union: The Civil War Diary and Letters of Elisha Hunt Rhodes.* New York, NY: Vintage, 1991.

Rosenblatt, Emil, ed. *Anti-Rebel: The Civil War Letters of Wilbur Fisk.* Croton-on-Hudson, NY: Published by Editors, 1983.

Scott, Robert Garth, ed., *Fallen Leaves: The Civil War Letters of Major Henry Livermore Abbott.* Kent, OH: The Kent State University Press, 1991.

Scott, Robert N. *The War of the Rebellion: A Compilation of the Official Records of the Union and Confederate Armies.* 128 vols. Washington, D.C.: Government Printing Office, 1880-1901.

Silliker, Ruth L. *Rebel Yell & the Yankee Hurrah: The Civil War Journal of a Maine Volunteer: Private John W. Haley, 17th Maine Regiment.* Bangor, ME: Down East Books, 1985.

Smith, James Power. "Stonewall Jackson's Last Battle." *Battle and Leaders of the Civil War.* 4 vols. New York, NY: Castle Books, 1956.

Stewart, Alexander Morrison. *Camp, March, and Battle-Field or Three and a Half Years with the Army of the Potomac.* Philadelphia, PA: A. R. Rodgers Printers, 1865.

Stewart, Robert L. *History of the One Hundred and Fortieth Pennsylvania Volunteers.* Pittsburgh, PA: Regimental Association, 1912.

Stevens, George T. *Three Years in the Sixth Corps: A Concise Narrative of Events in the Army of the Potomac, From 1861 to the Close of the Rebellion, April, 1865.* Albany, NY: S. R. Gray Publishing, 1866.

Stiles, Robert. *Four Years Under Marse Robert.* Marietta, GA: R. Bemis Publishing, 1995.

Stoeckel, Carl and Ellen, eds. *Correspondence of John Sedgwick Major-General.* 2 vols. New York, NY: De Vinne Press, 1903.

Survivors Association. *History of the Corn Exchange Regiment 118th Pennsylvania Volunteers: From Their First Engagement at Antietam to Appomattox.* Philadelphia, PA: J. L. Smith Map Publisher, 1905.

——. *History of the Twenty Third Pennsylvania Volunteer Infantry Birney's Zouaves: Three Months and Three Years Service in the Civil War 1861-1865.* Philadelphia, PA: Survivors Association Twenty Third Regiment Pennsylvania Volunteers, 1903-1904.

Thayer, George A. *History of the Second Massachusetts Regiment of Infantry.* Boston, MA: G. H. Ellis, 1882.

Tower, R. Lockwood, ed. *Lee's Adjutant: The Wartime Letters of Colonel Walter Herron Taylor, 1862-1865.* Columbia, SC: University of South Carolina Press, 1995.

Tremain, H. Edwin. *In Memoriam Major General Joseph Hooker.* Cincinnati, OH: Robert Clarke & Company, 1881.

Veil, Charles H. *An Old Boy's Personal Recollections and Reminiscences of the Civil War.* Dillsburg, PA: Dr. John V. Miller, 1958.

Walker, Francis A. *History of the Second Army Corps In the Army of the Potomac.* New York, NY: Charles Scribner's Sons, 1886.

Webb, Alexander S. "Meade at Chancellorsville." *Campaigns in Virginia, Maryland, and Pennsylvania, 1862-1863.* 3 vols. Boston, MA: Griffith-Stillings Press, 1903.

Westbrook, Robert S. *History of the 49th Pennsylvania Volunteers: A Correctly Compiled Roll of the Members of the Regiment and Its Marches From 1861-1865.* Altoona, PA: Altoona Times Print, 1898.

Westervelt, William B. *Lights and Shadows of Army Life: As Seen by a Private Soldier of 27th N.Y. Infantry and 17th N.Y. Veteran Zouaves.* Marlboro, NY: C. H. Cochrane Book and Pamphlet Printer, 1886.

White, Russell C., ed. *The Civil War Diary of Wyman S. White: First Sergeant Company F. 2nd United States Sharpshooters.* Baltimore, MD: Butternut & Blue, 1993.

Williams, Alpheus S. *From the Cannon's Mouth: General Alpheus S. Williams.* Ed. Milo M. Quaife. Lincoln, NE: University of Nebraska Press, 1995.

Secondary Sources

Allen, Thomas. *Intelligence in the Civil War.* Washington, D.C.: Government Printing Office, 2008.

Ambrose, Stephen E. *Upton and the Army.* Baton Rouge, LA: Louisiana State University Press, 1993.

Bates, Samuel. *The Battle of Chancellorsville.* Meadville, PA: Edward T. Bates, 1882.

——. "Hooker's Comments on Chancellorsville." *Battles and Leaders of the Civil War*. 4 vols. New York, NY: Castle Books, 1956.

Benedict, G. G. *Vermont in the Civil War. A History of the Part Taken by the Vermont Soldiers and Sailors in the War for the Union 1861-5*. 2 vols. Burlington, VT: The Free Press Association, 1886.

Bigelow, John. *The Campaign of Chancellorsville*. New Haven, CT: Yale University Press, 1910.

Bilby, Joseph. *Three Rousing Cheers: A History of the Fifteenth New Jersey from Flemington to Appomattox*. Hightstown, NJ: Longstreet House, 1993.

Brooks, Noah. *Washington in Lincoln's Time*. New York, NY: The Century Company, 1895.

Coffin, Howard. *Full Duty: Vermonters in the Civil War*. Woodstock, VT: The Countryman Press, Inc., 1993.

Conner, Jane Hollenback. *Lincoln in Stafford*. Fredericksburg, VA: Park Publishing LLC, 2006.

Crute, Joseph W., Jr. *Lee's Intrepid Army: A Guide to the Units of the Army of Northern Virginia*. Madison, GA: Southern Lion Books, 2005.

Davis, Danny. "Return to Fredericksburg." *America's Civil War*. September 1992, 30-37.

Dodge, Theodore Ayrault. *The Campaign of Chancellorsville*. New York, NY: Da Capo Press, 1999.

Doster, William E. *Lincoln and Episodes of the Civil War*. New York, NY: G. P. Putnam's Sons, 1915.

Ellis, Alden C. *The Massachusetts Andrew Sharpshooters*. Jefferson, NC: McFarland & Co., 2012.

Fordney, Ben F. *Stoneman at Chancellorsville: The Coming of Age of Union Cavalry*. Shippensburg, PA: White Mane Publishing, 1998.

Fox, William F. *Regimental Losses in the Civil War, 1861-1865*. Albany, NY: Albany Publishing Company, 1889.

Freeman, Douglas Southall. *Lee*. Ed. Richard Harwell. New York, NY: Scribner, 1997.

——. *Lee's Lieutenants: A Study In Command: Volume One*. Ed. Stephen W. Sears. Old Saybrook, CT: Scribner, 1998.

Frye, Dennis E. *Antietam Revealed: The Battle of Antietam and the Maryland Campaign As You Have Never Seen It Before*. Collingswood, NJ: C. W. Historicals, LLC, 2004.

Furgurson, Ernest B. *Chancellorsville 1863: The Souls of the Brave*. New York, NY: Vintage, 1993.

Gallagher, Gary W. *Lee & His Army in Confederate History*. Chapel Hill, NC: University of North Carolina Press, 2001.

——. "East of Chancellorsville: Jubal A. Early at Second Fredericksburg and Salem Church," in Gary W. Gallagher, ed., *Chancellorsville: The Battle and Its Aftermath*. Chapel Hill, NC: University of North Carolina Press, 1996.

Glatthaar, Joseph T. *General Lee's Army: From Victory to Collapse.* New York, NY: Free Press, 2008.

Gottfried, Bradley M. *Brigades of Gettysburg: The Union and Confederate Brigades at the Battle of Gettysburg.* Cambridge, MA: Da Capo, 2002.

Greene, A. Wilson. *J. Horace Lacy: The Most Dangerous Rebel in the County.* Richmond, VA: Owens Publishing Company, 1988.

Hand, Henry Wells, ed. *Centennial History of the Town of Nunda: With a Preliminary Recital of the Winning of Western New York, from the Fort Builders Age to the Last Conquest by Our Revolutionary Forefathers.* Rochester, NY: Rochester Herald Press, 1908.

Happel, Ralph. *Salem Church Embattled.* Washington, D.C.: Eastern National Park and Monument Association, 1980.

Harrison, Noel G. *Chancellorsville Battlefield Sites.* Lynchburg, VA: H. E. Howard, 1990.

——. *Fredericksburg Civil War Sites, Volume One: April 1861-November 1862.* Lynchburg, VA: H. E. Howard, 1995.

——. *Fredericksburg Civil War Sites, Volume Two: December 1862-April 1865.* Lynchburg, VA: H. E. Howard, 1995.

Harsh, Joseph L. *Sounding the Shallows: A Confederate Companion for the Maryland Campaign of 1862.* Kent, OH: The Kent State University Press, 2000.

Hebert, Walter H. *Fighting Joe Hooker.* Lincoln, NE: University of Nebraska Press, 1999.

Hodge, Robert. "The Story of the Rappahannock Canal." *The Fredericksburg Times*, January 1978, 24-25.

Hughes, Mark. *The New Civil War Handbook: Facts and Photos for Readers of All Ages.* New York, NY: Savas Beatie, 2011.

Hunt, Roger D. *Colonels in Blue: Union Army Colonels of the Civil War: The Mid-Atlantic States Pennsylvania, New Jersey, Maryland, Delaware, and The District of Columbia.* Mechanicsburg, PA: Stackpole Books, 2007.

Jordan, David M. *"Happiness Is Not My Companion": The Life of General G. K. Warren.* Bloomington, IN: Indiana University Press, 2001.

Keneally, Thomas. *American Scoundrel: The Life of the Notorious Civil War General Dan Sickles.* New York, NY: Doubleday, 2002.

Krick, Robert K. *Civil War Weather in Virginia.* Tuscaloosa, AL: University of Alabama Press, 2007.

Longacre, Edward G. *The Commanders of Chancellorsville: The Gentleman and the Rogue.* Nashville, TN: Thomas Nelson, 2005.

Mackowski, Chris. *Chancellorsville: Crossroads of Fire.* Gettysburg, PA: Thomas Publications, 2011.

Mackowski, Chris, and Kristopher D. White. "From Foxcroft to Fredericksburg: Captain Sewell Gray of the Sixth Maine Infantry." *Fredericksburg History & Biography.* Volume 7 (December 2008), 130-149.

——.*The Last Days of Stonewall Jackson*. 2nd ed. Sacramento, CA: Savas Beatie, 2013.

Maier, Larry B. *Rough & Regulars: A History of Philadelphia's 119th Pennsylvania Volunteer Infantry, The Gray Reserves*. Shippensburg, PA: Burd Street Press, 1997.

Martin, Eric B. *Salem Church Heights: The Loss of a Park Battlefield*. Frostburg, MD: Frostburg State University, 2003.

Matter, William D. *If It Takes All Summer: The Battle of Spotsylvania*. Chapel Hill, NC: The University of North Carolina Press, 1988.

McPherson, James M. *Ordeal by Fire: The Civil War and Reconstruction*. New York, NY: McGraw-Hill, 2001.

Miller, Richard F. *Harvard's Civil War: A History of the Twentieth Massachusetts Volunteer Infantry*. Lebanon, NH: University Press of New England, 2005.

Moe, Richard. *The Last Full Measure: The Life and Death of the First Minnesota Volunteers*. New York, NY: MHS Press, 1993.

Morrison Jr., James L. *"The Best School": West Point, 1833-1866*. Kent, OH: The Kent State University Press, 1998.

Morrow, Robert F., Jr. *77th New York Volunteers: "Sojering" in the VI Corps*. Shippensburg, PA: White Mane Publishing, 2004.

Mundy, James H. *No Rich Men's Sons: The Sixth Maine Volunteer Infantry*. Cape Elizabeth, ME: Harp Publications, 1994.

O'Reilly, Francis Augustin. *The Fredericksburg Campaign: Winter War on the Rappahannock*. Baton Rouge, LA: Louisiana State University Press, 2003.

Parsons, George W. *Put the Vermonters Ahead: The First Vermont Brigade in the Civil War*. Shippensburg, PA: White Mane Publishing Company, 2000.

Parsons, Philip W. *The Union Sixth Army Corps in the Chancellorsville Campaign: A Study of the Engagements of Second Fredericksburg, Salem Church and Bank's Ford, May 3-4, 1863*. Jefferson, NC: McFarland Press, 2010.

Pfanz, Donald. *History Through Eyes of Stone*. Fredericksburg, VA: The National Park Service, 2006.

Raus, Edmund J., Jr. *A Generation on the March: The Union Army at Gettysburg*. Gettysburg, PA: Thomas Publications, 1996.

Reece, Timothy J. *Sykes' Regular Infantry Division, 1861-1864: A History of Regular United States Infantry Operations in the Civil War's Eastern Theater*. Jefferson, NC: McFarland and Company, 1990.

Sauers, Richard. *Advance the Colors: Pennsylvania Civil War Battle Flags*. 2 vols. Harrisburg, PA: Capitol Preservation Association, 1991.

Sanders, C. C. "Chancellorsville." *Southern Historical Society Papers*. 52 vols. Richmond, VA: Virginia Historical Society, 1901.

Sears, Stephen W. *Chancellorsville*. New York: Mariner Books, 1996.

——. *Controversies and Commanders: Dispatches from the Army of the Potomac*. New York, NY: Mariner, 1999.

——. *To the Gates of Richmond: The Peninsula Campaign*. New York, NY: Mariner Books, 1992.

Siegel, Alan A. *For the Glory of the Union: Myth, Reality, and the Media in Civil War New Jersey*. Madison, NJ: Fairleigh Dickinson University Press, 1984.

Snell, Mark A. *From First to Last: The Life of Major General William B. Franklin*. New York, NY: Fordham University Press, 2002.

Stackpole, Edward J. *Chancellorsville: Lee's Greatest Battle*. Harrisburg, PA: Stackpole Books, 1992.

——. *The Fredericksburg Campaign: Drama on the Rappahannock*. Harrisburg, PA: Stackpole Books, 1991.

State of New York Historian. *Third Annual Report of the State Historian of the State of New York, 1897: Transmitted to the Legislature March 14, 1898*. Albany, NY: Wynkoop Hallenbeck Crawford, 1898.

Styple, William B., ed., *Generals in Bronze: Interviewing the Commanders of the Civil War*. Kearny, NJ: Belle Grove Publishing, 2005.

——. *Writing & Fighting The Civil War: Soldiers Letters from the Battlefront*. Kearny, NJ: Belle Grove Publishing Company, 2004.

Taaffe, Stephen R. *Commanding the Army of the Potomac*. Lawrence, KS: University of Kansas Press, 2006.

Tagg, Larry. *The Generals of Gettysburg: The Leaders of America's Greatest Battle*. Cambridge, MA: Da Capo, 2003.

Trask, Kerry A. *Fire Within: A Civil War Narrative from Wisconsin*. Kent, OH: The Kent State University Press, 1995.

Warner, Ezra J. *Generals in Blue: Lives of the Union Commanders*. Baton Rouge, LA: Louisiana State University Press, 2006.

——. *Generals in Gray: Lives of the Confederate Commanders*. Baton Rouge, LA: Louisiana State University Press, 2006.

Ward, David A. *Amidst A Tempest of Shot and Shell: A History of the Ninety-Sixth Pennsylvania Volunteers*. New Haven, CT: Southern Connecticut State University, 1988.

Waugh, John C. *The Class of 1846 From West Point to Appomattox: Stonewall Jackson, George McClellan and their Brothers*. New York, NY: Ballantine Books, 1994.

Welch, Emily Sedgwick. *A Biographical Sketch of John Sedgwick Major-General*. New York, NY: The De Vinne Press, 1899.

Wert, Jeffrey D. *The Sword of Lincoln: The Army of the Potomac*. New York, NY: Simon & Schuster, 2005.

Winslow, Richard E., III. *General John Sedgwick: The Story of a Union Corps Commander*. Novato, CA: Presidio Press, 1982.

Wise, Jennings Cropper. *The Long Arm of Lee*. 2 vols. Lincoln, NE: University of Nebraska Press, 1991.

Index

About the Authors

Chris Mackowski, Ph.D. is a professor in the School of Journalism and Mass Communication at St. Bonaventure University in Allegany, New York. He also works as a historian with the National Park Service at Fredericksburg and Spotsylvania National Military Park, where he gives tours at four major Civil War battlefields (Fredericksburg, Chancellorsville, Wilderness, and Spotsylvania), as well as at the building where Stonewall Jackson died.

Kristopher D. White is a historian for the Penn-Trafford Recreation Board and a continuing education instructor for the Community College of Allegheny County near Pittsburgh, Pennsylvania. He served for five years as a staff military historian at Fredericksburg and Spotsylvania National Military Park, and is a former Licensed Battlefield Guide at Gettysburg. Kristopher holds a Master of Arts degree in Military History from Norwich University in Northfield, Vermont.

*   *   *

Mackowski and White are longtime friends and have co-authored several books together, including *The Last Days of Stonewall Jackson* and *Simply Murder: The Battle of Fredericksburg*, along with monograph-length articles on the battle of Spotsylvania for *Blue & Gray* magazine. They have also written for *Civil War Times*, *America's Civil War*, and *Hallowed Ground*. Chris and Kris are co-founders of the popular blog "Emerging Civil War" (www.emergingcivilwar.com).